Regional Competitiveness

There is now a wide spread interest in regions as a key focus in the organisation and governance of economic growth and wealth creation. This book considers the factors that influence and shape the competitive performance of regions. This is not just an issue of academic interest and debate, but also of increasing policy deliberation and action. However, as the readings in this book make clear, the very idea of regional competitiveness is itself complex and contentious. Many academics and policy makers have used the concept without fully considering what is meant by the term and how it can be measured. Policy formulation has tended to rush ahead of understanding and analysis and the purpose of this book is to close this important gap in understanding

This book was previously published as a special issue of *Regional Studies*.

Ron Martin is Professor in Economic Geography in the Department of Geography, University of Cambridge

Michael Kitson is a University Lecturer in Global Macroeconomics, Judge Institute of Management, University of Cambridge

Peter Tyler is a Professor in Urban and Regional Economics, Department of Land Economy, University of Cambridge

Regional Development and Public Policy Series
Series editor: Ron Martin, University of Cambridge, UK, Gernot Grabher, University of Bonn, Germany, Maryann Feldman, University of Toronto, Canada

Regional Development and Public Policy is an international series that aims to provide authoritative analyses of the new significance of regions and cities for economic development and public policy. It seeks to combine fresh theoretical and empirical insights with constructive policy evaluation and debates, and to provide a definitive set of conceptual, practical and topical studies in the field of regional and urban public policy analysis.

Regions, Spatial Strategies and Sustainable Development
Graham Haugton and Dave Counsell (eds.)

Geographies of Labour Market Inequality
Ron Martin, Philip Morrison (eds.)

Regional Development Agencies in Europe
Henrik Halkier, Charlotte Damborg and Mike Danson (eds.)

Social Exclusion in European Cities
Processes, experiences and responses
Ali Madanipour, Goran Cars and Judith Allen (eds.)

Regional Innovation Strategies
The challenge for less-favoured regions
Kevin Morgan and Claire Nauwelaers (eds.)

Foreign Direct Investment and the Global Economy
Nicholas A. Phelps and Jeremy Alden (eds.)

Restructuring Industry and Territory
The experience of Europe's regions
Anna Giunta, Arnoud Lagendijk and Andy Pike (eds.)

Community Economic Development
Graham Haughton (ed.)

Out of the Ashes?
The social impact of industrial contraction and regeneration on Britain's mining communities
David Waddington, Chas Critcher, Bella Dicks and David Parry

Regional Competitiveness

Edited by Ron Martin, Michael Kitson and Peter Tyler

Routledge
Taylor & Francis Group

London and New York

First published 2006 by Routledge
2 Park Square, Milton Park, Abingdon, OX14 4RN

Simultaneously published in the USA and Canada
by Routledge
270 Madison Ave, New York, NY 10016

Routledge is an imprint of the Taylor & Francis Group

© 2006 Regional Studies Association

Typeset in Bembo by AccComputing, North Barrow, Somerset
Printed and bound in Great Britain by Antony Rowe Ltd., Chippenham, Wilts

British Library Cataloguing in Publication Data
A catalogue record for this book is available from the British Library

Library of Congress Cataloging in Publication Data
A catalog record for this book has been requested

ISBN10: 0-415-39190-3
ISBN13: 978-0-415-39190-0

Learning Resources
Centre

Regional Competitiveness

CONTENTS

Regional Competitiveness: An Elusive yet Key Concept?

RON MARTIN★, MICHAEL KITSON† and PETER TYLER‡

★Department of Geography, †Judge Institute of Management and ‡Department of Land Economy, University of Cambridge, Cambridge, UK. Emails: mk24@cam.ac.uk; rlm1@cam.ac.uk; pt23@cam.ac.uk

INTRODUCTION

There is now widespread agreement that we are witnessing the 'resurgence' of regions as key loci in the organization and governance of economic growth and wealth creation. A previous special issue of this journal ('Rethinking the Regions', *Regional Studies* (2003) **37**(6/7)) was devoted to recent developments and debates in regional development theory. The present special issue on 'Regional Competitiveness' is intended to complement that earlier collection of papers by focusing on what has become one of the most discussed aspects of the new concern with regions, namely their competitive performance. The competitiveness of regions is an issue not just of academic interest and debate, but also of increasing policy deliberation and action. However, as the papers in this issue make clear, the very notion of regional competitiveness is itself complex and contentious, and even though policymakers everywhere have jumped onto the regional and urban competitiveness bandwagon, we are far from a consensus on what is meant by the term and how it can be measured: as is often the case, policy has raced ahead of conceptual understanding and empirical analysis. The papers included in this issue are intended to advance that understanding and analysis. The purpose of this extended Editorial introduction is to provide some of the background to this project.

THE COMPETITIVENESS FAD

The credo of competitiveness has attracted a veritable host of believers and followers. Economists and experts everywhere have elevated 'competitiveness' to the status of a natural law of the modern capitalist economy. To assess a country's competitiveness and to devise policies to enhance it have become officially institutionalized tasks in many nations, e.g. the USA, the UK, Belgium, Italy, the Netherlands and Japan. The USA led the way in the early 1990s by setting up a governmental Competitiveness Policy Council to report regularly on and to promote the competitiveness of the US economy. In the same year, the European Commission established a European Council of Competitiveness, and it undertook to produce a regular Competitiveness Report on the performance of the economy of the European Union (the most recent being the seventh, for 2003). In the European Union, the issue of competitiveness has taken on particular significance in relation to its Lisbon 'growth strategy', with its highly ambitious aim to close the 'competitiveness gap' with the USA and to become the world's most dynamic and competitive knowledge-based economy by 2010. In addition, numerous private organizations and consultancies concerned with measuring and lobbying the cause of competitiveness have emerged recently, such as the World Economic Forum (Geneva, Switzerland), the Competitiveness Institute (Barcelona, Spain), the Council on Competitiveness (Washington, DC, USA) and the Institute for Strategy and Competitiveness (Harvard, MA, USA).

This focus on competitiveness has not just been a macroeconomic phenomenon, however. It has also assumed key significance at the regional, urban and local scales. Within governmental circles, interest has grown in the 'competitive performance' of individual regions and cities, with identifying the key determinants of regional and urban competitiveness, and with devising policies to promote and foster those determinants. In the UK, for example, the improvement of regional and urban competitiveness has moved to central stage in the policy statements of the Treasury, Department of Trade and Industry, and the Office of the Deputy Prime Minister (DTI, 2004; H. M. TREASURY, 2001, 2003, 2004; ODPM, 2003, 2004). Likewise, the EUROPEAN COMMISSION (2004) sees the improvement of competitiveness in Europe's lagging regions as vital to 'social cohesion'. At the same time, city and regional authorities are themselves increasingly obsessed with constructing local competitiveness indices so as to compare the relative standing of their localities with that of others, and with devising policy strategies to move their area up the 'competitiveness league table'. Thus, in the same way that the World Economic Forum produces annual global competitiveness indices that rank national economies, so a plethora of city and regional indices have appeared that rank places on the basis of this or that measure of competitiveness. The Progressive Policy Institute in Washington, DC, for example, compiles various 'new economy' indices for US cities and regions (ATKINSON and CODURI, 2002; ATKINSON and WILHELM, 2002). ROBERT HUGGINS ASSOCIATES (2004a, b) produces the World Knowledge Competitiveness Index that seeks to benchmark the globe's leading knowledge economy regions; it also produces a European Competitiveness Index that ranks cities and regions. Yet another of these indices of 'place competitiveness' is FLORIDA's (2002) 'creativity index', a proxy for an area's openness to different kinds of people and ideas.

However, this new focus on 'territorial competitiveness' is itself highly problematic. For despite the rush to measure, compare and promote 'regional competitiveness', the very notion is contentious and far from well understood. As GARDINER *et al.* (in this volume) ask: What, precisely, is meant by the competitiveness of regions, cities and localities? In what sense do regions and cities compete? How can regional competitiveness be measured? What are the connections between regional competitiveness and regional economic prosperity? Although the academic literature on regional and urban competitiveness has been expanding (e.g. STEINLE, 1992; CHESHIRE and GORDON, 1995; DUFFY, 1995; GROUP OF LISBON, 1995; STORPER, 1995, 1997; JENSEN-BUTLER *et al.*, 1997; BEGG, 1999, 2002; URBAN STUDIES, 1999; CAMAGNI, 2003; PORTER, 1998a, b, 2000, 2001, 2003), there is still no generally agreed theoretical or empirical framework for answering these questions. The concern is that there is an elusive concept, flawed indicators and over-prescribed policies.

COMPETITIVENESS: AN ELUSIVE CONCEPT

At its simplest, regional (and urban) competitiveness might be defined as the success with which regions and cities compete with one another in some way. This might be over shares of (national, and especially international) export markets. Or it might be over attracting capital or workers. Such notions would seem to underpin Michael STORPER's (1997, p. 20) definition of 'place competitiveness' as:

> The ability of an (urban) economy to attract and maintain firms with stable or rising market shares in an activity while maintaining or increasing standards of living for those who participate in it.

Similarly, in recent work on regional competitiveness, PORTER (1998a, b, 2000, 2001a, b) has emphasized the key role of export-orientated clusters as the basis for a high regional standard of living.

However, this focus on regional export shares as a

measure of regional competitiveness is problematic. First, it uses a concept of competitiveness defined originally for national economies without questioning whether this is the most useful or meaningful concept for use at the sub-national (urban and regional) scale. Second, as a consequence, it carries over all the problems and debates that surround the notion of national competitiveness as defined in trade and export terms.

For even at the national level, there is considerable disagreement over the idea of competitiveness (CELLINI and SOCI, 2002). As KRUGMAN (1996a, b) and others (e.g. GROUP OF LISBON, 1995) have pointed out, there may be less to the export market share view of competitiveness than meets the eye. The complaint is that while the notion of competitiveness may well be meaningful for an individual firm, it is misplaced to carry the concept over to the aggregate national economy: national economies do not go out of business such as uncompetitive firms, and international trade is far from being a zero-sum game.

Traditionally, in economics, the notion of *comparative advantage* (with roots going back to Ricardo and reformulated in modern guise by Heckscher and Ohlin) has been used rather than that of competitive advantage or competitiveness. The concept of comparative advantage holds that countries, through specialization, can benefit from trade even if they do not have an absolute advantage, so that trade can be a positive sum game. It acts as an antidote to some of the paranoia about globalization, the development of the newly industrializing countries and the rise in outsourcing. Under comparative advantage theory, trade reflects national differences in factor endowments (land, labour, natural resources and capital). Nations gain factor-based comparative advantage in industries that make intensive use of the factors they possess in abundance. But the concept of comparative advantage has limitations. It is a static concept based on inherited factor endowments and, in most forms, it assumes diminishing returns to scale and equivalent technologies across nations. Nevertheless, comparative advantage based on factors of production has intuitive appeal and has certainly played a role in determining trade patterns in many industries. It is also a view that has informed much government policy toward competitiveness, because governments believe they can alter factor advantage through various forms of intervention, especially by altering factor costs (through reductions in interest rates, efforts to hold down wages, currency devaluation, subsidies, export credits, etc.).

Over the past 20 years or so, however, there has been a growing sentiment that comparative advantage based on factors of production is not sufficient to explain patterns of trade. A new paradigm of *competitive advantage* has risen to the fore. This is meant to capture the view that nations can develop and improve their competitive position. It focuses on the decisive characteristics of a nation that allow its firms to create and sustain competitive advantage in particular fields. As Michael Porter, one of the prime exponents of this notion, and indeed the doyen of the whole competitiveness debate, puts it:

> I believe that many policy makers, like many corporate executives, view the sources of true competitiveness within the wrong framework. If you believe that competitiveness comes from having cheap capital, and low cost labour, and low currency prices and if you think that competitiveness is driven by static efficiency, then you behave in a certain way to help industry. However, my research teaches that competitiveness is a function of dynamic progressiveness, innovation, and an ability to change and improve. Using this framework, things that look useful under the old model prove counterproductive.
>
> (PORTER, 1992, p. 40)

For Porter, the only meaningful concept of competitiveness is *productivity*. The principal goal of a nation is to produce a high and rising standard of living for its citizens. The ability to do so depends, according to Porter, not on the fuzzy and amorphous notion of 'competitiveness', but on the productivity with which a nation's resources are employed. A rising standard of living depends on the capacity of a nation's firms to achieve high levels of productivity and to increase productivity over time. Sustained productivity growth requires that an economy continually upgrades itself.

Similarly, KRUGMAN (1990, p. 9) also argues that if competitiveness has any meaning, then it is simply another way of saying productivity:

> Productivity isn't everything, but in the long run it is almost everything. A country's ability to improve its standard of living over time depends almost entirely on its ability to raise its output per worker.

The focus on productivity is apparent throughout the industrialized world: for example, for the USA, see the COUNCIL ON COMPETITIVENESS (2001); for the UK, see DEPARTMENT OF TRADE AND INDUSTRY (DTI) (1998, 2003b, c), H. M. TREASURY (2000) and BROWN (2001); and for Europe, see EUROPEAN COMMISSION (2003) and O'MAHONY and VAN ARK (2003). Furthermore, the preoccupation with productivity is now firmly focused on the region: for the USA, see PORTER (2001a, b); for the UK, see H. M. TREASURY (2001, 2003) and DTI (2003a, 2004); and for Europe, see SAPIR *et al.* (2004). Indeed, one aspect of Porter's productivity approach to competitiveness is of particular interest: namely, his argument that 'competitive advantage is created and sustained through a highly localized process' (PORTER, 1990, p. 19; also PORTER, 1998a, 2001b). In fact, in recent years, his focus has shifted away from the competitive advantage of nations to the competitive advantage of regions.

THE COMPETITIVE ADVANTAGE OF REGIONS?

It is certainly possible to derive measures of regional productivity either from firm-based micro-data or from aggregate regional output figures, and such measures provide valuable information on a region's standard of living, both through time and relative to other regions. But although regional productivity is certainly a useful indicator of what might be termed 'revealed regional competitiveness' (GARDINER *et al.*, 2004), there are empirical problems in measuring it accurately (KITSON, 2004) as well as conceptual issues about how to interpret what is actually meant by *regional* productivity. All of the problems associated with measuring and interpreting national or sectoral productivity carry over the regional case. Thus, should one focus on labour productivity (possibly adjusted to take into account the number of hours worked) or on total (or multifactor) productivity (TFP)? Additional problems include the output indicator used, which at the regional level also raises the issue of residence- versus workplace-based measures. There is the difficulty of measuring the output of services and the government sector. The estimation and interpretation of regional TFP are even more problematic: TFP requires data that are rarely available at the sub-national scale, and the estimation of regional production functions that are themselves contentious. In addition, productivity on its own is only one aspect of revealed regional competitiveness, or competitive advantage. What also matters is the regional employment rate. The ability to sustain a high rate of employment amongst the working-age population is as important as having a high output per worker. Although the two usually go together, a focus just on the latter can be misleading. Examples abound of regions in which firms and industries have sought to raise labour productivity through the extensive shakeout of workers and closure of plants, that is by reducing employment. But it would obviously be perverse to view such regions as having improved their long-run competitive advantage if the cost of increased labour productivity is persistent high unemployment.

Beyond these issues, useful though regional productivity analyses might be – and even these are not that common – they tell us little about the meaning, sources or processes of regional competitive advantage (BUDD and HIRMIS, 2004; TUROK, 2004). If Porter is correct that competitive advantage is a highly localized process, then this requires further elaboration for it suggests that there is something distinctive and formative about regional and local economic development: that the regional economy is more than just the sum (or aggregate) of its parts.

As CELLINI and SOCI (2002) argue, the notion of regional competitiveness – or to use our terminology, regional competitive advantage – is neither macro-(national) nor micro-economic (firm-based). Regions are neither simple aggregations of firms, nor are they scaled-down versions of nations. These authors go on to suggest that competitiveness takes on a different meaning according to the scale or level at which the term is being used. Thus, they distinguish between the macro level (the competitiveness of a country), the micro level (the competitiveness of the individual firm) and the meso level (the competitiveness of local economic systems), where the latter is further divided into industrial districts (or what Porter would call 'clusters') and regions. They suggest that the regional level is possibly the most difficult and complex one at which to define competitiveness. They acknowledge that it means much more than the potential ability to export or the surplus in trade balance, and that it reaches far beyond the production of goods to include a wide range of material and immaterial inputs and their mobility, from housing and infrastructure to communications to social networks. Beyond this, however, they fail to provide much insight.

CAMAGNI (2002) offers a much more useful discussion. He takes the view that regions do indeed compete, over attracting firms (capital) and workers (labour), as well as over markets, but based on *absolute* advantage rather than comparative advantage. According to Camagni, a region may be thought of as having absolute competitive advantages when it possesses superior technological, social, infrastructural or institutional *assets* that are *external* to but which benefit individual firms such that no set of alternative factor prices would induce a geographical redistribution of economic activity. These assets tend to give the region's firms, overall, a higher productivity than would otherwise be the case. A similar view has been expressed by the EUROPEAN COMMISSION (1999, p. 5):

> [The idea of regional competitiveness] should capture the notion that, despite the fact that there are strongly competitive and uncompetitive firms in every region, there are common features within a region which affect the competitiveness of all firms located there.

The question is: what are these 'common features' and what makes them specifically regional in nature? One way of thinking about these question is in terms of 'regional externalities', or resources that reside outside of individual local firms but which are drawn on – directly or indirectly – by those firms and which influence their efficiency, innovativeness, flexibility and dynamism: in short, their productivity and competitive advantage.

There is now a considerable literature, within both economic geography and economics, that emphasizes the distinctive role of regions and cities as sources of key external economies. This interest is in fact part of a more general recognition of the role of geography as a source of increasing returns, and the rediscovery and extension of ALFRED MARSHALL's (1890/1920) original triad of external economies of industrial localization – skilled labour, supporting and ancillary industries, and knowledge spillovers – all held together by what he called 'something in the air' or 'industrial atmosphere'. Marshall's schema forms the basis of

Porter's 'cluster concept', in which regional competitive advantage derives from the presence and dynamics of geographically localized or clustered activities among which there is intense local rivalry and competition, favourable factor input conditions, demanding local customers, and the presence of capable locally based suppliers and supporting industries. The more localized are these industrial/business clusters, he argues, the more intense the interactions between these four components of the 'competitive diamond' and the more productive the region.

According to Porter, a key aspect of cluster formation and success – and hence of regional competitive advantage – is the degree of social embeddedness, the existence of facilitative social networks, social capital and institutional structures (PORTER, 1998a, b, 2001a, b). The formation and evolution of such 'soft' externalities is seen as crucial for the dynamic competitiveness of regions and cities. In economic geography, Storper's not dissimilar notion of 'untraded interdependencies' – such as flows of tacit knowledge, technological spillovers, networks of trust and cooperation, and local systems of norms and conventions – is also regarded as central to understanding the economic performance and competitive advantage of a region (STORPER, 1995; POLENSKE, 2004).

There is in fact an increasing tendency to explain regional growth and development in terms of such 'soft' externalities. In particular, considerable emphasis is now given to local knowledge, learning and creativity (PINCH *et al.*, 2003; MORGAN, 2004). The argument is that in a globalized economy, the key resources for regional and urban competitiveness depend on localized processes of knowledge creation, in which people and firms learn about new technology, learn to trust each other, and share and exchange information (MALECKI, 2004). Indeed, an assumed link between localization and tacit or informal, uncodified knowledge is now almost accepted axiomatically (PINCH *et al.*, 2003). While problems abound in all these discussions (on the cluster concept, see, for example, MARTIN and SUNLEY, 2003), one point is clear: that the definition and explanation of regional competitive advantage need to reach well beyond concern with 'hard' productivity, to consider several other – and softer – dimensions of the regional or urban socio-economy (Fig. 1). The quality and skills of the labour force (human capital), the extent, depth and orientation of social networks and institutional forms (social/institutional capital), the range and quality of cultural facilities and assets (cultural capital), the presence of an innovative and creative class (knowledge/creative capital), and the scale and quality of public infrastructure (infrastructural capital) are all just as important as, and serve to support and underpin, in the form of regional externalities, an efficient productive base to the regional economy (productive capital). For example, the ability of regions to attract

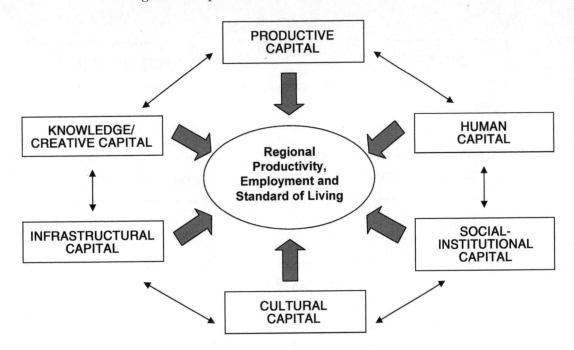

Fig. 1. *Bases of regional competitive advantage*

skilled, creative and innovative people; to provide high-quality cultural facilities; and to encourage the development of social networks and institutional arrangements that share a common commitment to regional prosperity, are all key regional 'externalities' or 'assets' that benefit local firms and businesses, and hence are major aspects of regional competitive advantage.

This is not to assume, however, that such externalities all operate at the same spatial scales, or that they can be nurtured or developed equally across all parts of a regional economic space. On the contrary, one of the most pressing research questions concerns the appropriate spatial scale at which to measure and analyse regional competitiveness. Do different externalities operate over different geographical scales? How do they interact across space? We actually know surprisingly little about such issues. Yet they are of critical importance given the need to ensure that policy interventions to improve regional competitiveness are meaningful and effective.

POLICY ISSUES

If there is no generally accepted definition or theory of regional competitiveness, this has not stopped policy-makers from devising policies designed to boost the competitiveness of this or that region or city. Just as productivity has been used as the dominant indicator of 'revealed competitiveness', so it has tended to be a prime target for policy intervention. The UK illustrates this tendency well. Over the past few years, the UK Treasury, the DTI and the Office of the Deputy Prime Minister, have all sought to identify the underlying determinants – or 'drivers' to use the fashionable policy

parlance – of the productive performance of the country's regions, cities and local authority areas. Five such drivers have been singled out in relation to policies at the regional level: skills, enterprise, innovation, competition and investment (H. M. TREASURY, 2001, 2004) (Fig. 2). In the case of urban competitiveness, the list of drivers is somewhat different: innovation, human capital, economic diversity and specialization, connectivity, strategic decision-making, and quality of life factors (ODPM, 2003, 2004). Why the drivers underpinning urban competitiveness should differ from those underpinning regional competitiveness is not explained when some of those listed for cities would seem just as relevant to regions.

The broad rationale for government intervention in relation to these drivers is to overcome the market and institutional failures that restrain their contribution to the growth of regional productivity. Thus, according to H. M. TREASURY (2004, p. 14):

there are important implications for the design and delivery of regional policy in two respects. First, it is essential that a comprehensive package of policy instruments be in place to strengthen each of the five drivers throughout the UK. Failure to do so would undermine efforts to strengthen individual drivers and overall economic performance. A region's economic underperformance could be perpetuated if, for example, policy makers failed to recognise the importance of a strong local skills base to the attraction and growth of new businesses. Secondly, it is vital that there is a coordinated approach to the design and implementation of policies designed to raise regions' productivity and growth. . . . There will be beneficial synergies from a coordinated effort to strengthen all of the drivers that may be holding back a particular region's growth.

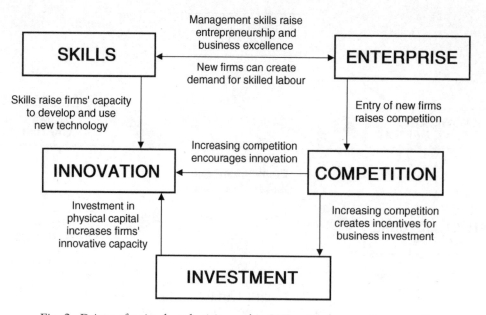

Fig. 2. Drivers of regional productivity used in UK regional competitiveness policy.
Source: H. M. TREASURY (2004).

One problem with this approach is that there appears to be no underlying coherent theoretical justification for the particular choice of 'drivers'. At best, different theories seem to be implicit in different drivers. The difficulty here, of course, is that several different candidates are available as theoretical underpinnings for conceptualizing and devising policy interventions to promote regional competitive advantage, and all have their limitations. Standard regional export-base theory offers far too narrow a view of the nature and determinants of regional competitive advantage. Likewise, standard regional growth theory, with its dependence on the idea of a regional production function subject to constant returns to scale, is of very limited usefulness. Much more promising are those approaches that emphasize the importance of increasing returns, since these at least allow for consideration of what was termed above 'regional externalities'. But even here there is a wide choice: from regional versions of endogenous growth models (MARTIN and SUNLEY, 1998), through the spatial agglomeration models of the so-called 'new economic geography' (FUJITA *et al.*, 1999; FUJITA and THISSE, 2002; BALDWIN *et al.*, 2003), cumulative causation models (SETTERFIELD, 1998), evolutionary theories (BOSCHMA, 2004), to cluster theory (PORTER, 1998a, b, 2001a, b). In the UK, there has certainly been more than a whiff of endogenous growth theory behind Treasury thinking in this area, while within the DTI Porter's cluster theory has been highly influential – both in focusing on regional productivity as the key indicator of regional performance and in advocating the promotion of clusters as an integral component of regional strategies.

Another problem is that policies – both in the UK and elsewhere – tend to be overwhelmingly supply-side in approach, and little attention is given to the demand side (FOTHERGILL, 2004). It is as if a sort of Say's law of regional competitive advantage is being invoked: if all the 'drivers' are in place, then demand for the region's products and services should follow. As Porter's work has emphasized, demand for a region's products is not simply an end result but is itself an important 'driver' of a region's competitive advantage. A low level of local demand tends to dampen local innovativeness and entrepreneurialism, encourages the exodus of skilled and educated workers in search of better employment prospects elsewhere, hinders the development of high-quality cultural and infrastructural capital, and generally weakens the competitive dynamics of the area. Tackling the supply side is certainly necessary to foster growth and development, but may not of itself be sufficient. Action may also be needed to help stimulate local demand (on the importance of markets, see CLARK *et al.*, 2004). In this context, favourable macroeconomic conditions and policies are also important.

A third limitation is the 'universalism' of many policies aimed at boosting regional or urban competitiveness, whereby it is assumed that the same 'drivers' are equally important everywhere, and hence the same basic policy model is applicable, the idea being that, in principle, the process of regional economic growth is governed by a series of universal economic rules (on the limitations of such universalism, see KENNY and WILLIAMS, 2001); thus, if you pull the right levers, the 'drivers' will respond in similar ways with similar outcomes. But both history and geography will have a major impact on the relevance of particular drivers and their impact. Thus, investing in 'innovation' (assuming such an investment could be adequately defined) may have beneficial effects in one region but have little impact in another. In the absence of a robust theoretical framework that takes account of spatial specificity, it is hard to gauge how policy initiatives targeted on any one specific driver contribute to final outcomes, how the policy drivers work together, what relative weight should be applied to each, and the time it takes for change to occur.

Yet a further problem is that alluded to above: namely, that there has been little research into what the appropriate spatial scale of intervention should be. Some processes of regional competitive advantage may be highly localized, while others may operate at a more broad regional scale, and some may be national or global. In most instances, however, polices are pursued on the basis of predefined administrative or political areas that may have little meaning as economically functioning units, and from which policy effects may 'leak out' into other regions. At the same time, by following similar strategies (based on similar 'drivers') different regions may end up competing one with another over a particular form of growth and development that has a very specific and geographically restricted form, as in the case, for example, of certain high-technology activities. Thus, many regions crave a biotechnology cluster as a key element to boost their region's competitive performance. Yet not only do few regions have any potential competitive advantage in this activity, arguably it is a sector that thrives most when concentrated in a limited number of large clusters. In other words, not every region can have a major biotechnology industry cluster, and for each to attempt to nurture such a cluster of its own may simply result in the failure to develop a strong national biotechnology sector at all. The same argument may well apply to other 'new economy' type activities, such as information and communication technologies (ICT), creative media, nanotechnology and the like. In short, there is no 'one-size fits all' regional competitiveness policy (on this, see also LOVERING, 1999).

To compound this problem, and again related to the question of what the appropriate scale of intervention should be, there is the issue of whether and how far policy should focus on particular localities within the region rather than on others. Is the best strategy one that focuses policy interventions and resources in just one or two growth zones (such as the major urban agglomerations or selected localized clusters)? If so, to what extent will any improvements in competitive performance spread out into other parts of the regional economy more generally? In other words, the focus on regional competitiveness should not ignore or neglect issues of intra-regional inequality. As the European Commission has recognized, social cohesion (the reduction of spatial socio-economic inequalities) should be an integral component of any policy aimed at improving regional competitiveness: indeed, social cohesion should rank equally with productivity and employment in any notion of regional competitive advantage.

CONCLUDING COMMENT

The issue of 'regional competitiveness' is thus ripe with theoretical, empirical and policy debate. In an era of 'performance indicators and rankings', it is perhaps inevitable that regions and cities should be compared against each other in terms of their economic performance. Such comparisons can serve a useful purpose in that they point up the fact that, and call for explanations of why, regions and cities differ in economic prosperity. But, to adapt Krugman's criticism of the idea of national competitiveness, it is at best potentially misleading and at worst positively dangerous to view regions and cities as competing over market shares as if they are in some sort of global race in which there are only 'winners' and 'losers'. This is not to deny the importance of competition. In economic life and beyond, competition is one of the fundamental sources of mobilization and creativity. But there are structural limits to, and negative consequences of, excessive competition as construed in narrow adversarial market terms (GROUP OF LISBON, 1995). Crucially, it is important to distinguish between 'competition' and 'competitiveness'.

As the papers in this issue make clear, if the notion of regional competitiveness has meaning and value, it is as a much more complex and richer concept; and one, moreover, that focuses more on the determinants and dynamics of a region's (or city's) long-run prosperity than on more restrictive notions of competing over shares of markets and resources. It is one that recognizes that ultimately competitive regions and cities are places where both companies and people want to locate and invest in. We are far from any agreed framework for defining, theorizing and empirically analysing regional competitive advantage. But given the current fashion for notions of regional and urban competitiveness in policy circles, the need for such a framework is all the more urgent. Without such a framework, policies lack coherent conceptual and evidential foundations, and policy outcomes may as a consequence prove variable and disappointing. The notion of regional competitiveness requires informed debate: the papers that follow are intended as contributions to this task.

Acknowledgements – The authors thank two anonymous referees for comments on an earlier version of this paper. The usual disclaimer applies.

REFERENCES

ATKINSON R. D. and CODURI R. (2002) *The 2002 State New Economy Index*. Progressive Policy Institute, Washington, DC.

ATKINSON R. D. and WILHELM T. G. (2002) *The Best States for E-Commerce*. Progressive Policy Institute, Washington, DC.

BALDWIN R., FORSLID R., MARTIN P., OTTAVIANO G. and ROBERT-NICOUD F. (2003) *Economic Geography and Public Policy*. Princeton University Press, Princeton.

BEGG I. (1999) Cities and competitiveness, *Urban Studies* **36**, 795–810.

BEGG I. (2002) *Urban Competitiveness: Policies for Dynamic Cities*. Policy Press, Bristol.

BOSCHMA R. A. (2004) Competitiveness of regions from an evolutionary perspective, *Regional Studies* (present issue).

BROWN G. (2001) The conditions for high and stable growth and employment, *Economic Journal* **111**, 30–44.

BUDD L. and HIRMIS A. (2004) Conceptual framework for regional competitiveness, *Regional Studies* (present issue).

CAMAGNI R. (2002) On the concept of territorial competitiveness: sound or misleading?, *Urban Studies* **39**, 2395–2411.

CELLINI R. and SOCI A. (2002) Pop competitiveness, *Banca Nazionale del Lavoro, Quarterly Review* **55**(220), 71–101.

CHESHIRE P. and GORDON I. R. (Eds) (1995) *Territorial Competition in an Integrating Europe*. Avebury, Aldershot.

CLARK G. L., PALASKAS T., TRACEY P. and TSAMPRA M. (2004) Globalization and competitive strategy in Europe's vulnerable regions: firm, industry and country effects in labour-intensive industries, *Regional Studies* (present issue).

COUNCIL ON COMPETITIVENESS (2001) *U.S. Competitiveness 2001: Strengths, Vulnerabilities and Long-term Priorities*. Council on Competitiveness, Washington, DC.

DEPARTMENT OF TRADE AND INDUSTRY (1998) *Our Competitive Future: Building the Knowledge Driven Economy*. Competitiveness White Paper. DTI, London.

DEPARTMENT OF TRADE AND INDUSTRY (2003a) *A Modern Regional Policy for the United Kingdom*. DTI, London.

DEPARTMENT OF TRADE AND INDUSTRY (2003b) *Prosperity for All: The Analysis*. DTI, London.

DEPARTMENT OF TRADE AND INDUSTRY (2003c) *Prosperity for All: The Strategy*. DTI, London.

DEPARTMENT OF TRADE AND INDUSTRY (2004) *Regional Competitiveness & State of the Regions*. DTI, London.

DUFFY H. (1995) *Competitive Cities: Succeeding in the Global Economy*. E & FN Spon, London.

EUROPEAN COMMISSION (1999) *Sixth Periodic Report on the Social and Economic Situation of Regions in the EU*. EC, Brussels.

EUROPEAN COMMISSION (2003) *European Competitiveness Report 2003*. EC, Luxembourg.

EUROPEAN COMMISSION (2004) *A New Partnership for Cohesion: Convergence, Competitiveness and Cooperation*. EC, Brussels.

FLORIDA R. (2002) *The Rise of the Creative Class*. Basic Books, New York.

FOTHERGILL S. (2004) A new regional policy for Britain and for Europe? [mimeo], *Regional Studies* (in press).

FUJITA M., KRUGMAN P. and VENABLES A. (1999) *The Spatial Economy; Cities, Regions and International Trade*. MIT Press, Cambridge, MA.

FUJITA M. and THISSE J.-F. (2002) *Economics of Agglomeration: Cities, Industrial Location and Regional Growth*. Cambridge University Press, Cambridge.

GARDINER B., MARTIN R. and TYLER P. (2004) Competitiveness, productivity and economic growth across the European regions, *Regional Studies* (present issue).

GROUP OF LISBON (1995) *Limits to Competition*. MIT Press, Cambridge, MA.

H. M. TREASURY (2000) *Productivity in the UK: The Evidence and the Government's Approach*. HMSO, London.

H. M. TREASURY (2001) *Productivity in the UK: 3 – The Regional Dimension*. H. M. Treasury, London.

H. M. TREASURY (2003) *Productivity in the UK: 4 – The Local Dimension*. H. M. Treasury, London.

H. M. TREASURY (2004) *Devolving Decision Making: Meeting the Regional Economic Challenge: Increasing Regional and Local Flexibility*. H. M. Treasury, London.

JENSEN-BUTLER C., SCHACHER A. and VAN WEESEP J. (Eds) (1997) *European Cities in Competition*. Avebury, Aldershot.

KENNY C. and WILLIAMS D. (2001) What do we know about economic growth? Or, why don't we know very much?, *World Development* **29**, 1–22.

KITSON M. (2004) Failure followed by success or success followed by failure? A re-examination of British economic growth since 1949, in FLOUD, R. and JOHNSON, P. (Eds) *The Cambridge Economic History of Modern Britain*, Vol. III: *Structural Change and Growth*, pp. 27–56. Cambridge University Press, Cambridge.

KRUGMAN P. (1990) *The Age of Diminished Expectations*. MIT Press, Cambridge, MA.

KRUGMAN P. (1994) Competitiveness: a dangerous obsession, *Foreign Affairs* **73**, 28–44.

KRUGMAN P. (1996a) *Pop Internationalism*. MIT Press, Cambridge, MA.

KRUGMAN P. (1996b) Making sense of the competitiveness debate, *Oxford Review of Economic Policy* **12**, 17–35.

LOVERING J. (1999) Theory led by policy? The inadequacies of the 'new regionalism', *International Journal of Urban and Regional Research* **23**, 379–395.

MALECKI E. J. (2004) Jockeying for position: what it means and why it matters to regional development policy when places compete, *Regional Studies* (present issue).

MARSHALL A. (1890) *Principles of Economics*, 8th Edn [1920]. Macmillan, London.

MARTIN R. and SUNLEY P. (1998) Slow convergence? The new endogenous growth theory and regional development, *Economic Geography* **74**, 201–227.

MARTIN R. and SUNLEY P. (2003) Deconstructing clusters: policy panacea or chaotic concept?, *Journal of Economic Geography* **3**, 5–35.

MORGAN K. (2004) The exaggerated death of geography: learning, proximity and territorial innovation systems, *Journal of Economic Geography* **4**, 3–22.

O'MAHONY M. and VAN ARK B. (Eds) (2003) *EU Productivity and Competitiveness: An Industry Perspective. Can Europe Resume the Catching-up Process?* European Commission, Luxembourg.

ODPM (2003) *Cities, Regions and Competitiveness.* Office of the Deputy Prime Minister, London.

ODPM (2004) *Competitive European Cities: Where Do the Core Cities Stand?* Urban Research Paper 13. Office of the Deputy Prime Minister, London.

PINCH S., HENRY N., JENKINS M. and TALLMAN S. (2003) From 'industrial districts' to 'knowledge clusters': a model of knowledge dissemination and competition in industrial agglomerations, *Journal of Economic Geography* **3**, 373–388.

POLENSKE K. R. (2004) Competition, collaboration and cooperation: an uneasy triangle in networks of firms and regions, *Regional Studies* (present issue).

PORTER M. (1990) *The Competitive Advantage of Nations.* Basingstoke, Macmillan.

PORTER M. E. (1992) *Competitive Advantage: Creating and Sustaining Superior Performance.* Issue 10. PA Consulting Group, London.

PORTER M. E. (1998a) *On Competition.* Harvard Business School Press, Boston.

PORTER M. E. (1998b) Location, clusters and the new economics of competition, *Business Economics* **33**, 7–17.

PORTER M. E. (2000) Location, competition and economic development: local clusters in the global economy, *Economic Development Quarterly* **14**, 15–31.

PORTER M. E. (2001a) Regions and the new economics of competition, in SCOTT, A. J. (Ed.) *Global City Regions*, pp. 139–152. Blackwell, Oxford.

PORTER M. E. (2001b) *Cluster of Innovation: Regional Foundations of US Competitiveness.* Council on Competitiveness, Washington, DC.

PORTER M. E. (2003) The economic performance of regions, *Regional Studies* **37**, 549–578.

PORTER M. E. and KETELS C. H. M. (2003) *UK Competitiveness: Moving to the Next Stage.* DTI Economics Paper 3. DTI, London.

ROBERT HUGGINS ASSOCIATES (2004a) *World Knowledge Competitiveness Index.* Robert Huggins Associates, Pontypridd.

ROBERT HUGGINS ASSOCIATES (2004b) *European Competitiveness Index.* Robert Huggins Associates, Pontypridd.

SAPIR A., AGHION P., BERTOLA G., HELLWIG M., PISANI-FERRY J., ROSATI D., VIÑALS J., WALLACE H. with BUTI M., NAVA M. and SMITH P. M. (2004) *An Agenda for a Growing Europe.* Sapir Report. Oxford University Press, Oxford.

SETTERFIELD M. (1997) *Rapid Growth and Relative Decline.* Macmillan, Basingstoke.

STEINLE W. J. (1992) Regional competitiveness and the single market, *Regional Studies* **26**, 307–318.

STORPER M. (1995) Competitiveness policy options; the technology–regions connection, *Growth and Change* **Spring**, 285–308.

STORPER M. (1997) *The Regional World: Territorial Development in a Global Economy.* Guilford Press, New York.

TUROK I. (2004) Cities, regions and competitiveness, *Regional Studies* (present issue).

URBAN STUDIES (1999) Special Issue on Competitive Cities, *Urban Studies* **36**(5/6).

Competitiveness of Regions from an Evolutionary Perspective

RON A. BOSCHMA

Department of Economic Geography, Faculty of GeoSciences, Utrecht University, PO Box 80 115, NL-3508 TC Utrecht, the Netherlands. Email: r.boschma@geog.uu.nl

(Received April 2003: in revised form April 2004)

BOSCHMA R. A. (2004) Competitiveness of regions from an evolutionary perspective, *Regional Studies* **38**, 993–1006. Do regions compete, as firms do? How does one deal with the fact that regions, unlike organizations, are entities that do not act? Does it make sense to talk about the ability of regions to generate new variety? This paper aims to address these questions from an evolutionary perspective. It is meaningful to talk about regional competitiveness when the region affects the performances of local firms to a considerable degree. This is especially true when the competitiveness of a region depends on intangible, non-tradable assets based on a knowledge and competence base embedded in a particular institutional setting that are reproduced and modified through the actions and repeated interactions of actors. Although regions are increasingly becoming collective players actively responding to an increasing exposure to extra-regional competition, the paper explains why there are serious limits in enhancing the competitiveness of regions. By doing so, it questions the usefulness of benchmarking practices with the purpose of improving regional competitiveness: there exists no 'optimal' development model, it is difficult to copy or imitate a successful model from elsewhere, and new trajectories often emerge spontaneously and unexpectedly in space.

Evolutionary economics   Economic geography   Regional competitiveness   Benchmarking   Lock-in
Institutions
BOSCHMA R. A. (2004) La compétitivité régionale du point de vue évolutionniste, *Regional Studies* **38**, 993–1006. Les régions, est-ce qu'elles se font concurrence, comme le font les entreprises? Comment tenir compte du fait que les régions, à la différence des établissements, constituent des entités qui n'agissent pas? A quoi sert de discuter de la capacité des régions à engendrer de nouvelles idées? Cet article cherche à aborder ces questions-là d'un point de vue évolutionniste. Il vaut la peine de discuter de la compétitivité régionale au moment où la région influe sensiblement sur la performance des entreprises locales. Cela est vrai notamment lorsque la compétitivité régionale dépend des ressources incorporelles, non-commercialisables fondées sur une connaissance et une compétence ancrées dans un contexte institutionnel particulier, et qui sont reproduites et modifiées à l'aide des actions et des interactions renouvelées des acteurs. Bien que les régions aient de plus en plus l'esprit d'équipe, réagissant sérieusement au contact croissant à la concurrence extrarégionale, cet article cherche à expliquer pourquoi l'amélioration de la compétitivité régionale a d'importantes limites. De cette façon, on remet en question l'emploi des points de repère afin d'améliorer la compétitivité régionale: il n'existe pas de modèle de développement 'optimal', il est difficile de copier ou d'imiter un modèle réussi emprunté, et de nouvelles trajectoires se font souvent jour spontanément et à l'improviste sur le plan géographique.

Economies évolutionnistes   Géographie économique   Compétitivité régionale   Points de repère enfermés
Lock-in   Organismes
BOSCHMA R. A. (2004) Die Konkurrenzfähigkeit von Regionen aus der Perspektive der Evolution, *Regional Studies* **38**, 993–1006. Konkurrieren Regionen miteinander wie Geschäftsfirmen? Wie soll man mit der Tatsache fertig werden, daß Regionen, im Gegensatz zu Organisationen, Einheiten sind, die nicht handeln? Hat es Sinn, über die Fähigkeit von Regionen zu sprechen, neue Vielfalt zu entwickeln? Dieser Aufsatz beabsichtigt, diese Fragen aus evolutionärer Sicht anzugehen. Es hat Sinn, über regionale Konkurrenzfähigkeit zu sprechen, wenn die Region die Leistung ortsansässiger Firmen in beträchtlichem Umfang beeinflußt. Dies ist besonders so, wenn die Konkurrenzfähigkeit einer Region von unbestimmbaren, nicht verkäuflichen Vermögenswerten abhängt, die auf einer Fachwissens-und Fähigkeitsgrundlage beruhen, die in einen besonderen institutionellen Rahmen eingebettet auftreten, und durch Einsatz und wiederholte Zusammenarbeit von Spielern neu inszeniert und abgewandelt werden. Obschon Regionen zunehmend zu Spielerkollektiven werden, die zunehmend von außerhalb der Region kommendem Wettbewerb ausgesetzt sind und aktiv darauf reagieren, erklärt der Aufsatz, warum es ernst zu nehmende Grenzen für die Anhebung der Konkurrenzfähigkeit einer Region gibt. Damit wird die Nützlichkeit der Normenpraxis zum Zwecke der Anhebung regionaler Konkurrenzfähigkeit in Frage gestellt: es gibt kein 'optimales' Entwicklungsmodell; es ist schwierig, anderorts erfolgreiche Modelle nachzuahmen oder zu kopieren, und neue Flugbahnen treten oft spontan und unerwartet im Raume auf.

Evolutionäre Wirtschaftswissenschaft   Wirtschaftsgeographie   Regional Kompetitiveness   Wettbewerbsfähigkeit
Normenfixierung   Institutionen

Boschma R. A. (2004) La competitividad de las regiones desde un punto de vista evolutivo, *Regional Studies* **38**, 993–1006. Compiten las regiones de la misma forma que lo hacen las empresas? Como debe uno tratar el hecho de que las regiones, a diferencia de las organizaciones, son entidades que no actúan? Tiene sentido hablar sobre la capacidad de las regiones para generar nuevas diversidades? El objetivo de este artículo es abordar estas cuestiones desde un punto de vista evolutivo. Hablar de competitividad regional tiene sentido cuando una región afecta el rendimiento de las empresas locales de forma considerable. Esto es especialmente cierto en aquellos casos en los que la competitividad de una región depende de activos que son intangibles y no-comercializables basados en una base de conocimiento y competencia que está incrustada en un contexto institucional particular, los cuales se reproducen y se modifican mediante las acciones y las interacciones repetidas de los actores. Aunque las regiones se están convirtiendo cada vez más en jugadores colectivos que responden activamente a una creciente exposición a la competición extra-regional, el artículo explica por qué existen serias limitaciones a la hora de optimizar la competitividad de las regiones. Cuestionamos así el grado de utilidad de las prácticas comparativas que tienen el propósito de mejorar la competitividad regional: no existe ningún modelo 'óptimo' de desarrollo, resulta difícil copiar o imitar un modelo que ha dado buenos resultados en otros contextos, y nuevas trayectorias emergen a menudo de forma espontánea e inesperadamente de forma espontánea.

Economía evolutiva   Geografía económica   Competitividad regional   *Benchmarking*   *Lock-in*   Instituciones

JEL classifications: O18, O33, R11, R58

INTRODUCTION

The notion of regional competitiveness has attracted a lot of attention since PORTER published *The Competitive Advantage of Nations* (1990). It has increasingly been adopted as a policy tool in the 1990s. Due to the process of globalization, cities and regions have been confronted with increasing competitive pressures, and this made policy-makers at the regional and urban level think about how to respond (BEGG, 2002).

Economic geographers have also been eager to embrace the concept because it promised to bring back the relevance of geography into economics, despite tendencies of globalization. There now exists a large body of literature stating that regions are an important resource of competitive advantage in a world of stronger interregional competition. Concepts like industrial districts (BECATTINI, 1990), innovative milieus (CAMAGNI, 1991), learning regions (ASHEIM, 1996) and regional innovation systems (COOKE *et al.*, 1998; COOKE, 2001) have described the crucial importance of externalities in maintaining competitiveness that extend or cross the boundaries of individual firms but which operate within the boundaries of a (loosely defined) territory. In this respect, the focus of attention has shifted from traded relationships to untraded interdependencies on which regional competitiveness is based (STORPER, 1997). This body of literature argues that non-economic factors (such as cognitive, social, cultural and institutional factors) are crucial for knowledge creation, learning and economic development. According to LAWSON (1999, p. 160), these underlying factors 'are somehow more enduring, but less "concrete" in some sense – factors which are "in the air" or "untraded" '. What is crucial is that these are believed to be spatially bounded, shaped and reproduced through the interaction between local actors.

The notion of regional competitiveness, however, is complicated and rather disputed (e.g. KRUGMAN, 1994). Basically, it comes down to the following questions. Do regions compete, as firms do? Is it meaningful to talk about the ability of regions to generate new variety and to engage in learning processes? It is not necessarily true that they do, despite the fact that some regions grow faster and show a better ability to develop new economic activities than other regions. How does one deal with the fact that regions are entities that do not act, like individuals or organizations do? Taking these remarks in consideration, does it make sense to talk about the competitiveness of regions?

The present paper aims to address these questions from an evolutionary perspective. Since the seminal work of NELSON and WINTER (1982), evolutionary economics has become a well-established field of research in economics that basically focuses on economic change in situations of bounded rationality (for a good overview, see NELSON, 1995). In economic geography, it is increasingly recognized that evolutionary thinking has a lot to offer (e.g. BOSCHMA and VAN DER KNAAP, 1997; COOKE *et al.*, 1998; BOSCHMA and LAMBOOY, 1999). One reason is that it fits rather well in the tradition of economic geography: it is well equipped to account for complexity and place-specific developments (MARTIN, 1999). An evolutionary economic geography approach aims to understand actions of economic actors and paths of change in a context of time and space. It explains how the behaviour of agents is situated and conditioned, but not determined, by structures accumulated at the level of the organization (e.g. routines) and the environment (e.g. social networks, institutions). In other words, these surrounding structures enable and constrain, but do not determine actions of agents: chance events and human agency, often in combination with increasing returns, may result in unforeseeable changes. That is, actions and repeated interaction of agents adapt, transform, upgrade or lock-in structures at the level of both the organization and the external environment. An evolutionary economic geography approach focuses on the dynamic interplay between structure and agency in particular settings: it aims to analyse how human action, organizational structures and the surrounding environment interact and co-evolve over time in different spatial contexts (BOSCHMA and LAMBOOY, 1999).

The main objective of the present paper is to explore from such an evolutionary perspective whether the region may conceptually be defined as a relevant and meaningful unit that affects the economic performance of firms. This objective requires an effort to extend the application of evolutionary thinking from the organizational to the territorial level. The paper proposes a conceptualization of the region based on evolutionary notions like routines, competences and lock-in that gives meaning to the competitiveness of regions. In doing so, it describes how the development of regions may give evidence of evolutionary features, such as path dependence and irreversibility.

Adopting an evolutionary perspective also has implications for what one means by a region. From an evolutionary point of view, it would be wrong to view the region as a static and fixed entity. The present paper will conceptualize the region as a dynamic rather than as a predefined entity that can only be considered relevant when co-evolutionary processes result in place-specific developments. Consequently, regions are portrayed as flexible rather than fixed units because its key assets, being constructed advantages based on inter-actions, may extend or shrink in space, or even disappear over time. In addition, regional competitiveness is a multidimensional phenomenon because many factors, operating simultaneously at various spatial levels, affect the performance of regions. For these reasons, it is argued that it is unlikely that place-specific developments take place at the level of administrative units, despite the fact that nation states (and sometimes regions at the sub-national level) have considerable institutional and administrative powers to affect the competitiveness of their companies.

The paper has three parts. Before it can be understood whether it is meaningful to talk about regional competitiveness, one first has to determine how firms compete, and what is their ability to engage in learning processes and innovation. The first part of the paper briefly unravels the relationships between routines, knowledge creation, learning and competitiveness at the organizational level under conditions of bounded rationality. The second part discusses whether or not regions compete. In doing so, it addresses the question of how to extend evolutionary economics from the organizational to the territorial level. It explains how the competitiveness of regions depends on the co-evolution of organizational capabilities and intangible resources at the regional level. The third part discusses

some policy implications of such a conceptualization of the region based on evolutionary thinking.

COMPETITIVENESS OF FIRMS

Evolutionary economics is founded on decision-making theory stressing that organizational behaviour is routinized because of fundamental uncertainty. At the micro-level, it explains the success and failure of organizations in terms of routines and competences. According to NELSON and WINTER (1982), market competition enables more efficient firms with 'fitter' routines to expand their production capacity at the expense of less efficient firms with 'unfit' routines. This is not to say that firms are subject to selection forces alone. On the contrary, they can change their routines to adapt to changing circumstances (e.g. a change in factor prices) or to exploit new technological opportunities. ALCHIAN (1950) explains that adaptive behaviour occurs because firms learn from their mistakes by trial and error, or because they observe and imitate the successful routines of other firms.

History matters in this respect. Mutations in routines (i.e. innovations) or learning behaviour at the firm level are affected by current routines. They influence the type of activities firms undertake, the strategies they follow and the opportunities they perceive. Search for new knowledge goes along with a high degree of uncertainty: outcomes of search processes are uncertain and often unexpected. That is why organizations rely and build on their existing knowledge base and experience, which have proven successful in the past (NELSON and WINTER, 1982). Searches for new technology are likely to be undertaken locally, i.e. directed to technologies and markets with which firms have become familiar in the past (ATKINSON and STIGLITZ, 1969; HEINER, 1983). According to DOSI (1982), innovative behaviour proceeds along narrowly defined trajectories that form a sort of framework of thought that guides the exploratory activities of firms and affects their ability to react to changing technologies or market circumstances. In other words, organizations search for new knowledge in close proximity to their existing knowledge base, which provides opportunities but also sets constraints for further improvement. This implies that change is often cumulative and localized: innovations are often incremental, piecemeal improvements.

As such, knowledge is considered a particular input: contrary to capital and labour, the stock of knowledge is not reduced when it is used. On the contrary, knowledge accumulates in time through usage due to learning from experience, trial-and-error processes, etc. This largely takes place within the firm: firms, for instance, undertake research and development activities, with the purpose of creating new knowledge. In this way, organizations build their core competences over time (PRAHALAD and HAMEL, 1990). Knowledge accumulates in the structure of the organizations, as embodied in organizational routines and procedures. NELSON and WINTER (1982) refer to routines as 'organizational memory' that are embedded in the skills of the employees, the fixed capital of the firm, etc. Knowledge may, of course, spill over across organizations. However, this is less likely to occur when the degree of tacitness and excludability of knowledge is high (ARROW, 1962). As a result, due to the cumulative, localized and tacit nature of knowledge, successful routines are difficult to imitate by competitors.

The firm-specific nature of routines implies that firms differ from each other. As a result, competition does not eliminate variety, although some firms will be forced to exit, and some routines will be imitated rather easily. Moreover, the cumulative, localized and tacit nature of knowledge has important consequences for the performance level of firms. On the one hand, it brings benefits to the firm, enabling the exploitation and further improvement of its competitive advantage. On the other hand, it may turn against the well-being of the organization (lock-in). This has been described by LEVITT and MARCH (1996) as the 'competency trap': 'becoming quite good at doing any one thing reduces the organization's capacity to absorb new ideas and to do other things' (LAWSON and LORENZ, 1999, p. 311). It often turns out to be difficult to unlearn habits or routines that have been successful in the past, but which have become redundant over time. This problem to break with lock-in situations might also have to do with vested interests in organizations opposing change that undermine their positions. Therefore, organizations need dynamic capabilities to ensure the successful implementation of new ideas (TEECE *et al.*, 1997).

The build-up of firm-specific core competences implies that required knowledge is dispersed among many different agents and organizations (ANTONELLI, 2000). In other words, knowledge creation and learning often depend on combining diverse, complementary capabilities of heterogeneous agents not only within, but also between organizations (NOOTEBOOM, 2000). The tacit and idiosyncratic nature of much knowledge implies that free access to external knowledge is not just enough. The effective transfer of knowledge requires a capacity to identify and exploit the new knowledge. If not, search and imitation costs will be too high. Moreover, it requires mechanisms to coordinate the exchange of complementary pieces of knowledge owned by a variety of actors. Knowledge may be readily bought on the market place. However, the market is often considered as not the most obvious mechanism to acquire tacit knowledge because of information asymmetry between supplier and buyer. Therefore, it is often argued that the transfer of tacit knowledge depends on reciprocal and stable arrangements because relationships based on understanding and trust make it easier to bridge communication gaps.

Thus, knowledge creation is a cumulative, localized and interactive process that occurs within and between organizations, and which affects their level of performance either positively or negatively (lock-in). As a result, firm-specific competences with a high degree of tacitness are created and reproduced through interactive learning based on past experience and sharing of knowledge between members within and between organizations. In other words, the competitiveness of firms depends both on intra-organizational resources (embodied in routines and competences) and extra-organizational assets (such as complementary knowledge sources and relational capital).

COMPETITIVENESS OF REGIONS

So far, it has been explained briefly how firms compete in an evolutionary framework. But do regions compete? To explore this issue, evolutionary approach needs to be extended from the organizational to the regional level. To put it differently, it has to be explored whether the cumulative, localized, and interactive nature of knowledge creation and learning may also have a geographical meaning.

There have been recent attempts to bridge the gap between the organization and the region as levels of analysis (e.g. LAWSON and LORENZ, 1999). MASKELL and MALMBERG (1999) claim that the notion of 'localized capabilities' might be useful to link the concepts of the region and the firm. LAWSON (1999, p. 158) draws on the competence perspective of Penrose to conclude that both firms and regions should be regarded as 'ensembles of competences that emerge from social interaction'. According to LAWSON (1999, p. 157), 'the region, as a productive system, may be differentiated as an ensemble of competences that "stretches" both through space and across organisations, and contains a degree of coherence in virtue of the nature of (localised) interaction constitutive of it'.

To elaborate on the concept of regional competitiveness, three topics have to be addressed. First, the problem of how to apply the notion of competition to the territorial level when one accounts for the fact that regions neither enter and exit markets, nor do they act, in contrast to firms. Second, from an evolutionary perspective, how regions can affect the competitiveness of firms. A distinction is made between two intangible sources of territorial competitiveness, i.e. the knowledge and competence base of regions, and their institutional setting. Third, the evolution of the long-term competitiveness of regions: to what extent are regional development paths likely to persist? In doing so, a real dynamic evolutionary approach on regional development is adopted.

Do regions compete?

It was explained above that competition results in varying growth rates of firms. This is also almost true for regions. It is a stylized fact that some regions grow faster than others. Like market shares shifting between firms, successful regions will increase their relative share in the (national or world) economy at the expense of lagging regions. A major difference between the evolution of firms and regions, however, is that firms enter and exit markets in contrast to regions. That is, market selection forces do not drive out regions (i.e. they do not disappear), like firms go broke. Moreover, regions do not emerge *ex nihilio*, like new firms enter markets, although there are exceptions, such as new acclaimed land such as in the case of the Dutch polders.

There is another feature that firms and regions share. Just like successful firms do not have to show profit-maximizing behaviour in order to be selected as 'winners' (ALCHIAN, 1950), differential growth rates of regions can also be just due to luck. Theoretically speaking, it is conceivable that it is merely the sum of the performances of all firms (in terms of, for example, productivity levels or profits) in a region that decides which region 'performs' better, or is 'more fit', in comparison with other regions. In this case, a successful region is just lucky to host more successful firms on average, and it does not have to be assumed that regions (like firms) act for this to happen.

But do regions compete like firms do? When regions have strong economic specializations in similar markets, regions would compete directly. A good example is competition between city harbours (such as Rotterdam and Antwerp in the Netherlands and Hamburg in Germany) that serve more or less the same hinterland, with direct implications for the growth rates of the regions involved. However, when economic growth rates between two regions differ (e.g. Sicily in Italy and Silicon Valley in California, USA), this does not necessarily mean that (firms within) both regions have been engaged in a direct, competitive struggle. Nevertheless, it could be claimed that regions are always in a state of competition (though less directly), trying to attract creative talent and investments from elsewhere (FLORIDA, 2002). A similar line of reasoning is more or less true for firms. Firms compete directly in product markets, operate in different markets (and market niches), and are competing for talented people and for capital for investments with other firms.

But do regions act like firms do? As explained above, the actions of firms are strongly affected by the intra- and inter-organizational context in which they operate. Nevertheless, they are not only subject to selection forces, but also they can act (e.g. they undertake search behaviour). Accordingly, it makes sense to talk about the behaviour and the adaptability of firms. Regions, however, are entities that do not act like individuals or organizations do. For instance, they are incapable of migrating when things get worse. Nevertheless, to an increasing extent regions are active players representing regional interests, with the goal of preserving or enhancing their competitiveness. Regional collective

strategies, in principle, can influence the outcome of the competition process, but some regions (e.g. due to their relative location or economic history) provide more opportunities for successful policy-making than do other regions.

Still, it would be meaningless to state that a region shows a higher performance when this has hardly anything to do with the region itself. As in the case of firms, it is essential to account for the role of history that enables, but also the constraints the actions, of firms. Since regions do not exit, they always carry with them a past that may affect the competitiveness of firms either positively or negatively. In this case, it would be more meaningful to conclude that some regions perform better than others. In other words, when actors and organizations are embedded in a territorial context that determines largely their behaviour and level of performance, the notion of regional competitiveness gets its most explicit meaning. In that case, the wider local context needs to be understood in order to understand the success or failure of firms. This logic allows it to be explained why some regions in contrast to others are characterized by a well-developed ability to adjust, but one does not have to assume that regions act.

The foregoing requires defining the region (at whatever spatial level) as a meaningful and relevant entity that affects the behaviour and performance of local organizations. This idea is elaborated below by proposing a conceptualization of the region based on evolutionary economics giving meaning to the competitiveness of regions under certain conditions. First, notions like connectivity, receptivity and variety are built on in order to claim that regions may be characterized by a specific knowledge and competence base that acts as an incentive and selection mechanism in a territorial context. Second, it is explained that regions accumulate different institutional environments over time. Institutions affect not only the intensity and nature of relations and, thus, the degree of interactive learning between agents, but also the capacity of regions to upgrade, transform or restructure specific organizations and institutions required for the development of new economic activities.

Region-specific knowledge and competence base

Because of the quasi-public nature of knowledge, as mentioned above, it is quite common that knowledge spills over across organizations. Moreover, it is increasingly recognized that knowledge externalities are also geographically bounded: firms in the vicinity of knowledge sources often take more benefit from these externalities and will most likely show a better innovative performance or higher productivity than firms located elsewhere (e.g. JAFFE *et al.*, 1993; AUDRETSCH and FELDMAN, 1996; VAN OORT, 2004).

First, this is a matter of connectivity, i.e. having

access to information flows. Co-location of similar activities makes sure that successful experiments by local firms do not remain unnoticed but are readily taken up almost without costs (MASKELL, 2001). This results in network externalities: the more (potential) knowledge sources in the territory, the larger the (potential) benefit for each local agent. Also, the more the knowledge sources in a region, the higher the number of (potential) connections with the outside world, and the more information there is available through extra-regional linkages to each local agent. This latter feature explains that connectivity is not necessarily restricted to a particular region: it means that local agents may benefit from linkages with the outside world through other local actors.

Second, effective knowledge transfer and interactive learning is not just a matter of being connected or not. It also requires receptivity (ANTONELLI, 2000). Local firms sharing similar competences in a particular knowledge field will have a better absorptive capacity and learning ability than non-local actors. This has much to do with the tacit and idiosyncratic nature of knowledge: the effective transfer of tacit (i.e. complex, uncodifiable and contextual) knowledge requires a common knowledge base, face-to-face interactions, and mutual understanding and trust (HOWELLS, 2002). This is not to say that geographical proximity is a necessary condition for tacit knowledge transfer (RALLET and TORRE, 1999). BRESCHI and LISSONI (2002) claim that dense social networks, rather than regions, may be effective vehicles of knowledge creation and diffusion. It is reminiscent of the fact that tacit knowledge is a common property or club good shared between members of an 'epistemic community' or 'community of practice' (BRESCHI and LISSONI, 2001; GERTLER, 2003). Nevertheless, since social networks are often (but not necessarily) geographically localized, the resulting knowledge spillovers will also be geographically localized. On the one hand, this accumulated body of regional knowledge acts both as incentive, offering opportunities for further improvement in familiar fields of knowledge. As a result, local actors search for new knowledge in close proximity to their own knowledge base, both in their own organization and in their surrounding environment. On the other hand, the regional knowledge base functions as a selection mechanism, impeding knowledge creation that does not fit into the local context. For instance, individuals and organizations may migrate to successful regions, but only some of them (most likely those with the required skills) will be able to participate in the social networks through which the local knowledge circulates. As a result, firms integrate regional knowledge with their own previously acquired knowledge base, resulting in new recombinations of knowledge.

Third, knowledge creation also requires variety, which acts as a stimulus, providing complementary capabilities. Neither connectivity nor receptivity is sufficient for interactive learning to take place. NOOTEBOOM (2000) states that too little cognitive distance means a lack of sources of novelty (a problem of lock-in). Organizations require access to heterogeneous sources of information both in their own region and beyond that provide new impulses and ideas, and bring new variety into the region. However, costs of coordinating separate bodies of knowledge increase and interactive learning ceases when the cognitive distance between organizations becomes too large (a problem of miscommunication).

Both problems can be dissolved, however, by a region endowed with a common knowledge base in which organizations have access to diverse, but complementary, knowledge resources either within the region or through extra-regional linkages. MASKELL (2001) explains how such a certain degree of variety may drive the development of clusters. At the horizontal dimension, variety between local competitors with similar capabilities in a cluster stimulates new experiments (as triggered by local rivalry), while it lowers the risk of unintended, undesirable spillovers to rivals. At the vertical dimension, a high degree of specialization of firms in clusters implies that the knowledge base of each firm has diverged to such an extent that interfirm learning takes place. Another way of avoiding both problems of lock-in and miscommunication is through the establishment of connections with other organizations outside the cluster, but only under two conditions. First, local actors need capabilities to absorb the external knowledge, i.e. some degree of cognitive proximity is required. Second, local firms need to share the same values and expectations with their non-local counterparts, i.e. some degree of institutional proximity is required (GERTLER, 1997).

In sum, regions may play an important role in the innovation process. They may accumulate a knowledge and competence base that acts as incentive and selection device. Regions provide not only access to local and non-local information (connectivity), but also a context in which regional capabilities (with a high degree of tacit knowledge) are accumulated, reproduced, and recombined through actions and interactions of local agents (receptivity). This further increases the level of variety within the region. Variety (both within the area and through extra-regional linkages) plays a fundamental role, both as a potential source of novelty and as a valuable asset providing complementary capabilities. In this way, the cumulative, localized nature of knowledge creation and learning has been extended from the organizational to the territorial level.

Region-specific institutional environment

A common knowledge and competence base, however, is not sufficient for bringing firms together and enabling interactive learning processes to take place. It also requires various mechanisms (e.g. markets, networks, firms) that coordinate the actions within and between organizations with complementary inputs. Beyond firms, there is a wide range of other actors and organizations (e.g. research institutes, the educational system, financial organizations) that provide complementary inputs essential to the innovation process. Building on the innovation system literature, the competitiveness of a region depends not only on the presence of a critical mass of (qualified) organizations within its boundaries, but also on its capacity to coordinate the actions of these organizations. It is assumed (if not explicitly than implicitly) that the greater the interaction between the different parts of the system, the more dynamic will be the system (CARLSSON *et al.*, 2002).

The most important type of relationship in an innovation system is beyond doubt the transfer of knowledge. There are various channels through which knowledge exchange can take place, such as labour mobility and inter-firm links (CAPELLO, 1999). However, there are a number of alternative mechanisms (e.g. the market, network, firm, public organization) that may establish these connections, enabling knowledge transfer through these various channels. In principle, innovating firms can buy the required knowledge and other inputs through the market. However, these inputs can also be acquired through network relationships, which are trust-based market relationships between organizations that are reciprocal and more stable (GRABHER, 1993). Besides market and network relationships, there is another mechanism of coordination that is possible, i.e. the firm. In principle, the firm can organize all the required inputs itself, especially when both markets and public organizations fail to ensure ownership rights and sufficient rewards for investments in new knowledge. However, in contrast to the two previously mentioned coordination mechanisms, the predominance of intra-firm relations is likely to reduce the degree of variety at the regional level, eroding the local base of potential sources of novelty.

It is essential to underline that the ways these (intra- and inter-organizational) relations are governed may be deeply embedded in a region-specific institutional environment. EDQUIST and JOHNSON (1997, p. 46) define institutions as 'sets of common habits, routines, established practices, rules, or laws that regulate the relations and interactions between individuals and groups'. Formal institutions (such as laws) and informal institutions (like cultural norms and habits) are enabling and constraining factors for the innovation process and, therefore, form a major part of the selection environment. The institutional environment affects the intensity and nature of knowledge creation and the (collective) learning mechanisms involved, such as the extent and nature of inter-firm cooperation. Or, as EDQUIST (1997, p. 20) puts it, 'when innovating, firms interact more or less closely with other organizations, they do so in the context of existing laws, rules, regulations and cultural habits'.

An institutional environment often consists of an interdependent set of institutions within a particular region. HALL and SOSKICE (2001) write about 'institutional complementarities', which means that the effectiveness of one institution (e.g. the way the labour market is organized) increases the returns from other complementary institutions (e.g. the way the financial market operates). At the international level, a distinction is often made between liberal market economies and coordinated market economies, or what ERGAS (1984) called 'exit-based' and 'voice-based' countries, with widespread implications for the speed and nature of the Schumpeterian process of creative destruction.

In liberal market economies, labour and capital markets are much more responsive to the development of radical innovations (HALL and SOSKICE, 2001). Governments show a pro-market attitude, as reflected, for instance, in restrictive anti-trust policy and a system of decentralized labour regulation. Labour markets are very flexible, but discourage both firms and people to invest heavily in highly specialized skills, resulting in a labour force with more generic skills (ESTEVEZ-ABE *et al.*, 2001). Labour mobility is relatively high, and labour relations are more short-term based: employees are less loyal to firms (if they can earn higher wages elsewhere, they change jobs), while labour poaching is more common practice. In contrast, in coordinated market economies, financial and labour markets are more rigid and more focused on the longer term, and the government is more active. Labour markets give more employment security for employees, and firms are more inclined to invest in their personnel, leading to a labour base with more specialized skills (GERTLER, 1997). Financial relations are more trust based, with large commitments on both sides. This kind of environment is more likely to generate incremental innovations: these are the deeper, long-term relationships that encourage more specialization of firms and labour skills and more commitment from the main players involved (HALL and SOSKICE, 2001).

However, the region-specific institutional environment not only affects the nature of interaction patterns and (thus) the way collective learning mechanisms take shape, but also it impacts on the intensity of relations, and thus the degree of interactive learning and the economic performance of local firms. It has been argued that a situation of institutional lock-in in old industrial regions has led to an inability to make the transition from one development trajectory to another (GRABHER, 1993). Moreover, a regional institutional environment characterized by a culture of shared trust has often been regarded as a local capability that supports learning and innovation: information is transmitted more easily when agents share cultural features such as language and common values (MASKELL and MALMBERG, 1999). This stands in contrast to an institutional environment with a low

degree of social capital that neither stimulates networking and inter-organizational learning nor provides
a sound basis for effective market transactions (lacking
basic requirements such as the enforcement of security),
as in the case of the South of Italy (PUTNAM, 1993).

In sum, regions accumulate different institutional
environments over time, which act as incentive and
selection mechanisms. Institutions affect not only the
intensity and nature of relations and, thus, the degree
of interactive learning between agents in a regional
context, but also the capacity of regions to upgrade,
transform or restructure specific institutions (such as
specific laws) required for the development of new
economic activities. What matters is whether institutions are flexible and responsive to change when
required: the implementation and diffusion of novelty
often requires the restructuring of old institutions and
the establishment of new institutions (FREEMAN and
PEREZ, 1988). This dynamic capability of institutions
affects the long-term competitiveness of a region
considerably.

*Evolution of long-term competitiveness of regions: stability
and dynamics*

Since the knowledge and competence base tends to
accumulate within a region, and the regional institutional setting is quite durable due to its systemic nature
and high sunk costs, their impact on the competitiveness of regions may last for a considerable period.
In fact, both region-specific assets are intangible forces
that are hard to copy or imitate by other territories.
For example, regional institutional settings (such as a
culture of shared trust) are the outcome of a long
history in a specific context and are neither for sale on
the market nor can they be designed instantaneously
by public policy. GERTLER (2003) notes that regional
institutions (such as practices, attitudes, values, etc.),
similar to knowledge, contain a certain degree of
tacitness, whose pervasive influence is so subtle that
local actors themselves are unaware of it. The regional
institutional setting is sustained and reinforced by
experience and frequent, repeated interaction within
the region, which is quite similar to the way the
regional knowledge base accumulates. In other words,
both sources of regional competitiveness are passed on
and reproduced in the course of time. According to
MASKELL (1998, p. 112), 'this transferability over time,
but not over space, can enable localized industries to
sustain their competitiveness'.

In other words, one needs to understand the wider
local context in order to understand the success or
failure of firms. The behaviour and performance of
firms are firmly rooted in a regional base of (shared
and diverse, complementary) knowledge resources and
a particular institutional setting, which are durable
and irreversible. Both region-specific assets provide

incentives and set constraints within which the innovation process takes place. In this respect, the region,
operating as a selection device, has become an entity
on its own. It consists of a variety of firms within a
technological field (or covering several, partly overlapping fields) that have differentiated themselves through
the use of unique regional resources. Moreover, firms
come and go without affecting the knowledge and
competence base of the region and its institutional
setting, and thus its level of competitiveness. Therefore,
it is not the individual or the organizational but the
territorial level that matters.

Regional development is therefore path dependent
and irreversible: a region moves along a specific development trajectory that affects (as an incentive and
selection structure) the kind of competences that are
most developed and reproduced, and how the institutional set-up co-evolves, and influences the way
production, learning and innovation take place. Consequently, there exists a wide diversity of regional
trajectories that differ with respect to which key organizations are involved in the innovation process (e.g.
large or small firms, universities, public agencies), how
knowledge is transmitted and diffused through the
area (through inter-firm cooperation or other means),
which institutions affect the innovation process, and
how institutions themselves are shaped, modified and
transformed.

As a result, regions develop different economic
structures, resulting in spatial variety of industries. In
Germany, for instance, most innovative effort takes
place in industries like chemicals, machine tools and
luxury cars, while the USA excel in sectors like
computers, software and aerospace. What is even more
interesting, and quite understandable from an evolutionary perspective, is that intra-sectoral specialization
of regions also exists and often persists for a long time
(COOKE *et al.*, 1998). For instance, ESSLETZBICHLER
(2002) has demonstrated in a long-term analysis of four
mature industries in the USA that interregional variety
(measured as technological variation in input–output
coefficients between US states) often persists even
within the same industry. This is a fine example of what
a true evolutionary approach can offer to economic
geography when analysing the spatial evolution of
a population of non-identical firms (with different
competences and routines) in a sector: Does there
emerge a spatial pattern in which regions specialize in
particular routines (do routines differ more between
rather than within regions)? Does the surrounding
environment (such as supportive organizations and
institutions) co-evolve differently in different regional
contexts? And to what extent do routines converge
across space due to imitation and selection, and at what
spatial levels? (BOSCHMA and FRENKEN, 2003).

This possibility of multiple spatial outcomes brings
to one's attention that different regions, with different
economic structures and institutional contexts, may

yield similar levels of economic performance and development, or what SAVIOTTI (1996) calls 'multi-stability'. As conventional economists would put it, the economic system displays multiple equilibria. Italy provides a strong case that high levels of innovative performance of regions (in this case in the North and in the Third Italy) may be produced by diverse systems. Broadly speaking, the Third Italy is characterized by strong learning systems at the level of the industrial district, characterized by informal and loosely structured relationships between (mainly small- and medium-sized) organizations that stimulate collective learning. In contrast, the North of Italy is mainly characterized by a science-based system focused on large firms with a high amount of research and development efforts and a strong capability to innovate (EVAN-GELISTA *et al.*, 2002).

This has implications for the way one looks at the influence of the institutional framework. The various coordination mechanisms dealt with above (such as markets or networks) may generate similar levels of economic performance, but the way this is achieved differs considerably. This questions the (often implicit) assumption in the literature that shared trust is a prerequisite and a superior condition for a high level of economic and innovative performance. For sure, it affects the kind of organizations found in regions, the ways relationships within and between organizations are coordinated, and how interactive learning take shape. However, it does not imply that places with no significant trust levels cannot be economically successful. This is illustrated by the example of Silicon Valley, where such a lack of shared culture has not prevented the existence of significant knowledge spillovers. COHEN and FIELDS (1999) claim that knowledge circulation in Silicon Valley has been enhanced by mechanisms like reputations and the reliability of firms. As long as formal institutions such as (physical and intellectual) property rights and the enforcement of contracts are in place and function well, knowledge may be traded through market transactions (e.g. through contractual arrangements between universities and firms).

Consequently, it would be wrong to search for a superior or optimal model. It is typically found that one innovation system performs well in one subset of dimensions while another performs well in another subset of dimensions. It can be argued that due to the systemic nature, an innovation system cannot be optimal in all dimensions at the same time, i.e. there are trade-offs (FRENKEN, 2001). This is not to deny that some institutional models are better than others. Building on the work of MYRDAL (1957) on negative feedback effects in developing countries, NOISI (2002) states there are regions where a lack of institutional efficiency is paramount and difficult to change. As noted above, the South of Italy provides a well-known case: it is considered a backward and vulnerable region,

characterized by a poor endogenous capability, a high dependency on external knowledge, and weak coordination among organizations due to a lack of social capital and poor institutional performance (EVANGELISTA *et al.*, 2002).

Thus, interregional variety is likely to be a persistent feature of economies. In the foregoing, emphasis has been put on self-reinforcing processes, in which the environment of a region (in terms of a specific knowledge and institutional base) is upgraded and becomes more valuable for local firms. However, it may also work oppositely. For example, a mismatch may develop between the local economic structure and the (once effective) institutional set-up. Regional differences may evaporate, a process described by MASKELL and MALMBERG (1999) as 'ubiquitification'. There are several reasons why the competitive position and prosperity of regions may be gradually undermined. First, globalization may result in the availability of production inputs at more or less the same costs everywhere. Second, (tacit) knowledge not only accumulates, but also may become standardized (i.e. more explicit and codified). Since this process of codification of knowledge encourages interregional diffusion of knowledge, the knowledge base of the region may lose its rareness and, therefore, its unique value for local firms. Third, effective institutions (such as specific laws, or the enforcement of property rights) may be copied or imitated by other regions.

However, there is another reason why regional dynamics are more likely to be the rule than the exception when applying a long-term evolutionary perspective. New technological trajectories often tend to emerge spontaneously and unexpectedly in space. Because chance events may be involved, the long-term competitiveness of regions is likely to be rather unpredictable. Evolutionary concepts such as chance, human agency and increasing returns are extremely powerful when explaining the spatial formation of new industries (BOSCHMA and FRENKEN, 2003). Basically, such an evolutionary approach describes a self-reinforcing and irreversible mechanism that 'organizes' the initial chaos of a firm's behaviour into a pattern of spatial concentration, which is unpredictable beforehand (ARTHUR, 1994). The impact of the local environment is considered to be of minor importance at the initial stage of development of a new industry (although this differs between industries): there exists a gap between the requirements of the new industry (in terms of knowledge, skills, etc.) and its surrounding environment. Instead, historical accidents, creative strategies of new industries and their further growth are considered to bring increasing returns (i.e. agglomeration economies) into the local environment (BOSCHMA and LAMBOOY, 1999). This may be based on purely evolutionary mechanisms, in which routines and knowledge spill over between organizations due to labour mobility, supplier–buyer linkages, spin-offs, imitation behaviour, etc. However, non-evolutionary mechanisms may also stimulate this self-reinforcing process, such as the increase of more specialized suppliers, better infrastructure and a more diversified labour market. As such, a supportive regional environment (such as a specific knowledge base and institutional set-up) is more likely the outcome of a long process of co-evolution (BOSCHMA and VAN DER KNAAP, 1997).

This is reminiscent of an important issue concerning the competitiveness of regions. One should be cautious not to overestimate the role of the (local) environment. Organizations and their surrounding environment co-evolve over time: region-specific assets are constantly transformed, upgraded or are locked-in by the actions and repeated interactions of agents. Thus, organizations are not only subject to selection forces that operate at the level of a regional trajectory, which enable and constraint possible actions and future paths of change. Actions of organizations may also deviate from existing paths, resulting in unexpected changes. That is, organizations continually adapt and transform, intentionally or not, their environment (METCALFE, 1994). Or, to put it differently, path dependence both produces and is produced by place-specific developments (MARTIN, 1999).

Space sometimes even plays a very marginal role, even in the case of spatial clustering. KLEPPER (2002) demonstrates in an empirical study using survival rates of different cohorts (time of entry) and types of firms (e.g. techno-economic background of entrepreneurs) that the early spin-off process largely determines the location of automobile manufacturing in Detroit. The essence of his approach is that spin-offs of successful firms inherit successful routines of their parents. This is regarded as a purely evolutionary process: knowledge creation occurs and remains within the boundaries of firms, while knowledge is reproduced through the growth of the firm involved and through its giving birth to new spin-offs. Rather than agglomeration effects per se, it was instead the 'accidental' presence of a number of early, highly successful entrants in the Detroit region, generating many successful spin-offs in the same location, that largely determined the spatial clustering of automobiles in the USA. In other cases, space plays a more prominent, complementary role, as a recent study of the software industry in the Netherlands suggests: both firm characteristics (such as dynamic capabilities of firms and spin-off dynamics) and spatial factors (measured as urbanization economies) played a significant role in the emerging spatial pattern of the Dutch software industry (BOSCHMA and WETERINGS, 2004).

In sum, interregional variety may be a persistent feature of an economy due to the dynamic interplay between two intangible factors (i.e. a specific knowledge and institutional base) at the regional level. However, it is more a rule than an exception that the knowledge and competence base of a region eventually becomes codified and therefore may lose its rareness and unique value for local firms. Overall, the long-term competitiveness of a region depends on its ability to upgrade its economic base by creating new variety (through new entries and innovation by incumbents) in order to offset variety-destroying processes (due to exits and imitation). As history tells, some regions are more capable of coping with this Schumpeterian process of creative destruction. Nevertheless, new technological trajectories often tend to emerge spontaneously and unexpectedly in space due to the importance of chance events, human agency and increasing returns. Consequently, the long-term competitiveness of regions is likely to be rather unpredictable.

BENCHMARKING AND POLICY-MAKING

As there exists no superior or optimal model, one has to think over the consequences for policy-making. This is especially relevant because regions pursue to an increasing extent a collective policy strategy to enhance the competitiveness of local firms (BEGG, 2002).

As noticed above, in advanced countries, sources of territorial competitiveness are constantly undermined, and regions have to cope with this. Following Schumpeter, it makes sense to distinguish between weak and strong competition (STORPER, 1997). This partly represents a distinction between competition on 'hard' factors (through the means of, for example, relative wages or tax levels) and competition on 'soft' factors (e.g. identity, culture, institutions). Weak competition means static price competition. Regions can pursue a strategy that concentrates on relative low labour costs, or they may exploit institutional differences between regions (such as differences in subsidies or labour regulation systems) that affect price competition between firms directly. However, a strategy of strong competition based primarily on exploiting the 'soft', intangible, region-specific assets described above is likely to be more effective in the long run (FOSS, 1996).

However, as noticed above, path dependence and lock-in situations are reflected in region-specific assets that provide opportunities but also set constraints for effective policy-making. Consequently, there are serious limits in enhancing the competitiveness of regions. Moreover, as there exists no optimal development model, there are no ready-made blueprints that can be universally applied to whatever local context (AMIN, 1999). As a result, it is a rather complicated task to identify and formulate preconditions for good and effective regional policy-making.

This implies benchmarking (i.e. a popular method to monitor competitors aiming at identifying best practices for the purpose of enhancing the competitiveness of firms and regions; e.g. HUGGINS, 2003) is unlikely to be much of a help either. This is not to deny that it is useful to compare the structure and performance of regions and to derive general policy implications from such benchmarking studies. For example, such studies provide considerable insights in the wide range of successful development paths available to regions. Policy-makers, however, should be reluctant to imitate a successful (institutional) model (such as the Silicon Valley model) that has its origin in a different environment without accounting for region-specific contexts. As explained above, there is no such thing as an optimal model in evolutionary thinking, and benchmarking studies are, therefore, unlikely to reveal one. In this respect, benchmarking may be very useful as a learning tool for policy-makers when it makes them aware of the dangers of simply copying best practices developed elsewhere.

The core problem of regional policy by imitation of best practices concerns the (often subtle) inter-dependencies that exist between the different factors contributing to a successful model. This implies that imitation of a subset of factors that contributed to success in one region may be detrimental for another region because of the mismatch between the new subset and the existing structures and routines. The historical trajectory of a region sets serious limits on copying an external model that owed its success to its deep roots in an alien environment. This is true not only for the whole system (such as the Silicon Valley model), but also for transferring one successful part of an innovation system from one local context to another. For example, the set-up of a research centre of excellence in a technology field (such as biotechnology) is likely to remain a cathedral in the desert in a region that lacks the required competences (in organizations like firms, educational facilities, financial institutes, etc.) and institutional context (e.g. cultural resistance against genetic engineering). Policy efforts to stimulate joint research between firms are also more likely to fail in regions where the set of institutions governing, for instance labour and capital markets is largely focused on short-term returns.

Even so, policy-makers are necessarily adapters rather than optimizers (METCALFE, 1994). Like firms, they have to cope with a great deal of uncertainty. New development paths cannot be planned or foreseen. As explained above, one should be cautious to overestimate the role of the (local) environment: new industries have often emerged quite spontaneously somewhere due to chance events and increasing returns. This is not to deny the important and active role governments have always played in this respect (e.g. through defence expenditures), but they have not determined (at least not consciously) the place where these new growth paths took place (LAMBOOY and BOSCHMA, 2001). Therefore, it remains uncertain where the new industries with the highest growth potentials emerge in space.

Nevertheless, there might be room for effective policy-making. Since regional policy is likely to fail when local strategies deviate from the regional context, there is a need for an innovation policy with an explicit territorial dimension. The potential impact might be the larger the more the policy objectives are embedded in the surrounding environment. This comes down to a bottom-up policy directed at upgrading the regional context where necessary (i.e. strengthening weak elements, redesigning existing institutions), while building on existing regional competences and relational capital. In this respect, government policy in principle might be effective: not only has it an impact on the importance and structure of organizations (for instance, knowledge organizations are often publicly owned), but also it affects the interaction patterns of organizations in many ways (e.g. policies stimulating close industry–university links).

Policy-makers might also be more in favour of such a kind of policy. Since they are not optimizers, they are more inclined to pursue a policy of trial and error. As firms, policy-makers learn and adopt in the light of experience. Consequently, they are more inclined to embrace a policy that is focused on geographically localized change: there is less risk involved, local support will be much stronger and the guarantee of success may be higher (BOSCHMA, 2004). However, this might easily lead to a situation of regional institutional lock-in that leaves no room for new basic variety to develop. There is a serious risk that the ideal circumstances for regional policy-making (i.e. a specialized region with a few strong players) are accompanied with a situation of institutional lock-in, with adverse impacts on regional competitiveness in the long run. Or, as CHESHIRE and GORDON (1996, p. 388) have put it:

> a relatively specialized urban economy, with a high degree of integration among long-established businesses may be the most promising economic base for the organization of competitive activity, but that activity will tend to reflect the perceptions and interests of those particular businesses rather than a strategic view of current competitive prospects.

One could also argue that since the local environment exercises only a minor influence on the location of new industries subject to increasing returns, there is room for human agency (including policy-makers) to act effectively and to contribute to the build up of a favourable environment (LAMBOOY and BOSCHMA, 2001). According to CAMAGNI (2002, p. 2405), in such a world of increasing returns, regional competitiveness should reside in dynamic factors that 'are all artificial or created advantages, open to the proactive, voluntary action of local communities and their governments'. However, as stated above, it is uncertain where these new industries will emerge in space, since chance events and increasing returns are involved.

Therefore, in principle, there is room for policy-makers, but there are good reasons to presume that the effectiveness of policy-making remains uncertain and rather unpredictable.

CONCLUSIONS

Based on evolutionary thinking, the present paper has made an attempt to explore under what circumstances it might be meaningful to talk about the competitiveness of regions. This is true when the prosperity of firms depends on region-specific intangible assets embodied in a knowledge and competence base with a high degree of tacitness, which is sustained and reproduced by interaction patterns that are firmly rooted in a particular institutional setting. It explains why collective learning mechanisms may be localized, cumulative and geographically bounded, and why regional development is path dependent. Regions offer a set of opportunities and constraints that not only directs the search process of local firms, but also acts as a selection environment that promotes firms whose core competences fit into the local context. In that case, firms in other regions are excluded from competition in that particular field because they have no local access to these intangible factors, and they have not accumulated an absorptive capacity to imitate the technology required and to copy its institutional foundation. Due to its systemic and non-tradable nature, these region-specific assets are hard to replicate or transfer to places elsewhere.

Thus, interregional variety is a persistent feature in the world economy. However, it is more a rule than an exception that the knowledge base of a region eventually loses its rareness and unique value for local firms. In sum, the competitiveness of a region depends on its ability to upgrade its economic base by creating new variety in order to offset variety-destroying processes. Contrary to localized and cumulative change along existing trajectories, new technological trajectories often emerge spontaneously in space, resulting in unforeseeable changes and spatial leapfrogging. Consequently, the long-term competitiveness of regions is likely to be rather unpredictable.

However, this way of describing the region as a meaningful entity needs further refinements both at the conceptual and at the empirical levels. First, it would be wrong to portray regions as predefined, static and fixed entities. When a region is defined in terms of competence and institutional features, the boundaries of these features (when delineated) are not very likely to show a great deal of overlap with the boundaries of a spatial unit. It was explained above that it is quite likely that successful regions have developed extra-regional linkages that may bring in new variety in the region. It is common that economic transactions cross regional borders, which may go along with knowledge flows and the creation of institutions such as shared values and norms. Moreover, since region-specific assets are largely constructed advantages, these assets extend and shrink in space, or may even disappear, over time. What is more, many geographical scales are involved in interactive learning processes at the same time (MALMBERG and MASKELL, 2002). For example, inter-firm networks (such as research and development partnerships) often tend to operate at higher, more aggregate spatial levels than spin-off dynamics and labour mobility. Informal institutions stimulating the everyday, informal exchange of information and ideas are often geographically localized. In contrast, the impact of formal institutions (e.g. laws) that regulate the interaction between agents tends to operate at the level of the nation state, or even beyond (BATHELT, 2003). As a result, it would be misleading to select (or assume) a priori a particular geographical scale when analysing interactive learning and innovation processes. Instead, empirical analyses have to decide at what spatial levels these dynamic processes take place, and to what extent regions are relevant in this respect. In other words, there is a strong need to account for (the interaction of) various spatial scales that may influence the competitiveness of regions (e.g. ASHEIM and ISAKSEN, 2002).

There are still quite a few empirical challenges that need to be addressed concerning the economic impact of regions at the level of the firm. Empirical studies have often been more inclined to assume that knowledge externalities are geographically bounded rather than providing direct empirical evidence at the firm level. Moreover, they shed little empirical light on the question whether pure knowledge spillovers rather than pecuniary externalities are involved (MALMBERG and MASKELL, 2002). Such research would certainly help to be more specific on the question under what circumstances geographical proximity plays a role in the transfer of tacit knowledge, and when it does not. Especially, there needs to be more understanding of how to determine empirically the impact of institutions on the competitiveness of firms. This is an urgent matter because it is not always straightforward what are the relationships between institutions and the performance of local firms. For instance, HUDSON (1999), among others, has argued that 'institutional thickness' not only facilitates, but also can constrain collective learning and regional growth. This is especially difficult to determine for the 'grey mass' of regions that do not fit into the two ideal-type categories of the bad (i.e. no regional system) and the beautiful (i.e. a highly developed regional system). Overall, there is a strong need for real comparative studies that analyse systematically (i.e. making use of identical methodology) the impact of different regional contexts on the performance of firms (COOKE, 2001). Such a comparative approach would really contribute to unravel the mechanisms that lay at the root of regional competitiveness.

REFERENCES

ALCHIAN A. A. (1950) Uncertainty, evolution, and economic theory, *Journal of Political Economy* **58**, 211–221.

AMIN A. (1999) An institutionalist perspective on regional economic development, *International Journal of Urban and Regional Research* **23**, 365–378.

ANTONELLI C. (2000) Collective knowledge communication and innovation: the evidence of technological districts, *Regional Studies* **34**, 535–547.

ARROW K. J. (1962) The economic implications of learning by doing, *Review of Economic Studies* **29**, 155–173.

ARTHUR W. B. (1994) *Increasing Returns and Path Dependence in the Economy*. University of Michigan Press, Ann Arbor.

ASHEIM B. T. (1996) Industrial districts as 'learning regions': a condition for prosperity, *European Planning Studies* **4**, 379–400.

ASHEIM B. T. and ISAKSEN A. (2002) Regional innovation systems: the integration of local 'sticky' and global 'ubiquitous' knowledge, *Journal of Technology Transfer* **27**, 77–86.

ATKINSON A. B. and STIGLITZ J. E. (1969) A new view of technological change, *Economic Journal* **79**, 573–578.

AUDRETSCH D. B. and FELDMAN M. (1996) Spillovers and the geography of innovation and production, *American Economic Review* **86**, 630–640.

BATHELT H. (2003) Geographies of production: growth regimes in spatial perspective 1 – innovation, institutions and social systems, *Progress in Human Geography* **27**, 763–778.

BECATTINI G. (1990) The Marshallian industrial districts as a socio-economic notion, in PYKE F. (Ed.) *Industrial Districts and Inter-firm Co-operation in Italy*, pp. 37–51. International Institute for Labour Studies, Geneva.

BEGG I. (2002) *Urban Competitiveness*. Policy Press, Bristol.

BOSCHMA R. A. (2004) Rethinking regional innovation policy: the making and breaking of regional history, in FUCHS G. and SHAPIRA P. (Eds) *Rethinking Regional Innovation and Change: Path Dependency or Regional Breakthroughs?* Kluwer, Dordrecht (forthcoming).

BOSCHMA R. A. and FRENKEN K. (2003) Evolutionary economics and industry location, *Review for Regional Research/Jahrbuch fur Regionalwissenschaft* **23**, 183–200.

BOSCHMA R. A. and LAMBOOY J. G. (1999) Evolutionary economics and economic geography, *Journal of Evolutionary Economics* **9**, 411–429.

BOSCHMA R. A. and VAN DER KNAAP G. A. (1997) New technology and windows of locational opportunity. Indeterminacy, creativity and chance, in REIJNDERS J. (Ed.) *Economics and Evolution*, pp. 171–202. Edward Elgar, Cheltenham.

BOSCHMA R. A. and WETERINGS, A. (2004) The spatial formation of the software sector in the Netherlands. Working Paper Urban & Regional Research Centre Utrecht.

BRESCHI S. and LISSONI F. (2001) Knowledge spillovers and local innovation systems: a critical survey, *Industrial and Corporate Change* **10**, 975–1005.

BRESCHI S. and LISSONI F. (2002) Mobility and social networks: localised knowledge spillovers revisited. Paper presented at the Workshop 'Clusters in High-technology: Aerospace, Biotechnology and Software Compared', Montreal, Canada, 1 November 2002.

CAMAGNI R. (Ed.) (1991) *Innovation Networks. Spatial Perspectives*. Bellhaven, London.

CAMAGNI R. (2002) On the concept of territorial competitiveness: sound or misleading?, *Urban Studies* **39**, 2395–2411.

CAPELLO R. (1999) Spatial transfer of knowledge in high technology milieux: learning versus collective learning processes, *Regional Studies* **33**, 353–365.

CARLSSON B., JACOBSSON S., HOLMEN M. and RICKNE A. (2002) Innovation systems: analytical and methodological issues, *Research Policy* **31**, 233–245.

CHESHIRE P. C. and GORDON I. R. (1996) Territorial competition and the predictability of collective (in)action, *International Journal of Urban and Regional Research* **20**, 383–399.

COHEN S. and FIELDS G. (1999) Social capital and capital gains in Silicon Valley, *California Management Review* **41**, 108–130.

COOKE P. (2001) Regional innovation systems, clusters, and the knowledge economy, *Industrial and Corporate Change* **10**, 945–974.

COOKE P., URANGA M. G. and EXTEBARRIA G. (1998) Regional innovation systems: an evolutionary perspective, *Environment and Planning A* **30**, 1563–1584.

DOSI G. (1982) Technological paradigms and technological trajectories. A suggested interpretation of the determinants and directions of technical change, *Research Policy* **11**, 147–162.

EDQUIST C. (1997) Systems of innovation approaches. Their emergence and characteristics, in EDQUIST C. (Ed.) *System of Innovation. Technologies, Institutions and Organizations*, pp. 1–35. Pinter, London.

EDQUIST C. and JOHNSON B. (1997) Institutions and organizations in systems of innovation, in EDQUIST C. (Ed.) *System of Innovation. Technologies, Institutions and Organizations*, pp. 41–63. Pinter, London.

ERGAS H. (1984) *Why Do Some Countries Innovate More Than Others?* CEPS, Brussels.

ESSLETZBICHLER J. (2002) Competition, variety, and the geography of technology evolution. Paper presented at the 9th Conference of the European Association of Evolutionary Political Economy, Aix-en-Provence, France, 9–13 November 2002.

ESTEVEZ-ABE M., IVERSEN T. and SOSKICE D. (2001) Social protection and the formation of skills: a reinterpretation of the welfare state, in HALL P. A. and SOSKICE D. (Eds) *Varieties of Capitalism. The Institutional Foundations of Comparative Advantage*, pp. 145–183. Oxford University Press, Oxford.

EVANGELISTA R., IAMMARINO S., MASTROSTEFANO V. and SILVANI A. (2002) Looking for regional systems of innovation: evidence from the Italian Innovation survey, *Regional Studies* **36**, 173–86.

FLORIDA R. (2002) The economic geography of talent, *Annals of the Association of American Geographers* **92**, 743–755.

FOSS N. J. (1996) Higher-order industrial capabilities and competitive advantage, *Journal of Industry Studies* **3**, 1–20.

FREEMAN C. and PEREZ C. (1988) Structural crisis of adjustment, business cycles and investment behaviour, in DOSI G., FREEMAN C., NELSON R., SILVERBERG G. and SOETE L. (Eds) *Technical Change and Economic Theory*, pp. 38–66. Pinter, London.

FRENKEN K. (2001) Understanding product innovation using complex systems theory. PhD thesis, University of Amsterdam/University of Grenoble.

GERTLER M. S. (1997) The invention of regional culture, in LEE R. and WILLS J. (Eds) *Geographies of Economies*, pp. 47–58. Arnold, London.

GERTLER M. S. (2003) Tacit knowledge and the economic geography of context, or the undefinable tacitness of being (there), *Journal of Economic Geography* **3**, 75–99.

GRABHER G. (Ed.) (1993) *The Embedded Firm. On the Socioeconomics of Industrial Networks*. Routledge, London.

HALL P. A. and SOSKICE D. (2001) An introduction to varieties of capitalism, in HALL P. A. and SOSKICE D. (Eds) *Varieties of Capitalism. The Institutional Foundations of Comparative Advantage*, pp. 1–68. Oxford University Press, Oxford.

HEINER R. A. (1983) The origin of predictable behaviour, *American Economic Review* **73**, 560–595.

HOWELLS J. R. L. (2002) Tacit knowledge, innovation and economic geography, *Urban Studies* **39**, 871–884.

HUDSON R. (1999) The learning economy, the learning firm and the learning region. A sympathetic critique of the limits to learning, *European Urban and Regional Studies* **6**, 59–72.

HUGGINS R. (2003) Creating a UK competitiveness index: regional and local benchmarking, *Regional Studies* **37**, 89–96.

JAFFE A. B., TRAJTENBERG M. and HENDERSON R. (1993) Geographic localization and knowledge spillovers as evidenced by patent citations, *Quarterly Journal of Economics* **108**, 577–598.

KLEPPER S. (2002) The evolution of the U.S. automobile industry and Detroit as its capital. Paper presented at the 9th Congress of the International Joseph A. Schumpeter Society, Gainesville, FL, USA, March.

KRUGMAN P. (1994) Competitiveness. A dangerous obsession, *Foreign Affairs* **73**, 28–44.

LAMBOOY J. G. and BOSCHMA R. A. (2001) Evolutionary economics and regional policy, *Annals of Regional Science* **35**, 113–131.

LAWSON C. (1999) Towards a competence theory of the region, *Cambridge Journal of Economics* **23**, 151–166.

LAWSON C. and LORENZ E. (1999) Collective learning, tacit knowledge and regional innovative capacity, *Regional Studies* **33**, 305–317.

LEVITT B. and MARCH J. (1996) Organizational learning, in COHEN M. D. and SPROULL L. S. (Eds) *Organizational Learning*, pp. 516–541. Thousand Oaks, Sage.

MALMBERG A. and MASKELL P. (2002) The elusive concept of localization economies: towards a knowledge-based theory of spatial clustering, *Environment and Planning A* **34**, 429–449.

MARTIN R. (1999) The new 'geographical turn' in economics: some critical reflections, *Cambridge Journal of Economics* **23**, 65–91.

MASKELL P. (1998) Low-tech competitive advantages and the role of proximity. The Danish wooden furniture industry, *European Urban and Regional Studies* **5**, 95–118.

MASKELL P. (2001) Towards a knowledge-based theory of the geographical cluster. Paper presented at the Third Congress on Proximity 'New Growth and Territories', Paris, France, 13–14 December 2001.

MASKELL P. and MALMBERG A. (1999) The competitiveness of firms and regions. 'Ubiquitification' and the importance of localized learning, *European Urban and Regional Studies* **6**, 9–25.

METCALFE S. (1994) Evolutionary economics and technology policy, *Economic Journal* **104**, 931–944.

MYRDAL G. (1957) *Economic Theory and Under-developed Regions*. Duckworth, London.

NELSON R. R. (1995) Recent evolutionary theorizing about economic change, *Journal of Economic Literature* **33**, 48–90.

NELSON R. R. and WINTER S. G. (1982) *An Evolutionary Theory of Economic Change*. Harvard University Press, Cambridge, MA.

NOISI J. (2002) National systems of innovation are 'x-efficient' (and x-effective). Why some are slow learners, *Research Policy* **31**, 291–302.

NOOTEBOOM B. (2000) *Learning and Innovation in Organizations and Economies*. Oxford University Press, Oxford.

PENROSE E. (1959) *The Theory of the Growth of the Firm*. Oxford University Press, Oxford.

PORTER M. E. (1990) *The Competitive Advantage of Nations*. Macmillan, London.

PRAHALAD C. and HAMEL G. (1990) The core competence of the organization, *Harvard Business Review* **68**, 79–91.

PUTNAM R. D. (1993) *Making Democracy Work. Civic Traditions in Modern Italy*. Princeton University Press, Princeton.

RALLET A. and TORRE A. (1999) Is geographical proximity necessary in the innovation networks in the era of the global economy?, *GeoJournal* **49**, 373–380.

SAVIOTTI P. P. (1996) *Technological Evolution, Variety and the Economy*. Edward Elgar, Cheltenham.

STORPER M. (1997) *The Regional World. Territorial Development in a Global Economy*. Guilford, New York.

TEECE D., PISANO G. and SHUEN A. (1997) Dynamic capabilities and strategic management, *Strategic Management Journal* **18**, 509–33.

VAN OORT F. G. (2004) *Urban Growth and Innovation. Spatially Bounded Externalities in the Netherlands*. Ashgate, Aldershot.

Conceptual Framework for Regional Competitiveness

LESLIE BUDD★ and AMER K. HIRMIS†

★Open University Business School, Open University, Michael Young Building, Walton Hall, Milton Keynes MK7 6AA, UK. Email: l.c.budd@open.ac.uk
†48 Kelso Close, Rayleigh, Essex SS6 9RT, UK. Email: amerhirmis@hotmail.com

(Received May 2003: in revised form July 2004)

BUDD L. and HIRMIS A. K. (2004) Conceptual framework for regional competitiveness, Regional Studies 38, 1007–1020. The concept of territorial competitiveness has gained ground in academic, policy and practitioner circles. In particular, urban competitiveness has generated a large literature. However, there is a danger that competitiveness at a territorial level becomes a conceptual chimera. The essential problem is that territorially based actors and agencies seek to position and maintain the utility of their regions and subregions by reference to a set of measures and indicators that are conceptually suspect and often empirically weak. The degree to which regions compete depends on a manifold set of factors. The paper proposes a conceptual framework for regional competitiveness based on combining the competitive advantage of firms and the comparative advantage of a regional economy. The conceptual transmission mechanism to regional competitiveness combines Liebenstein's theory of 'X-inefficiency' and agglomeration economies. The paper begins with a review of competitiveness and its literature. It then investigates the regional balance of payment constraint in the absence of a real regional exchange rate. In conclusion, it asks whether the conceptual approach was appropriate for a study of benchmarking indicators for the London region in comparison with other metropolises.

Competitiveness   Competitive and comparative advantage   X-inefficiency   Agglomeration economies
Regional competitiveness

BUDD L. et HIRMIS A. K. (2004) La compétitivité régionale: un cadre conceptuel, Regional Studies 38, 1007–1020. Dans les milieux intellectuels, de politique générale et professionnels, la notion de compétitivité territoriale a gagné du terrain. En particulier, la compétitivité urbaine a suscité une documentation importante. Cependant, il y a un risque que la compétitivité devienne une chimère conceptuelle sur le plan géographique. Le problème primordial c'est que les acteurs et les organismes territoriaux cherchent à positionner et à maintenir l'utilité des régions et des sous-régions par rapport à un ensemble de mesures et d'indicateurs conceptuellement douteux et souvent empiriquement faibles. La compétitivité des régions dépend de nombreux facteurs. Cet article cherche à proposer un cadre conceptuel de la compétitivité régionale fondé sur une combinaison de l'avantage compétitif des entreprises et de l'avantage comparatif d'une économie régionale. Le mécanisme de transmission conceptuel de la compétitivité régionale combine la théorie de l'innefficience X d'après Liebenstein et les économies d'agglomération. Primo, l'article fait la critique de la compétitivité et de la documentation correspondante. Il s'ensuit une étude de la contrainte régionale en l'absence d'un taux de change régional réel. Pour conclure, l'article pose la question suivante: l'approche conceptuelle, est-elle appropriée à l'étude des points de repère relatifs à Londres et ses environs par rapport à d'autres métropoles?

Compétitivité   Avantages compétitif et comparatif   Inefficience X   Economies d'agglomération
Compétitif régionales

BUDD L. und HIRMIS A. K. (2004) Ein begrifflicher Rahmen für regionalen Wettbewerb, Regional Studies 38, 1007–1020. Der Begriff eines regional geprägten Konkurrenzgeistes hat in akademischen, politischen und Praktikerkreisen an Boden gewonnen. Besonders der städtische Konkurrenzgeist hat eine umfangreiche Literatur erzeugt. Es besteht jedoch Gefahr, daß Konkurrenzgeist auf Gebietsebene zur begrifflichen Schimäre wird. Das Grundproblem ist, daß gebietsgebundene Spieler und Agenturen bestrebt sind, die Nützlichkeit ihrer Regionen und Teilregionen durch Hinweis auf eine Reihe von Maßnahmen und Meßlatten zu positionieren und zu erhalten, die begrifflich verdächtig sind und empirisch auf unsicheren Füßen stehen. Das Ausmaß der Konkurrenz unter Regionen hängt von einem Bündel vielfältiger Faktoren ab. Dieser Aufsatz schlägt einen begrifflichen Rahmen für regionale Konkurrenz vor, der sich auf ein Durchkämmen der Wettbewerbsvorteile von Firmen und auch die vergleichbaren Vorteile eine Regionalwirtschaft stützt. Der begriffliche Mechanismus der Übertragung auf einen regionalen Konkurrenzgeist verbindet Liebensteins Theorie der 'X-Unwirksamkeit' mit Ballungswirtschaften. Der Aufsatz bringt zuerst einen Überblick über Konkurrenz und ihre Literatur. Dann untersucht er die regionalen Bilanzbeschränkungen im Lichte des Fehlens eines echten regionalen Wechselkurses. Abschließend wird die Frage aufgeworfen, ob der begriffliche

Ansatz der Autoren für eine Untersuchung der Maßstabsindikatoren der Region London im Vergleich zu anderen Metropolen geeignet war.

Konkurrenzgeist   Wettbewerbs-und vergleichbarer Vorteil   X-Unwirksamkeit   Ballungswirtschaften
regionale Kompetenzen

BUDD L. y HIRMIS A. K. (2004) Un marco conceptual para la competitividad regional, *Regional Studies* **38**, 1007–1020. El concepto de competitividad territorial ha ganado terreno en círculos académicos, de política y practicantes. En particular, el concepto de competitividad urbana ha generado una extensa literatura. Sin embargo, existe el riesgo de que la competitividad a nivel territorial se convierta en una quimera conceptual. El principal problema radica en que los actores y los órganos territoriales aspiran a posicionar y a mantener la polivalencia de sus regiones y sub-regiones tomando como referencia un conjunto de medidas e indicadores que son conceptualmente dudosos y sin mucho fundamento empírico. El grado hasta el cual las regiones compiten depende de múltiples factores. Este artículo propone un marco conceptual para la competitividad regional basado en la combinación de la ventaja competitiva de las empresas y la ventaja comparativa de una economía regional. El mecanismo de transmisión conceptual a la competitividad regional combina la teoría de 'ineficiencia-X' de Liebenstein y las economías de aglomeración. El artículo comienza con una revisión del concepto de competitividad y la literatura existente en torno a dicho concepto. A continuación investiga la restricción de balance regional en la ausencia de un tasa de cambio regional real. Por último, el artículo plantea la cuestión de si nuestro enfoque conceptual fue el apropiado para un estudio de indicadores comparativos para la región de Londres en comparación a otras metrópolis.

Competitividad   Ventaja competitiva y comparativa   Ineficiencia-X   Economías de aglomeración
Competencias regionales

JEL classifications: D24, F10, R0, R12

INTRODUCTION

The notion of competitiveness is one that informs every economic policy document at every level of government and governance. Rather like globalization, the repetition of the term 'competitiveness' sheds much heat but little light. Competitiveness has become a generic term that is applied widely to a variety of business and economic circumstances. Consequently, it means different things to different people. In public fora, many policy-makers tend to conflate the terms of trade performance with the productivity of firms and industries into a single entity of competitiveness.

The purpose of this paper is to make a contribution to the debate surrounding regional competitiveness. It also aims to further the research agenda, that to date has been conceptually wanting.

Definitions

The paper starts by setting out some definitional problems.

In the UK, the DEPARTMENT OF TRADE AND INDUSTRY (1998) defines competitiveness as:

> the ability to produce the right goods and services of the right quality, at the right price, at the right time. It means meeting customer needs more efficiently and more effectively than other firms.

For the ORGANIZATION FOR ECONOMIC CO-OPERATION AND DEVELOPMENT (1996), a working definition of national competitiveness is:

> The degree to which it can, under free and fair market conditions, produce goods and services which meet the

test of inter-national markets, while simultaneously maintaining and expanding the real incomes of its people over the long term.

DUNNING *et al.* (1998) argue that:

> Competitiveness is a way of discussing the relative performance of economies in a benchmarking sense. It can help identify areas of the economy that are lagging behind but not the reasons for those lags.

They found it difficult to define competitiveness beyond identifying the level and growth of Gross Domestic Product (GDP) per head the most frequently cited and used measure. There are a number of studies of competitiveness, particularly national competitiveness, that start from the same conceptual point (GUDGIN, 1996; DEPARTMENT OF TRADE AND INDUSTRY, 1998; BROOKSBANK and PICKERNELL, 1999; HEALEY & BAKER, 1999; INTERVIEW, 1999). The present staring point is PORTER's (1998) 'diamond' framework, which consists of the following:

- Factor conditions.
- Demand conditions.
- Related and supporting industries.
- Firm strategy, structure and rivalry.

According to Porter, strong national diamond is essential to the competitive advantage of a national economy. The use of this framework is useful in that it takes the measurement of competitiveness at national and regional levels beyond the limitations of GDP per head and unemployment rates. It opens up the possibility of including manifold factors in the measurement of regional competitiveness. The problems with many of the measurement studies are that they tend to accept, fairly uncritically, Porter's diamond as the conceptual framework of territorial competitiveness.

The present paper seeks critically to build on and interrogate this approach in order to create a conceptual framework for regional competitiveness. It does so by investigating the role of agglomeration economies as the indirect transmission mechanism of regional competitiveness from combining competitive advantage at the firm level with comparative advantage at the regional economy level. It integrates the theory of 'X-inefficiency' to provide a conceptual datum against which the performance of the regional economy can be measured. In providing this conceptualization, the authors hope to contribute to an important research agenda.

CHALLENGE OF TERRITORIAL COMPETITIVENESS AT THE REGIONAL SCALE

Territorial competition appears to cause the most theoretical and conceptual difficulty. Business commentators and policy-makers tend to swallow wholeheartedly such generalized nostrums as competitiveness at national and subnational levels. By not being clear about what is and is not competitiveness, it can end up as a chimera.

Many of the problems associated with defining territorial competitiveness are that the definition of territory itself is narrowly geographical. If one conceives of industrial *filieres*, many of their activities are distributed over industrial space. Similar arguments can be made for supply chains in certain industries. These territories are geographically constrained because of access to market reasons, but the dominance of Euclidean space in national and regional policy often renders policy-makers' objectives redundant because of spillover effects not being contained within administrative boundaries.

One needs to establish a first-principles approach to investigate competitiveness if it is to have any analytical purchase and resonance. Much of the literature on competitiveness, at different territorial levels, is rooted within the discourses of strategy, strategic management, industrial economics and trade theory. The trajectory of firm competition to industry competitiveness to national competitiveness has been accompanied by a burgeoning literature, as well as concomitant confusion, as a number of disciplinary approaches have entered the debate and collided. These approaches include the following:

- Microeconomics and industrial organization.
- 'New competition'.
- Institutional economists.
- Economic retardation debate.
- Excellence and turnaround.

Their associated literature is set out in Fig. 1 (PETTIGREW and WHIP, 1993). Within an industry context,

interfirm competition is central to the industrial organization tradition (SCHUMPETER, 1950; BAIN, 1956). For industrial organization theorists, returns to the firm are correlated with industry structure, not only firm size, but also barriers to entry into the market. The Schumpetarian approach concerns revolutionary technological, market and product disruption, expressed by Schumpeter as 'creative destruction'. In the field of strategy, the industrial organization approach to competition has been extended by CAVES (1980) and PORTER (1981) to include a number of contingent factors.

The new competition literature arose out of a stringent critique of the competitive performance of US industry in the 1980s (HAYES and ABERNATHY 1980; ABERNATHY *et al.*, 1981). These commentators and their disciplinary base focussed on management issues and the scope for action in addressing the competitive performance of US industry compared with the developing Asian economies

Schumpeter, the Austrian School (HAYEK, 1956) and the Transaction Cost Economics approach (WILLIAMSON, 1985), have influenced institutional economics. Institutionalists do not assume that economic agents are rational as do neo-classical economists. Instead, they focus on the relationship between market opportunism and bounded rationality: rationality that is limited by the nature of the organizational environment. Competition is not explained by the process of allocating resources through a price-discovery process, but by the interaction of a set of social institutions.

The economic retardation debate has focussed primarily on the long run economic decline of the UK. The reasons for this decline include a poor entrepreneurial culture (WIENER, 1981), the lack of US-style mass production techniques and forms of corporate managerial coordination (ELBAUM and LAZONICK, 1986). This literature looks at the scale and scope, costs and benefits of government intervention in addressing institutional factors of retardation. Its weakness is its over-concentration on national competitive performance.

The excellence and turnaround approaches developed from the 1980s shock to US industry of overseas competitors rapidly penetrating their markets. Successful companies are given as examples whose experience forms a set of generic rules to be applied to declining firms and industries (PETERS and WATERMAN, 1982). This literature is heavily influenced by studies of the apparently outstanding record of Japanese management in the post-Second World War period (PASCALE and ATHOS, 1981). Company turnaround is closely related to the excellence approach. A checklist of requirements to rescue a failing company is the basis of turnaround, in this view. The problem with these two allied approaches is that they focus exclusively on the management of companies rather than on the competitive environment.

One of the foremost proponents of competitiveness,

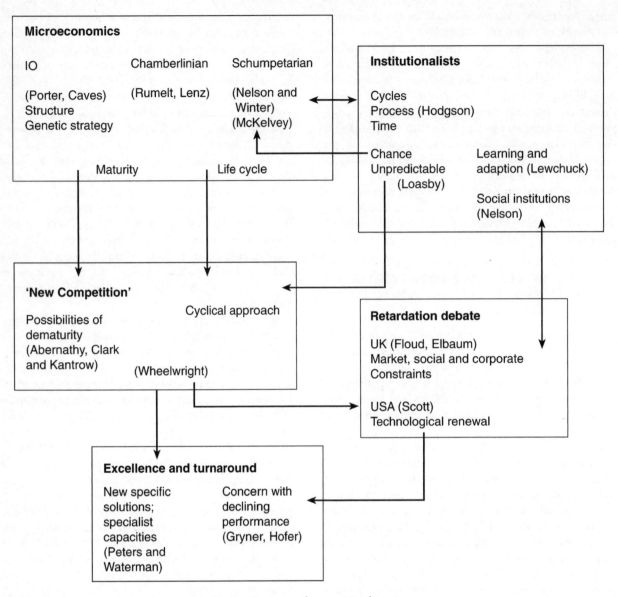

Fig. 1. *Strategy and competition literature*

on a national and regional scale, is Porter. In his influential *The Competitive Advantage of Nations* (1998), Porter has adapted his concept of the strategic competitive advantage[1] of firms and industries to the analysis of the competitive position of nations. He claims that the new paradigm of competitive advantage has replaced Ricardian theory of comparative advantage in trade.[2] Both supporters and critics of Porter's analysis have tended to talk past each other, leading to a confusion over the precise nature of concept and terms. This lack of definitional clarity has in itself set up a debate over the validity of Porter's work at different territorial levels. This issue will be returned to below.

There are essentially two parts to achieving competitive advantage. First, the ways in which firms organize and undertake distinct activities is the basis for the growth of competitive advantage. Second, by a process of discovering novel and enhanced ways of competing

in a market. This constitutes innovation that includes not only technical progress, but also improved working and managerial methods.

This duality at the firm level is extended by Porter into the national sphere. He asks what are the circumstances in which firms and industries achieve international success in discrete sectors and industries? The search for these national circumstances constitutes the competitive advantage of nations. Second, nations will generate improved competitive advantage when a proper national strategy is pursued where circumstances are created that support the competitive advantage of these internationally exposed sectors and industries (PORTER, 1998, p. 10):

> Our central task, then, is to explain why firms based in a nation are able to compete successfully against foreign rivals in particular segments and industries. Competing internationally may involve exports and/or locating some

company activities abroad. We are particularly concerned with the determinants of international success in relatively sophisticated industries and segments of industries involving complex technology and highly skilled human resources, which offer the potential for high levels of productivity as well as productivity growth.

PORTER (2000) states that the only basis of national competitiveness is productivity, namely: 'The only meaningful concept of competitiveness is productivity' and that 'productivity is the prime determinant in the long run of a nation's standard of living. For it is the root cause of per capita income'. Productivity is defined as output per unit of input, including both capital and labour inputs. For some economists, productivity and competitiveness become the same thing at the full-employment level of national income (BEGG, 1999). In Porter's account, it is productivity in the internationally traded goods and services sector that determines national competitiveness. Porter, however, tends to shift his ground between 'competitiveness as the productivity of a nation' (DAVIES and ELLIS, 2000) and competitiveness as the ability of some firms and industries to acquire global markets share. Despite Porter's assertion that competitive advantage represents a new and superior paradigm to comparative advantage there is elision between the two concepts in his work on national competitiveness. Furthermore, by arguing that national competitiveness is determined by comparative productivity, Porter is confusing comparative advantage with absolute advantage (DAVIES and ELLIS, 1999). Porter ascribes the trade deficit of motor vehicles in the USA to the higher levels of productivity in the Germany and Japanese motor vehicle industries. To meet German and Japanese competition, US firms must meet the absolute productivity standards of these countries (PORTER, 1998, p. 8). This represents the Adam Smith theory of absolute advantage of trade.

Porter appears to take the theory of comparative advantage in trade and the Heckscher–Ohlin[3] thesis of comparative factor endowment (labour and capital) and at the same time mould it for the 'global' era, whilst stressing international competition. By not being explicit about the relationship between the concept of competitive advantage and the theory of comparative advantage, confusion is sown for both proponents and opponents of Porter's position on national competitiveness.

Porter rightly points out the weakness of comparative advantage in explaining intra-industry trade, but trade theory has moved on since Heckscher–Ohlin (HELPMAN and KRUGMAN, 1985). The assertion that exchange rates and wages are unimportant in the determination of national competitiveness is refuted if national competitiveness is defined as the ability to secure global export market share. As competitiveness is also defined as comparative productivity, for which exchange rates are not directly important, it is impossible to refute or deny the role of exchange rates

when the two definitions are conflated. However, real exchange rate considerations become important in meeting the challenge of conceptualizing, defining and measuring regional competitiveness, as the present paper seeks to demonstrate below.

Porter's work on competitiveness is heavily determined by his role as a strategist with mercantilist tendencies and not as an economist (KRUGMAN, 1996). Porter's colleagues at the Harvard Business School took a similar view and represented the school's 75th anniversary colloquium 'US Competitiveness in the World Economy':

> National competitiveness refers to a nation state's ability to produce, distribute, and service goods in the international economy in competition with goods and services produced in other countries, and to do so in a way that earns a rising standard of living. The ultimate measure is not a 'favorable' balance of trade, a positive current account, or an increase in foreign exchange reserves: it is an increase in the standard of living. To be competitive as a country means to be able to employ national resources, notably the nation's workforce, in such a way as to earn a rising level of real income through specialization and trade in the world economy.
>
> (SCOTT and LODGE, 1985, p. 15)

Despite the cavils about trade competitiveness, this measure of national competitiveness is essentially derived from labour productivity in the internationally traded goods and service part of the economy. It is therefore not really a measure of *national* competitiveness. Furthermore, the Scott and Lodge position puts them in the economic retardation camp.

The weakness in the Porter position relates to the balance of payments constraint in international trade and the perspective that economists take on competitiveness. The role of macroeconomic policy is usually to achieve internal and external balance in the economy in the short run. Internal balance is ensured if there is the lowest level of unemployment being reached that is consistent with a reasonable level of inflation. External balance should be consistent with current-account equilibrium. In the long run, the role of macroeconomic policy is the best achievable rate of economic growth. In this context, international competitiveness is:

> The desirable degree of international competitiveness in this context could be defined as the level of the real exchange rate which, in conjunction with appropriate domestic policies, ensured internal and (broadly defined) external balance.
>
> (BOLTHO, 1996, p. 2)

Boltho goes on to argue that domestic forces drive higher incomes, through labour productivity growth, adjusted for the terms of trade. Consequently, concerns with international competitiveness, per se, are irrelevant in this context. The only potential link is if productivity growth is associated with unfavourable trends in the income elasticities of demand for the nation's exports and imports. Boltho, however, assumes that changes in the real exchange rate can overcome the balance-of-payments constraint. The role of this constraint in limiting economic growth has been identified in a significant body of literature (KRUGMAN, 1989; THIRLWELL, 1991; McCOMBIE and THIRLWELL, 2003). Its importance at a regional level has also been recognized (McCOMBIE and THIRLWELL, 2003), although there has been little discussion of this issue in the regional economics literature.[4] The essential point, in contradiction to Boltho's, is that changes in the real exchange rate have little impact on the growth of import and exports:

> income elasticities determine the balance-of-payments constrained growth rate, but the supply characteristics of goods (such as their technical sophistication, quality etc.) determine the relative income elasticities. In this important respect, there can be a marrying of demand- and supply-side explanation of the growth performance of nations.
>
> (THIRLWELL, 1991, p. 27)

The choice of exchange rate is constrained by maintaining external balance. In the context of the balance-of-payments growth constraint, a concept of competitiveness determined by relative productive growth in the internationally traded goods and services sector cannot be sustained unless it explicitly incorporates balance-of-payments constraint considerations in the context of a sustainable real exchange rate.

A virulent critic of national competitiveness is Paul Krugman:

> But what does national competitiveness mean? For the great majority of those who use the term, it means exactly what it seems to mean; it is the view that nations compete for world markets in the same way that corporations do, that a nation which fails to match other nations in productivity or technology will face the same kind of crisis as a company that cannot match the costs or products of its rivals.
>
> (KRUGMAN, 1996, p. 17)

As in the new competition, excellence and turnaround literature reviewed above, Krugman points to the strategic trade perspective that informs the demand that the competitive position of firms and industries of an economy in global markets should be sustained through policy intervention. Yet Porter himself is constantly opposed to government intervention, in the form of public expenditure, administrative fiat or protection to shift resources to more internationally competitive industries or industry mixes. Paradoxically, governments have espoused Porter's approach in advancing strategies of global positioning. Wittingly or unwittingly, Krugman points to the strategic roots that inform the position of Porter and those holding similar views (REICH, 1990, THUROW, 1992):

> Strategists want the government to stand behind domestic firms wherever there seems to be winner-take-all competition for future monopoly profits; they want promotion of industries that pay exceptionally high wages, or seem likely to generate strong spill-overs.
>
> (KRUGMAN, 1996)

The creation and distribution of strong spillovers are clearly important for regional economic development. The creation and ability of indigenously regional firms to avail themselves of the benefits spillovers generate does not of itself illustrate or indicate regional competitiveness. Krugman concludes his damning critique by stating:

> Economists, in general, do not use the word 'competitiveness'. Not one of the textbooks in international economics, I have on my shelves contains the word in its index. So why are there so many councils on competitiveness, White Papers on competitiveness and so on? ... It seems too cynical to suggest that the debate over competitiveness is simply a matter of time-honoured fallacies about international trade being dressed up in new and pretentious rhetoric.
>
> (KRUGMAN, 1996)

Krugman's original critique was published in *Foreign Affairs* (1994). In a later edition of the same year, the targets of Krugman's opprobrium retorted under the title 'The fight over competitiveness: a zero-sum debate?' (DORNBUSCH, 1994). Their retort centres on the following:

• In some cases, trade may be a zero-sum game, unlike Krugman's assertion.
• Although trade only accounts for 11% of Gross National Product, it accounts for half of US manufacturing output, so that consideration of domestic competitiveness is important.
• Status and power of nations relate to their economic performance because loss of competitiveness lends itself to political vulnerability.
• Nations do have a bottom line in the form of the living standards of its citizens.

A detailed analysis of the critique of Krugman is not central to the purpose of the present paper. The main weakness of the attack on his position is that his critics are talking about comparative productivity levels between nations and not competitiveness in the sense used by economists, an issue returned to below when discussing regional competitiveness. The crucial issue is that competition and competitiveness are used interchangeably, muddying the analytical waters further. The irony of the 'zero-sum debate' presumably has not passed by Krugman. These debates and the discourse that Porter's *The Competitive Advantage of Nations* has engendered, however, have focused critical minds on the question of competitiveness and its territorial variants. For this contribution, Porter's role should be more generously noted.

It is when one moves into the subnational levels that analytical, conceptual, and operational difficulty and some confusion increase. Regional competitiveness appears squeezed between the rock of the national competitiveness debate and the hard place of the plethora of the volume of work on territorial competitiveness at an urban scale.

There is a large and growing literature of urban or city competitiveness (KRESL, 1995; CHESHIRE and GORDON 1995; LEVER, 1993, CIAMPI, 1996; BUDD, 1998, BEGG, 1999, 2002, GORDON, 1999). The notion of city competitiveness appears able to withstand the Krugman critique rather better than can national or regional competitiveness. This is primarily because of the combination of functional specialization and agglomeration benefits of urbanization. The combination of both can be described as cities competing over locational assets. GORDON and CHESHIRE (1998) suggest that:

> territorial competition may be conceived of as involving attempts by agencies representing particular areas to enhance their locational advantage by manipulating some of the attributes which contribute to their area's value as a location for various activities.

Firms compete on the price and non-price characteristics of their output, so that competitiveness at the firm level is pretty well understood. Both price and non-price factors are influenced by firm location, particularly with regard to input costs. These costs are direct and indirect. Direct locational costs include rent, labour and cost of capital. The greater the degree of city specialization, the larger these costs are likely to be, e.g. the City of London. Indirect costs are usually external to the firm but are influenced by: 'miliuex – external, unmarketed influences on the productivity innovativeness and dynamism of local businesses' (BEGG, 1999).

External economies of scale and scope and the degree to which firms can exploit them in a location will also determine firm competitiveness in a particular location. The aggregation of firm-level competitiveness and non-price and indirect cost advantages can be said to constitute urban competitiveness. One of the few authors who have attempted to pin down urban competitiveness is Peter Kresl. In identifying a competitive urban economy, he sets out six attributes (KRESL, 1995, p. 51):

- High-skill, high-income job creation.
- Goods and services produced should be environmentally orientated.
- Goods and services with high-income elasticity of demand and similar characteristics should be the basis of production.
- Full-employment considerations should determine the suitable rate of growth, without overheating markets.

- Specialization of activities should be based on future potential of the city, not on acceptance of present configurations.
- Potential of the city to move up the urban hierarchy.

Kresl organizes the determinants of competitiveness into two categories:

- Quantitative: 'economic' determinants (factors of production, infrastructure, etc.).
- Qualitative: 'strategic' determinants (policy factors, design of institutions, etc.).

This approach suggests that a balance sheet of city assets and liabilities can be generated. For example, on the asset side, the benefits of agglomeration are more easily gained in a city than in a region. Whether these characteristics can be transferred to the regional scale is open to question.

Conceiving of competitiveness and using a balance sheet-type measure at the regional scale presents a challenge. The next section reviews the attempt to take up this challenge.

POSSIBILITIES FOR REGIONAL COMPETITIVENESS?

This section attempts to negotiate around some of the cross-cutting issues. It also discusses the possibilities of conceptualizing regional competitiveness in a regional economy. In what sense do regions compete? MARTIN and TYLER (2003) cite three instances on which regions compete:

- For investment through regions' ability to attract foreign, private and public capital.
- For labour by being able to attract skilled employees, entrepreneurs and creative workers, thereby enabling innovation environments within local labour markets.
- For technology through regions' ability to attract knowledge and innovation activity.

Martin and Tyler also conceive of regions as sites of comparative advantage through export specialization; as sources of increasing returns enabled by agglomeration economies; and as hubs of knowledge and innovation developed and sustained by local innovations milieu. This threefold conception can also be read from three theoretical perspectives: neo-classical theory; increasing returns theories; and endogenous growth theory. This reinforces their conclusion that 'there is no theoretical perspective that captures the full complexity of "regional competitiveness"' (MARTIN and TYLER, 2003).

Regional competitiveness appears to be neither the simple aggregation of firms nor a weighted disaggregation of the national economy. The 6th Periodic Report on the Social and Economic Situation and Development of the Regions in the Community

(EUROPEAN COMMISSION, 1996) defines regional competitiveness as follows:

> the ability to produce goods and services which meet the test of international markets, whilst at the same time maintaining high and sustainable levels of income, or more generally, the ability of (regions) to generate, while being exposed to external competition, relatively high incomes and employments levels. In other words, for a region to be competitive it is important to ensure both quality and quantity of jobs.

Although clearly complex, regional competitiveness can be seen as the cumulative outcome of a number of factors. These include the traditional factors of labour market conditions and transport costs (VICKERMAN, 1989), as well as company size, research and intensity, innovative capacity, and export orientation as important locational endowments (STEINLE, 1992).[5] Studies of Wales and of Baden-Wurtemeburg, Germany, as a 'learning regions' in the international economy argued that future economic success was expected to come from firms that were active exporters, had competitive products and processes, and were innovators through research and development (COOKE, 1997). The competitiveness of these 'learning regions' rests on 'untraded inter-dependencies' (STORPER, 1995). These include formal and informal collaborative and information networks, shared labour market intelligence, and shared conventions and rules for developing communications and interpreting knowledge.

As noted above, one of the issues at the heart of the debate over national competitiveness is the role of exchange rates and the balance of payments constraint. The balance of payments constraint at the regional level is also important to any conception and ultimately to the measurement of regional competitiveness. The regional implications of the argument advanced above are that non-price competition is important in understanding trade flows. Changes in relative regional prices will be ineffective if pricing policies of firms are nationally determined or a function of imperfect competition where price leadership is a primary objective.[6] Therefore, attempting to change relative regional prices to make declining regions more competitive will be ineffective. Consequently, increased competitiveness will be determined by locational advantage, which depends on non-price and non-trade factors like the degree of institutional embeddedness, governance structures and demonstration effects that can be assessed as part of the external economies that a place may derive. These form part of the agglomeration economies that are central to locational advantage and can thus be said to be integral to the potential competitiveness of a city or region. PORTER (2003) points to the importance of traded clusters and their spillover effects in regional economic performance. Furthermore, Porter suggests that economic policy needs to be decentralized at the regional level, with development policies being used to encourage traded clusters and the upgrading of their productivity.

What this means is that in effect, the comparative productivity of industries as a measure of national competitiveness is being devolved to the comparative productivity of traded clusters as a measure of regional competitiveness, including institutional and governmental externalities.

In developing a regional perspective, the present paper focuses on the role of comparative factor endowments, including location, in interregional trade. Intraregional transactions are also important. The argument is summarized in Fig. 2, and proceeds as follows:

- The relative prices of goods produced in a region will determine the level of interregional trade.
- The competitiveness of firms' output in terms of relative productivity will determine income and employment.
- The regional terms of trade are, therefore, determined by relative costs expressed as regional deflators in the absence of a regional exchange rate.

However, the countervailing role of an exchange rate in equilibrating regional trade imbalances is missing. Therefore, what proxies as the balance of payments constraint where there is no real exchange rate is the level of factor endowments including locational factor advantages, notwithstanding the degree to which interregional transfers partly compensate for trade imbalances.[7] In the first instance, it is the mobility of capital and labour. In the second, it is agglomeration economies, including external economies of scale and scope. The extent to which the latter are availed of by local firms will determine the degree to which they translate into regional prices. In doing so, the regional balance of trade constraint is exerted, but through secondary transmission mechanisms.

As MARTIN and TYLER (2003) correctly point out, productivity is not necessarily a good measure or indicator of regional competitive advantage. The relationship is complex and proceeds via indirect effects. Increasing returns, external economies and endogenous growth effects have greater influence on regional success. Furthermore, competitive advantage at the firm level relates to superior performance (MA, 2000). Equally, competitive advantage at the regional level does not directly lead to superior performance.

It is apparent that locational factors are crucial to a conceptualization of regional competitiveness. Despite the present criticism of the conceptual and methodological aspects of the Porter position, the paper attempts to construct a conceptual framework that includes competitive advantage and comparative advantage. This is done in the context of the transmission mechanism of agglomeration economies, in particular localization, urbanization and activity-complex economies, in combination with the theory of X-inefficiency providing the conceptual benchmark.

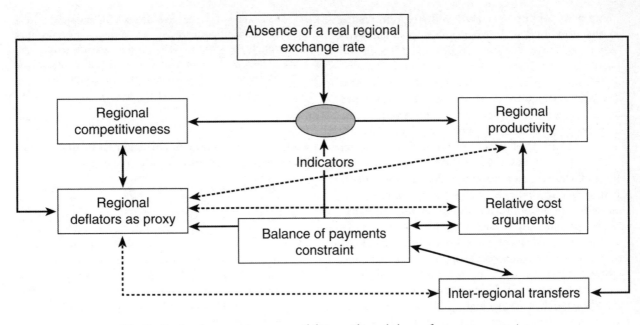

Fig. 2. Regional competitiveness possibilities within a balance of payments constraint

REGIONAL COMPETITIVENESS CAPACITY AS A CONCEPTUAL FRAMEWORK

It is apparent that regional competitiveness invites difficulty and confusion at the conceptual level. There is the possibility of regional competitiveness via indirect transmission mechanisms, through agglomeration economies bestowing locational advantage. This is recognized in some studies of measuring regional competitiveness that go beyond GDP per head and employment levels. HUGGINS (2003) uses a three-factor model of regional competitiveness, which includes the following:

- Inputs business density (firms per capita); knowledge-based business (as a percentage of all businesses) and economic participation (activity rates).
- Outputs productivity (measured as GDP per capita).
- Outcomes: earnings (full-time wages); unemployment (International Labour Organization measure).

In contrast the present conceptual framework is built upon regional competitiveness capacity (RCC). It is a regional variant of the concept of urban competitiveness capacity the authors introduced in the Global Cities Benchmarking feasibility study for the London Skills Forecasting Unit in 2000.[8] RCC is formulated by combining the theory of comparative advantage, Porter's concept of competitive advantage and LIEBENSTEIN's (1966) theory of X-inefficiency in the context of the three types of agglomeration economy into a single framework. The starting point is as follows:

- Comparative advantage is the classical theory of comparative costs that provides the underlying logic

of gains from international trade. Differences in the opportunity costs of producing, say, two commodities in two countries forms the basis of gains in trade for both countries. Underlying the comparative advantages of each nation, region or city are factors such as the initial endowments of resources, the environment and technical knowledge. Conventionally, comparative advantage operates at the level of the national economy.

- Competitive advantage is created in the act of generating novel and improved ways of competing in an industry and bringing these ways to market. For Porter, this is an act of innovation. However, competitive advantage is 'created and sustained through a highly localised process' (LIEBENSTEIN, 1966) in which externalities are the determining factor at subnational levels. The basis of a locality's competitive success – whether national, regional or urban in this view – rests on the manner in which the combination of differences in opportunity costs and the endowment of externalities are combined to generate improvements in productivity. The Porter view of competitive advantage, at the firm level, comes from the industrial organization tradition, with its stress on cost leadership and differentiation. The resource-based view (RBV) of competitive advantage is used. The RBV perspective suggests unique resources are the source of sustained competitive advantage of a firm (BARNEY, 1991). But heterogeneity in resource endowments provides competitive advantage (PETERAF, 1993). In the context of the competitive advantage of firms and industries in a region, non-price and non-traded locations factors are part of these heterogeneous resources. Taking an RBV perspective allows one to relate competitive advantage more directly to performance in the firms in a region being able to sustain economic rents than a cost leadership and differentiation approach.

- X-efficiency arises out of imperfectly competitive markets, characteristic of the modern economy, where absolute cost efficiency of the firm cannot be substantiated. In the language of economic theory, the combination of factors of production – capital and labour – do not push the firm to operate at the edge of its production possibility frontier.[9] In essence, a firm is said to be X-efficient if it maximizes its outputs whilst minimizing its inputs. Improvements in the productivity of factor inputs will reduce X-inefficiencies. The correlation is introducing 'novel and improved ways of competing in an industry and bring those to market' to maximize outputs. An important source of X-inefficiency is 'managerial slack', whereby management and workers pursue their own objectives rather than those of external shareholders who seek profit maximization as an efficiency objectives. For LIEBENSTEIN (1966), production costs rise as markets become more imperfectly competitive. Raising total factor productivity (TFP) is then an important component in reducing X-inefficiency and increasing competitive advantage. Where increases in X-efficiency are generalized across an economy, the potential to increase comparative advantage for traded commodities is also enhanced. In imperfect markets, non-price competition increases so that the ability to absorb the benefits bestowed by externalities is an important source of sustaining firms' competitive advantage. In a regional economy, the degree to which externalities are distributed among all sectors and activities reduces the degree to which dominant activities appropriate externalities and therefore sustain their X-inefficiency.

The three types of external economies are set out below. Their importance to place cannot be underestimated because, first, the localization of industry provides support for specialized local providers of inputs to production. Second, the diffusion of information is speedier where there is localized concentration of industry, thereby generating technological spillovers. Third, the pooling of specialized labour in a locality creates important local demand (MARSHALL, 1920).

One can organize these economies into three distinct but related types of agglomeration economies: localization, urbanization and activity-complex, otherwise known as complexity economies:

- Localization economies are internal to an industry or sector in an area but external to the firm:

  Localization economies refer to the advantages accruing to the firm in the same activity which result form their joint location. On the revenues side... are the

  possibilities for the cross-referral of business among firms and the emergence of particular specialisations within the activity; while on the cost side, advantages include the existence of a pool of skilled labour, the availability of specialise business services specific to the activity under consideration and access to high quality information, often on an informal basis.

  (PARR and BUDD, 2000, p. 603)

- Urbanization economies are internal to the area but external to the sector or industry or firm.

  Urbanisation economies ... are concerned with the range of advantages to the individual firms which result from the joint location of firms in different and unrelated activities ... the availability of transport and communications facilities and municipal services may provide important savings Also important is the availability of a specialised business service not specific to a particular activity, as well as the advantage of an urban amenity and the derived or indirect advantage of a pool of qualified labour.

  (PARR and BUDD, 2000, p. 603)

- Activity-complex economies: sometimes known as complexity economies.

  These refer to economies that emerge from the joint location of unlike activities which have substantial trading links with one another. In the case of manufacturing, such economies typically occur within industrial complexes, involving structure of a vertical or convergent nature.

  (PARR and BUDD, 2000, p. 603)

For example, in the garments industry, there is a degree of vertical integration that is distributed across local space.

Localization economies tend to be associated with external economies of scale, whilst urbanization economies tend to be associated with external economies of scope. Economies of scope result from a variation of products being made from the same or shared inputs.

In a regional economy, shared inputs are supplied by both the public and private sectors, so that most urbanization economies can be seen as predominantly external economies of scope. Activity-complex economies reduce coordination and transaction costs for firms within industrial complexes or other agglomerations, and as such could be thought of important external economies in contributing to greater competitiveness of a region. Once these external economies are availed of at the firm level, the challenge is to understand how they can be reproduced within a region to sustain its supposedly regional competitiveness.

The present paper attempts to bring these elements together in its RCC framework (Fig. 3).

Starting at the economy level, a Heckscher–Ohlin approach is taken in the context of comparative locational factor endowments whilst loosening the assumptions of their neo-classical model.[10] The comparative

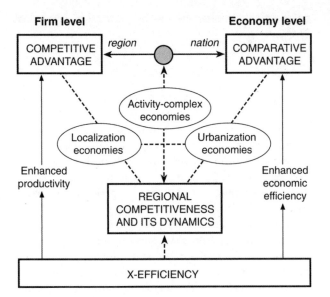

Fig. 3. Framework for assessing regional competitiveness capacity

advantage of regions derives from their capacity to use and sustain factors of production and, consequently, to generate output and trade. The more these factor endowments generate productivity gains, the larger will be the region's share of employment and income gains. In addition, the larger the share of capital-intensive industries in a region, the larger will be the region's share of interregional trade, as demonstrated by the Heckscher–Ohlin theorem (SÖDERSTEN, 1980). In an era of globalization or internationalization, factors are more mobile. To sustain factors endowments that make a region competitive in terms of relative prices, extra-firm and industry factors, including non-price and non-trade ones, are crucial. They help to enhance the region's capacity to absorb further growth. The total internal economies and the scale of agglomeration economies and the ability of trading firms to avail themselves of the latter and gain price benefits make up the locational endowments (or regional assets). The relative scale and scope of locational endowments is crucial to maintaining comparative advantage and competitiveness at the level of the regional economy.

At the firm level, the competitive advantage of firms in a region will be enhanced by the degree to which productivity gains in the production of goods result from and further create innovative means of production. From the RBV perspective, the unique and heterogeneous resources that create competitive advantage for a firm will include its ability to exploit external economies as well as non-price and non-traded factors.

The present paper uses the theory of X-inefficiency as a conceptual datum to integrate the competitive advantage at the firm level with comparative advantage at the economy level of the region. The promotion of external economies is important in enhancing the productivity potential of a region by increasing TFP.

X-inefficiency conventionally works at the level of the firm and industry where pricing regulation is important. The relationship between X-inefficiency and the competitive advantage at the firm level seems straightforward. The scale and degree to which 'managerial slack' can be overcome, in the form of better production and managerial practices, the greater the scope for productivity improvements and thus gains in X-efficiency for the firm and industry. For firms and industries engaged in interregional trade, these X-efficiency gains are translated into more competitive prices and the welfare gains in the form of income and employment in the host region, thereby enhancing comparative advantage. Despite this apparently straightforward link, the application of the theory of X-inefficiency at the regional economy level poses more difficulties, particularly measurement ones, but these are beyond the scope of the paper.

A more X-efficient region is one in which total locational endowments, including agglomeration economies, are exploited optimally by indigenous firms and industries.

Therefore, the size and scope of comparative locational factor endowments can be related to comparative X-efficiency at the regional economy level. The three types of agglomeration economy provide the indirect transmission mechanism that brings together the competitive advantage at the firm level and the comparative advantage at the economy level of a region. Localization economies are relevant at the firm level and urbanization economies at economy level, whilst activity-complex economies are relevant to both.

The relationship between productivity, external economies, price, traded, and non-price and non-traded factors is complex. Growth in TFP is a function of market and non-markets factors, in particular the formation of skills and the sharing of tacit knowledge. Work done by the National Institute for Economic and Social Research (NIESR) on productivity, however, has demonstrated the role played by externalities in increasing TFP. In particular, TFP growth has been associated with the following:

- Advances in scientific and technical knowledge.
- Learning by doing and learning from others.
- Organizational changes.
- Legislation and regulatory changes.

None of the above factors is compensated by the market mechanism (OULTON, 1997). The first factor arises from spillovers from non-commercial organizations or from commercial research and development activities. For the second factor, skills formation from educational attainment generates increased productivity, as individual learning becomes generalized as sector-specific and tacit knowledge. The third factor includes corporate restructuring, just-in-time inventory systems and total quality management. The fourth factor includes enhancing labour flexibility legislation and lowering transaction costs for firms. One can identify these four elements with the three types of agglomeration economy detailed above.

The role of a region's spatial structure is often overlooked in discussions of regional competitiveness, particularly as a regional asset. Growth occurs in activities that are 'place orientated' in real places and real time. The sources of growth are associated with agglomeration activities and the appropriation of localization and urbanization economies rather than with the input of resources subject to competition, as argued above. That is, it is spatial efficiency rather than additional inputs of factors of production that is the greater determinant of regional growth and thus the basis of competitiveness. The importance of the spatial structure to regional competitiveness cannot be underestimated. It determines regional capacity to absorb, or constrain, further growth. There are circumstances under which the spatial structure can retard or enhance regional development, particularly in the short run, where the spatial structure affects the regional supply function of the significant factors of production. The spatial structure can therefore be considered as part of the regional production function, in addition to the conventional inputs of labour, capital and land. The analogy is with the physical layout of an industrial plant: the more efficient the use of space, the higher the output (PARR, 1979).

In other words, two regions with the same factor endowments and apparent competitiveness will differ in output, income and employment if they have different spatial structures. The greater the scale of urban and metropolitan areas in a region, the greater the degree to which agglomeration economies can be realized in regional externalities and economic welfare in the form of income and employment. This would suggest that city regions are more competitive than non-city regions. However, the clustering of economic activities in non-urban areas might compensate less urbanized regions by generating agglomeration economies. A similar argument applies to the regions with more efficient spatial structures.

The concept of RCC, therefore, rests on combining the theory of comparative advantage and the concept of competitive advantage into a single framework. The three types of agglomeration economies act as an indirect transmission mechanism between the comparative advantage of the regional economy and the competitive advantage of its firms. The theory of X-inefficiency provides a conceptual benchmark against which to assess efficiency at the firm and economy level. The interaction of X-efficiency and the realization of benefits derived from agglomeration economies then provides a concept of regional competitiveness and its dynamics. In the study of the London region's competitiveness, RCC was found to be a feasible framework on which to build indicators. The London Skills Forecasting Unit shared this conclusion. Further work and iterations will test the practical challenges of RCC.

CONCLUSION

The present paper has attempted to conceptualize regional competitiveness by combining competitive advantage *at the firm level* and the balance of payments constraint, implicit in comparative advantage, *at the regional level* into a single framework. In developing the concept of RCC, it stresses that regional competitiveness is an outcome of economic performance, based on manifold factors in a particular locale, not a basis for economic performance, *sui generis*. One cannot say that regions as economic entities are engaged in a process of comprehensive and direct competition. Regions can be said to compete for economic activities at various levels, but the mediation processes are complex and often incomplete. By not being clear about the limits of regional competitiveness as a concept, it may fall into the 'intellectual play zone' because of the proliferation of meaning in concept and practice.

There are lessons to be learnt from the debates and range and depth of the literature produced on urban and city competitiveness that apply at the regional level:

> To propose cities or regions competing with each other presuppose a unity of purpose between the constituent economic and social interests and that city governance has an autonomy and freedom of manoeuvre. If one were speaking of city-states or Hayek's 'catallaxies' this might be a possibility (HAYEK, 1961). Instead we are faced with a cross-cutting form of regulation between the international division of labour, national political interests and the way these factors are played out in urban territories.
>
> (BUDD, 1998)

The present paper has attempted critically to interrogate the debates and literature about territorial competition in a regional context in order to propose a conceptual framework of regional competitiveness. It might have actually created a concept of capacity for competitiveness or competition between regional competences and not regional competitiveness per se.[11] Three future directions suggest themselves that might take the debate further over the concept of regional competitiveness. First, attempting to construct comparative regional balance sheets of assets and liabilities. These can then be translated into indicators of regional competitiveness, on the one hand, and constraints to growth, on the other. Second, using a Transactions Cost Economics framework to investigate the relationship between opportunism and bounded rationality within and between regions, in the context of theorizing the region as an informal organization. Finally, constructing a set of criteria with which to measure the capacity of a region to absorb further investment and growth, thus taking the spatial structure of a region to a new level.

If nothing else, the authors hope that the questions and issues raised herein contribute to a research agenda of growing importance.

Acknowledgements – The authors are grateful for comments made by anonymous referees, and for comments made by John Parr, John McCombie and Ron Martin. Amer Hirmis works for DTZ Pieda Consulting, and he is writing in a personal capacity, and the views expressed may not necessarily reflect that of DTZ Pieda.

NOTES

1. Competitive advantage is the concept most notably associated with Porter. Sometimes used interchangeably with competitiveness, it usually refers to the ability of domestic firms and industries to gain and retain share in contested global markets.
2. David Ricardo's theory of international trade is familiar to all students of economics. In the simplest model, if two countries, X and Y, produce two goods A and B, then if country X has an absolute advantage in the production of both goods, it will still benefit both countries to trade if the opportunity cost of producing good A (in terms of foregone production) is lower in country X than in country Y. Country X then has a comparative advantage in the production of good A, and vice versa. In other words, a country has a comparative advantage in producing a good if the opportunity cost is lower at home than producing in the other country.
3. The Heckscher–Ohlin model assumes two factors of production: labour and capital. What accounts for international trade in this model is the factor endowments of the trading countries. Countries rich in capital will export capital-intensive goods, whilst those with an abundance of labour will export labour-intensive goods. Four assumptions underlie the Heckscher–Ohlin theory that restrict the model. It differs from Ricardo's model in respect of being a two-factor model in which trade is determined by factor prices. In Ricardo, labour is the only factor of production and trade is determined by production conditions alone. Factor prices cannot be inferred form productions conditions per se.
4. The authors are grateful to John McCombie for bringing these points and the associated literature to their attention. They trust they do his insights justice.
5. Some benchmarking studies ignore the issue of export performance (e.g. Boston Consulting Group, 1998, quoted in GORDON, 1999).
6. Again, the authors are grateful to John McCombie for this point.
7. The authors are grateful to John Parr for making this point, which was absent from earlier drafts of the paper.
8. The study was undertaken on behalf of the London Skills Forecasting Unit of the Learning and Skills Council.
9. The analogy for an urban economy, like London's, is that improvement in the competitiveness and thus productivity of its firms and sectors will push the whole economy towards its production possibility curve in any one period. Increases in total factor productivity in the next period will extend the productive potential of the urban economy by pushing the frontier further out.
10. There are five assumptions: (1) there are no transport costs or other impediments to trade; (2) there is perfect competition in both factor and commodity markets; (3) all production functions are homogeneous to the first degree; (4) the production functions are such that the two commodities show different factor intensities; and (5) the production functions differ between commodities but not between countries.
11. The authors are grateful to Ron Martin for pointing out this possibility.

REFERENCES

ABERNATHY W. J., CLARK K. and KANTROW A. (1981) The new industrial competition, *Harvard Business Review* **September/October**, 69–81.

BAIN J. S. (1956) *Barriers to New Competition.* Harvard University Press, Cambridge, MA.

BARNEY J. B. (1991) Firm resources and sustained competitive advantage, *Journal of Management Studies* **17**, 99–120.

BEGG I. (1999) Cities and competitiveness, *Urban Studies* **36**, 795–809.

BEGG I. (Ed.) (2002) *Urban Competitiveness: Policies for Dynamic Cities.* Polity, Cambridge.

BOLTHO A. (1996) The assessment: international competitiveness, *Oxford Review of Economic Policy* **12**, 1–16.

BROOKSBANK D. J. and PICKERNELL D. G. (1999) Regional competitiveness indicators – a reassessment of method, *Local Economy* **13**, 310–326.

BUDD L. (1998) Territorial competition and globalisation: Scylla and Charybdis of European cities, *Urban Studies* **35**, 663–686.

CAVES R. (1980) Corporate strategy and structure, *Journal of Economic Literature* **18**, 64–92.

CHESHIRE P. and GORDON I. R. (Eds) (1995) *Territorial Competition in Integrating Europe.* Avebury, Aldershot.

CIAMPI C. A. (1996) Enhancing European competitiveness, *Banca nazioanle di Lavoro Quarterly Review* **197**, 143–164.

COOKE P. (1997) Regions in a global market: the experience of Wales and Baden-Wurtemeburg, *Review of International Political Economy* **4**, 349–381.

DAVIES H. and ELLIS P. (2000) Porter's *Competitive Advantage of Nations*: time for the final judgement, *Journal of Management Studies* **37**, 1189–1215.

DEPARTMENT OF TRADE AND INDUSTRY (1998) *Regional Competitiveness Indicators.* HMSO, London.

DORNBUSCH R. (1994) The fight over competitiveness: a zero-sum debate?, *Foreign Affairs* **July/August**.

DUNNING J., BANNERMAN E. and LUNDAN S. M. (1998) *Competitiveness and Industrial Policy in Northern Ireland.* Monograph 5, March. Northern Ireland Research Council.

ELBAUM B. and LAZONICK W. (1986) *The Decline of the British Economy.* Cambridge University Press, Cambridge.

EUROPEAN COMMISSION (1996) *Cohesion and Competitiveness: Trends in the Regions.* 6th Periodic Report on the Social and Economic Situation and Development of the Regions in the Community. European Commission, Luxembourg.

EUROPEAN COMMISSION (1996) *Cohesion and Competitiveness: Trends in the Regions.* 6th Periodic Report on the Social and Economic Situation and Development of the Regions in the Community. Luxembourg, EC.

GORDON I. R. (1999) Internationalisation and urban competition, *Urban Studies* **36**, 1001–1016.

GORDON I. R. and CHESHIRE P. C. (1998) Locational advantage and the lessons of territorial competition in Europe. Paper prepared for the International Workshop on 'Theories of Regional Development: Lesson for Policies of Economic Renewal and Growth', Udevalla, Sweden, 14–16 June.

GUDGIN G. (1996) Prosperity and growth in UK Regions, *Local Economy* **11**, 7–26.

HAYEK F. A. (1956) The road to serfdom after twelve years, in *The Road to Serfdom.* University of Chicago Press, Chicago.

HAYEK F. A. (1961) Freedom and coercion: some comments and Mr. Hamowy's criticism, *New Individualist Review* **2**, 28–32.

HAYES R. H. and ABERNATHY W. (1980) Managing our way to economic decline, *Harvard Business Review* **59**, 66–77.

HEALEY & BAKER (1999) *European Cities Monitor – Europe's Top Cities.* Healey & Baker, London.

HELPMAN E. and KRUGMAN P. (1985) *Market Structure and Foreign Trade.* MIT Press, Cambridge, MA.

HUGGINS R. (2003) *Creating a UK Competitiveness Index: Regional and Local Benchmarking.* .

INTERVIEW (1999) *The Competitive Advantage of Ten Major Cities in Europe.* INTERVIEW, Amsterdam.

KRESL P. (1995) The determinants of urban competition, in KRESL P. and GAPPERT G. (Eds) *North American Cities and the Global Economy: Challenges and Opportunities.* Sage, London.

KRUGMAN P. (1989) Differences in income elasticities and trends in real exchange rates, *European Economic Review* **33**, 1031–1046.

KRUGMAN P. (1994) Competitiveness: a dangerous obsession, *Foreign Affairs* **March/April**.

KRUGMAN P. (1996) Making sense of the competitiveness debate, *Oxford Review of Economic Policy* **12**, 17–25.

LEVER W. (1993) Competition within the European urban system, *Urban Studies* **30**, 935–948.

LIEBENSTEIN H. (1966) Allocation vs 'X-Efficiency', *American Economic Review* **56**, 392–461.

MA H. (2000) Competitive advantage and firm performance, *Competitiveness Review* **10**, 1–25.

MARSHALL A. (1920) *Principles of Economics.* Macmillan, London.

MARTIN R. and TYLER P. (2003) Regional competitiveness: an elusive concept. Paper presented at the Regional Studies Conference, 'Reinventing the Region in the Global Economy', University of Pisa, Italy, April.

McCOMBIE J. S. L. and THIRLWELL, A. P. (2003) *Essays in Balance of Payment Constrained Growth.* Routledge, London.

ORGANIZATION FOR ECONOMIC CO-OPERATION AND DEVELOPMENT (1996) *Industrial Competitiveness.* OECD, Paris.

OULTON N. and O'MAHONEY M. (1994) *Productivity and Growth: A Study of British Industry.* Occasional Paper 47. Cambridge University Press/National Institute of Economic and Social Research, Cambridge.

PARR J. B. (1979) Regional economic change and regional spatial structure: some interrelationships, *Environment and Planning A* **11**, 825–837.

PARR J. B. and BUDD L. (2000) Financial services and the urban system: an exploration, *Urban Studies* **37**, 593–610.

PASCALE R. T. and ATHOS A. G. (1981) *The Art of Japanese Management.* Simon & Schuster, New York.

PETERAF M. A. (1993) The cornerstones of competitive advantage: a resource-based view, *Strategic Management Journal* **14**, 179–191.

PETERS T. J. and WATERMAN R. H. (1982) *In Search of Excellence: Lessons from America's Best-run Companies.* Harper & Row, New York.

PETTIGREW A. and WHIPP R. (1993) *Managing Change for Competitive Success.* Blackwells, Oxford.

PORTER M. E. (1981) The contributions of industrial organization to strategic management: a promise beginning to be realized, *Academy of Management Review* **6**, 609–620.

PORTER M. (1998) *The Competitive Advantage of Nations*, 2nd edn. Macmillan, London.

PORTER M. E. (2000) Location, competition and economic development: local clusters in a global economy, *Economic Development Quarterly* **14**, 15–34.

PORTER M. E. (2003) The economic performance of regions, *Regional Studies* **37**, 549–578.

REICH R. (1990) But we're global, *Times Literary Supplement* **30 August**, 925–926.

SCOTT B. R. and LODGE G. C. (1985) *US Competitiveness in the World Economy.* Harvard Business School Press, Boston.

SCHUMPETER J. A. (1950) *Capitalism, Socialism, and Democracy*, 3rd Edn. Harper & Row, New York.

SÖDERSTEN B. (1980) *International Economics*, 2nd edn. Macmillan, Basingstoke.

STEINLE W. J. (1992) Regional competitiveness and the single market, *Regional Studies* **26**, 307–318.

STORPER M. (1995) Institutions in a learning economy. Paper presented to the OECD Conference 'Employment Growth in a Knowledge-based Economy', Copenhagen, Denmark, November.

THIRLWELL A. P. (1991) Professor Krugman's 45-degree rule, *Journal of Post Keynesian Economics* **14**, 23–28.

THUROW L. (1992) *Head to Head.* William Morrow, New York.

VICKERMAN R. (1989) Measuring changed in regional competitiveness: the effects of international infrastructure investments, *Annals of Regional Science* **23**, 275–286.

WIENER M. J. (1981) *English Culture and the Decline of the Industrial Spirit 1850–1980.* Cambridge University Press, Cambridge.

WILLIAMSON O. E. (1985) *The Economic Institutions of Capitalism.* Free Press, New York.

Competition, Collaboration and Cooperation: An Uneasy Triangle in Networks of Firms and Regions

KAREN R. POLENSKE

Department of Urban Studies and Planning, Massachusetts Institute of Technology, Room 9-535, Cambridge, MA 02139, USA. Email: krp@mit.edu

(Received January 2003: in revised form February 2004)

POLENSKE K. R. (2004) Competition, collaboration and cooperation: an uneasy triangle in networks of firms and regions, *Regional Studies* **38**, 1021–1035. Many analysts maintain that firms can meet the challenges of global competition by establishing improved competitive, collaborative or cooperative activities, hereafter called 'the 3Cs'. The paper proposes that effective industrial and regional competition is often constrained by perceived and real spatial, labour, and organizational boundaries that limit the 3C relationships within the networks of firms and regions. The paper makes three contributions to the literature. First, it distinguishes collaboration from cooperation as collective types of behaviour and asserts that both can form part of an uneasy triangle of industrial interrelationships with competition. Second, it uses the 3C relationships to help explain the 'success' of industrial organizations as portrayed by analysts in alternative industrial and regional restructuring models, namely the Italian, Japanese and Global models. It examines how analysts deal with the spatial, labour and organizational boundaries in these alternative models. Third, it shows that none of the models was sufficiently general to cover all the restructuring issues as the world has moved into the globalization form of development. Throughout, the paper asserts that an understanding of the interrelationships among the 3Cs and the primary constraints affecting those relationships will help local and national government and industrial decision-makers make effective firm, labour and regional policies.

Competition   Collaboration   Cooperation   Industrial and regional restructuring   Networks

POLENSKE K. R. (2004) La concurrence, la collaboration, et la coopération: une alliance boîteuse triangulaire au sein des réseaux d'entreprises et de régions, *Regional Studies* **38**, 1021–1035. De nombreux analystes affirment que les entreprises peuvent relever le défi de la concurrence mondialisée par établir de meilleures activités du point de vue de la concurrence, de la collaboration et de la coopération, appelées ci-après 'les trois C'. On laisse supposer que la concurrence industrialo-régionale efficace se voit entraver par des contraintes géographiques perçues et réelles à l'emploi et à l'organisation qui limitent les rapports 3C au sein des réseaux d'entreprises et de régions. L'apport à la documentation est à trois temps. Primo, on distingue la collaboration de la coopération comme un comportement plutôt collectif, et on affirme que tous les deux peuvent faire partie d'une alliance boîteuse triangulaire de relations industrielles avec la concurrence. Secundo, on se sert des rapports 3C afin d'expliquer la 'réussite' des établissements industriels que présentent les analystes dans divers modèles de la restructuration industrielle et régionale, à savoir les modèles italien, japonais, et mondial. Tertio, on laisse voir que pas un modèle n'était suffisamment général pour embrasser toutes les questions de restructuration au fur et à mesure de la mondialisation. Tout au long de l'article, on affirme qu'une meilleure compréhension des relations parmi les 3C et parmi les principales contraintes qui touchent ces relations-là aidera les administrations nationale et régionale, et les décideurs industriels, à mettre au point des politiques efficaces visant les entreprises, l'emploi, et les régions.

Concurrence   Collaboration   Coopération   Restructuration industrielle et régionale   Réseaux

POLENSKE K. R. (2004) Konkurrenz, Kollaboration und Kooperation: eine problematische Dreiecksbeziehung in Netzwerken von Firmen und Regionen, *Regional Studies* **38**, 1021–1035. Manche Analytiker behaupten, daß Firmen der Herausforderung des globalen Wettbewerbs nachkommen können, indem sie verbesserte, konkurrenzfähige, kollaborative und kooperative Betätigungsfelder aufbauen, die im Folgenden als 'die 3 C' (=competitive, collaborative-comparative) zusammengefaßt werden. Es wird die These aufgestellt, daß wirksamer industrieller und regionaler Wettbewerb oft durch so aufgefaßte und tatsächliche räumliche Arbeits-und Organisationsgrenzen eingeengt wird, welche auch die 3C Beziehungen innerhalb der Firmen und Regionennetzwerke einschränken. Es werden drei Beiträge zur diesbezüglichen Literatur vorgelegt: erstens eine Unterscheidung von Kollaboration und Kooperation als kollektive Verhaltenstypen, sowie die Behauptung, daß beide Teil eines problematischen Dreiecks industrieller Beziehungen mit Konkurrenz bilden können; zweitens werden die 3C Beziehungen dazu benutzt, den 'Erfolg' industrieller Organisationen erklären zu helfen, wie von Analytikern in alternativen industriellen und regionalen Umstrukturierungsmodellen, z.B. den italienischen, japanischen und globalen Modellen bereits vorgestellt. Es wird untersucht, wie Analytiker mit den räumlichen, arbeitstechnischen und organisatorischen Grenzen in diesen alternativen Modellen fertig werden. Drittens wird gezeigt, daß keins dieser Modelle ausreichend allgemeine Ziele aufwies, um alle Umstrukturierungsfragen behandeln zu können, da die Welt sich auf die Entwicklungsform der Globalisierung zubewegt hat. In der ganzen Arbeit wird betont, daß Verständnis der Beziehungen zwischen den 3Cs und den Hauptbeschränkungen, denen diese unterliegen, Gemeinde-und Landesverwaltungen sowie Industriellen, die Entscheidungen zu treffen haben, helfen werden, eine wirksame Firmen-, Arbeits- und Regionalpolitik zu entwerfen.

Konkurrenz   Kollaboration   Kooperation   Industrielle und regionale Umstrukturierung   Netzwerke

POLENSKE K. R. (2004) Competición, colaboración y co-operación: un incómodo triángulo en las redes de empresas y regiones, *Regional Studies* **38**, 1021–1035. Muchos analistas mantienen que las empresas pueden hacer frente a los desafíos que conlleva la competición global mediante una mejora en sus actividades competitivas, colaborativas y co-operativas, a lo que de aquí en adelante se referirá como las 3Cs. El artículo propone que una competición regional e industrial efectiva se ve a menudo restringida por límites organizativos, laborales y espaciales tanto reales como percibidos que limitan las relaciones entre las 3Cs dentro de las redes de empresas y regiones. Este artículo contribuye a la literatura de tres formas. En primer lugar, hace una distinción entre colaboración y co-operación como tipos de comportamiento colectivo, y afirma que ambos pueden formar parte de un incómodo triángulo de interrelaciones industriales con competición. En segundo lugar, hace uso de las relaciones entre las 3Cs para explicar el éxito de las organizaciones industriales tal y como las presentan los analistas en los modelos alternativos de reestructuración regional e industrial, siendo estos el modelo italiano, el japonés y el global. Examina cómo los analistas tratan los límites organizativos, laborales y espaciales en estos modelos alternativos. En tercer lugar, muestro que ninguno de estos modelos fue lo suficientemente general como para abarcar todas las cuestiones de reestructuración a medida que el mundo se ha encaminado hacia una forma globalizadora de desarrollo. En todo momento, se afirma que un entendimiento de las interrelaciones entre las 3Cs y de las principales restricciones que afectan dichas relaciones ayudará a lo tomadores de decisiones tanto locales, nacionales como idustriales a diseñar políticas regionales, laborales y de empresa efectivas.

Competición   Colaboración   Co-operación   Reestruturación regional e industrial   Redes

JEL classifications: L6, M0, M2, R30

INTRODUCTION

Major changes in global markets are affecting the way in which networks of firms and regions operate. In the late 1980s and 1990s, many analysts (e.g. AMIN and ROBBINS, 1990; AOKI, 1990; BEST, 1990; DORE, 1986; GERTLER, 1988; HARRISON, 1992, 1994; HIRST and ZEITLIN, 1992; IMAI and KOMIYA, 1994; MARKUSEN, 1996; ODAGIRI, 1992; PIORE and SABEL, 1984) analysed industrial and regional growth and attributed successful restructuring of firms/regions to how they could meet the new challenges posed by establishing improved competitive, collaborative or cooperative activities, hereafter called the '3Cs'. It is proposed that effective industrial and regional growth is often constrained by perceived and real labour, organizational and spatial boundaries that limit the 3C relationships within the local, national and global networks of firms.[1]

The present paper makes three contributions to the literature. First, it distinguishes collaboration from cooperation as collective types of behaviour and asserts that both can form part of an uneasy triangle of industrial/regional interrelationships with competition. Second, the 3C relationships are used to help explain the 'success' of industrial organizations as portrayed by analysts in alternative industrial and regional restructuring models, namely the Italian, Japanese and Global models. It is examined how analysts deal with the spatial, labour and organizational boundaries in these alternative models. Third, it is shown that none of the models is sufficiently general to cover all the restructuring issues as the world has moved into the globalization form of development. Throughout, it is asserted that an understanding of the interrelationships among the 3Cs and the primary constraints affecting those relationships will help local and national government and industrial decision-makers make effective firm, labour and regional policies.

The following series of questions has driven the present author's research for the paper. Do collaboration and/or cooperation help a firm attain a competitive advantage over other firms? Do they have an effect on regional boundaries, specifically on the types of networks and regional and global supply chains being established? How do these relationships constrain or enhance local, national and global networks of firms? What effect do the constraints and enhancements have on industrial and regional restructuring? The paper does not explicitly furnish answers to these questions, but they did provide the impetus for much of the author's thinking.

UNEASY 3C TRIANGLE

As the global economy is rapidly being created and restructured, analysts have altered their view on the relationship between competition, collaboration and cooperation. Initially, analysts were prone to think of competition as being the ideal type of behaviour for the firm, in that it was the one that maximized profits.

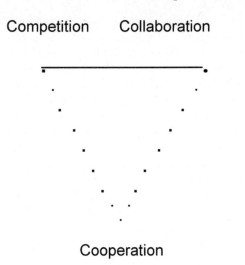

Fig. 1. *Uneasy 3C triangle*

Today, as shown above, many analysts think that collaboration and/or cooperation are needed for a competitive firm to be effective. The author believes that the three types of behaviour are best viewed as being on different end points of a triangle (Fig. 1). When a relationship exists, such as between competition and collaboration in Fig. 1, a solid line is used; when it does not exist, as between collaboration and cooperation and competition and cooperation, a dotted line is used.

An analyst can shorten or lengthen the sides of the triangle as the relationship varies from being a closer to a more distant relationship, respectively; thus, it is an uneasy triangle over space, organizational entity and time. In some periods and regions or for some organizational structures of firms, collaboration and competition can occur almost in tandem; in other cases, cooperation and competition can be the closest of the three; in still other cases, collaboration and cooperation can be almost united. Illustrations of such cases will be given below and this simple diagram will be used to help illustrate an important dimension of the differences among the industrial and regional restructuring models analysts posed in the latter 20th century.

COLLABORATION, COOPERATION AND COMPETITION: CHANGES IN BOUNDARIES

Collaboration and cooperation are similar forms of collective behaviour in some ways. First, either collaboration or cooperation may occur among actors (e.g. private or public firms, the public sector, local organizations, members of the labour force or other agents) within the entity or region or across regional, national and international boundaries. Second, in both cases, the interaction may occur among firms in the private sector, between a private firm and the public sector, and/or among other types of agents, such as trade

associations and unions. Third, they may or may not be adopted to enhance the competitiveness of a firm. Fourth, either one may last a long or a short time, depending upon many economic, social and political factors. The similarities may be part of the reason many scholars treat the two concepts as synonymous, but the present paper stresses the distinctions that separate collaborative from cooperative forms of behaviour.

Collaborative relationships are defined to include direct participation by two or more actors in designing, producing and/or marketing a product (process). The relationships among these actors are often internal arrangements that are usually vertical, sometimes among divisions in the same firm or along supply chains. They may include joint ventures. The WORD dictionary (Version 4.1, thesaurus) gives the words 'teamwork' and 'partnership' as synonyms. Those collaborative arrangements that require firms to perform in teams or to form partnerships usually take far longer to build than those cooperative ones that may just require firms to assist each other voluntarily.

Cooperation relationships are defined to include when two or more actors agree through formal or informal arrangements to share information, support managerial and technical training, supply capital, and/or provide market information. The relationships among these actors are usually external and horizontal, i.e. the actors do not work together on designing, producing and/or marketing a product (process). Cooperative arrangements are similar to public goods because they allow for the provision of collective goods under the non-exclusion principle (LORENZ, 1992, p. 195), whereas collaborative arrangements are generally exclusionary. Collaborative and cooperative arrangements are two of many ways a firm has to expand its organizational and spatial boundaries.

Both types of arrangements affect costs. Here, the way in which these two forms of behaviour affect, especially the cost structure of a firm, will be shown, noting that these ideal types do not always fit the reality as well as they should.

Costs of collaboration and cooperation

There are several ways to distinguish the costs facing a firm. Typically, economists have looked at internal and external economies to distinguish movements along the average cost curve from changes in the position of the average cost curve, respectively. Others now are looking at adaptive costs (DONER and SCHNEIDER, 1997; HAGE and ALTER, 1997, McCORMICK, 1998) versus transactions costs (NORTH, 1981, pp. 18–19; NORTH, 1990, p. 28; POLENSKE, 2001; WILLIAMSON, 1975). Adaptive costs are those associated with a firm acquiring new products, skills and capital, in addition to learning to innovate and to diffuse new technologies fast. Transaction costs are those costs, such as banking, communication, compliance, exchange, finance, insurance, retail and wholesale trade, transportation, and any other transfer costs, other than production costs, that result from the trading of goods or services.

The ability to lower costs, of course, is only one of the objectives the firm may have when entering into a collaborative or cooperative arrangement. Firms often enter into these two types of collective agreements to obtain access to information, goods, particular labourers, services, funds, etc. Internationally, automobile firms, for example, made collaborative agreements to maintain their competitive edge, in order to gain market access or market control, rather than for cost-reduction reasons (SCHOENBERGER, 1994, p. 56). With a collaborative agreement, the firm usually obtains unique access to one or more of these factors; whereas for the cooperative agreement, all firms that sign the agreement have access, often equal access, to the factors. One reason for trying to distinguish between collaborative and cooperative arrangements is because each type of behaviour will affect costs in different ways.

Collaborative arrangements often lead to internal economies of scale, affecting the position the firm has on its long-run, average-cost curve; in other words, by entering into a collaborative agreement, firms expect to move to a lower position on their long-run, average-cost curve. By collaborating on designing and producing a product, for example, two firms can lower their adaptation costs and innovate new products faster, have workers acquire new skills and obtain more capital investment. Another possibility is that by having an agreement that a supplier will design a particular product, a firm can pass the design costs on to the supplier, which may benefit by agreeing to do this only if the customer agrees to purchase a given amount of the product.

Examples of collaborations are many, some formal and others informal. Joint ventures between two or more private firms and the establishment of public–private corporations by the state and a private firm are a prevalent type of collaboration today. Other types noted by restructuring analysts (e.g. ANGEL, 2002; KELLEY and ARORA, 1996) include the offering of a product or process engineering by customer firms to supplier firms, setting up industry councils of small and medium enterprises to assist supplier firms to fulfil industry quality-control standards, and demonstrating technologies and training workers at centres that make products for the client firm, with incentives given through leasing arrangements to encourage the client firm to buy the machinery for installation in their own firm. These training centres have been established with support from the US National Institute of Standards and Technology (NIST) for a number of years. As I note below, firms now are using some of these types of collaborative arrangements to increase their competitiveness in a global economy.

Industrial–organization scholars document numerous other types of collaborative activities focused on adaptive costs, such as the technology transfer of computer numerical control equipment (KELLEY and BROOKS, 1992) and the adoption of advanced manufacturing technology (CHEW *et al.*, 1991). All these affect adaptive costs. In the study by the Massachusetts Institute of Technology multiregional planning research team of the restructuring of the Chicago metalworking and transportation sectors, POLENSKE *et al.* (1996) identified additional ones, such as the computer transfer of production specifications among firms and participation on problem-solving teams. In addition, some Midwest automotive producers collaborate with Midwest metalworking firms that are designing certain parts for the automotive firm, i.e. the metalworking supplier offers engineering and design assistance to the automotive customer (MCCORMICK, 1996a). MYTELKA (2001, pp. 130–131) indicates that in Europe, the initial one-way linkages between customers and suppliers in the 1980s changed into two-way collaborative relationships in the 1990s. Mytelka attributes this to three factors affecting the pattern of production and the nature of competition, a trend that started in the 1970s: (1) the increased knowledge-intensity of production, (2) the increased speed with which new products are developed and (3) the increased speed of innovation diffusion. The globalization, Mytelka maintains, led to mergers and acquisitions that reduced the firms' flexibility. To overcome this inertia, firms build strategic alliances (partnerships and oligopolies) and learn through these partnerships. ZELLER (2002) provides illustrations of the collaborative arrangements for the exchange of knowledge and technologies between initially competitive biotechnology and pharmaceutical firms.

In contrast to these collaborative agreements, cooperative arrangements often lead to external economies of scale, affecting the overall position and shape of the cost curve, helping a firm to reduce the average cost of producing at all scales of production. Firms frequently enter these arrangements to lower their transaction costs. A cooperative arrangement differs from a collaborative one in that information about the research and development, product and process engineering, etc., may be shared among many firms, because of the non-exclusionary nature of the arrangement, but each firm works separately from the other. For example, some firms in the Italian industrial districts, as discussed below, share training costs or have credit associations to which the given firms can apply for funding. Other examples include the enhancement of information exchange (SABEL, 1993; MCCORMICK, 1996a, b; LINCOLN *et al.*, 1992) and capacity building within a sector (KELLEY and ARORA, 1996). ASHEIM and ISAKSEN (2002) show how industries in two of the three Norwegian regions they studied, namely the shipbuilding industry in Sunnamøre and the electronics/

micro-electronics sector in Jæren, have close inter-firm (technological) cooperation. In both regions, cooperation occurs both within the firm/region and externally with technical research institutes in Norway or internationally. By reducing transaction costs, a cooperative type of collective arrangement usually helps to reduce costs for each firm that makes use of the information/product.

Collaboration or cooperation normally takes time and money, making the firm weigh the costs against the benefits gained. 'The opportunity for mutual gain from cooperation comes into play when the gains from the other's cooperation are larger than the costs of one's own cooperation' (AXELROD, 1984, p. 173). If feasible, firms can compare the overall economic, political, and social benefits and costs of cooperative versus collaborative behaviour against purely competitive behaviour. Many non-market forces also play an important role in making collaboration or cooperation successful. Many of these can be grouped under the concepts of 'trust' and 'learning', including inter- and intra-firm learning, learning regions, and learning economies.

PROXIMITY, TRUST AND LEARNING

In the current globalization and flexible versus lean-production era, managers and workers often encounter new codes of behaviour and need to consider new work rules, norms and many other differences in customs, laws and behaviour. 'Proximity', 'trust' and 'learning' all seem to have important implications for both collaborative and cooperative arrangements.

Regional political economists and geographers often emphasize the importance of geographic proximity for firms within an industry to grow rapidly. Among others, GERTLER (1995) finds that different work ethics and the 'rules of the game' are usually easiest with which to deal if those who are collaborating or cooperating with one another come from the same country (or region), culture, and social, religious or political groups. Within different sectors, different types of proximity may be important. ZELLER (2002), for example, discusses different types of proximity required in the pharmaceutical and biotechnology sectors, separating those that are internal to the firm from those external to it. From Gertler, Zeller and other analysts, the present paper distinguishes the six types of proximity that appear most to affect industrial and regional development: (1) physical (geographical), (2) organizational (interaction, shared workplace practices, training), (3) cultural (common language, modes of communication, customs, conventions, social norms), (4) temporal (the time that elapses), (5) technological (shared perceptions of technology) and (6) electronic (the form and intensity of electronic communication between economic agents).[2] ZELLER (2002, p. 286)

indicates that the second to fifth proximities may become substitutes for diminishing spatial proximity. Because the actors come from different economic, political and/or social domains with respect to any of these types of proximity, effective interaction may be hindered, even if the producers supposedly belong to the same network of firms, as discussed below.

'Trust' is a critical component of collective relationships (TEUBAL *et al.*, 1991; LORENZ, 1992; SABEL 1992). ZELLER (2002) emphasizes its need for the building of collaborative relationships. Trust probably is most needed if firms are collaborating; it is less needed if firms are cooperating; and, it is even less needed if firms are competing individually in the market place.[3] The basis of trust between firm owners, workers and others may change over time, evolving from an 'ascribed' trust among those in the same social group within a region to 'earned' trust among outsiders in the global market (SCHMITZ, 1996). 'Learning' is another important characteristic for collaborative and/or cooperative activities. The present paper argues, along with others (e.g. ASHEIM, 1996, 1998; LUND-VALL and JOHNSON, 1994; PIORE and SABEL, 1984), that a major qualitative change is taking place as capitalist economies make the transition from Fordism to Post-Fordism, as collective learning enters the workplace. The learning may be intrafirm, interfirm and/or regional. Thus, one can adapt the Lundvall–Johnson concept of the learning economy to Asheim's learning region. Within the learning region, the firm, local government, educational establishments and community all work together to determine the industrial and regional development policies for the region.

Both managers and workers sometimes need special training in how to work together in collective-learning environments. KELLEY and BROOKS (1992) state that the best adoption of computer-numerical-control technology occurs through interfirm learning, and if the innovation source is external to the firm, networks of sources, e.g. firms and non-market institutions, are the best way to facilitate the transfer. Appropriate training, however, may be difficult for policy-makers to implement. As GLASMEIER and FUELLHART (1996, p. 28) maintain, analysts have not been able to measure 'what type of learning occurs within different geographic spaces and across different organizational configurations'.

ASHEIM (1998, p. 3) persuasively argues that learning regions promote innovation through interlinking cooperative partnerships that range from work organizations within a firm to activities outside the firm, all of which he defines as 'regional development coalitions'. These coalitions change over time, as collective interactive learning leads to cooperation as a strategy to promote innovations in regionally based networks (LAZONICK, 1993, p. 4). To sustain a global competitive advantage, PORTER (1990) argues that firms need continuously to initiate organizational and institutional innovations that promote cooperation or collaboration. The organizational form in Scandinavia of learning regions is, according to ASHEIM (1998, p. 7), a group of firms in which there are high levels of worker participation in the decisions of the firm, helping to create loyalty to the firm by the workers and the managers. This intrafirm cooperation is supported by interfirm cooperation, which takes the form of inter-firm networks. Thus, collaborative and/or cooperative activities are important ways in which a firm can enhance its competitive position in the market.

NETWORKS

If three or more firms collaborate or cooperate, they almost always form a formal or informal network. Scholars analyse several distinct types of networks, such as social networks (GRANOVETTER, 1985; FRIEDLAND and ALFORD, 1991) and innovation networks (DEBRESSON and AMESSE, 1991; MARCEAU, 1995; MATHEWS, 1995; ANGEL, 2002), and they discuss networks of firms, information, labourers, organizations, etc. The present paper mainly discusses the network of firms, the main purpose being to see if a network of firms differs from firms forming a collective through collaboration or cooperation efforts and if the network enhances the competitive advantage of firms that collaborate or cooperate.[4]

How do these networks of firms differ from older types of alliances? According to HAGE and ALTER (1997, p. 95), they differ in four ways: (1) the coordination tasks are more complex; (2) the alliances span industrial sectors rather than being within one sector; (3) a given firm may be involved in more than one alliance, such as a joint venture to produce products and a strategic alliance to set national standards; and (4) alliance memberships are more diverse, often involving a member who oversees enforcement of agreements. A fifth difference could be added in that interfirm networks generally span across regions or even countries.

Either collaboration or cooperation can be done by two or more firms alone or as part of a network of firms. In many ways, both modes of behaviour start to change the 'rules of the game' concerning competitive economic behaviour, regardless of whether the firm is inside or outside a network. In the above discussion of collaboration and cooperation, it was implied that such collective actions make analysts think differently about the model of a competitive firm operating in isolation from other firms, and if the firm is part of a network of firms, analysts also must alter the earlier image of a firm. The production boundaries of the firm that is part of a network may be expanded backwards or forwards along the 'supply chain' of the firm and/or over space. As an example, MCCORMICK (1996a) cites the case where previously an automobile firm in

Detroit, USA, designed and produced a particular part for the vehicle, but now it has a metalworking firm in Chicago design and produce the part. This is an expansion of the boundaries of the firm both along the supply chain and across regions.

What is known about network formation? When are they more or less likely to form? Firms establish/join a network for many reasons. They may want to reduce technological and market uncertainties or to participate in additions to their knowledge that reduce information costs, both of which may improve profits (DEBRESSON and AMESSE, 1991, pp. 367–368). Alternatively, they may join a network to reduce their risk and uncertainty, switching costs, and sunk costs. As noted above, networks can be distinguished from the long-term supplier and customer relationships that have always existed (ODAGIRI, 1992; DORE and WHITTAKER, 1994).

Networks of firms may be established among firms in the same sector, among firms within a politically defined region or in an industrial district, among firms across national and international boundaries, and/or among firms and labourers, public agencies, or non-profit groups (DEBRESSON and AMESSE, 1991; HERRIGEL, 1992; LOCKE, 1995; SAXENIAN, 1994). To assist these networks, the US NIST established numerous manufacturing centres throughout the USA to aid firms in obtaining access to advanced technology, training, credit, etc. (SABEL, 1996).

Firms use networks as a way to expand their spatial and organizational boundaries. These are still basically economic considerations. Although a review of the numerous social, cultural and political factors is beyond the scope of this paper, these considerations may also influence the firm to form and/or join a network by taking part in collaborative or cooperative activities.

The use of networks may increase 'in periods of acute technological, institutional, and market turbulence' (DEBRESSON and AMESSE, 1991, p. 370), for economic, political or social reasons. Some networks of firms, such as that of Chicago metalworking firms, which has been formalized into a trade association, have been in place for years (MCCORMICK, 1996b). Others are being established for the first time, as partially indicated by an entire issue of the *Journal of Industry Studies* (1995) covering 'Innovation Networks: East Meets West'.

Japan is one country well known for its use of networks of firms, including the *keiretsu*, formed through relationships among managers and other officials in Japanese industrial firms and financial institutions. Many of these have existed since the 1950s. These networks form collaborations that are said to 'reduce costs and risk, facilitate communication, ensure trust and reliability, and provide insulation from outside competition' (LINCOLN *et al.*, 1992, p. 561). There are two types of *keiretsu* networks: those horizontally organized among the large companies and those vertically organized between each large manufacturing firm and its suppliers and distributors. These networks are credited with having allowed Japanese firms in the past to undertake risky, low-profit-margin, high-growth ventures (NAKATANI, 1984).

Networks may disband and/or their scope of responsibility may be drastically reduced especially, but not exclusively, in cases where an industry or sector is in decline (KELLEY and ARORA, 1996, pp. 21–22; MCCORMICK, 1996b; SABEL, 1992) and/or in turbulence (GLASMEIER and FUELLHART, 1996) for, at least, the following three reasons.

First, networks are difficult to establish and maintain. They seem to be more difficult to establish than originally anticipated, and firms become discouraged or place severe restrictions on the types of information that can be exchanged. In Michigan, for example, Continuous Improvement User Groups (CIUG) have been established among firms using common-process technologies by the Michigan Manufacturing Technology Center, but the exchange of information is very limited (KELLEY and ARORA, 1996, p. 21). In addition, internal tensions can lead networks to disband or threaten to disband. In the 1940s, for example, in the network of Chicago's metalworking machinist union and shop owners, the two groups stopped cooperating with one another, and there was even a conflict among the metalworking shop owners as a group (MCCORMICK, 1996b, pp. 140–185).

Second, firms may change their production practices, which may result in breaking previous alliances or creating new ones. By instituting a captive shop, for example, a metalworking or an automotive firm breaks its alliance to machinists in contract shops. This occurred in the 1950s when the Chicago metalworking firms expanded their in-house captive tool rooms, transferring work from small, outside, custom-toolmaking contract shops that had made their production machinery and tools (MCCORMICK, 1996b, pp. 186–224).

Third, competition may adversely affect the network of firms. If industries are in decline and experiencing competitive pressures, attempts to cooperate among members of the network may fail when firms decide to conduct price-cutting practices. Price cuts adversely affected a network of automotive suppliers in Michigan, of apparel manufacturers in Pennsylvania, and of furniture makers in Mississippi (KELLEY and ARORA, 1996, p. 22). Also, the network of firms may disband because of some of the very reasons that make them attractive, namely, they may become overly specialized and/or entrenched in the use of new technologies or processes that soon become old and/or obsolete (GLASMEIER and FUELLHART, 1996, p. 19). Often, in these cases, it seems that competitive forces of one form or another lead to a break-up of the network and the collaboration or cooperation occurring.

One way to help prevent dissipation of the network is to develop measures of 'trust', because, as noted above, trust is a critical component of collective relationships (TEUBAL *et al.*, 1991; LORENZ, 1992; SABEL 1992). Through repeated encounters in the network, producers build up a judgement as to the participants who are trustworthy and those who are not. At times, this trust can be subverted, as shown by HERRIGEL (1990, pp. 403–408) for the industrial districts in Germany in the 1930s, and by SABEL and ZEITLIN (1985, pp. 158–159) for the Sheffield cutlery industry in the late 1800s, the Birmingham metalworking shops in the 1890s, and the Saint Etienne silk-ribbon industry in the 1930s. Producers' sense of trust in each other was eroded either through long periods of recession and violence (Germany and Saint Etienne) or in periods of rapidly rising expectations (Sheffield and Birmingham). Prevention of this erosion may be difficult.

In general, producers who collaborate or cooperate respect the property-rights' distributions implicitly or explicitly set out by 'norms of competition' and the sharing, behavioural and contractual obligations implied by 'norms of reciprocity' (LORENZ, 1992, p. 195). Reciprocity norms create a trust among firms that share information, labour and/or suppliers and customers; however, reciprocity requirements in a supplier/purchaser arrangement may reduce the accessibility to those firms outside a network (LINCOLN *et al.*, 1992, p. 577). The network of firms is a form of 'community', which has ways to retaliate through withdrawal of reciprocity and/or the imposition of sanctions. According to SABEL (1993, p. 46), 'Economic cooperation results in innovation and growth, therefore, [it occurs] only when networks are neither under- nor over-socialized'.

Overall, insufficient information is available concerning the benefits and costs associated with belonging to a network of firms, the causes for some networks to be transitional while others are permanent, and the factors causing networks to cross spatial, political and/or social boundaries. Both collaboration and cooperation, thus the formation of networks of firms, seem in opposition to some competitive instincts of the marketplace, but the present paper has shown ways in which they may be seen, in many cases, to be undertaken to enhance a firm's competitive advantage.

The relationship, which is termed here an uneasy 3C triangle, among the three modes of behaviour obviously requires more intensive theoretical and empirical study. The rudimentary features of the uneasy 3C triangle are evident in the restructuring literature, which are now examined in detail.

RESTRUCTURING DEBATE

In the 1980s, many analysts began to study how industrial restructuring was being implemented through changes in industrial organization. These changes came to be known as 'flexible manufacturing'. PIORE and SABEL (1984) made this topic well known with their combined models of technological innovation and market stability. Others (e.g. AMIN and ROBBINS, 1990; GERTLER, 1988; HARRISON, 1992, 1994; HIRST and ZEITLIN, 1992; MARKUSEN, 1996) seriously questioned what the principal factors are behind this restructuring and/or if all manufacturing firms are using processes that help to enhance small, rather than large, firms, and/or what role certain regions play in the restructuring.

By using one of three models, the present paper will show how restructuring scholars analysed the boundaries among collaboration, cooperation and/or competition to create 'success' in the industrial organization of firms: (1) small firms that innovate, cooperate and form particular regions – the Italian model; (2) competitive firms that practice just-in-time (JIT) production, with collaboration between the large customer and the small supplier – the Japanese model; and (3) large, especially multinational, firms that practice collaborative behaviour globally – the Global model. Networks and spatial boundaries also begin to play a major role in some of the analyses. It will be explained how the three sets of analysts differ as to the relationship among competition, collaboration and cooperation, and in their emphasis on the role regions play in the relationships. It is concluded that no one model adequately portrayed the entire industrial/regional restructuring process, which probably contributed to the emergence of some of the later models of learning regions (LUNDVALL and JOHNSON, 1994; ARCHIBUGI and LUNDVALL, 2001).

How do the restructuring scholars deal with competition, collaboration, cooperation, networks, and changes in regional and organizational boundaries? The alternative views are summarized in Fig. 2 by portraying an uneasy triangle for each model. For analysts supporting the purely competitive model, collaborative and cooperative activities are usually not considered as part of the behaviour firms display. Thus, the lines for this triangle are just dots.

Success of small firms and cooperation: the Italian model

Some restructuring analysts focused on the success of small firms that cluster in particular regions and thrive in an innovative, cooperative environment. These analysts are referred to by the term 'Italian model' because many of the early studies were conducted in Italy. Why did these scholars identify this success with small firms with cooperative activities and with particular regions? Most firms they studied had the following characteristics. They were often small craft-based firms with flexible multi-use equipment, labour-intensive production processes, constant product and process innovations, and, of special importance for this study, they created specialized, cooperative, regional organizations to share production costs.

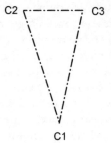

Perfectly competitive model

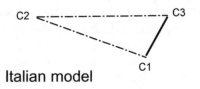

Italian model

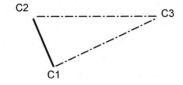

Japanese model

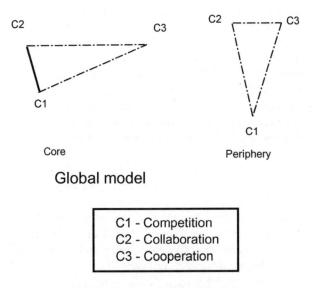

Core   Periphery

Global model

```
C1 - Competition
C2 - Collaboration
C3 - Cooperation
```

Fig. 2. Uneasy triangle of the 3Cs

Although this is an idealized description, the main attribute of a successful region in this model is a spatial network of firms that helps to foster and maintain an innovative and cooperative spirit within the geographical boundaries of an industrial district. In fact, Alfred Marshall is the first analyst to have used the term 'industrial district'. In the so-called 'Third Italy', a term used since the late 1970s to refer to the regions in the centre/north-east of the country, industries from the early 1960s were growing far faster than those in Piedmont and Lombardy in the North and than those in the South (BIANCHI, 1994; SABEL, 1989). Given that the North was the traditional industrial base in Italy, this finding was surprising to analysts. By the end of the 1980s, Italian scholars seemed to have agreed that the Third Italy was transforming itself (BIANCHI, 1994). Whether this leads to its demise or to a new invigorated region is yet to be seen.

The same type of clustering of small firms was found in the Silicon Valley in California, USA (SAXENIAN, 1991), although STORPER (1997) and a few other analysts dispute this portrayal by Saxenian of Silicon Valley firms. In addition, such clustering has been documented in areas in France, Germany, Spain and elsewhere (HERRIGEL, 1990, 1992; PYKE *et al.*, 1990), indicating that the industrial district is not an isolated phenomenon. Small firms seem to cluster and thrive in each environment. The industrial district becomes a region; thus, it has spatial boundaries, and it becomes an entity recognized in the economic world as much as a province or state is recognized as a region in the political world (SABEL, 1989).

What causes these firms to flourish? Some analysts (e.g. SAXENIAN, 1991, 1994; GERTLER, 1993, 1995) maintain that innovation is important and is partially responsible for the growth and survival of firms in these regions. SAXENIAN (1994) provides one example by comparing the innovative, cooperative aspects of firms in Silicon Valley with the hierarchical, centralized decision-making of the firms along Route 128 in Massachusetts. Firms in both regions started producing electronics: semiconductors (1960s) and chips (1970s) in Silicon Valley, and transistors and other solid-state devices (1960s) and microcomputers (late 1970s) on Route 128, but, according to SAXENIAN (1994), firms in Silicon Valley soon dominated the semiconductor field and also took a lead with small workstations and personal computers, partly as a result of the innovative, cooperative arrangements they established.

GERTLER (1993, 1995) provides another example by examining the restructuring of particular innovative sectors, such as advanced-technology machinery producers, to determine the causes of successful relationships between the producers and users of this machinery, maintaining that they are enhanced by the three types of proximity mentioned above. Gertler found that long and extended interactions between producers and users are very important for small enterprises and those that are domestically owned, single-plant establishments. He also found that a lack of any of the three first types of proximity reduced the effectiveness of the interaction. According to Gertler, even large enterprises feel the need for closeness, in terms not only of distance, but also organizationally and culturally. More recently, FRITSCH (2001, p. 297), who examines a broad array of German manufacturing firms in three regions, concludes that spatial proximity enhances horizontal cooperation among firms and helps firms to obtain public funding for the research institutions.

Other scholars (e.g. DeBRESSON and AMESSE, 1991, p. 388) argue that a network of innovators is needed to ensure the success of these industrial districts. This network can help reduce transaction costs, foster collective learning, link the innovation to the market, overcome failures in market creation for technological services, establish social norms and standards for the new market, and generate trust (TEUBAL *et al.*, 1991; SABEL, 1992). Continuous innovation, timeliness and rapid product development in turn require cooperation among firms (SAXENIAN, 1994).

Innovation is only one part of the picture. To compete effectively, firms must cooperate to meet the market demands and because of the need for production specialization. Firms in Silicon Valley, for example, form a regional network where there is collective learning, dense social networks, open labour markets, with considerable horizontal communication among firm divisions, and with outside suppliers, trade associations and universities (SAXENIAN, 1994). These practices enable firms in Silicon Valley to capture economies of scale and scope simultaneously at the level of the district rather than within the individual firm. The present author supports SABEL's (1993) and SAXENIAN's (1994) view that a key feature is cooperation, because it allows firms to reduce transaction costs by sharing research and development and by gaining access to credit, training, etc.[5] This sharing reduces production costs of each small firm, which otherwise would not have low-cost access to such services.

Fig. 2 shows the uneasy triangle for the Italian model. Because cooperation among the small firms is assumed to occur to enhance the competitive position of the firms, cooperation and competition have a short link. Collaborative arrangements might exist, but they have less influence on the competitive behaviour of the firms.

Success of competitive firms and collaboration: the Japanese model

The present paper calls the analysis by scholars of the success of JIT production and competitive firms the Japanese model. These scholars (e.g. AOKI, 1990; BEST, 1990; DORE, 1986; IMAI and KOMIYA, 1994; ODAGIRI, 1992) were aware of the major transition occurring in the industrial organization of the firm during the 1980s. From their studies, primarily of Japanese firms, they identify the following chief characteristics of industrial organization: large firms outsource to small firms through long-term contracts, which provides a collaborative mechanism for risk sharing.

These long-term relationships reduce adaptive and transaction costs and enhance the efficiency of transmitting information from the large to the small firms. Small firms cluster near large firms to allow for JIT production, and by taking larger risks because of their high degree of diversification and financing capability, the risk-taking firm gets a greater risk premium in the form of profits. In addition, there is relative control of labour by the owners, and the Japanese cultural influence is significant. These analysts deal with regions only implicitly in their analyses.

The establishment of quality circles or work teams is one of the early methods SABEL (1993, pp. 14–15) mentions as a means for Japanese firms to get workers to do their own industrial engineering and to organize their own means of collaborating with outside suppliers and coordinating other logistical functions.[6] SABEL (1993, p. 26) also claims that in Japan, joint programmes are enhanced by the creation of enduring mutual interests and by building ways to encourage reciprocity.

The complexity of the Japanese production system has led some researchers to question whether it represents a capitalistic and competitive system. KOMIYA (1994) argues that because of the various collective support mechanisms, the prevailing industrial organization system in Japan cannot be referred to as 'capitalism'. Many cultural and social factors, such as the security afforded by long-term employment and a desire for social equality, add stability to the life of the workers, a factor not found in purely competitive environments (DORE, 1973),[7] even though some of the job security is beginning to erode (ITOH, 1992; ODAGIRI, 1992). Also, some scholars (e.g. GLASMEIER and FUELLHART, 1996) note that the dependency ties that develop between suppliers and customers, because of the joint equipment purchases, mutual design, etc., might work against selection of the best supplier.

Others argue that the system in Japan is 'capitalistic' and competitive. They base this on the view that competition prevails even on the shop floor (KOIKE, 1994), that extensive control exists between the providers of finance and the employees (AOKI 1990), that the traditional Japanese style of management is being dismantled (ITOH 1992), and that there is an increase of purchases from non-contract, including foreign, suppliers (ODAGIRI 1992).

This new competition posed by the Japanese system results from many non-economic factors. These include shared cultural norms; relations of trust between managers and permanent employees; JIT technologies; process efficiency (measured by processing-time factors); the social embeddedness of technology (based upon the way in which technological and organizational learning are embedded in the machinery); and decentralized supplier networks, mostly comprised of small- and medium-sized firms (BEST, 1990, pp. 144–166). SCHOENBERGER (1994, 1997) maintains that control by the managers over time and space plays an

important role in formulating the new competition. Additional characteristics of the Japanese setting are an extensive amount of subcontracting between large and small manufacturing firms, formation of regional complexes, the important role of the state,[8] and the social division of labour (GLASMEIER and SUGIURA, 1991). Finally, other Japanese transformation scholars (e.g. IMAI, 1989; SAMUELS, 1987) maintain that with the growing importance of information technology, alternatives to the markets and hierarchies posed by WILLIAMSON (1975) will be needed.

In Fig. 2, the Japanese model is almost a mirror image of the Italian model, with the closest link in the uneasy triangle being between collaboration and competition. Collaboration takes the form of long-term contractual agreements between large and small firms and between the firm and its employees. Whereas Italian model analysts emphasize the important role played by the industrial district as a region, spatial relationships are mainly neglected by the Japanese model analysts, although, in fact, the contracting parties may be in different regions.

Success of large transnational firms and collaboration: the Global model

The present paper refers to the third group of restructuring analysts by the term 'Global model' because, in their early work, the present authors studied the success of multinational corporations in the post-Fordist period (e.g. AMIN and ROBBINS, 1990; GEREFFI, 1994; HARRISON, 1994; HELPER, 1991; MARTINELLI and SCHOENBERGER, 1991; SCOTT, 1993). These authors agreed that restructuring is occurring and that flexibility is being incorporated into the production and distribution processes, but they maintain that many of the other restructuring analysts place too much emphasis on the role of small firms. In order for flexible specialization to thrive, the Global-model analysts argue that networks among all sizes of firms are critical (CASTELLS and HALL, 1994).

How do these scholars view restructuring within a global context? They argue that multinational firms are participating in an increased internationalization of capital, more effective corporate integration, increased control over markets and finance, pushing of risks and costs along the supply chain over spatial and organizational boundaries onto small suppliers, and that multinationals need support from both the public and private sectors to establish collaborative arrangements.

An important forerunner to this global perspective is the work by CHANDLER (1977) on the rise of large firms. These firms, states Chandler, were greatly assisted in developing their dominant competitive position by the creation of the hierarchical organization of the firm, the presence of managers who oversaw the entire supply chain from the raw-material supplier to the ultimate consumer, and the resulting ability to use these attributes and scientific-management procedures to reap 'economies of time'.

What ways does the large firm use to adopt more flexible production techniques and flourish? HARRISON (1994, pp. 9–10) suggested four ways. First, they are downsizing both the number of activities and the number of employees, thus reducing costs. Second, they segment the remaining employees by keeping the core workers at the headquarters and getting them to collaborate in the production decisions, and by dispersing the others to the periphery. Third, they network both within their own corporation and with other corporations, thus obtaining up-to-date information. Finally, managers are using computers increasingly both for manufacturing and management information systems to help coordinate and monitor their activities and employees and to increase the flexibility of production and marketing.[9]

What role, if any, do regions play? Many of the Global-modal analysts deal with regions in terms of the way the corporations develop a network of supplier/customer firms across space and allocate core workers to the urban centres and peripheral workers to the suburbs. ETTLINGER (1992), for example, investigates the way in which large corporate organizations affect the regional geography by clustering in certain locations. Also, GEREFFI (1994) developed a global commodity-chain framework, specifically studying segments of the chain, from the core region, where the innovating firms locate, to the peripheral regions, where the low-cost firms locate and employ low-skilled workers. Rather than looking at networks of firms in a region, Gereffi studied the network of large transnational firms and their customers across political, hence

regional, boundaries. These large producers, states Gereffi, control the supply chain.

Thus, most of the global analysts did not dispute the adoption of flexible manufacturing techniques among the small producers, but they maintained that large transnationals also determine ways to become flexible. The large firms dominate many of these small firms, with collaboration occurring only among managers and workers in the core. Workers on the periphery are not brought within this collaboration network, but are controlled by the firm in the core.

In Fig. 2, the Global model has two uneasy triangles. The first is like that of the Japanese model, with a close collaboration-competition link, in this case representing the arrangement between the managers and the employees in the core region. The second triangle for the Global model represents the behaviour for the part of the firm located in the peripheral regions. It resembles that of the competitive model, in which neither collaboration nor cooperation occur to any significant extent. Thus, Italian, Japanese and Global-model analysts tend to view regions, the 3Cs (competition, collaboration and cooperation) and networks in different ways (Table 1).

The Italian restructuring scholars state that small firms cluster to benefit from localization and social economies, forming industrial districts, hence regions. The firms in this region establish a network and cooperate with other firms within the cluster, developing trust relationships; in the process, they create both new internal organization boundaries within the district and new spatial boundaries. For these analysts, the region and the network are defined by the industrial district, which is comprised of small, often craft-based,

Table 1. Alternative industrial/regional restructuring models

Attribute	Success of small firms, Italian model	Success of competitive firms, Japanese model	Success of large multinational firms, Global model
Competition	Downplayed in favour of cooperation	Prevails even on shop floor Only some contracts are long term Control over time and space; very competitive in a global marketplace	Driving force of the global firm Oversee (control) entire supply chain of large and small suppliers
Collaboration	Joint work on project limited, but can occur	Long-term contracts between large and small firms	After downsizing, in core, employer–employees collaborate
Cooperation	Prevalent form of behaviour Constant product-process innovation Regional organizations: credit unions, research and development training, and information dispersion	Limited forms may exist	Limited forms may exist
Networks	Occur for small firms in an industrial district	Not stressed, but exist Small firms 'cluster' near large firms to achieve Just-in-Time and information sharing	Important for firms of all sizes
Regional	Industrial district as a region is as important as politically determined regions Network operates within this 'region' Strong regional identity	Small and large firms cluster Government influential in location decisions, but no specific role for the region	Core region has innovators and collaborators Peripheral region has low-cost firms that employ low-wage and low-skilled workers Networks cross spatial boundaries

firms that use various forms of cooperative behaviour to create effective competition.

In contrast, the Japanese restructuring scholars stress the competition among the firms and the contractual arrangements of large and small firms, regardless of location. These arrangements can be considered forms of collaboration. The small firms must be able to deliver supplies JIT. For the Japanese analysts, spatial boundaries do not seem to be seriously considered, while the organizational boundary goes beyond the internal structure of the large firm to incorporate contracts with small firms. The network of collaborating supplier–customer firms might cross regional boundaries, but the analysts do not deal with this fact explicitly.

For the global-restructuring scholars, the core and the periphery become the regional form. They view the large firms as conducting competitive behaviour from dispersed core locations around the world and having control over the small firms. Networks occur within the large corporation, among the large firms, and among the large corporation(s) and the small firms, mostly through supply chains, which cross spatial boundaries as they are extended globally. Collaboration is done by the managers and workers in the core, but it is not usually done with the periphery. The organizational boundary extends along the supply chain, with the large producer controlling the market.

Thus, each of the three sets of restructuring analysts stress different interrelationships (Fig. 2) among competitiveness, collaborative and/or cooperative behaviour. In addition, the role of regions varies among the three sets of analysts. Regions play a major role for the Italian analysts in that the industrial district helps to define the region. At the other extreme, the region in which the firm is located does not seem to matter for the Japanese analyst. For the global analyst, regions are the core and the periphery, which form the beginning and the end of the supply chain. The uneasy triangular relationship changes for each industrial/regional restructuring perspective, and, for each, it changes over time.

CONCLUSIONS

The paper stresses throughout that the interrelationships among the 3Cs can change from sector to sector, and over time, space and organizational entity, including among different types of networks. For the three restructuring models, it is concluded that no one model ever becomes sufficiently general to cover all the industrial and regional restructuring issues. By distinguishing between collaborative and cooperative relationships, it is illustrated how industrial and regional analysts use both types of behaviour to enhance the third type of behaviour, i.e. competition.

In today's global world, policy-makers who understand the distinction between these three types of behaviour should be able to design relevant industrial and regional policies to help firms compete in the global marketplace. These policies may be ones that help firms overcome the constraints imposed by competition by making it easier for firms to establish rules of reciprocity for the exchange of information, to change production practices and adopt new technologies and/or to develop cooperative or collaborative relationships across spatial, organizational and labour boundaries. It has been indicated that if a firm undertakes collaborative or cooperative activities, it might be able to reap internal or external economies of scale and enhance its competitive position, but that the lowering of costs might not be the prime reason why a firm enters into such relationships. Instead, it might be to enhance its market access and market control or to maintain its regional connections.

Work on the present paper was started towards the end of the restructuring era in the mid-1990s as a way to understand the restructuring models, but the present author now (in 2003) views the paper not only as a reflection on the past, but also as a way to look into the future. Today, analysts are no longer emphasizing restructuring, but are looking into the future and discussing the role that LUNDVALL and JOHNSON's (1994) learning regions or networks and other types of new relationships might play in industrial and regional development. AMSDEN (2001) maintains that the countries she examined had an unorthodox economic model governed by an innovative control mechanism. AMSDEN (2001, p. 11) states that the main reason for the rise of these countries is that they got the control mechanism 'right' rather than getting the prices 'right'.[10] Although Amsden does not explicitly mention collaborative or cooperative relationships, it can be that as with the Third Italy, Silicon Valley and other successful regions, the establishment of such relationships in the country or among the countries helped them to compete successfully.

Empirical testing of the ideas presented here would be possible, but it is beyond the scope of the study. In addition to empirical tests, considerably more theoretical work is needed to understand the basic economic, political, social and psychological forces creating the 3C modes of behaviour and their interactions within and outside of the network of firms and regions. The restructuring process as it was known in the 1990s has changed. How will the competitive, collaborative and/or cooperative relationships be affected in the future? There are as yet no definitive answers. Firms and regions may find potential policies to enhance the interrelationships among competition, collaboration and cooperation, thus stabilizing the uneasy triangle of the 3Cs.

Acknowledgements – Work on the paper was deeply influenced by many years of teaching regional economic theories to planning students, by issues raised by Lynn E. McCormick, Alvaro E. Pereira and Nicolas O. Rockler as we studied the Chicago metalworking and transportation sectors' restructuring in the 1990s, by detailed comments by

Professors Björn Asheim, Meenu Tewari, Chris DeBresson and others on an earlier version of the paper, and, most recently, by students in the author's seminar, Globally Linked Regional Centers of Innovation. The author also sincerely thanks two anonymous reviewers for their insightful comments. Research was partially funded by the Joyce Foundation, Chicago Manufacturing Center, the National Institute of Standards and Technology, and the Alliance for Global Sustainability.

NOTES

1. Industrial and regional restructuring is defined as the deliberate, sometimes planned, process by which the economic, social, cultural and/or political organization (structure) and boundaries of an industry or region are significantly altered. The industry usually does not move from its current location.

2. The last one is cited by FINE *et al.* (1995, p. 5), and ZELLER (2002) adds other types of proximity, such as institutional and relational.

3. One reviewer disagrees, but the author thinks it is because of the difference in interpretation of what is collaboration and what is cooperation and what is meant by trust. Analysts seem to indicate that a formal contract required for collaboration will not be signed unless the two or more parties signing the agreement 'trust' each other.

4. It will be shown below how the 3Cs are viewed by restructuring analysts to help develop networks.

5. One reviewer disagrees with the author's interpretation of the role of cooperation and collaboration in the Italian model. The author thinks this disagreement might be related to the interchanging by many authors of the terms 'collaboration' and 'cooperation' without distinguishing the differences in the types of behaviour. Another reason for the difference of opinion might be that each of the 'models' presented herein is undergoing transition; collaborative relationships are emerging in these industrial districts in Italy, but, as indicated above, the present interpretation is idealized and based on work by many analysts, including Saxenian and Sable.

6. SABEL (1993), at times, seems to confuse cooperation and collaboration. The present paper will take the liberty throughout of reinterpreting Sabel's terms to fit with the definitions used herein.

7. Consistent throughout Dore's writing is a healthy scepticism that the Japanese companies will become more like their Western counterparts, or that the two forms of industrial organization will ever converge (e.g. DORE and WHITTAKER, 1994, pp. 1–15; DORE, 1986).

8. AMSDEN (1989) maintains that in Korea, the state encouraged, and even forced, firms to collaborate.

9. Even in Japan, the large corporation is flourishing as it enters into the global marketplace. ITOH (1992) maintains, however, that as these large firms increase in importance, instability and income stagnation also increase for most Japanese workers, partially because of the lack of trade unions and limited state welfare policies.

10. According to ANTHONY and GOVARINDARAJAN (1995), the four control mechanisms are a sensor, an assessor, an effector and a communication network.

REFERENCES

AMIN A. and ROBBINS K. (1990) Industrial districts and regional development: limits and possibilities, in PYKE F., BECATTINI, G. and SENGENBERGER, W. (Eds) *Industrial Districts and Inter-Firm Cooperation in Italy*, pp. 185–237. International Labour Organization, Geneva.

AMSDEN A. H. (1989) *Asia's Next Giant: South Korea and Late Industrialization*. Oxford University Press, New York.

AMSDEN A. H. (2001) *The Rise of 'the Rest': Challenges to the West from Late-Industrializing Economies*. Oxford University Press, Oxford.

ANGEL D. P. (2002) Inter-firm collaboration and technology development partnerships within U.S. manufacturing industries, *Regional Studies* **36**, 333–344.

ANTHONY R. N. and GOVARINDARAJAN V. (1995) *Management Control Systems*. Irwin, Chicago.

AOKI M. (1990) Toward an economic model of the Japanese firm, *Journal of Economic Literature* **33**, 1–27.

ARCHIBUGI D. and LUNDVALL B.-Å. (2001) *The Globalizing Learning Economy*. Oxford University Press, Oxford.

ASHEIM B. T. (1996) Industrial districts as 'learning regions': a conduction for prosperity, *European Planning Studies* **4**, 379–400.

ASHEIM B. T. (1998) Learning regions as development coalitions: partnerships as governance in European workfare states? Paper presented at the Second European Urban and Regional Studies Conference on 'Culture, Place, and Space in Contemporary Europe', University of Durham, UK, 17–20 September.

ASHEIM B. T. and ISAKSEN A. (2002) Regional innovation systems: the integration of local 'sticky' and global 'ubiquitous' knowledge, *Journal of Technology Transfer* **27**, 77–86.

AXELROD R. (1984) *The Evolution of Cooperation*. Basic Books, New York.

BEST M. H. (1990) *The New Competition: Institutions of Industrial Restructuring*. Harvard University Press, Cambridge, MA.

BIANCHI G. (1994) Requiem for the Third Italy? Spatial systems of small firms and multi-regional differentiation of the Italian development. Paper presented at the 34th European Regional Science Congress, Gröningen, Sweden, 23–26 August.

CASTELLS M. and HALL P. (1994) *Technopoles of the World: The Making of 21st Century Industrial Complexes*. Routledge, London.

CHANDLER A. D., JR (1977) *The Visible Hand*. Harvard University Press, Cambridge, MA.

CHEW W. B., LEONARD-BARTON D. and BOHN R. E. (1991) Beating Murphy's law, *Sloan Management Review* **32**, 5–16.

DEBRESSON C. and AMESSE F. (1991) Networks of innovators: a review and introduction to the issue, *Regional Policy* **20**, 363–379.

DONER R. F. and SCHNEIDER B. R. (2000) Business associations and economic development: why some associations contribute more than others, *Business and politics* **2**, 261–288.

DORE R. (1973) *British Factory–Japanese Factory: The Origins of National Diversity in Industrial Relations.* University of California Press, Berkeley.

DORE R. (1986) *Flexible Rigidities: Industrial Policy and Structural Adjustment in the Japanese Economy 1970–80.* Stanford University Press, Stanford.

DORE R. and WHITTAKER H. (1994) Introduction, in IMAI K. and KOMIYA R. (Eds) *Business Enterprise in Japan: Views of Leading Japanese Economists*, pp. 1–15. MIT Press, Cambridge, MA.

ETTLINGER N. (1992) Modes of corporate organization and the geography of development, *Papers in Regional Science* **71**, 107–126.

FINE C., GILBOY G., OYE K. and PARKER G. (1995) *The Role of Proximity in Automotive Technology Supply-Chain Development: An Introductory Essay.* MIT Press, Cambridge, MA.

FRIEDLAND R. and ALFORD R. R. (1991) Bringing society back in: symbols, practices and institutional contradictions, in POWELL W. W. and DIMAGGIO P. J. (Eds) in *The New Institutionalism in Organizational Analysis*, pp. 232–263. University of Chicago Press, Chicago.

FRITSCH M. (2001) Cooperation in regional innovation systems, *Regional Studies* **35**, 297–307.

GEREFFI G. (1994) The organization of buyer-driven commodity chains: how U.S. retailers shapes overseas production networks, in GEREFFI G. and KORZENIEWICZ M. (Eds) *Commodity Chains and Global Capitalism*, pp. 95–122. Praeger, Westport.

GERTLER M. S. (1988) The limits to flexibility: comments on the Post-Fordist vision of production and its geography, *Transactions: Institute of British Geographers*, **13**, 419–432.

GERTLER M. S. (1993) Implementing advanced manufacturing technologies in mature industrial regions: towards a social model of technology production, *Regional Studies* **27**, 665–680.

GERTLER M. S. (1995) 'Being There': proximity, organization, and culture in the development and adoption of advanced manufacturing technologies, *Economic Geography* **71**, 1–26.

GLASMEIER A. and FUELLHART K. (1996) *What Do We Know About How Firms Learn?* Department of Geography, Pennsylvania State University, University Park.

GLASMEIER A. and SUGIURA N. (1991) Japan's manufacturing system: small business, subcontracting, and regional complex formation, *International Journal of Urban and Regional Research*, **15**, 395–414.

GRANOVETTER M. (1985) Economic action and social structure: the problem of embeddedness, *American Journal of Sociology* **91**, 481–510.

HAGE J. and ALTER C. (1997) A typology of interorganizational relationships and networks, in ROGERS HOLLINGSWORTH J. and BOYER R. (Eds) *Contemporary Capitalism: The Embeddedness of Institutions*, pp. 94–126. Cambridge University Press, New York.

HARRISON B. (1992) Industrial districts: old wine in new bottles?, *Regional Studies* **26**, 469–483.

HARRISON B. (1994) *Lean and Mean: The Changing Landscape of Corporate Power in the Age of Flexibility.* Basic Books, New York.

HELPER S. (1991) Strategy and irreversibility in supplier relations: the case of the U.S. automobile industry, *Business History Review* **65**, 781–824.

HERRIGEL G. (1990) Industrial organization and the politics of industry centralized and decentralized production. PhD dissertation, Massachusetts Institute of Technology, Cambridge, MA.

HERRIGEL G. (1992) Industry as a form of order: a comparison of the historical development of the machine tool industries in the United States and Germany, in STREEK W., SCHMITTER P. and ROGERS HOLLINGSWORTH J. (Eds) *Comparing Capitalist Economies: Variation in the Governance of Sectors*, pp. 97–128. Oxford University Press, New York.

HIRST P. and ZEITLIN J. (1992) Flexible specialization versus Post-Fordism: theory, evidence, and policy implication, in STORPER M. and SCOTT A. J. (Eds) *Pathways to Industrialization and Regional Development*, pp. 70–115. Routledge, London.

IMAI K. (1989) Evolution of Japan's corporate and industrial networks, in CARLSSON B. (Ed.) *Industrial Dynamics*, pp. 123–155. Kluwer, Dordrecht.

IMAI K. and KOMIYA R. (Eds) (1994) *Business Enterprise in Japan: Views of Leading Japanese Economists.* MIT Press, Cambridge, MA.

ITOH M. (1992) The Japanese model of Post-Fordism, in STORPER M. and SCOTT A. J. (Eds) *Pathways to Industrialization and Regional Development*, pp. 116–134. Routledge, London.

KELLEY M. R. and ARORA A. (1996) The role of institution-building in U.S. industrial modernization programs, *Research Policy* **25**, 265–279.

KELLEY M. R. and BROOKS H. (1992) Diffusion of NC and CNC machine-tool technologies in large and small firms, in AYRES R. U., HAYWOOD W. and TCHIJOV I. (Eds) *Computer-Integrated Manufacturing*, Vol. III: *Models, Case Studies, and Forecasts of Diffusion*, pp. 117–135. Chapman & Hall, New York.

KOIKE K. (1994) Intellectual skills and long-term competition, in IMAI K. and KOMIYA R. (Eds) *Business Enterprise in Japan: Views of Leading Japanese Economists*, pp. 261–274. MIT Press, Cambridge, MA.

KOMIYA R. (1994) The life insurance company as a business enterprise, in IMAI K. and KOMIYA R. (Eds) *Business Enterprise in Japan: Views of Leading Japanese Economists*, pp. 365–386. MIT Press, Cambridge, MA.

LAZONICK W. (1993) Industry cluster versus global webs: organizational capabilities in the American economy, *Industrial and Corporate Change* **2**, 1–24.

LINCOLN J. R., GERLACH M. L. and TAKAHASHI P. (1992) Keiretsu networks in the Japanese economy: a dyad analysis of intercorporate ties, *American Sociological Review* **57**, 561–585.

LOCKE R. M. (1995) *Remaking the Italian Economy.* Cornell University Press, Ithaca.

LORENZ E. H. (1992) Trust, community, and cooperation: toward a theory of industrial districts, in STORPER M. and SCOTT A. J. (Eds) *Pathways to Industrialization and Regional Development*, pp. 195–204. Routledge, New York.

LUNDVALL B. Å. and JOHNSON B. (1994) The learning economy, *Journal of Industry Studies* **1**, 22–42.

MARCEAU J. (1995) A networked nation or a complexes issue? Reshaping industry analysis, *Journal of Industry Studies* **2**, 19–34.

MARKUSEN A. (1996) Sticky places in slippery space: a typology of industrial districts, *Economic Geography* **72**, 293–313.

MARSHALL A. (1920) *Industry and Trade*. Macmillan, London.

MARTINELLI F. and SCHOENBERGER E. (1991) Oligopoly is alive and well. Notes for a broader discussion on flexible accumulation, in BENKO G. and DUNFORD M. (Eds) *Industrial Change and Regional Development*, pp. 117–133. Belhaven, London.

MATHEWS J. (1995) Introduction to the Special Issue: Innovation networks, East meets West, *Journal of Industry Studies* **2**, 1–18.

McCORMICK L. E. (1996a) Clustering and the future of Chicago's metalworking sector. Paper presented at the 43rd Annual Meetings of the North American Regional Science Association, Washington, DC, USA, 14–17 November.

McCORMICK L. E. (1996b) A life-cycle model of manufacturing networks and Chicago's metalworking industry. PhD dissertation, Department of Urban Studies and Planning, Massachusetts Institute of Technology, Cambridge, MA.

McCORMICK L. E. (1998) *Are They 'Rent-seekers' or Innovators: Assessing the Capacity of Interfirm Networks*. Hunter College, New York.

MYTELKA L. K. (2001) Mergers, acquisitions, and inter-firm technology agreements in the global learning economy, in ARCHIBUGI D. and LUNDVALL B.-A. (Eds) *The Globalizing Learning Economy*, pp. 127–144. Oxford University Press, Oxford.

NAKATANI I. (1984) The economic role of financial corporate groupings, in AOKI M. (Ed.) *The Economic Analysis of the Japanese Firm*, pp. 227–258. Elsevier, Amsterdam.

NORTH D. C. (1981) *Structure and Change in Economic History*. W. W. Norton, New York.

NORTH D. C. (1990) *Institutions, Institutional Change and Economic Performance*. Cambridge University Press, Cambridge.

ODAGIRI H. (1992) *Growth Through Competition: Competition Through Growth. Strategic Management and the Economy in Japan*. Clarendon, Oxford.

PIORE M. J. and SABEL C. F. (1984) *The Second Industrial Divide*. Basic Books, New York.

POLENSKE K. R. (2001) Taking advantage of a region's competitive assets: an asset-based regional economic-development strategy, in *Entrepreneurship, Firm Growth, and Regional Development in the New Economic Geography*. Proceedings of the Uddevalla Symposium, Trollhättۘen, Sweden, 15–17 June 2000, pp. 527–544.

POLENSKE K. R., McCORMICK L. E., PEREIRA A. E. and ROCKLER N. O. (1996) *Industrial Restructuring, Infrastructure Investment, and Transportation in the Midwest*. Department of Urban Studies and Planning for the Joyce Foundation, Chicago Manufacturing Center, and National Institute for Science and Technology, Cambridge, MA.

PORTER M. E. (1990) *The Competitive Advantage of Nations*. Free Press, New York.

PYKE F., BECATTINI G. and SENGENBERGER W. (Eds) (1990) *Industrial Districts, Interfirm Cooperation in Italy*. International Labour Organisation, International Institute for Labour Studies, Geneva.

SABEL C. and ZEITLIN J. (1985) Historical alternatives to mass production: politics, markets, and technology in nineteenth century industrialization, *Past and Present* **108**, 131–176.

SABEL C. F. (1989) Flexible specialization and the re-emergence of regional economics, in HIRST P. and ZEITLIN J. (Eds) *Reversing Industrial Decline*, pp. 17–70. Berg, Oxford.

SABEL C. F. (1991) Moebius-strip organizations and open labor markets: some consequences of the reintegration of conception and execution in a volatile economy, in BOURDIEU P. and COLEMAN J. S. (Eds) *Social Theory for a Changing Society*, p. 23–63. Westview, Boulder.

SABEL C. F. (1992) Studied trust: building new forms of co-operation in a volatile economy, in PYKE F. and SENGENBERGER W. (Eds) *Industrial Districts and Local Economic Regeneration*, pp. 215–249. International Institute for Labour Studies, Geneva.

SABEL C. F. (1996) A measure of federalism: assessing manufacturing technology centers, *Regional Policy* **25**, 281–307.

SAMUELS R. (1987) *The Business of the Japanese State*. Cornell University Press, Ithaca.

SAXENIAN A. (1991) The origins and dynamics of production networks in Silicon Valley, *Regional Policy* **20**, 423–438.

SAXENIAN A. (1994) *Regional Advantage: Culture and Competition in Silicon Valley and Route 128*. Harvard University Press, Cambridge, MA.

SCHMITZ H. (1996) *From Ascribed to Earned Trust in Exporting Clusters*. Institute of Development Studies, University of Sussex, Falmer.

SCHOENBERGER E. (1994) Competition, time and space in industrial change, in GEREFFI G. and KORZENIEWICZ M. (Eds) *Commodity Chains and Global Capitalism*, pp. 51–66. Praeger, Westport.

SCHOENBERGER E. (1997) *The Cultural Crisis of the Firm*. Blackwell, Cambridge, MA.

SCOTT A. J. (1993) *Technopolis: High-Technology Industry and Regional Development in Southern California*. University of California Press, Berkeley.

STORPER M. (1997) *The Regional World: Territorial Development in a Global Economy*. Guilford Press, Oxford.

TEUBAL M., YINNON T. and ZUSCOVITCH E. (1991) Networks and market creation, *Regional Policy* **20**, 381–392.

WILLIAMSON O. E. (1975) *Markets and Hierarchies: Analysis and Industry*. Free Press, New York.

ZELLER C. (2002) Project teams as means of restructuring and development in the pharmaceutical industry, *Regional Studies* **36**, 275–289.

Competitiveness, Productivity and Economic Growth across the European Regions

BEN GARDINER⋆, RON MARTIN† and PETER TYLER‡

⋆*Cambridge Econometrics, Covent Garden, Cambridge CB1 2HS, UK. Email: bg@camecon.com*
†*Department of Geography, University of Cambridge, Downing Site, Downing Place, Cambridge CB2 3EN, UK.*
Email: rlm1@cam.ac.uk
‡*Department of Land Economy, University of Cambridge, 19 Silver Street, Cambridge CB3 9EP, UK.*
Email: pt23@cam.ac.uk

(Received February 2004: in revised form July 2004)

GARDINER B., MARTIN R. and TYLER P. (2004) Competitiveness, productivity and economic growth across the European regions, *Regional Studies* **38**, 1037–1059. During the last few years, there has been a significant interest by both academics and policy-makers in the notion of regional competitiveness. Yet, despite the relative popularity of the term, there is a surprisingly lack of consensus about what is meant by the competitiveness of regions and cities. The paper discusses some of the key issues that arise in operationalizing the concept and it focuses on the central relevance of productivity in the debate about regional competitiveness. It then examines the pattern and dynamics of regional productivity across the European Union (EU) including the new Central and East European Enlargement (CEEE) enlargement states, and in particular it addresses the issue of whether, and to what extent, there has been regional convergence in productivity levels over the past two decades. Regional convergence in the EU-15 has been remarkably slow, and while recent regional productivity growth has been rapid in CEEE Member States, suggesting possibilities for catch-up in those countries, it seems to have been accompanied and, indeed, in part achieved by falls in regional employment rates, a combination hardly sustainable in the long run. The persistence of regional disparities in productivity across the EU clearly raises key issues for policy at the very time that intense debate surrounds the scale and allocation of the Structural Funds.

Regional competitiveness   Productivity   Growth   European Union   Convergence   Enlargement states

GARDINER B., MARTIN R. et TYLER P. (2004) La compétitivité, la productivité et la croissance économique à travers les régions européennes, *Regional Studies* **38**, 1037–1059. Dans les dernières années, et les universitaires et les décideurs ont prêté une attention particulière à la notion de compétitivité régionale. En dépit de la popularité relative de cette notion, il est à s'étonner que tout le monde ne soit pas d'accord pour reconnaître ce que veut dire la notion de compétitivité quant aux régions et aux grandes villes. Cet article cherche à examiner quelques-unes des questions clé qui se posent suite à la mise en exploitation de la notion et porte sur le rôle central que joue la productivité dans le débat sur la compétitivité régionale. Il s'ensuit une étude de la distribution et de la dynamique de la productivité régionale à travers l'Union européenne, y compris les nouveaux pays-membres, et aborde en particulier la question de si, oui ou non, et dans quelle mesure il y a eu une convergence régionale des niveaux de la productivité dans les deux dernières décennies. Il s'avère que la convergence régionale au sein de l'Ue à 15 a été très lente, et tandis que la croissance récente de la productivité régionale a été rapide dans les nouveaux pays membres, ce qui laisse supposer la possibilité pour ces pays-là de rattraper leur retard, il semble que cela s'associe à, et dans une certaine mesure s'explique par, des baisses des taux d'emploi régionaux, une combinaison qui n'est guère à maintenir à long terme. La persistance des écarts régionaux de la productivité à travers l'Ue soulève des questions clé quant à la politique, juste au moment où on discute de l'importance et de l'octroi des Fonds structurels.

Compétitivité régionale   Productivité   Croissance   Union européenne   Convergence
Nouveaux pays-membres

GARDINER B., MARTIN R. und TYLER P. (2004) Wettbewerbsfähigkeit, Produktivität und Wirtschaftswachstum in den europäischen Regionen, *Regional Studies* **38**, 1037–1059. In den letzten Jahren hat die Idee einer regionalen Wettbewerbsfähigkeit erhebliches Interesse unter Akademikern und Wirtschaftspolitikern ausgelöst. Doch trotz der verhältnismäßigen Popularität des Ausdrucks besteht ein überraschender Mangel an Übereinstimmung, was Wettbewerbsfähigkeit von Regionen und Städten eigentlich bedeutet. Dieser Aufsatz bespricht einige der Hauptfragen, die bei der Anwendung des Begriffes auftauchen, und konzentriert sich auf die zentrale Relevanz der Produktivität in der Debatte über regionale Wettbewerbsfähigkeit. Er untersucht sodann die Muster und Dynamik regionaler Produktivität in der gesamten europäischen Union einschließlich der neuen CEEE Vergrößerungsstaaten, und beschäftigt sich vorallem mit der Frage, ob, und in welchem Ausmaß eine regionale Konvergenz der Produktionshöhen während der beiden letzten Jahrzehnte stattgefunden hat. Es wird festgestellt, daß regionale Konvergenz in den 15 Staaten der EU außergewöhnlich langsam vonstatten gegangen ist, und obschon in letzter Zeit in den CEEE Mitgliedstaaten eine rasche regionale Produktionszunahme festzustellen war, die Möglichkeiten des Aufholens in jenen Staaten nahelegt, dies von einer Abnahme in regionalen Beschäftigungsraten begleitet, und sogar teilweise durch sie erreicht worden zu sein scheint, eine Kombination, die sich auf lange Sicht kaum als nachhaltig erweisen dürfte. Das Fortbestehen regionaler Ungleichheiten der Produktivität in der EU wirft offensichtlich grundlegende Fragen für die Politik auf, und das genau zu dem Zeitpunkt, da Umfang und Zuweisung des Strukturfonds ernsthaft diskutiert werden.

Regionale Wettbewerbsfähigkeit   Produktivität   Wachstum   Europäische Union   Konvergenz
Vergrößerungsstaaten

GARDINER B., MARTIN R. y TYLER P. (2004) Competitividad, productividad y crecimiento económico a través de las regiones europeas, *Regional Studies* 38, 1037–1059. En los últimos años se ha prestado un interés significativo a la noción de competitividad regional tanto por parte de académicos como de diseñadores de políticas. Aún así, a pesar de la relativa popularidad de este término, existe una sorprendente falta de consenso en lo que al significado de competitividad de regiones y ciudades se refiere. Este artículo discute algunas de las principales cuestiones que emergen a la hora de operacionalizar el concepto y se centra en la relevancia central de la productividad en el debate sobre competitividad regional. A continuación se examina el patrón y la dinámica de la productividad regional a través de la Unión Europea, incluyendo los nuevos estados del Centro y Este europeos (CEEE) tras la ampliación, y, en particular, aborda la cuestión de si, y hasta qué punto, ha existido convergencia regional en los niveles de productividad durante las dos últimas décadas. Los resultados muestran que la convergencia regional en los UE-15 ha sido remarcablemente lenta, y mientras que el reciente crecimiento de la productividad regional en los estados miembros del Centro y Este europeos (CEEE) ha sido rápido, lo cual sugiere posibilidades de recuperación en esos países, esto parece haberse visto acompañado, y ciertamente logrado en parte, por caídas en los índices de empleo regional, una combinación que es casi insostenible a largo plazo. La persistencia de disparidades regionales en productividad a través de la UE plantea de forma muy clara un número de cuestiones clave para cuestiones de política, precisamente en este mismo momento en que existe un intenso debate en torno a la escala y a la asignación de los Fondos Estructurales.

Competitividad regional   Productividad   Crecimiento   Unión Europea   Convergencia
Estados de la ampliación

JEL classifications: R0, R1, R5

REGIONAL COMPETITIVENESS AND PRODUCTIVITY

Recent years have seen a surge of academic and policy attention devoted to the notion of 'competitiveness': nations, regions and cities, we are told, have no option but to strive to be competitive in order to survive in the new global marketplace and the 'new competition' (BEST, 1990, 2001) being forged by the new information or knowledge-driven economy. Policy-makers at all levels have been swept up in this competitiveness fever. Thus, the importance of competitiveness has been a recurring theme in Organization for Economic Co-operation and Development assessments of the advanced economies. Similarly, the European Commission has become much exercised by what it sees as the inferior competitiveness of the European Union (EU), and has set as one of its goals the catch-up of EU competitiveness with that of the USA by 2010. Likewise, the UK government has placed the need to boost national competitiveness at the centre of its policy agenda.

This concern with competitiveness has quickly spread to regional, urban and local policy discourse. Growing interest has emerged in the 'regional foundations' of national competitiveness and with developing new forms of regionally based policy interventions to help improve the competitiveness of every region and major city, and hence the national economy as a whole.

In the UK, for example, the government has assigned increasing importance to the competitiveness of the country's regions and cities as part of its reorientation of national and regional policy (H. M. TREASURY, 2001, 2003; DEPARTMENT OF TRADE AND INDUSTRY, 2004; OFFICE OF THE DEPUTY PRIME MINISTER, 2003, 2004). In the EU, the issue of regional competitiveness has taken on particular significance not only in relation to its aim to close the 'competitiveness gap' with the USA, but also as part of its pursuit of social and economic cohesion. Raising the competitiveness of Europe's lagging and less prosperous regions is regarded as crucial to social cohesion, especially in the context of monetary union and EU enlargement. In fact, although still small, the literature on 'territorial competitiveness' is now growing rapidly.

However, this new focus on 'place competitiveness' raises a host of questions about what precisely is meant by the competitiveness of regions, cities and localities. In what sense can one talk of regional competitiveness? In what sense do regions and cities compete? Traditionally, neither economists nor economic geographers have tended to frame their discussions of regional growth and development in terms of such questions, or certainly not explicitly in the language of competitiveness. Only recently has this state of affairs begun to change (e.g. STEINLE, 1992; CHESHIRE and GORDON, 1995; DUFFY, 1995; GROUP OF LISBON,

1995; STORPER, 1995, 1997; JENSEN-BUTLER *et al.*, 1996; PORTER, 1998a, b, 2000, 2001, 2003; BEGG, 1999, 2002; URBAN STUDIES, 1999; CAMAGNI, 2002). However, these contributions notwithstanding, we are still far from any general consensus about the nature and measurement of regional competitiveness. A not uncommon theme, nevertheless, is that regional (and urban) competitiveness has to do with the success with which regions and cities compete with one another over shares of national and, especially, global export markets. This notion would seem to underpin the European Commission's interpretation of the term:

> [Competitiveness is defined as] the ability to produce goods and services which meet the test of international markets, while at the same time maintaining high and sustainable levels of income or, more generally, the ability of (regions) to generate, while being exposed to external competition, relatively high income and employment levels. . . .
>
> (EUROPEAN COMMISSION, 1999, p. 4)

Given that regional economies are almost certain to be more open (to trade) than the national economies of which they are a part, this focus on export performance would seem to be warranted. The 'export base' of a region or city has long been viewed as key to regional and urban prosperity, as recently re-emphasized by ROWTHORN (1999, pp. 22–23):

> The prosperity of a region is determined primarily by the strength of its export base ... all those activities which bring income into the region by providing a good or service to the outside world. ... The alternative term 'tradables' is also used to denote such activities.

The implication of this line of argument would seem to be that a reduction in the size of a region's export base, or a deterioration in the region's trade balance, or both, would signal a decline in regional competitiveness. This approach is very similar to that found in many definitions of national competitiveness, as for example in TYSON's *Who's Bashing Whom* (1992), where (US) national competitiveness is defined as 'our ability to produce goods and services that meet the test of international competition while our citizen's enjoy a standard of living that is both rising and sustainable' (p. 10).

Yet, as KRUGMAN (1996a, b) and others (e.g. GROUP OF LISBON, 1995) have pointed out, there might less to this view of competitiveness than meets the eye. Thus, KRUGMAN (1996a, p. 5), making frequent reference to the USA, has argued that:

> Concerns about competitiveness are, as an empirical matter, almost always completely unfounded. ... The obsession with competitiveness is not only wrong but dangerous ... thinking in terms of competitiveness leads to bad economic policies on a range of issues.

KRUGMAN raises three points of opposition to the idea of national competitiveness. In the first place, he argues that it is misleading and incorrect to make an analogy between a nation and a firm, whereas, for example, an unsuccessful firm will ultimately go out of business; there is no equivalent 'bottom line' for a nation. Second, whereas firms can be seen to compete for market share, and one firm's success will often be at the expense of another, the success of one country creates rather than destroys opportunities for others, and trade between nations is well known not to be a 'zero-sum' game. Third, if competitiveness has any meaning, then it is simply another way of saying *productivity*; that growth in national living standards is essentially determined by the growth rate of productivity.

Michael Porter, who has been amongst the most influential writers on 'competitive advantage' – of firms, industries, nations, and regions and cities – also suggests that the best measure of competitiveness is productivity:

> Competitiveness remains a concept that is not well understood, despite widespread acceptance of its importance. To understand competitiveness, the starting point must be the sources of a nation's prosperity. A nation's standard of living is determined by the productivity of its economy, which is measured by the value of its goods and services produced per unit of the nation's human, capital and natural resources. Productivity depends both on the value of a nation's products and services, measured by the prices they can command in open markets, and the efficiency with which they can be produced. *True competitiveness, then, is measured by productivity.* Productivity allows a nation to support high wages, a strong currency and attractive returns to capital, and with them a high standard of living.
>
> (PORTER and KETELS, 2003, p. 7, emphasis added)

The issue is whether this line of argument applies equally to regions and cities. CELLINI and SOCI (2002) argue that the notion of regional competitiveness is neither a macro-economic (national) nor a micro-economic (firm-based) one: regions are neither simple aggregations of firms nor are they scaled-down versions of nations. CAMAGNI (2002) takes a similar view, suggesting that regions do indeed compete, but based on absolute advantage rather than of comparative advantage. A region might be thought of as having absolute competitive advantages when it possesses superior technological, social, infrastructural or institutional assets that are external to but which benefit individual firms such that no set of alternative factor prices would induce a geographical redistribution of economic activity. These assets tend to give the region's firms, overall, a higher productivity than would otherwise be the case. As the EUROPEAN COMMISSION (1999, p. 5) puts it:

> [The idea of regional competitiveness] should capture the notion that, despite the fact that there are strongly competitive and uncompetitive firms in every region, there are common features within a region which affect the competitiveness of all firms located there.

This is not to suggest that the export performance of regions is unimportant: on the contrary, the comparative advantage of a region's export sectors is still key to its overall growth and prosperity. Competition between regions (both within and between nations) may exclude a region from an industry in which it could have established a comparative advantage, or drive a region from an industry in which comparative advantage could have been maintained (especially bearing in mind that regions do not have recourse to currency devaluation, nor posseses the price-wage flexibility that might alleviate competitive disadvantage in the short run). But the basic point is that regional competitive advantage is both absolute and comparative in nature, and that productivity is not only important in influencing the comparative advantage of a region's export sectors, but also is important across the whole range of its industries and services, not just to keep up with external competitors.

The present paper focuses attention on the pattern and dynamics of regional productivity across the EU. As noted above, the European Commission has highlighted the importance of regional competitiveness for its goal of social cohesion. In addition, the competitiveness of the EU regions is of key significance for the success of the new Single Currency (monetary union) and the major phase of membership enlargement that is now underway (MARTIN, 2001, 2003). The next section reviews some of the conceptual

issues involved in thinking about regional productivity differences and evolutions. To undertake empirical analysis, the third section constructs a new hours-worked measure of productivity for the EU regions, and examines the pattern and scale of regional productivity differences across the EU, including the Central and East European Accession States. The fourth section addresses the important question of whether regional productivity is converging across the Union. The fifth section relates both productivity growth and changes in employment rates to the pattern of regional per-capita Gross Domestic Product (GDP) growth across the EU. The final section outlines some of the implications of the findings. Throughout, analysis refers to the NUTS2-level regions and it draws on historical time-series data collated and compiled by Cambridge Econometrics.

REGIONAL PRODUCTIVITY: SOME CONCEPTUAL ISSUES

At the outset, it should be stressed that the concept of productivity is itself far from straightforward. The standard notion of productivity refers to the productive efficiency of a given workforce, i.e. labour productivity, measured in terms of output per input of labour. This is an aggregate notion, and as Fig. 1 suggests, in a regional context, labour productivity is the outcome of a variety of determinants (including the sort of

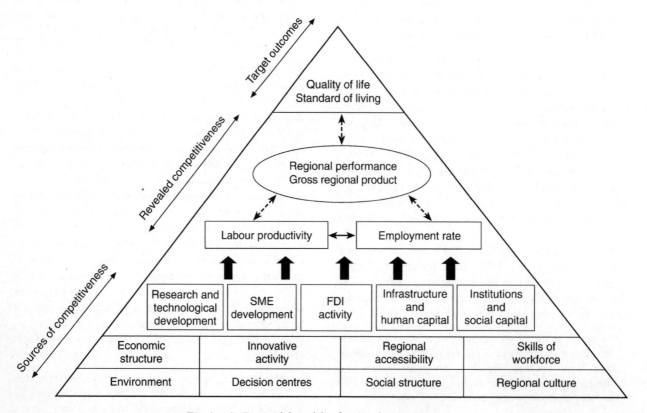

Fig. 1. A 'Pyramidal model' of regional competitiveness

Sources: Based on BEGG (1999), EUROPEAN COMMISSION (1999), JENSEN-BUTLER (1996), LENGYEL (2000, 2003).

Table 1. Three theoretical perspectives on regional productivity growth

Theory	Explanation of regional productivity differences	Evolution of regional productivity differences
Neoclassical Growth Theory	Regional differences in productivity due to different factor endowments, and especially differences in capital/labour ratios and technology	Assumes constant returns to scale; diminishing returns to factors of production; free factor mobility and geographical diffusion of technology, so that low-productivity regions should catch up with high productivity ones, i.e. regional convergence in productivity
Endogenous Growth Theory	Regional differences in productivity due to differences in capital/labour ratios, knowledge base and the proportion of the workforce in knowledge-producing industries	Implications for regional productivity evolutions depend on the extent to which low-technology regions catch up with high-technology regions, and this on the degree of geographical diffusion of technology and knowledge, and flows of knowledge workers. The more knowledge/technology spillovers are localized, and the more knowledge workers move to leading technology regions, the more productivity differences between regions will persist or even widen
'New Economic Geography' models	Spatial agglomeration/specialization/clustering are key sources of externalities and increasing returns (labour, knowledge spillovers, specialist suppliers, etc.) that give local firms higher productivity	Economic integration (trade, factor flows) increases the tendency to spatial agglomeration and specialization of economic activity, leading to 'core–periphery' equilibria and persistent regional differences in productivity

regional assets alluded to above). Many of these regional factors and assets also determine a region's overall employment rate. Together, productivity and employment rate are measures of what might be termed 'revealed competitiveness', and both are central components of a region's economic performance and its prosperity (as measured, say, by GDP per head), though obviously of themselves they say little about the underlying regional attributes (sources of competitiveness) on which they depend. For it would be somewhat perverse to describe a 'competitive' region solely in terms of its productivity, because a region's productivity can increase significantly if the firms located there underwent a major phase of rationalization and downsizing, involving the closure of the least efficient firms and layoff of the least efficient workers. Such one-off rationalization-induced increases in productivity may not be associated with any overall increase in the output of the region (nor with any improvement in the region's absolute competitive advantage), but with a rise in unemployment that may end up being very difficult to solve. In such circumstances, employment reduction is a 'negative' route to raising regional productivity, and is to be contrasted with regions with both high productivity and employment.

Fig. 1 suggests that productivity may differ between regions for a host of different reasons. But equally important is how such differences are predicted to evolve over time. In the standard Neoclassical model, the growth of productivity (output per worker) depends on the growth of capital per worker and the (exogenous) rate of technical progress (or total factor productivity). Hence, regional differences in productivity growth are explained by regional differences in the rate of (exogenous) technical progress and by regional differences in the growth of the capital–labour

ratio. But given that the model also assumes constant returns to scale, diminishing returns to labour and capital, and complete factor mobility – including the unimpeded diffusion of technological advance – regional productivity disparities are predicted to narrow over time, as initially low-productivity regions catch up with initially high-productivity ones (Table 1). Neoclassical growth models of regional convergence have been much researched in recent years with varying empirical results (for a survey, see MARTIN and SUNLEY, 1998).

In endogenous growth models, on the other hand, where technical change is argued to be itself determined by the growth process, the implications for the evolution of regional variations in productivity over time depend on the assumptions made about the process of technical progress. For example, in the Romer version of the endogenous growth model, the rate of growth of technological knowledge is assumed to be a function of the growth in the numbers of workers employed in knowledge-producing activities. If it is further assumed that technological progress diffuses rapidly across geographical space, then one might expect that technical progress in any given region will depend on the extent to which its own technology lags behind the technology of the most advanced region(s). Low technology regions, therefore, should experience the fastest growth in output per worker, which means that regional convergence in productivity is predicted to occur in this version of the endogenous growth model. However, there is now ample empirical work that suggests that the spatial diffusion of technology is far from instantaneous as assumed in the Neoclassical model. It is well known that certain regions appear to be innovation leaders. They are the sources of basic inventions and take the lead in applying these innovations in the form of new products and services, or more efficient ways of producing existing products. It seems that technology spillovers tend to be localized, and an important source of geographically concentrated externalities and increasing returns. Regional convergence in productivity may thus be a slow process. The more so if the leading innovative regions also attract knowledge and highly skilled workers from other regions. Under such conditions, not only may productivity differences between regions persist, but also they might even widen over time (for a review of regional endogenous growth models, see MARTIN and SUNLEY, 1998).

Not unrelated to endogenous growth theory, the 'new economic geography' models that have become popular in recent years (FUJITA *et al.*, 1999; BRACKMAN *et al.*, 2001; FUJITA and THISSE, 2002; BALDWIN *et al.*, 2003) attribute regional differences in growth to localized increasing returns arising from the spatial agglomeration of specialized economic activity and the external economies and endogenous effects such localized specialization generates (accumulation of skilled labour, local knowledge spillovers, specialized suppliers and services, etc.). The existence of localized externalities, and hence the limited geographical range of knowledge spillovers, may be due to locally embedded socio-cultural, political and institutional structures and practices that can all contribute to the localization of these external economies (MARTIN, 2000). They can help to explain not only why some regions (and cities) have a higher productivity and growth rate than others (for an early but cogent account of why productivity varies between cities, see SVEIKAUSKAS, 1975), but also why such differences might not diminish over time. Many of the new economic geography models in fact predict a 'core–periphery' equilibrium pattern of productivity (DAVIS and WEINSTEIN, 2001).

The different prognoses of long-run trends in regional productivity and incomes given by these various models are not simply of academic interest. All three types of model have been used to predict what is likely to happen to regional productivity and per-capita incomes across the EU as the process of economic and monetary union (EMU) deepens. As integration proceeds – and trade, factor flows and regulatory harmonization all increase – so Neoclassical models predict accelerating convergence. The endogenous growth and new economic geography models, on the other hand, predict increasing regional specialization and spatial concentration of economic activity and growth, and hence no necessary convergence. The different models also carry different implications for the trajectories of regional development in the new Accession States as they become exposed to and integrated with the EU market. Examining the temporal evolution of regional productivity disparities across the EU is thus crucial to resolving this theoretical debate.

REGIONAL PRODUCTIVITY: SOME MEASUREMENT ISSUES

There are several measures of productivity, but the most common is output per employed worker. In the European case, this is the easiest to calculate because regional data on output and employment are readily available from Eurostat's Regio database. However, this employment measure suffers from not being a direct measure of labour input. Hours worked is the better indicator as people work different weekly hours in different countries and this should be taken account of when measuring productivity. In the past, it has not been possible to distinguish regional productivity as output per hour due to data limitations, but two versions of an hours-worked measure of productivity can be estimated. One is a new data series of regional hours work derived from the Labour Force Survey (LFS), which takes account of differences in part- and full-time employment. These data were supplied by the European Commission. The alternative measure of hours worked is a composition-derived estimate based on regional sectoral structure and national sectoral average hours worked.

The sectoral hours-worked measure, calculated by applying national sectoral hours-worked data to a region's industrial structure to build up a total hours worked series, represents an improvement on just using employment, but there is still the problem of distinguishing between part- and full-time employment, as the sectoral hours-worked series relates only to full-time employees. If the relative proportions of workers in each category were the same across countries/ regions, this would not be a problem. But Fig. 2 clearly shows that significant differences exist.

The effect would be that for countries such as the Netherlands and the UK, which have a relatively high proportion of part-time employment, productivity would be artificially deflated while the employment rate would be correspondingly inflated. To correct for this distortion, an adjusted (i.e. averaging across part- and full-time employment categories) regional weekly hours-worked series is used. It has been combined with the headcount employment measure to create a more accurate representation of labour input and, hence, productivity.

Fig. 3 shows the correlation between the sectoral and LFS hours-worked measures of productivity, both based on purchasing power parities (PPS) and EU-15 = 100 normalization. Although the correspondence between the two measures is quite close, for some regions the differences between the two definitions are quite large. As Fig. 4 indicates, these differences run mainly along national lines, with regions in the Netherlands, Italy, the UK and much of Germany recording a higher productivity per hour worked using the LFS measure than using the sector-based one; and vice versa for regions in Belgium, Denmark, Spain and some new Accession

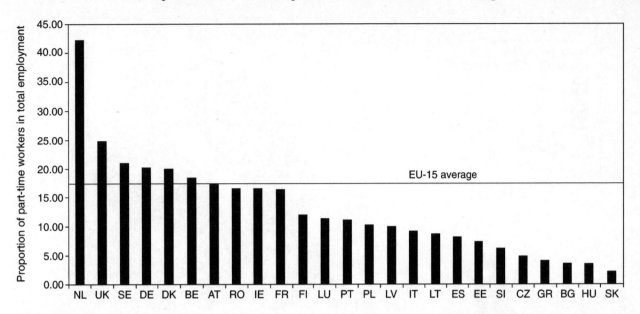

Fig. 2. *Share of part-time in total employment across European Union Member States (including CEEE States), 2001: AT, Austria; BE, Belgium; BG, Bulgaria; CZ, Czech Republic; DE, Germany; DK, Denmark; EE, Estonia; ES, Spain; FI, Finland; FR, France; GR, Greece; HU, Hungary; IE, Ireland; IT, Italy; LT, Lithuania; LU, Luxembourg; LV, Latvia; NL, the Netherlands; PL, Poland; PT, Portugal; RO, Romania; SE, Sweden; SI, Slovenia; SK, Slovakia; UK, the United Kingdom.*

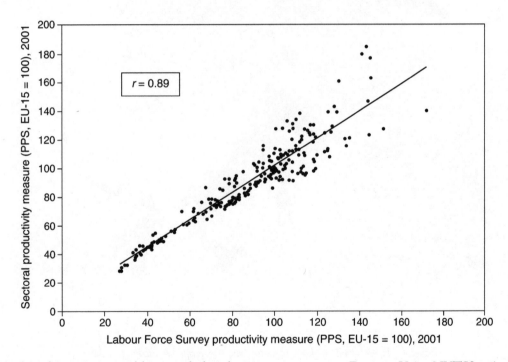

Fig. 3. *Labour force versus sectoral hours-worked productivity measures, across European Union NUTS2 regions, 2001.*

States. The results are broadly in line with the national differences in the relative importance of part-time employment shown in Fig. 2, and confirm that failure to take proper account of part-time employment could lead to incorrect estimates of regional productivity.

The LFS hours-based measure of productivity is not without its problems, however. The LFS data refer to an individual's main job rather than all work carried

out. In addition, the data are residence based, whereas GDP data are occupation based, so the two do not necessarily match precisely. Nonetheless, the results seem an improvement on the sectorally constructed hours-worked series.

Estimates of regional productivity using the LFS hours-worked measure are shown in Fig. 5. Regional differences in labour productivity across the EU are

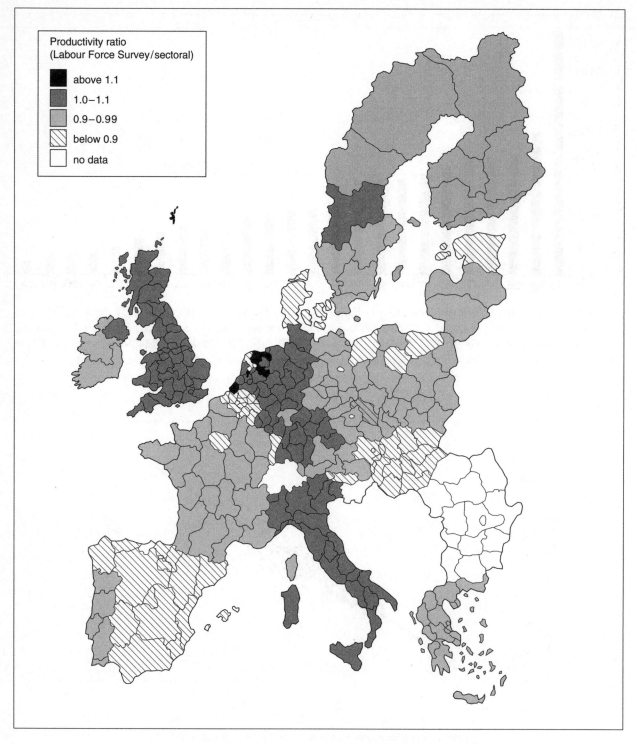

Fig. 4. Ratio of labour force to sector-based regional productivity, 2001

substantial. Within the EU-15 group of countries, productivity ranges from only around 50% of the EU-15 in some regions of Portugal and Greece to about 150% of the EU-15 average in certain regions of the Netherlands, Austria, France and Belgium. Almost the whole of France, northern Italy, Austria, Denmark, much of Finland and parts of Ireland, the South East of England and some areas in southern Germany emerge as having the highest productivity. These differences are only partly accounted for by regional differences in industrial structures and specialization (CAMBRIDGE ECONOMETRICS, 2003). The former East Germany, the Central and East European Accession States, and Portugal have the lowest productivity. There is some indication of a broad 'core–periphery' pattern of regional productivity across the EU, although the high productivity outliers found in southern Ireland and Finland complicate any such generalization.

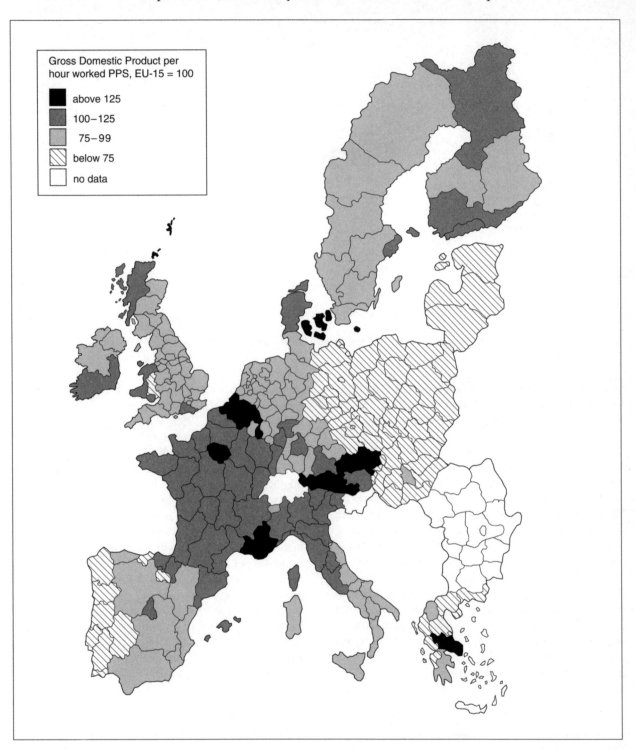

Fig. 5. Regional productivity across the European Union, 2001 (Labour Force Survey hours-worked measure)

At the same time, it is apparent that regional disparities in productivity are a characteristic feature of almost every EU-15 country, including those in which regional productivity levels in general are high by EU-15 standards. Indeed, regional productivity disparities in productivity are noticeably wider than in the new Accession States, which tend to have almost uniformly low-productivity levels. In effect, the enlargement of the EU to include the Central and East European states will add a large low-productivity periphery to the economic landscape of the EU, in which productivity will be only around half of the EU-15 average and in some regions only around 40%. The key issue, of course, is whether these regional differences in productivity across the EU have been narrowing or widening over time, and it is to this question that the discussion will now turn.

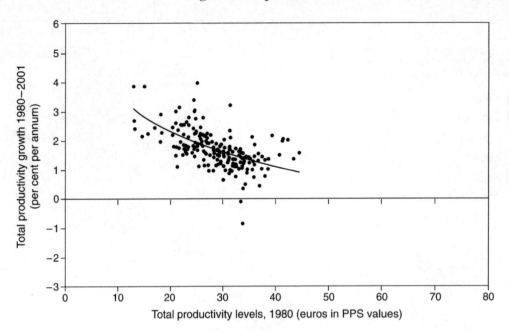

Fig. 6. Slow convergence in regional productivity across European Union regions, 1980–2001

EVIDENCE ON THE CONVERGENCE OF REGIONAL PRODUCTIVITY ACROSS THE EUROPEAN UNION

The standard Neoclassical growth model predicts the catch-up of initially low-productivity regions, on the grounds of factor price equalization across regions, rapid technology transfer, and diminishing returns to labour and capital, i.e. initially low-productivity regions should record higher rates of growth than initially high-productivity regions. Other alternative models of regional growth, of the sort discussed above, do not necessarily predict any convergence at all. Almost all of the empirical analyses that have been conducted thus far have focused on regional GDP per capita, rather than on regional productivity, and have tended to suggest that regional convergence in the EU is at best a very slow process typically only 1–2% per annum, implying that it would take several decades for any

significant narrowing of regional disparities in per-capita GDP to occur (DUNFORD, 1993; ARMSTRONG and VICKERMAN, 1995; MARTIN and SUNLEY, 1998; BUTTON and PENTECOST, 1999; EVANS, 2000; DUNFORD and SMITH, 2002).

The LFS hours-worked measure of productivity for the NUTS2 regions of the basic EU-15 countries shows some measure of convergence over the 1980s and 1990s (Fig. 6). It has been the regions with the lowest productivity levels in 1980 that have registered the highest productivity growth – in many cases of between 2 and 4% per annum in real terms – while many of the initially high productivity regions have recorded productivity growth rates of only around 1% per annum. A Barro-type growth regression (BARRO and SALA-I-MARTIN, 1995) fitted to the data in Fig. 6 yields a β-convergence parameter of only -0.0095, which whilst significantly different from zero, suggests a rate of convergence of barely 1% per annum (Table 2).

Table 2. Barro growth regression of regional productivity in the EU-15, 1980–2001

Ordinary least squares estimation
Dependent variable is productivity growth (output per hour worked)
197 out of 211 regions are used for estimation

Parameter	Coefficient	Standard error	T ratio	T probability
α	0.0424	0.0030	14.0688	0.0000
β	-0.0095	0.0011	-8.7552	0.0000
R^2		0.28217		
R_{bar}^2		0.27849		
Aikaike Information Criterion		731.89		
Schwartz Bayesian Criterion		728.61		
Moran statistic (spatial autocorrelation)		0.673		

Note: Expected Moran statistic is given as $E(I) = -1/(n-1)$, where n is the number of regions. In this case, the expected value is -0.0005.

This would seem to imply that if the regional productivity trends within the EU-15 are following a Neo-classical growth process, it is an extremely slow one.

If the Central and East European Enlargement (CEEE) states are included so that the data are restricted to the more recent 1993–2001 period, it has been the regions in these countries that have experienced the most rapid growth in productivity, with real growth rates in excess of 4% per annum in some cases. Above average rates of growth have also been recorded by regions in Sweden, Greece, throughout much of Italy and in Ireland (Fig. 7). Thus, while the regional pattern of productivity growth is rather mixed across the EU as a whole, the evidence indicates that since the dissolution of the former Communist states in the early 1990s, the very low-productivity regions of the CEEE countries have managed to improve their labour productivity much faster than most other regions of the EU, although, of course, they have a very long way to catch up with the core regions of the EU-15.

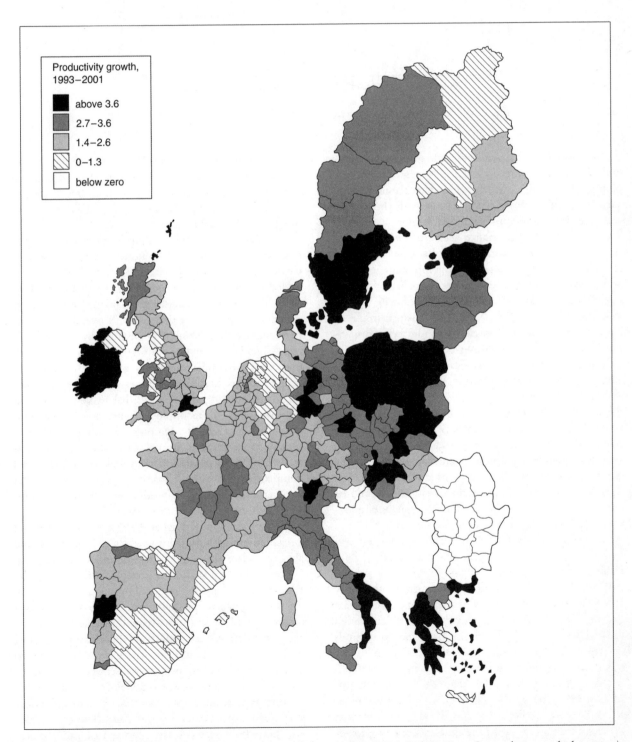

Fig. 7. Regional productivity growth across the European Union, 1993–2001 (Labour Force Survey hours-worked measure)

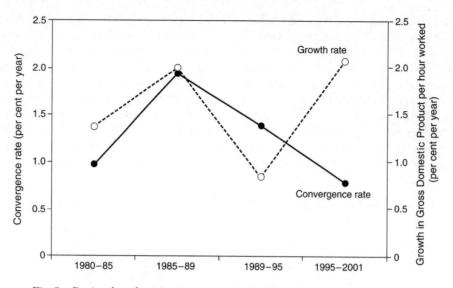

Fig. 8. *Regional productivity convergence in the EU-15 over two economic cycles*

Two issues that have received surprisingly little empirical analysis in the literature on regional convergence are whether and to what extent convergence varies with the economic cycle, and with the relative specialization of regions in traded (export) sectors of activity as against non-traded sectors. With regard to the effect of the economic cycle, it has been noted that absolute regional differences in unemployment in EU countries' rates tend to vary counter-cyclically, widening during recessions and narrowing during booms (BADDELEY *et al.*, 1998; MARTIN, 1998). It might be expected therefore that regional productivity disparities might also narrow during boom periods, as low-productivity regions are particularly well placed to take advantage of the expansionary economic conditions and to expand their output per worker accordingly. On the other hand, given such regions are also likely to be those with the highest unemployment, and hence ready pools of available labour, it could be that the main impact of general economic boom in such areas is the expansion of output via increases in employment rather than by a major boost in productivity. This would be consistent with the tendency for regional unemployment disparities to narrow in boom periods.

Between 1980 and 2001, the EU experienced two major economic cycles: recession in the early 1980s, followed by a strong recovery and boom in the second half the 1980s; then another downturn in the early 1990s, followed by recovery in the second half of that decade. Overall EU productivity growth has varied pro-cyclically, being higher in both boom periods (averaging 2% per annum in real terms) than in the recessionary periods (just under 1.5% in the 1980–85 recessionary period, and less than 1% in the first half of the 1990s) (Fig. 8). The rate of convergence in regional productivity across the EU-15 also followed the economic cycle up to the mid-1990s, being lower in recession and faster in recovery, but it failed to

increase again in the boom of the second half of the decade. In effect, the rate of convergence in regional productivity across the EU has been falling since the late 1980s, precisely the time when EU economic integration has accelerated.

Another aspect of regional productivity convergence concerns the impact of economic structure, and in particular the relative importance of traded and non-traded sectors. Recall from Section 1 that the productivity of a region's tradable (export) base is often regarded as the key to that region's overall economic performance and prosperity. Because by definition a region's export activities are directly exposed to competition from similar activities in other regions, the supposition is that this openness should expose the sectors in question to pressures that make for constant improvements in technology, efficiency, investment, product design, etc. if a region's exporting firms are to remain competitive. Regional non-traded activities that serve local markets are not exposed to such external competitive pressure. Thus, the expectation is that regional convergence in productivity should be faster in traded sectors than in non-traded ones.

Sectoral data limitations at the regional level prevent a detailed evaluation of this issue, in the sense of being able to isolate the export base of individual regions, but a preliminary analysis is possible in the case of the EU-15 by recalculating regional productivity separately for two aggregate sectors that correspond in broad terms to 'traded' and 'non-traded' activities. The former was defined to include manufacturing, energy, business services and intermediate services; the latter to include construction, household services and public sector services. This is obviously only an approximate decomposition, since not all local manufacturing industries need export, while some construction activities and household services are exported out of regions. Nevertheless, these broad divisions should be sufficient

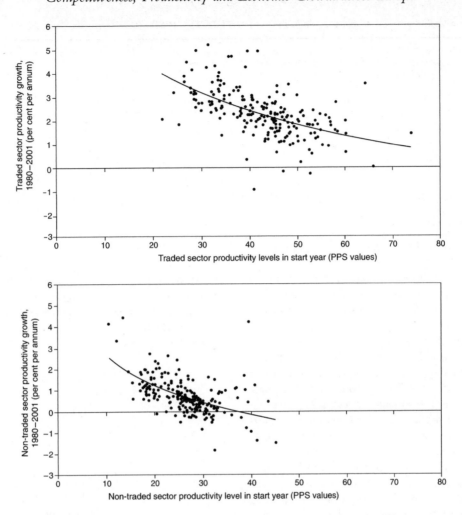

Fig. 9. Regional productivity convergence in traded and non-traded sectors, EU-15 states

to allow one to detect any significant differences in regional convergence between the traded and non-traded sectors of the economy.

The results are quite instructive (Fig. 9). First, as perhaps expected, start-year average productivity levels in the EU-15 regions were noticeably higher in traded activities than in non-traded ones. But second, the evidence suggests that regional productivity convergence in traded activities has been no faster, in fact slower, than that in the non-traded sector (Table 3). This is perhaps surprising given that traded activities are likely to be much more exposed to external competition. On the other hand, since the composition of household and public services tends to be similar across regions, one might expect productivity differences to be small and diminish over time. Interestingly, productivity levels in non-traded activities were noticeably less variable across regions to begin with. Third, regional productivity growth rates have tended to be lower in non-traded than in traded activities. Clearly, these findings are highly tentative, and more detailed analysis is needed before any definitive statements can be made about the impacts of openness and the 'export base' on long-run regional productivity trends.

Table 3. Convergence estimates from Barro growth regressions of regional productivity in the EU-15, 1980–2001: traded and non-traded sectors are compared

Model (estimated on 197 of 211 NUTS2 regions)	Convergence parameter (β estimate)	R^2	Standardized Moran statistic
All sectors	−0.0095 (0.0011)	0.282	0.673
Traded sectors	−0.0081 (0.0013)	0.275	0.710
Non-traded sectors	−0.0114 (0.0009)	0.324	1.023

Notes: Standard errors are in parentheses.
Expected Moran statistic is −0.005.

All of the regressions exhibit positive and statistically significant spatial autocorrelation (Table 3). Both endogenous growth and new economic geography models give strong grounds for expecting productivity to display geographical contiguity (for different perspectives on this issue, see, for example, FINGLETON and MCCOMBIE, 1998; FINGLETON, 2004; DAVIS and WEINSTEIN, 2001; KAMARIANAKIS and LE GALLO,

Table 4. Barro growth regression of regional productivity in the EU-15, 1980–2001, with the 'contiguity/spillover' variable

Ordinary least squares estimation
Dependent variable is productivity growth (output per hour worked)
197 of 211 regions are used for estimation

Parameter	Coefficient	Standard error	T ratio	T probability
α	0.0451	0.0030	15.0376	0.0000
β	−0.0120	0.0012	−9.7198	0.0000
γ	0.0082	0.0022	3.8130	0.0002
R^2		0.33222		
R_{bar}^2		0.32534		
Aikaike Information Criterion		738.01		
Schwartz Bayesian Criterion		733.09		
Moran statistic (spatial autocorrelation)		0.353		

Note: Expected Moran statistic is −0.005.

2003). Such spatial clustering might reflect a range of factors and processes. Contiguous regions may have similar degrees of access to transport and other modes of communication; they may have similar proximity to major markets; they might share similar socio-institutional set-ups that influence firm performance and entrepreneurship; there may be localized spillovers of knowledge and technology, through interfirm networking, employee movement and technology sharing, local trading relationships, access to common technology centres, universities, and the like; and contiguous regions might share similar industrial structures and thereby similar responses to common external demand, technology and policy shocks. It is beyond the scope of this paper to explore all these possible influences, and, indeed, one of the problems in the EU context is the lack of consistent data on many such factors. Instead, it simply attempts to capture any conditioning spatial autocorrelation effects by means of a contiguity/'spillover' variable defined for each region as the distance weighted sum of all other regions' initial productivity, with weights given as the inverse of the distance between the region in question and each other region in the EU, where distance was measured between regional centroids (CAMBRIDGE ECONOMETRICS, 2003). The hypothesis is that spatially contiguous regions are more likely to exhibit similar productivity growth than are geographically distant ones. The results are shown in Table 4, where γ is the coefficient on the contiguity/'spillover' variable just defined. The contiguity/'spillover' effect is itself statistically significant, though small, and improves the overall fit of the regression and increases the convergence rate, but only slightly. Much more detailed research is needed on this key issue of spatial clustering/autocorrelation of productivity levels and growth.

CONTRIBUTION OF PRODUCTIVITY TO REGIONAL ECONOMIC PERFORMANCE

Following the logic of Fig. 1, the outcome of regional competitive success can be defined as a high level of GDP per capita. This in turn can be decomposed into four elements, each of which has a direct economic interpretation: productivity (measured as GDP per hour worked), employment rate, dependency rate and work–leisure trade off:

$$\frac{GDP}{Population}$$
$$= \frac{GDP}{Total\ hours\ worked}$$
$$(Productivity)$$
$$\times \frac{Total\ hours\ worked}{Employment}$$
$$(Work\text{–}leisure)$$
$$\times \frac{Employment}{Working\ age\ population}$$
$$(Employment\ rate)$$
$$\times \frac{Working\ age\ population}{Population}$$
$$(Dependency\ rate)$$

As indicated above, productivity is one of two key measures of 'revealed competitiveness' – the other being employment rate. These in turn are also two of the components of the conventional indicator of regional per-capita GDP. This section explores the contribution of productivity and employment rate to regional per-capita GDP growth across the EU.

Since the early 1990s, growth in GDP per capita has tended to be fastest in the peripheral areas of Europe, particularly those in Central and Eastern European countries, together with Spain, Ireland, Portugal and part of Greece (Fig. 10). These areas also tend to be those with lower levels of GDP per capita, with the exception of Ireland, which has overtaken the EU-15 average. Notable exceptions to this rule include the South East region of the UK and southern Sweden, areas that are prosperous and which have had high rates of economic growth. Overall, the rate of convergence

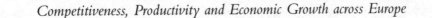

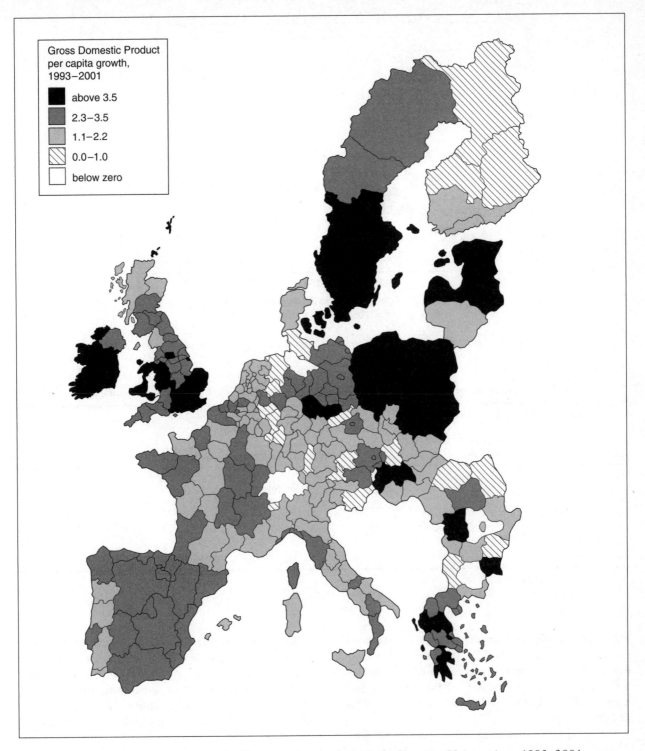

Fig. 10. Real Gross Domestic Product per-capita growth across the European Union regions, 1993–2001

of per-capita GDP across regions of the EU-15 has been less than 1% per annum over the 1980s and 1990s.

And this seems to have been almost entirely due to the rapid convergence that took place during the pronounced economic boom of the second half of the 1980s. Outside this subperiod, convergence has been negligible or non-existent, in much the same way as for productivity. Thus, regional disparities in per-capita

GDP across the EU display a high degree of persistence, with the pattern in 2001 bearing a strong similarity with that in 1980 (also MARTIN, 2001): the correlation between the two is high (Fig. 11). In fact, the regional dispersion of productivity within Member States has not changed significantly (Fig. 12). What is also evident is that while average productivity levels may have become more similar between nations,

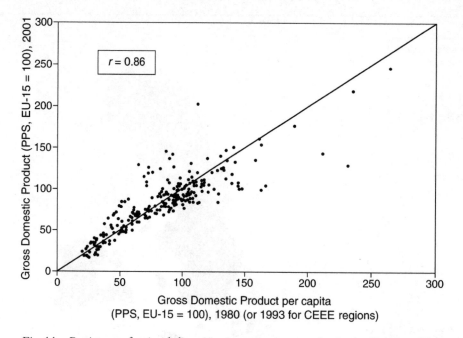

Fig. 11. *Persistence of regional disparities in economic prosperity in the European Union*

Table 5. *Components of Gross Domestic Product per capita by relative level of regional prosperity, 2001*

Gross Domestic Product (GDP) component

Regional GDP per capita group	Number of regions	GDP per capita	Productivity		Hours worked		Employment rate	Dependency rate
			Sectoral	LFS	Sectoral	LFS		
Less than 75% European Union average	48	64.86	76.85	73.74	102.97	107.63	84.64	99.82
More than 75% but less than European Union average	87	88.07	96.59	94.85	99.05	100.26	95.86	98.53
More than European Union average	71	121.78	112.92	111.37	99.68	100.21	110.53	100.12

Note: LFS, Labour Force Survey.

Values are relative to the EU-15 average ($=100$).

within-nation regional differences have not narrowed and in some cases (in the UK, Italy, the Netherlands, Austria, Germany) have actually increased. Also evident is the fact that the vast majority of the CEEE regions have GDP per-capita levels well below 75% of the EU-15 average.

How do productivity and employment rate influence these regional differences in per-capita GDP growth? Table 5 examines the components of per-capita GDP by three broad groups of regions: those with a per-capita GDP less than 75% of the EU-15 average (what has been the threshold for eligibility for Structural Fund support); those with a per-capita GDP between 75% and the EU-15 average; and those with a per-capita GDP greater than the EU-15 average. The dependency rate shows little variation across these three regional groups, while the hours worked component shows only minor variation, and what exists indicates a negative association with GDP per capita, i.e. regions

with lower GDP per capita have a higher than average level of working hours. The explanation might lie in the sectoral structure of production. For example, regions that specialize in agriculture have a higher number of weekly hours worked, and so the lower productivity of such activities leads to a lower level of GDP per capita.

Productivity and employment rate clearly account for most of the variation in average GDP per capita across the three regional groups. In terms of levels, both employment rate and productivity share a common association with GDP per capita, largely because both are positively linked to economic development, i.e. more successful regions have well-developed economies with reasonably high labour participation rates (in particular a higher participation rate among women), and by and large a productive workforce (Fig. 13). Once growth rates are analysed, however, it quickly becomes apparent that productivity and not employment is the

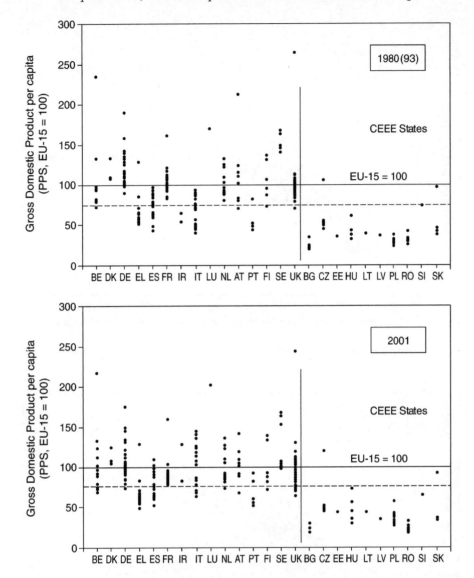

Fig. 12. Regional disparities in Gross Domestic Product per capita across the European Union, 1980 and 2001. For the upper graph, data for Central and East European Enlargement (CEEE) States are for 1993. For abbreviations, see Fig. 2

main link with GDP per-capita growth (Fig. 14). This result supports the argument that ultimately (in the long term) it is technological progress that drives growth. Bringing more people into the labour market can produce a short-term effect, but, migration issues aside, there is a natural constraint on how far such an effect can go. This leaves productivity as the main driver of per-capita GDP.

However, this result combines both western European regions and those in the CEEE states. As already noted, the latter have recorded some of the highest growth rates in per-capita GDP across the European economic space in recent years. But this appears to have been primarily due to marked increases in productivity rather than to improvements in employment rates. Indeed, since 1993, employment rate growth in many of the CEEE regions has been negative (Fig. 15 and Table 6). This implies that the high rates of productivity growth found amongst many of the regions in the

CEEE states has been attributable in part to 'labour shake-out' (rationalization) effects. Such effects may give a boost to productivity over the short run, but cannot be the source of sustained productivity growth and catch-up with the rest of the EU over the longer term. In addition, of course, labour shake-out exacerbates unemployment, which in turn frustrates the pursuit of social cohesion.

SOME CONCLUSIONS AND IMPLICATIONS

Although there is considerable debate amongst academics and policy-makers as to the precise definition of regional competitiveness, there can be little doubt that productivity represents one of its most important 'revealed' measures. In the light of the adoption of the Single Market from 1992 and the more recent establishment of a single currency space, it is perhaps

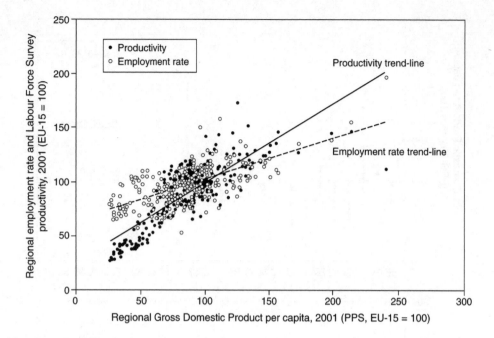

Fig. 13. *Gross Domestic Product per capita, productivity and employment rates across European Union regions*

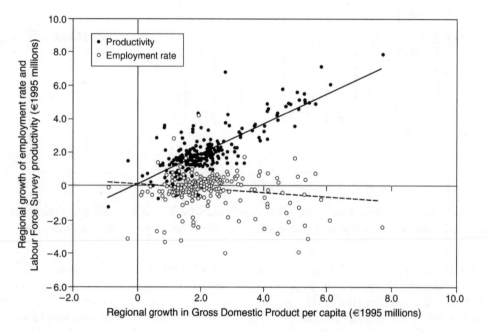

Fig. 14. *Growth of Gross Domestic Product per capita, productivity and employment rates across European Union regions, 1980–2001. Note the average growth (per cent per annum) is over 1980–2001, except for some German regions (1993–2001), Flevoland (1986–2001) and all enlargement countries (1993–2001)*

not surprising that policy-makers across Europe have been keen to establish what has been happening to regional disparities in productivity and whether there is evidence of convergence, i.e. whether the weaker regions are catching up with the stronger ones. This interest reflects not only a desire by policy-makers to enhance the overall efficiency of the Union so that its economic performance is more in line with that of the USA, but also a genuine concern that regions with relatively poor productivity performance should not be

at a disadvantage in the context of monetary union and EU enlargement.

This paper has sought to investigate some of the conceptual and measurement problems that arise in measuring regional variations in productivity and, for the first time, it has used new evidence based on an output per hour worked measure that, whilst not without its own problems, provides a better indication of the underlying concept relative to previous indicators (such as output per head or output per employee). The

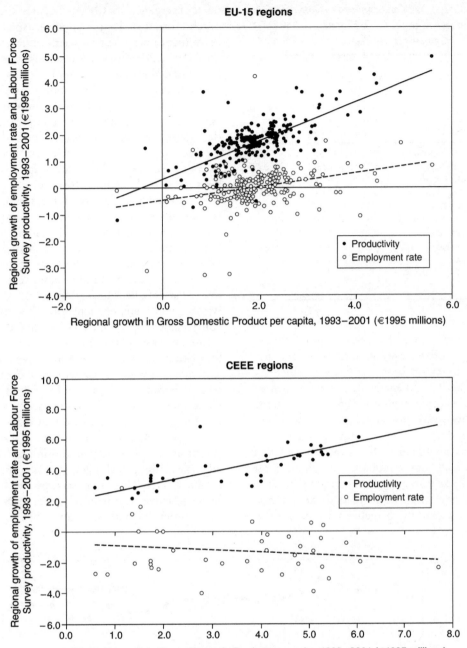

Fig. 15. *Regional Gross Domestic Product per capita, productivity and employment in the EU-15 and CEEE States*

output per hour worked measure reveals a number of areas of higher-than-average productivity: much of France, and especially the Paris subregion and Provence–Alpes–Cote d'Azur; almost all of Belgium; northern and central Italy; almost all of Austria; Denmark; much of Finland, southern Ireland, parts of South East England; and some areas in southern Germany. The former East Germany, the Central and East European Accession States, and Portugal have the lowest productivity. There is thus some indication of a broad 'core–periphery' pattern of regional productivity across the EU, although there are high productivity outliers found in southern Ireland and Finland. What

is all too clear, however, is that the enlargement of the Union to include the Central and East European states will add a large low-productivity periphery to the economic landscape of the EU.

There are widely differing views amongst economists as to the determinants of regional productivity and what happens to regional disparities in productivity over time. Standard Neoclassical theory predicts that with increasing economic and monetary integration, low-productivity regions should catch up with high-productivity regions. In the context of the EU, such convergence is an important dimension of the goal of 'cohesion'. However, other economic theories, which

Table 6. Productivity growth and employment rate decline in the top ten growth regions in the CEEE States, 1993–2001 (annual per cent rates)

Country	Region	Gross Domestic Product per head growth	Produc- tivity growth	Employ- ment rate growth
Poland	Mazowieckie	7.93	7.81	−2.48
Hungary	Nyugat-Dunántúl	5.78	6.05	−1.84
Bulgaria	Yugoiztochen	5.45	5.78	−1.96
Poland	Wielkopolskie	5.44	5.63	−2.05
Hungary	Közép-Dunántúl	5.04	4.43	−0.55
Hungary	Közép-Magyarország	4.57	4.53	−0.41
Poland	Malopolskie	4.23	4.50	−2.37
Poland	Pomorskie	4.22	3.99	−0.51
Poland	Lódzkie	4.10	3.77	−3.12
Czech Republic	Prague	4.10	3.93	−1.26

emphasize the importance of various forms of increasing returns, suggest that increasing integration does not necessarily lead to regional convergence in productivity (or GDP per head), and might in fact reproduce or even reinforce existing regional differences, leading to regional divergence or growing core–periphery patterns of productivity and competitiveness. The empirical results presented in this paper suggest that while some initially low-productivity regions (most notably Ireland) have improved their relative position within the EU over the past 20 years or so, a period of accelerating integration, the general degree of catch up (convergence) has been disappointingly slow (not much more than 1% per annum). And much of what convergence has occurred seems to have taken place in the boom conditions of the second half of the 1980s. Since then, there has been very little if any convergence. Furthermore, if the total variation in productivity across the regions of the EU-15 is decomposed into within and between Member State components, it appears that there has been no discernible reduction in the former, and that the slight fall in total region dispersion over the period has been entirely due to a reduction in between state differentials (Fig. 16).

What is evident, however, is that productivity growth is a key determinant of regional economic prosperity: there is a strong positive relationship across regions between productivity growth and growth in per-capita GDP. Yet, the rate of convergence of per-capita GDP across EU regions has been even slower than of productivity. Part of the explanation seems to reside in the way in which employment growth – the other main component of per-capita GDP growth – has varied across regions. In the EU-15, regions appear to fall into two main groups: those that have enjoyed growth in productivity and employment, and those that have recorded productivity growth but falls in their employment rate. This latter combination suggests that in many regions across the EU, productivity advances have come about as much through industrial rationalization, labour shakeout and capital substitution effects, as from efficiency-raising technological progress, higher value products, etc. This is most apparent in the CEEE regions, where high rates of productivity advance have been associated with significant falls in employment.

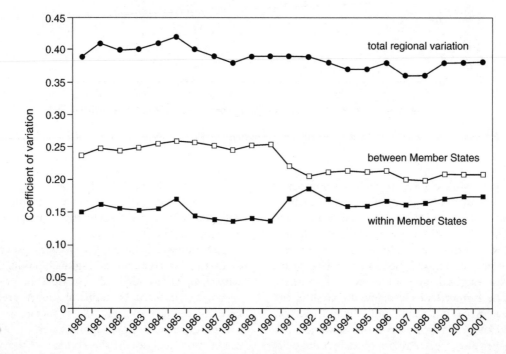

Fig. 16. Regional dispersion of productivity across the EU-15, 1980–2001: total and decomposition into within and between Member States

Intense rationalization and restructuring – that is, eliminating inefficient enterprises and expelling inefficient workers – may give a marked boost to productivity over the short run, but are obviously not a viable means of securing high rates of productivity growth over the longer term. As mentioned above, regional competitiveness implies both high productivity and a high employment rate. Neoclassical theory would suggest that the cheap labour and low productivity of the CEEE regions (40% or less of the EU-15 average) make these regions attractive to the inflow of foreign capital and investment, and thus that there is considerable scope for rapid productivity catch-up with the rest of the EU. New economic geography models, however, suggest that it is equally likely that with enlargement, economic growth could continue to concentrate and agglomerate in the existing core regions of the EU-15, and that the CEEE countries themselves could well experience increasing regional inequalities in growth, productivity and incomes as they adjust to the competitive market forces that membership of the EU will expose them to.

The lack of any sustained and significant convergence in productivity across the EU-15 regions over the 1980s and 1990s obviously raises questions about the efficacy of EU regional policy. Despite the positive assessments by the EUROPEAN COMMISSION (2004) that EU regional policy has helped to narrow regional inequalities, and the fact that there have undoubtedly been some notable individual regional improvements, in general, it is difficult to claim that the empirical evidence suggests policy has been a resounding success. It is of course problematic, if not impossible, to construct a meaningful counterfactual of what would have happened to regional productivity differences across the EU-15 in the absence of the Structural and Cohesion Funds. But if the hope was that increasing integration and regional policy together would promote greater regional cohesion and enhance the competitive performance of the poorer, lagging regions, then the lack of any real substantial convergence in productivity or GDP per head must be disappointing. On the other hand, it might be that the EU regional funds have served to prevent the demand and competitive shocks associated with increasing economic integration, technological change and accelerating globalization from exacerbating regional inequalities in productive performance. Or, again, it might be argued that the scale of EU regional aid has simply not been sufficient to make much of an impact on productivity convergence across the regions, and that a large financial commitment would have yielded the desired results. At the very time when the productive performance and competitiveness of the EU and its regions, and the integration of the new enlargement states into the Union, are rightly of central concern to the European Commission, it seems that the role, effectiveness and funding of regional policy are coming under increasingly critical review and reassessment (e.g. BOLDRIN and CANOVA, 2001; PUGA, 2002; SAPIR *et al.*, 2003). Understanding the determinants of regional productivity and competitiveness across the EU is thus a highly pertinent research task.

Acknowledgements – This paper is based in part on a larger project on 'The Factors of Regional Competitiveness' for the European Commission. The authors are grateful to the commission for permission to draw upon that research. An earlier version of the paper was presented at the Regional Studies Association's 'Regional Productivity Forum Seminar', London, UK, January 2004. The authors acknowledge the helpful comments made on that occasion, as well as the useful suggestions made by two anonymous referees.

REFERENCES

ARMSTRONG H. and VICKERMAN R. (Eds) (1995) *Convergence and Divergence Among European Regions*. Pion, London.

BADDELEY M., MARTIN R. L. and TYLER P. (1998) European regional unemployment disparities: convergence or persistence?, *European Urban and Regional Studies* 5, 195–215.

BALDWIN R., FORSLID R., MARTIN P., OTTAVIANO G. and ROBERT-NICOUD F. (2003) *Economic Geography and Public Policy*. Princeton University Press, Princeton.

BARRO R. and SALA-I-MARTIN X. (1995) *Economic Growth*. McGraw-Hill, New York.

BEGG I. (1999) Cities and competitiveness, *Urban Studies* 36, 795–810.

BEGG I. (2002) *Urban Competitiveness: Policies for Dynamic Cities*. Policy Press, Bristol.

BEST M. (1990) *The New Competition*. Harvard University Press, Cambridge, MA.

BEST M. (2001) *The New Competitive Advantage: The Renewal of American Industry*. Oxford University Press, Oxford.

BOLDRIN M. and CANOVA F. (2001) Inequality and convergence: reconsidering European regional policies, *Economic Policy* 16, 207–253.

BRACKMAN S., GARRETSEN H. and VAN MARREVIJK C. (2001) *An Introduction to Geographical Economics*. Cambridge University Press, Cambridge.

BUTTON K. and PENTECOST E. (1999) *Regional Economic Performance Within the European Union*. Edward Elgar, Cheltenham.

CAMAGNI R. (2002) On the concept of territorial competitiveness: sound or misleading?, *Urban Studies* 39, 2395–2411.

CAMBRIDGE ECONOMETRICS (2003) *A Study of the Factors Determining Regional Competitiveness in the EU*. European Commission, Brussels.

CELLINI R. and SOCI A. (2002) Pop competitiveness, *Banca Nazionale del Lavoro, Quarterly Review* 55, 71–101.

CHESHIRE P. and GORDON I. R. (Eds) (1995) *Territorial Competition in an Integrating Europe*. Avebury, Aldershot.

DAVIS D. R. and WEINSTEIN D. E. (2001) Market size, linkages and productivity: a study of Japanese regions. Working Paper 8516. National Bureau of Economic Research, Cambridge, MA.

DEPARTMENT OF TRADE AND INDUSTRY (2004) *Regional Competitiveness and the State of the Regions.* DTI, London.

DUFFY H. (1995) *Competitive Cities: Succeeding in the Global Economy.* E & FN Spon, London.

DUNFORD M. (1993) Regional disparities in the European Community: evidence from the REGIO databank, *Regional Studies* **27**, 263–275.

DUNFORD M. and SMITH A. (2002) Catching up or falling behind? Economic performance and the trajectories of economic development in an enlarged Europe, *Economic Geography* **76**, 169–195.

EUROPEAN COMMISSION (1999) *Sixth Periodic Report on the Social and Economic Situation of Regions in the EU.* European Commission, Brussels.

EUROPEAN COMMISSION (2004) A *New Partnership for Cohesion: Convergence, Competitiveness and Cooperation,* European Commission, Brussels.

EVANS P. (2000) Income dynamics in countries and regions, in HESS G. D. and VAN WINCOOP E. (Eds) *Intra-national Macro-economics,* pp. 131–155. Cambridge University Press, Cambridge.

FINGLETON B. (2004) Regional economic growth and convergence: insights from a spatial econometrics perspective, in ANSELIN L., FLORAX R. and REY S. (Eds) *New Advances in Spatial Econometrics,* pp. 397–432. Springer, Berlin.

FINGLETON B. and MCCOMBIE J. (1998) Increasing returns and economic growth: some evidence for manufacturing from the European Regions, *Oxford Economic Papers* **50**, 89–105.

FUJITA M., KRUGMAN P. and VENABLES A. (1999) *The Spatial Economy: Cities, Regions and International Trade.* MIT Press, Cambridge, MA.

FUJITA M. and THISSE J.-F. (2002) *Economics of Agglomeration: Cities, Industrial Location and Regional Growth.* Cambridge University Press, Cambridge.

GROUP OF LISBON (1995) *Limits to Competition.* MIT Press, Cambridge, MA.

H. M. TREASURY (2001) *Productivity in the UK: 3 – The Regional Dimension.* H. M. Treasury, London.

H. M. TREASURY (2003) *Productivity in the UK: 4 – The Local Dimension.* H. M. Treasury, London.

JENSEN-BUTLER C. (1996) Competition between cities. Urban performance and the role of urban policy: a theoretical framework, in JENSEN-BUTLER C., SCHACHER A. and VAN WEESEP J. (Eds) *European Cities in Competition,* pp. 3–42. Avebury, Aldershot.

KAMARIANAKIS Y. and LE GALLO J. (2003) The evolution of regional productivity disparities in the European Union, 1975–2000. Mimeo. Department of Economics, University of Crete, Heraklion.

KRUGMAN P. (1994) Competitiveness: a dangerous obsession, *Foreign Affairs* **73**, 28–44.

KRUGMAN P. (1996a) *Pop Internationalism.* MIT Press, Cambridge, MA.

KRUGMAN P. (1996b) Making sense of the competitiveness debate, *Oxford Review of Economic Policy* **12**, 17–35.

LENGYEL I. (2000) A regionalis versenykepessegrol [Regional competitiveness]. *Kozgazdasagi Szemle* **47**, 962–987.

LENGYEL I. (2003) The pyramid model: enhancing regional competitiveness in Hungary. Mimeo.

MARTIN R. L. (1998) Regional dimensions of Europe's unemployment problem, in LAWLESS P. MARTIN R. L. and HARDY S. (Eds) *Unemployment and Social Exclusion: Landscape of Labour Inequality,* pp. 11–48. Jessica Kingsley, London.

MARTIN R. L. (2000) Institutional approaches in economic geography, in SHEPPARD E. and BARNES T. J. (Eds) *A Companion to Economic Geography,* pp. 77–94. Blackwell, Oxford.

MARTIN R. L. (2001) EMU versus the regions? Regional convergence and divergence in Euroland, *Journal of Economic Geography* **1**, 51–80.

MARTIN R. L. (2003) EMU and enlargement: twin threats to Europe regional cohesion?, in ARNULL A. and WINCOTT D. (Eds) *Accountability and Legitimacy in the European Union,* pp. 345–363. Oxford University Press, Oxford.

MARTIN R. L. and SUNLEY P. J. (1998) Slow convergence? The new endogenous growth theory and regional development, *Economic Geography* **74**, 201–227.

OFFICE OF THE DEPUTY PRIME MINISTER (2003) *Cities, Regions and Competitiveness,* ODPM, London.

OFFICE OF THE DEPUTY PRIME MINISTER (2004) *Competitive European Cities: Where Do the Core Cities Stand?* Urban Research Paper 13, ODPM, London.

PORTER M. E. (1998a) *On Competition.* Harvard Business School Press, Boston.

PORTER M. E. (1998b) Location, clusters and the new economics of competition, *Business Economics* **33**, 7–17.

PORTER M. E. (2000) Location, competition and economic development: local clusters in the global economy, *Economic Development Quarterly* **14**, 15–31.

PORTER M. E. (2001) Regions and the new economics of competition, in SCOTT A. J. (Ed.) *Global City Regions,* pp. 139–152. Blackwell, Oxford.

PORTER M. E. (2003) The economic performance of regions, *Regional Studies* **37**, 549–578.

PORTER M. E. and KETELS C. H. M. (2003) *UK Competitiveness: Moving to the Next Stage.* Economics Paper 3. Department of Trade and Industry, London.

PUGA D. (2002) European regional policies in light of recent location theories, *Journal of Economic Geography* **2**, 373–406.

ROWTHORN R. E. (1999) The political economy of full employment in modern Britain. Kalecki Memorial Lecture, University of Oxford, Oxford.

SAPIR A., AGHION P., BERTOLA G., HELLWIG M., PISANI-FERRY J., ROSATI D., VINALS J. and WALLACE H. (2003) *An Agenda for a Growing Europe: Making the EU Economic System Deliver.* Report of an Independent High Level Study Group for the European President, Brussels.

STEINLE W. J. (1992) Regional competitiveness and the single market, *Regional Studies* **26**, 307–318.

STORPER M. (1995) Competitiveness policy options; the technology–regions connection, *Growth and Change* **Spring**, 285–308.

STORPER M. (1997) *The Regional World: Territorial Development in a Global Economy.* Guilford Press, New York.

SVEIKAUSKAS L. A. (1975) The productivity of cities, *Quarterly Journal of Economics* **89**, 393–413.

TYSON L. (1992) *Who's Bashing Whom? Trade Conflicts in High-Technology Industries.* Institute for International Economics, Washington, DC.

URBAN STUDIES (1999) Special Issue on 'Competitive Cities', *Urban Studies,* **36**(5/6).

Cities, Regions and Competitiveness

IVAN TUROK

Department of Urban Studies, University of Glasgow, Glasgow G12 8RS, UK. Email: I.Turok@socsci.gla.ac.uk

(Received February 2003: in revised form November 2003)

TUROK I. (2004) Cities, regions and competitiveness, *Regional Studies* **38**, 1061–1075. Competitiveness is a complex concept used in a variety of ways and contexts. The paper reviews some of the main ideas, particularly as they apply to cities and regions. Its definition should include the relative position of a region's firms in external markets, the productivity of local resources and the extent to which they are used. Competition takes both an institutionalized form (local public agencies competing overtly for investment and other resources) and, more importantly, a less organized form involving firms trading in wider markets. There are two contrasting perspectives on the competitive advantages of city-regions. One emphasizes the benefits of scale and diversity that flow from concentrations of economic activity. The other stresses the quality of the interactions between firms and supporting institutions. Recent studies suggest that the significance of localized business networks or clusters might be exaggerated and that a broader perspective of city-region competitiveness is required.

City-region competitiveness   Productivity   Agglomeration economies   Business networks   Clusters

TUROK I. (2004) Les grandes villes, les régions et la compétitivité, *Regional Studies* **38**, 1061–1075. La compétitivité est une notion complexe que l'on emploie dans diverses façons et contextes. Cet article cherche à faire la critique de quelques-unes des principales idées, notamment en ce qui concerne les villes et les régions. Sa définition devrait inclure le positionnement relatif des entreprises régionales sur les marchés extérieurs, la productivité des ressources locales, et leur taux d'utilisation. La concurrence prend et un caractère institutionnalisé (sous forme d'organismes gouvernementaux qui se font ouvertement concurrence pour l'investissement et d'autres ressources) et, plus important encore, un caractère moins organisé impliquant des entreprises qui font du commerce sur des marchés plus vastes. Il y a deux points de vue opposés quant à l'avantage compétitif des cités-régions. L'un souligne les atouts de l'échelle et de la diversité qui proviennent de la concentration de l'activité économique. L'autre met l'accent plutôt sur la qualité des rapports entre les entreprises et les services d'assistance technique. Des études récentes laissent supposer que l'importance des réseaux ou des regroupements commerciaux de proximité s'exagère et qu'il faut une interprétation plus large de la compétitivité des cités-régions.

Compétitivité des cités-régions   Productivité   Economies d'agglomération   Réseaux commerciaux
Regroupements

TUROK I. (2004) Großstädte, Regionen und Konkurrenzfähigkeit, *Regional Studies* **38**, 1061–1075. Konkurrenzfähigkeit ist ein komplexer Begriff, der auf verschiedene Arten und in verschiedenen Zusammenhängen angewandt wird. Dieser Aufsatz bespricht einige der meist gebrauchten Ideen, besonders im Hinblick auf Großstädte und Regionen. Seine Definition sollte die relative Stellung der Firmen einer Region im Außenhandel enthalten, sowie die Produktivität einheimischer Mittel, und das Ausmaß, in dem sie verwertet werden. Wettbewerb erscheint sowohl in institutionalisierter Form (wenn ortsansässige öffentliche Agenturen sich offen um Investierungen und andere Mittel bewerben), und, was wichtiger ist, in weniger organisierter Form, wenn Firmen auf weiter entfernten Märkten handeln. Man kann die Wettbewerbsvorteile einer Großstadtregion aus zwei gegensätzlichen Perspektiven sehen: die eine betont die Vorteile von Umfang und Vielfalt, die sich aus Konzentrationen wirtschaftlicher Betätigung ergeben, die andere legt Gewicht auf die Qualität der gegenseitigen Einwirkungen auf Firmen und Rückhalt gewährenden Institutionen. In jüngster Zeit durchgeführte Untersuchungen legen nahe, daß die Bedeutung örtlich begrenzter Geschäftsnetzwerke oder Cluster übertrieben sein dürfte, und durch eine breitere Perspektive der Konkurrenzfähigkeit von Großstadtregionen ersetzt werden sollte.

Konkurrenzfähigkeit von Großstadtregionen   Produktivität   Ballungswirtschaften   Geschäftsnetzwerke
GER clusters

TUROK I. (2004) Ciudades, regiones y competitividad, *Regional Studies* **38**, 1061–1075. El concepto de competitividad es un concepto complejo que se ha utilizado de muchas formas y en muchos contextos distintos. Este artículo revisa algunas de las ideas principales, particularmente aquellas que se aplican a ciudades y regiones. Su definición debería incluír la posición relativa que las empresas de una región ocupan en los mercados externos, la productividad de los recursos locales, y el grado hasta el cual se hace uso de ellos. La noción de competición adquiere tanto una forma institucionalizada (organismos públicos locales que compiten abiertamente por inversiones y otros recursos) y, más importante todavía, una forma menos organizada que implica el comercio en mercados más amplios por parte de las empresas. Existen dos perspectivas opuestas sobre las ventajas competitivas de las ciudades-regiones. Una de ellas enfatiza los beneficios de la escala y la diversidad que fluyen de las concentraciones de actividad económica. La otra acentúa la calidad de las interacciones entre las empresas y las instituciones de apoyo. Estudios recientes sugieren que puede que se haya exagerado la significancia de redes comerciales o de clusters localizados y que se requiere una punto de vista más amplio cuando se habla de competitividad ciudad-región.

Competitividad ciudad-región   Productividad   Economías de aglomeración   Redes comerciales   *Clusters*

JEL classifications: O18, R11, R38, R58

INTRODUCTION

The notion of competitiveness has become pervasive in urban, regional, and national economic analysis and policy during the last decade. However, its prolific use has outstripped coherent definition or robust evidence of its validity. In fact, the term is far from straightforward and has been used in many different ways and contexts. The purpose of this paper is to review and provide a preliminary assessment of some of the main interpretations of the concept, particularly as they apply to cities and regions. Two key questions explored are: in what sense do such places compete, and what are their underlying sources of competitive advantage in contemporary advanced economies?

The idea of competitiveness implies identification of a fundamental determinant of place prosperity, i.e. the basis for sustainable growth in modern economies. Competitiveness is not really an end in itself, more an indication of the drivers and dynamics of economic success. It is important therefore to go beyond descriptive economic measures, such as income per capita or employment trends, to explore the underlying sources of improved economic performance. What are the common physical, economic, social and institutional resources or assets of a city-region that influence the performance of its firms?

It can be argued that the notion encompasses three important determinants of economic development, particularly the following:

- Ability of local firms to sell their products in contested external markets ('trade').
- Value of these products and the efficiency with which they are produced ('productivity').
- Utilization of local human, capital and natural resources (e.g. the 'employment rate').

Competitiveness is a function of complex inter-relationships between these variables. If it is reduced to any single one of them, it risks representing the determinants of place prosperity too narrowly. There remain further questions about the factors underlying these features that require deeper analysis, such as the determinants of productivity (innovation, investment, skills, infrastructure, entrepreneurship, etc.), as well as many difficult measurement issues. The term can conceal important variations between the competitive positions of different branches of the regional economy (diversity). It can also obscure variable economic performance over time (volatility) and the uneven consequences of competitive success for different social groups and areas (inequality).

The structure of the paper is as follows. The next two sections outline why competitiveness has become such a widespread concern among local, regional and national authorities. The third and fourth sections consider the functions of overt competition between places involving public organizations. The following three sections explore the changing sources of and obstacles to urban and regional competitiveness involving firms. The conclusion provides some reflections on the most recent ideas.

ORIGINS OF COMPETITIVENESS

Two of the main reasons for the notion of competitiveness gaining currency are the increasing international mobility of capital and more open national markets – *globalization* for short. Economies have become more interconnected through rising exports and imports and increasing foreign direct investment. This has occurred because of declining trade barriers, falling transport costs and the growth of transnational corporations (TNCs). The emergence of new economic powers, particularly in Asia, and generally more competitive markets for products and services have intensified the pressure on costs and increased economic insecurity and the risk of instability. More integrated financial markets and international agreements between governments have made it more difficult to pursue traditional macro-economic policies independently.

Consequently, a variety of micro-economic, supply-side measures have been put forward to improve the efficiency of firms' internal processes and to enhance the quality and value of their products, and thereby secure their share of world markets and jobs. Productivity in this broad sense of creating or enhancing competitive advantage has been portrayed as central to long-term economic progress. It is important for regions and nations to pay their way in the world in terms of exporting sufficient goods and services to pay for imports. Therefore, productivity and trade performance are closely related to competitiveness.

Some governments have tended towards a low-cost, laissez-faire approach to raising competitiveness, including liberalization of domestic markets, privatization of public utilities, relaxation of environmental standards and withdrawal of other 'burdens on business' (H. M. GOVERNMENT, 1994, 1995). By reducing the levels of regulation and taxation, they have tried to lower the costs of production and create more flexible labour markets to establish a business context conducive to greater price competitiveness and higher profitability. This is intended to generate growth by stimulating private investment, encouraging enterprise and attracting foreign capital.[1]

Other governments have recognized limitations in low-cost competition, including the diminishing returns from cost cutting, the ease with which competitor nations may react in the same way, and the fact that the burden of lower costs may have to be borne by individual tax payers and workers in lower earnings, poorer working conditions and inferior public services. To protect people and places from a 'race to the bottom', they have pursued more active policies to enable firms to compete abroad through 'non-price' or quality-based competitive advantages intended to be more enduring, such as more sophisticated and reliable products or greater customer responsiveness. They have supported the development and application of new technologies, better workforce and management skills, or singled out key industries for special assistance to help them move up the value chain. In some high-income economies, there has been a tendency to demote the role of manufacturing, on the assumption that standardization of volume production techniques and falling transport costs favour cheaper locations abroad (e.g. DEPARTMENT OF TRADE AND INDUSTRY, 1998, 2001).[2] The alternative high-value, knowledge-intensive services are said to require more emphasis on building scientific expertise, enhancing technological innovation and strengthening human capital – 'technology and skills' for short. These strategies vary in their implications for different regions and social groups in ways that need to be spelt out more explicitly for judgements to be made about their adequacy.

Similar things have happened at sub-national levels. More intense competition within product markets, greater mobility of capital and rising unemployment have heightened awareness of external threats. Some policy responses have been overtly competitive in a defensive sense, including attempts to protect vulnerable industries or to discourage business relocation by offering subsidies in some form (CHESHIRE and GORDON, 1996). Others have been proactive, including 'place marketing' and incentives to attract mobile private investment. City boosterism reflects more aggressive competition to promote flagship events, build iconic projects and attract tourism, skilled mobile population and public investment, using both price and the quality of the environment. It follows a tradition of policies that were less explicitly competitive, including increasing the business formation rate and strengthening the managerial and technical capabilities

of local firms to help them enhance their market position and grow.

Recent initiatives seek to exploit novel 'urban assets', such as specialized labour pools, university research, institutional networks and even the lifestyle, cultural amenities and tolerant social milieu of cities (LEADBEATER and OAKLEY, 1999; LANDRY, 2000; FLORIDA, 2002). By developing distinctive indigenous strengths and promoting business learning, they seek to avoid vulnerability to mobile capital and a race to the bottom. They aim to attract and retain talented people and to develop special technologies in order to export knowledge-intensive products. Indeed, an emerging literature suggests that cities contain unique resources that make firms in the knowledge economy more internationally competitive: 'city-regions are coming to function as the basic motors of the global economy' (SCOTT, 2001, p. 4). According to a recent government report, 'the factors of productivity in advanced knowledge based economies are concentrated in cities' (OFFICE OF THE DEPUTY PRIME MINISTER [ODPM], 2003, p. 1; also H. M. TREASURY, 2001).

GOVERNMENT VIEWS OF COMPETITIVE LOCAL AND REGIONAL POLICIES

European governments have traditionally been ambivalent about competitive sub-national initiatives because of their uncertain net contribution to the national economy. Some have become more supportive over time, hoping to shape them to serve national purposes and for political expedience when macro-economic policies have been more constrained. Indeed, local development has increasingly replaced traditional equity-based regional policies in countries such as the UK (ANYADIKE-DANES *et al.*, 2001; H. M. TREASURY, 2001, 2003a; ORGANIZATION FOR ECONOMIC CO-OPERATION AND DEVELOPMENT, 2001). These sought to reduce spatial disparities by guiding investment away from congested areas to lagging regions with underused resources. Such carrot-and-stick policies have been scaled back because of concerns about their cost effectiveness and fears about firms being diverted out of the country through growth restrictions in buoyant areas.[3]

Instead, the focus of spatial policy has switched to encouraging development from within by exploiting indigenous strengths. There is less emphasis on mobile investment and the transfer of jobs between regions and more on creating environments where high-quality businesses can start and succeed. This draws on endogenous growth theory where growth is seen to arise from enhanced local productivity and innovation through investment in human capital and research in leading areas of the economy (CRAFTS, 1996; MARTIN and SUNLEY, 1998). This is supported by various arguments that innovation, institutional learning and the exchange of creative ideas (knowledge spillovers) occur most effectively in industrial clusters organized at the city-region level (MOSS KANTER, 1995; COOKE and MORGAN, 1998; PORTER, 1998).

The shift in approach occurred initially within the framework of 'top-down' regional and national policies. The main business development and training programmes were delivered locally but controlled centrally to prioritize national objectives. Over time, the aim has been to decentralize economic responsibilities to regional and local organizations in order to permit greater responsiveness to variable conditions on the ground and increased effectiveness rather than having a centralized 'one size fits all' approach (H. M. TREASURY, 2001, 2003a, b).[4] These bodies now cover the whole country rather than selected 'assisted areas' to maximize growth potential wherever it exists. This 'bottom-up', locally led approach encourages more explicit territorial competition, prompting a concern that localities in a weak position at the outset will lose out to areas with greater resources and competitive strengths (ANYADIKE-DANES *et al.*, 2001; HOUSE OF COMMONS, 2003). It is another sign of a shift in emphasis in spatial policy from equity considerations to national efficiency.

Governments have also sought to ensure that sub-national policies reinforce national competitiveness by encouraging a focus on skills, productivity and international markets. The first Competitiveness White Papers devoted special attention to London because of its supposed unique contribution to the UK economy as an international financial centre and tourist attraction (H. M. GOVERNMENT, 1994, 1995). The UK's other cities were bundled together and relegated by the statement that they required regeneration to become more internationally competitive. Their role as important centres of manufacturing with a substantial contribution to UK exports was ignored. The Urban White Paper stated that English cities needed 'to compete on a global scale for jobs and investment' (DEPARTMENT OF ENVIRONMENT, TRANSPORT AND THE REGIONS, 2000, p. 13). This fails to recognize that most branches of most urban economies do not and need not compete in international markets. Many cities could prosper by serving predominantly regional and national markets, especially as services become a larger share of their economies (TUROK and BAILEY, 2004b). At least as important a challenge for many of them is to maintain an adequate supply of property, land and infrastructure to avoid unnecessary relocation of expanding firms to surrounding towns.

Local public policies have also been affected by wider national reforms, which were influenced in part by government belief in competitive markets. Some reforms have sought to alter the culture of the public sector through greater emphasis on enterprise and opportunity at the expense of need and entitlement (KEARNS and TUROK, 2000). Competition has been used for resource allocation in transport, regional policy and special urban initiatives in education, health, housing and employment (H. M. GOVERNMENT, 1994, 1995; OATLEY, 1998). Competitive bidding is intended to provide pressure and rewards for public organizations to be more imaginative and efficient in service design and delivery. Privatization and contracting out of services and utilities have also opened new areas of the urban economy to market forces, including transport, water, environmental maintenance and catering. Competition has increased between all sorts of organizations *within* cities as well as between them, making strategic planning and coordination of policy implementation more difficult. There has been insufficient consideration of the circumstances in which competition is appropriate and where it is not.

FUNCTIONS OF COMPETITION BETWEEN CITIES AND REGIONS

Competition *between firms* is believed to have two main benefits for economic development (CARLIN *et al.*, 2001; BEATH, 2002). First, it provides a *selection* mechanism; firms with out-dated products or inefficient processes do not survive, while new entrants introduce better products and techniques. Selection by exit and entry reallocates resources from inefficient producers and declining sectors to more efficient and growing ones (H. M. TREASURY, 2001). Second, it provides strong *incentives* to existing firms to improve their technology and organization. The threat posed by rivals encourages them to become more innovative and efficient, which increases their market share, lowers the average cost of production in the industry and reduces the price to consumers.

Both mechanisms are said to improve productivity and growth across the economy. Firms often try to limit competition by securing a dominant position in their markets or by colluding to agree prices or market share. Government regulation is needed to prevent this. Competition may also have important costs arising from market failure – neglect of research and development (R&D), training, derelict land and other externalities – which also calls for government action. In practice, competition often coexists with various forms of cooperation. For instance, firms under pressure may collaborate with their suppliers and customers to expand their expertise, develop specialist products and improve their access to markets (KITSON and MICHIE, 2000; PORTER, 1990). Beyond a certain point, some forms of collaboration become collusion, which is why business associations have sometimes aroused suspicion.

Competition between places cannot operate in the same way. The agents and their powers are different and competition is moderated by other resource-allocation mechanisms. Considering *selection* first, cities cannot go bankrupt if they are uncompetitive, unlike businesses. New entrants also emerge infrequently and are insignificant compared with most markets in which firms operate, since building new urban economies is obviously costly and slow. Most countries have public finance systems that cushion the impact of economic decline. Local authorities in the UK and many other parts of Europe are insulated because most of their funds originate from central government based on their resident population, which is slow to adjust to decline. There is an element of need in their funding allocation, which partially compensates deprived areas. Areas of job loss also gain from social welfare expenditure for people out of work, which is another economic stabilizer. This centralized financial system protects UK cities and regions from the spiral of decline that can face distressed US cities within a more decentralized regime (HILL and NOWAK, 2002).

Yet, places still stagnate and decline, even if they do not 'close down'. There may be local reasons, such as exhausted natural resources or wider shifts in the demand for their products (BEGG *et al.*, 2002). National transfer payments may delay the process, but they will not reverse it without productive investment. New urban areas also emerge over time, showing a dynamic process of change at work that must affect the functioning of the economy in the long term. Edge cities and new towns may grow on the back of the amenities, services and markets of their neighbouring cities, without their physical and financial costs. Some of the fiscal stabilizers have also been pared back to cut government expenditure. Greater reliance on private finance for infrastructure and competitive bidding are bound to have more uneven spatial outcomes than previous procedures. Growth pressures and property shortages in successful regions mean that local authorities are often encouraged to respond to market demand and allow new development, not try to steer private investment through planning restrictions or strategic use of public infrastructure (TUROK and BAILEY, 2004b). So, although selection in territorial competition is unlikely to alter the structure and efficiency of the economy in the short-run, it may be becoming more relevant. Some of the consequences are discussed below.

Similar observations can be made about *incentives*. At issue are the benefits to the area from engaging in competitive policies in relation to the costs (CHESHIRE, 1999). This calculation is much more complex for cities than for firms since they are not single entities driven by the objective of profitability.[5] Even productivity is an insufficient over-arching aim since it can be increased simply by using fewer resources (e.g. labour shedding), which increases neither real prosperity nor an area's competitiveness. Some places would find it easier to enhance their prosperity (and their contribution to national output and prosperity) by activating underemployed resources (such as increasing the employment rate) than by raising productivity (BAILEY *et al.*, 2002; BEGG *et al.*, 2002). In addition, city

authorities have less control over their assets and liabilities than firms, so the links between what they do and the outcome is more indirect and uncertain. The calculation is bound to vary between the markets in which cities compete, depending on the characteristics of the competitive process and who experiences the benefit and burden. It is also likely to vary in different countries depending on the link in the financial system between a city's economic performance and its tax receipts. In general, one might expect cities with inherent economic advantages at the outset to be more inclined to participate in competitive activities than those in weaker positions, because they stand more chance of success.

There is little or no direct incentive for UK cities and regions to promote economic growth because the revenue from business rates is pooled nationally and distributed as part of local authorities' overall funding allocation, which is driven by a formula.[6] This grant system generally cancels out the effects of changing property values on local authority revenues and household deprivation on their expenditure. Only population growth has any real fiscal effect and this is not necessarily positive. Growth imposes costs through transport congestion and environmental damage, and requires investment in physical and social infrastructure (H. M. TREASURY, 2003b). Lack of public funds to tackle congestion and shortages of housing and schools may limit the capacity of places to grow. In addition, administrative boundaries separating residential suburbs from commercial cores complicate assessment of the effects of growth since the costs falls unevenly and the benefits leak out. Public authorities often encounter considerable political opposition to new development, particularly towards new roads and housing around existing suburbs, and especially in pressurized regions. Therefore, decision-makers face many considerations that can more than offset the gains from growth.

Nevertheless, a competitive political system, electoral pressures to create and safeguard jobs, and lobbying by selected business interests to help them grow mean that all except the most prosperous dormitory suburbs and towns normally make some effort to maintain or enhance their economic position. The intensity of their effort is bound to be sensitive to the economic cycle. The form it takes may also be symbolic as much as substantial. There are opportunities for most areas to access special resources for this purpose, such as regeneration budgets from central government, European funds or Lottery money, although the scale may be limited in non-assisted areas.

One of the difficulties facing local decision-makers is uncertainty about *what* policies to pursue. Their choice may be influenced by central government controls, the rules of other external funders, the pressure for visible actions, fashionable ideas or advice from consultants. They may also be swayed by special interests for whom the payoffs from development are more clear cut, such as major property owners or other business groups that stand to benefit from increasing demand and rising land prices and rents (LOGAN and MOLOTCH, 1987; STONE, 2001). Other economic interests with larger numbers, smaller individual stakes and more diverse concerns tend to find it harder to organize for collective action. This raises the obvious danger that the selected policies favour narrow interests. Overall, there is little doubt that there has been a steady growth in sub-national policies in the UK as in other European countries that are explicitly or implicitly competitive, even if the rationale is sometimes open to question and the incentives are not clear cut, as they are in North America.

NEGATIVE AND POSITIVE FEATURES OF INSTITUTIONALIZED COMPETITION

Overt competition between places has not traditionally been considered important for understanding the dynamics of economic growth. Common descriptions of the process as 'displacement' and 'zero-sum' imply it is unproductive and to be discouraged, since one area's success may only come at the expense of others (CHESHIRE and GORDON, 1998). This has long been the Treasury view of urban policy (MACLENNAN, 2000), and it now appears to be its view of traditional regional policy. Place-based competition may be wasteful if subsidies are provided to encourage business relocation, especially is this prompts retaliation in the form of inflated subsidies or concessions on environmental or employment standards (a negative-sum game). There is a history of predatory poaching or beggar-my-neighbour behaviour in the US through sizeable inducements offered for firms to move between areas (ORGANIZATION FOR ECONOMIC CO-OPERATION AND DEVELOPMENT, 2001). The European Union has become concerned about Member States subsidizing such movement, or being blackmailed by firms threatening to move. Limits have been imposed on state aid in recognition that governments may turn a blind eye to such behaviour by local authorities if their competitor locations are abroad. Yet, European integration and business mobility mean that competition occurs increasingly on an international basis. TNCs are more proficient than local firms at extracting subsidies by playing places off against each other (WIN, 1995).

There are other instances where place-based competition may lead to a misallocation of resources from a national or even a local perspective. Civic pride and rivalry can cause unnecessary imitation and wasteful duplication of public facilities, especially between adjacent areas. They can lead to expensive promotional efforts for symbolic purposes and unwarranted incentives to host major sporting and cultural events. Meanwhile, support for sectors that are much bigger generators of sustainable economic activity may be

neglected because they have a lower profile or the competition is less visible. Rivalry between neighbouring cities and towns can also mean they undermine the reputation and image of both, and fail to recognize or develop complementary assets that would be beneficial all round. By sharing their knowledge, financial and physical resources in collaborative ventures, they might benefit from economies of scale and scope, and thereby gain a collective competitive advantage in relation to other places (TUROK and BAILEY, 2004a). Efforts are currently being made to encourage collaboration between the eight major regional cities in England, and between each of them and their surrounding subregions (ODPM, 2003).

Finally, competition between cities and regions can generate substantial human costs and widen social inequalities if there are consistent losers. Places may be at a disadvantage at the start, perhaps through a peripheral location, a burden of physical dereliction, or outmoded educational or technical institutions. Market forces may exacerbate disparities by skewing resources towards areas with more immediate commercial prospects or confidence among investors. Decline may be self-reinforcing with weakened corrective mechanisms. Privileged cities and regions may become increasingly prosperous by attracting away investment, entrepreneurial skills and talent. This will fuel their development process, at some wider cost in imbalanced labour and housing markets, inflation and slower national economic growth. There is evidence of consistent disparities across Britain's cities and regions over the long post-war period (BEGG et al., 2002; PARKINSON et al., 2003). The distributional consequences arising from an unequal spread of competitive assets are usually ignored in documents promoting a decentralized, implicitly competitive approach to economic development (e.g. H. M. TREASURY, 2001). A recent Select Committee inquiry recognized the contradiction in the government's target to encourage the growth of all regions and at the same time to reduce the gap between them: 'To reduce differences, emphasis must be given to the less prosperous regions. Treating unequal regions equally is not a recipe for reducing disparities' (HOUSE OF COMMONS, 2003, p. 26).

Competition, of course, can also have positive consequences. Pressure on local bodies may prevent complacency and encourage timely delivery of suitable economic infrastructure, services and skills. It is important for cities to maintain their economic base, especially with public resources under scrutiny. Cities may seek to develop special areas of technological expertise and institutions to help firms access new markets. Provision of serviced land and property can facilitate business growth and avoid disruptive relocation of firms to surrounding areas. Similar points apply to the retention and attraction of mobile population. City authorities may build on their distinctive features, physical heritage and cultural traditions to develop new and original ways of attracting external visitors and investors. This can extend the range of investment opportunities, widen the choice of tourist destinations and enrich the quality of life for local residents. An emphasis on quality, diversity and differentiation (dynamic advantages) is much more likely than imitation and cost-cutting (static advantages) to produce a positive developmental effect overall, rather than zero-sum. The possibility remains that weaker cities will be less well equipped to compete on aspects of quality and better positioned to compete on cost for lower-value projects, because of their cheaper property and lower wages.

There is understandable ambivalence among commentators about deliberate encouragement of institutionalized competition (OATLEY, 1998; TUROK and HOPKINS, 1998). Competition is unlikely to be always or inevitably beneficial, or indeed harmful. Much depends on the form it takes and the context in which it is pursued, including regulation of counterproductive and underhand competitive practices by national authorities and the existence of compensating policies where appropriate. Governments have a role to play in creating an environment that encourages desirable practices, such as enhancing productive capacity, maximizing the use of underemployed human and physical resources, and stimulating institutional innovation. Simple diversionary activities may be discouraged, unless there are sound economic and social reasons. For instance, it could be argued that spreading development more equitably across the UK regions would increase sustainability in economic, social and environmental terms by reducing development pressures, overcrowding and investment requirements for additional housing, schools, transport and other infrastructure in the South East, while making better use of under-used resources and economizing on transfer payments to lagging regions (HOUSE OF COMMONS, 2003). Employment transfers between regions of course could occur through deliberate dispersal policies towards the public sector as well as through territorial competition.

Competition between places is a reality, especially in an unorganized form through firms trading in wider markets. Indirect competition for population through labour and housing markets is also important. The ongoing performance of firms can be influenced by various attributes of their areas – as will be discussed below – in ways that vary from sector to sector. This is a more important feature of territorial competition, with more significant economic consequences, than the visible battles between public agencies to host prominent events or to win challenge funds. The concept of competitiveness can help one understand these dynamics by prompting questions about the local conditions and resources that help firms sell their products in wider markets. It has become popular to suggest that specifically *urban* assets have become

important sources of competitive advantage for firms in an era of more integrated markets and higher quality products and services. According to PORTER (1998, p. 90), for example, 'The enduring competitive advantages in a global economy are often heavily localised, arising from concentrations of highly specialised skills and knowledge, institutions, rivalry, related businesses, and sophisticated customers'.

URBAN SIZE AS A SOURCE OF COMPETITIVE ADVANTAGE

One of the striking features of modern societies is the geographical concentration of economic activity. In England, for instance, 80% of the population lives in towns and cities of over 10 000 population covering only some 7% of the land area (DEPARTMENT OF ENVIRONMENT, TRANSPORT AND THE REGIONS, 2000). Nearly half (43%) of Britain's jobs are still in its 20 largest cities (TUROK and EDGE, 1999). This tendency for firms and population to concentrate in a limited number of places suggests that cities and towns have advantages as economic locations, although the influence of land-use planning controls, institutional inertia and the inherited infrastructure need also to be borne in mind. At the risk of over simplification, one can distinguish two contrasting interpretations of concentration. The differences between them underlie current debates about the development of cities and regions. They share a common view that location affects economic processes and that city-regions contribute positively to the national economy. However, they emphasize different ways in which geography influences economic performance. They also have different implications for policy, including whether to promote industrial diversity or specialization, to devote priority to enhancing hard assets (e.g. infrastructure or labour availability) or soft assets (e.g. institutional networks or specialized knowledge), and to foster competition or cooperation between firms and other local organizations.

The emphasis in the first perspective (discussed below) is on the benefits of size and diversity that flow from having a concentration of economic activity and population within easy reach. The second perspective (also discussed below) stresses the quality of the relationships between firms. The classic concept of *agglomeration economies* emphasizes the 'positive externalities', or external economies of scale, scope and complexity, that follow from co-location of many businesses. Geographical proximity and size increase the opportunities available to firms and reduce the risks to which they are exposed (STORPER, 1997; GORDON and McCANN, 2000; PARR, 2002). Size and proximity reduce the cost of labour and business services, and help to improve the efficiency with which inputs are used via better management, improved workforce skills or better production techniques. Agglomeration also increases the opportunities available to workers and to organizations that provide business and personal services, so the gains extend beyond individual firms and increase the overall productivity and growth rate of city economies.

There are three principal kinds of economic benefits, or 'centripetal forces' (KRUGMAN, 1998), originally identified by MARSHALL (1920). First, firms gain from access to a more extensive labour pool, which makes it easier to find specialist skills. Workers also benefit from a bigger choice of potential employers and better career prospects. Second, firms can gain access to a greater range and quality of shared inputs and supporting industries, such as specialized maintenance, marketing or design services, transport and communications facilities, and venture capital. Cities are good locations for suppliers and distributors of all sorts of business and commercial services because of the size of the market available. Third, firms gain from a greater flow of information and ideas. There is efficient transfer of trade knowledge and intelligence between firms through informal contacts, chance meetings or movement of skilled labour and management. These knowledge spillovers help to disseminate good practice and facilitate the development of new products and higher quality processes. A further important distinction is often drawn between 'localization' economies, which are associated with specialized infrastructure, services and skills geared to particular branches of economic activity, and 'urbanization' economies, which relate to generalized urban assets (such as airports, educational institutions and municipal services) that serve a diverse industrial structure.

To gain most of these benefits, a city requires no particular organization acting on its behalf, or any special loyalty or shared values between firms, apart from the provision of public goods or non-traded infrastructure and services. Companies are independent units operating with flexibility in a market environment. Competition is the driving force and firms do not tend to cooperate on matters beyond their short-term interests (GORDON and MCCANN, 2000). Proximity increases the opportunities for them to trade, recruit suitable labour, access specialized know-how and reduce market uncertainties, all of which help to improve their performance. The scale of activity in the city and the number of firms determines the significance of these benefits – basically the larger the better. The density and heterogeneity of firms are also sources of dynamism and creativity in strengthening the 'critical mass'. City-regions may acquire cumulative advantages over other places as a result of these 'regional externalities' (PARR, 2002), leading to self-reinforcing growth.

A recent study of the competitiveness of the London metropolitan region supported this perspective: 'The real strength of the London agglomeration effect ... seems to consist in the random possibilities for connections and stimuli made possible by its sheer scale and diversity' (BUCK *et al.*, 2002, p. 136). Another study of innovation in London, Paris and Amsterdam reaffirmed the importance of size and diversity in these metropolitan regions in allowing firms to 'pick and mix' their inputs and connections with suppliers, research establishments, technology transfer institutions and technical training centres (SIMMIE *et al.*, 2002). Firms also benefited from access to international airports, enabling them to gain 'time proximity' for face-to-face contact and effective knowledge transfer with international suppliers and customers.

Until a few decades ago, urban growth was the dominant trend throughout the world. Few doubted the advantages of cities and the connection between industrialization and urbanization. The received wisdom was that scale and diversity were central to successful cities, and that cities, in turn, enhanced national economic performance. Writers such as JACOBS (1969, 1984) explored in detail the role of cities in economic development as a result of their versatility and dynamism. The variety of skills and productive capacities enabled cities to improvise, adapt and innovate across many products and processes. This led to the successful replacement of imports by local production, boosted exports and it caused explosive growth, including manufacturing, and business and consumer services. Moreover, economic development was not a smooth, consensual process. The practical problems and inefficiencies of large cities induced creative responses and generated new goods and services for export that fuelled further growth. Jacobs also studied cities that had become more specialized over time. Although this enabled efficiency gains, Jacobs argued it was a recipe for stagnation in the long run because of the loss of adaptive capacity. The message was that the city had enormous strengths as a diverse, but interconnected, system.

COMPETITIVE DISADVANTAGES OF CITIES

Two important processes challenged this thinking from around the 1970s and raised doubts about the value of cities to the national economy. First, *deurbanization* caused a shift in population and firms out of many city cores towards suburbs and surrounding towns. Dispersal was partly a reflection of urban land constraints hampering the needs of modern production for extensive plant layouts, coupled with a shift from transporting freight by rail to motorway. There was also a search for cheaper premises and compliant labour for routine assembly work and back-office functions. Relocation of jobs was accompanied by residential decentralization, which had its own momentum with rising incomes, car ownership and people's preferences for more space, gardens and their own homes. Deurbanization suggested that economic success did not require proximity and urban density; the friction of distance seemed less important than had been understood. It also coincided with a growing interest in regions rather than cities as units of analysis and explanation.

Yet, deurbanization was more pervasive in some countries than others, depending on car and home ownership levels, public transport and attitudes to sprawl. It did not necessarily contradict the advantages of agglomeration, bearing in mind changes in the organization of industry and falling transport costs. There were also costs, or *diseconomies of agglomeration*, which had been neglected by Marshall and some of his successors, and which offset the advantages. Two diseconomies operate as the scale of a city increases. First, dense concentrations of activity increase the demand for local land, which force up property prices and rents for all land uses. Competition for land also causes displacement of lower-value industrial uses and routine office-based services by commercial and residential uses. Second, concentration causes congestion, which adds to business costs and worsens the quality of everyday life for residents. It is often difficult for established cities to improve their basic infrastructure radically to cope with congestion because of the disruption caused.

The relative importance of the centralizing and decentralizing forces can be expected to vary over time and between different industries and functions, depending on prevailing communication technologies and industrial organization. Governments can influence the outcome, as many European cities demonstrate (PARKINSON *et al.*, 2003). Investment in a good public transport system can alleviate congestion, improve commuting, and facilitate internal information and trade flows. Maintenance of quality public spaces, vibrant central squares and landscaped parks may help to retain residents and attract private investment. A pragmatic approach to building controls, land-use zoning and development on the urban edge can relieve inflated property prices and help accommodate urban growth through incremental expansion along transport corridors.

Britain's core cities have been disadvantaged in at least two respects. First, tight Greenbelt controls and the new towns have encouraged development to leapfrog to less accessible locations beyond the urban fringe (BREHENY, 1999; BEGG *et al.*, 2002). In addition, investment in their economic infrastructure has been neglected over the years because of an anti-urban ethos coupled with a perception that urban problems are essentially social and related to poor living conditions, so priority in capital investment has been given to building houses and improving neighbourhoods (e.g. BAILEY *et al.*, 1999). There has also been resistance from established residential communities to major infrastructure works on the grounds of dislocation, and a legacy of negative experiences following comprehensive redevelopment programmes in the 1960s and 1970s.

Meanwhile, a second and more traumatic process of *de-industrialization* hit the economic base of many cities from around the same period. Facing increasingly difficult circumstances, manufacturers in the UK closed many older inner-city plants to cut costs. This caused large-scale loss of manual employment, curtailed the markets of local supporting industries and damaged the environment through physical dereliction. The scale and speed of the contraction impacted old industrial areas particularly hard, making it difficult to replace lost opportunities or to retrain the workforce (BREHENY, 1999; TUROK and EDGE, 1999). Many cities were badly positioned in relation to surrounding towns, with a legacy of contaminated land, out-dated infrastructure and obsolete skills. Extensive manual job loss also contributed to a range of wider problems, the full extent of which has only recently become apparent, disguised unemployment, inactivity, ill health, premature mortality, personal and community stress, debt, racial tension, family break-up, and neighbourhood abandonment (SHAW *et al.*, 1999; WEBSTER, 2000; AMIN, 2002).

Some interpreted urban de-industrialization partly as the outcome of a new spatial division of labour among large corporations in which production was dispersed to lower cost locations while cities retained higher level managerial and service functions (MASSEY, 1984). These functions had comparative advantage in remaining in the core cities since face-to-face contact mattered to them and they were less dependent on proximity to or demand from production plants. London and the South East benefited particularly from a centralization of strategic control and R&D functions, while regional cities lost many of their corporate headquarters through mergers and takeovers. Others saw de-industrialization as the outcome of a similar process but on an international scale. It was the logical consequence of a new *international* division of labour in which much production went offshore to emerging economies while successful global cities developed a new strategic role. This was to control, finance and support the international network of factories, service operations and markets: 'Alongside the well-documented spatial dispersal of economic activities, new forms of territorial centralisation of top-level management and control operations have appeared' (SASSEN, 1994, p. 1).

CASTELLS (1996) devoted more emphasis to radical shifts in technology in conjunction with internationalization. He portrayed de-industrialization as part of a necessary transition towards a new 'informational' phase of capitalism whereby European and US cities become centres of advanced services dealing predominantly in information processing and control, and serving as nodes within new global networks. 'The new economy is organised around global networks of capital, management, and information, whose access to technological know-how is at the roots of productivity and competitiveness' (CASTELLS, 1996, p. 471). These shared the basic premise that economic relationships within cities had become less important than the position of cities within wider international networks (AMIN and THRIFT, 2002). Cities had become more open systems while still remaining the foci of extensive networks of power and information (MASSEY *et al.*, 1999). The 'presence or absence in the network and the dynamics of each network vis-à-vis others are critical sources of domination and change in our society' (CASTELLS, 1996, p. 469).

NEW SOURCES OF COMPETITIVE ADVANTAGE?

Another set of ideas emerged in parallel, shifting the balance of emphasis back somewhat towards the benefits of interfirm relationships within cities, while still recognizing the influence of global conditions and the role of cities in the wider national and international system. Three new features attracted attention: the importance of collaboration between firms as much as competition; sectoral specialization over urban size and diversity; and soft or intangible locational assets rather than hard or physical assets.

During the 1980s, several writers argued that the economy was moving from an era of mass production to one of *flexible specialization* or *post-Fordism* (PIORE and SABEL, 1984; HALL and JACQUES, 1989; AMIN, 1994). A growth in demand for less standardized consumer products was said to have coincided with changes in industrial technology and the labour process, including the application of computers to various stages of design, production and distribution. A key feature of the argument was that these shifts supported the establishment of local networks of specialized and interdependent firms. According to PIORE and SABEL (1984, p. 265), 'small enterprises bound in a complex web of competition and co-operation' had the flexibility to adapt more readily to changing market conditions, especially in high-technology and design-intensive sectors.

SCOTT (1988, 2002) pursued a similar argument about the horizontal and vertical disintegration of functions in industries facing unstable and competitive markets as a result of the breakdown of Fordism. One of his key propositions was that the shift from large, integrated corporations relying on internal-scale economies to supply secure markets towards smaller, fragmented firms favoured re-agglomeration. Specialization increased their focus and flexibility, and agglomeration reduced their costs. The outcome was a dense local network of producers engaged in subcontracting and service relationships and benefiting from a specialized labour pool, typically located in cities. Scott has argued that industries such as clothing in cities like Los Angeles and New York can only survive increasing competition from low-cost producers offshore by

upgrading their technological capabilities and becoming more fashion oriented, which requires closer collaboration between firms.

SAXENIAN (1994) also emphasized the importance of local social relationships and the institutional context for business. Industrial performance was greatly enhanced where there was a culture of 'co-operative competition'. In a study of the US electronics industry, Saxenian concluded that Silicon Valley's (California) greater success over Boston's (Massachusetts) Route 128 was its decentralized, network-based system that encouraged informal communication, collaboration and learning between firms. This culture fostered greater innovation and adaptation to changing markets and technologies than the hierarchical, vertically integrated and excessively rigid institutional structure of Route 128.

> Paradoxically, regions offer an important source of competitive advantage even as production and markets become increasingly global. Geographic proximity promotes the repeated interaction and mutual trust needed to sustain collaboration and to speed the continual recombination of technology and skill.
>
> (SAXENIAN, 1994, p. 161)[7]

STORPER (1995, 1997) extended this to include a wider range of interactions between firms (untraded interdependencies). These were essential for mutual learning and adaptation in a context of economic uncertainty and rapid technological change. Storper included underlying conventions or common rules and routines for developing, communicating and interpreting knowledge about all aspects of production. These interactions were distinctive to each locality and gave it a particular competitive advantage that got stronger and became more specialized over time. These intangible assets discouraged business dispersal, despite many industrial inputs becoming more standardized and processes more routine. Consequently, 'the region is a key source of development in capitalism ... the region has a central theoretical status in the process of capitalist development which must be located in its untraded interdependencies' (STORPER, 1995, pp. 191, 221).

Similar arguments were developed about a range of phenomena variously termed innovative milieu, new industrial spaces, learning regions, regional innovation systems, and the concept with the biggest impact on public policy, *industrial clusters* (COOKE and MORGAN, 1998; PORTER, 1990, 1998). Porter has been the most prominent advocate of the argument that place matters to international competitiveness because firms benefit from their surrounding environment through competitive and collaborative relationships with other firms and associated institutions. '[T]he drivers of prosperity are increasingly sub-national, based in cities and regions. ... Many of the most important levers for competitiveness arise at the regional level, and reside in clusters that are geographically concentrated' (PORTER, 2001, pp. 141, 156).

At the heart of these arguments is the idea that active cooperation between firms in business networks promotes trust and longer-term decision-making. This enables them to overcome some of the limitations of pure market relationships and to undertake risky ventures without fear of opportunism (GORDON and McCANN, 2000). Firms are willing to act together for mutual benefit, creating institutions to lobby on their behalf or to provide common support services. Proximity fosters some of the conditions for social interaction and collaboration, or 'social capital'. It can help interpersonal relationships and trust to develop, and promote a sense of belonging and shared interest. It can also help networks to build upon the distinctive cultural traditions and identity of places, and facilitate practical organization around collective action. The result may be strong urban or regional industrial clusters represented by their own business associations.

Although there has been surprisingly little systematic empirical research to substantiate these arguments, they have nevertheless proved highly attractive to recent city and regional policies (e.g. H. M. TREASURY, 2001; DEPARTMENT OF TRADE AND INDUSTRY, 2001; ODPM, 2003). The English Regional Development Agencies and related organizations have devoted considerable effort to identifying clusters and developing initiatives to assist leading-edge, knowledge-based industries, such as biotechnology, telecommunications and new digital media. There have been schemes to create trade associations and encourage business networking; to promote a more entrepreneurial culture among scientists and professionals; to develop specialized business districts and science parks; to enhance workforce skills and qualifications; to improve the provision of venture capital; and to accelerate the flow of knowledge from universities to business.

Policies towards the creative or cultural industries illustrate the enthusiasm with which these ideas have been taken up.

> [T]he cultural industries based on local know-how and skills show how cities can negotiate a new accommodation with the global market, in which cultural producers sell into much larger markets but rely upon a distinctive and defensible local base. ... Cultural industries and entrepreneurs will play a critical role in reviving large cities that have suffered economic decline and dislocation over the past two decades.
>
> (LEADBEATER and OAKLEY, 1999, pp. 14–16)

These industries' success is said to depend above all on the creativity, ingenuity and talent of individuals. Their skills and tacit know-how are fostered by a proximity to related people and enterprises, and to strong local networks. Cultural entrepreneurs share ideas and collaborate on joint projects by forming flexible, multi-skilled teams. Cities are said to be conducive environments because they offer scope for people and ideas to mix and mingle. They are places where knowledge is created, tested, adapted and disseminated (HALL, 1998; LANDRY, 2000). Cities can provide the shared space or 'milieu' within which connections are made and firms can learn, compare and cooperate. They house the institutions and infrastructure to bring together designers, producers, suppliers, educators, investors, distributors and customers in a complex web of relationships that are both competitive and collaborative. This is supposed to create a certain atmosphere, buzz or self-reinforcing dynamism that spurs innovation, attracts mobile capital and mobile people, and generates growth from within. This enhances the distinctiveness, profile and reputation of the city, which adds to its attractiveness and vitality. More detailed empirical research on the creative industries indicates weaknesses in these arguments, including the importance of external business connections, major public institutions, and powerful TNCs that control access to key technology and distribution channels (BASSETT *et al.*, 2002; TUROK, 2003).

CONCLUSION: TOWARDS A BROADER PERSPECTIVE

The recent literature explores different ways in which city-regions can contribute to national economic development. This is a useful counter to their previous portrayal as a burden on the economy. However, there is a danger of overstating the generative effects of localized networks, soft urban assets and spatial concentration as sources of international competitiveness, as indicated below. Certainly, evidence of the significance of these new competitive advantages for cities is rather thin at present (BUCK *et al.*, 2004). In addition, such notions may divert attention from the responsibilities of national and supra-national public institutions for contributing to economic and social development, and inadvertently foster unproductive competition between city and regional authorities. In a quality-based, knowledge-intensive competitive environment, the decentralized policy approach inevitably favours some kinds of cities over others to improve their performance. There is clearly a balance to be struck between locally led economic policies and national spatial development policies, with neither offering a simple panacea.

Recent theories of business networks and knowledge spillovers are open to several criticisms. In stressing the importance of ongoing interactions between firms, they may neglect historical linkages and processes (COE and TOWNSEND, 1998). Decisions about business location, reinvestment and new firm formation may reflect inertia or conditions inherited from pre-existing industrial structures as much as contemporary opportunities for trade and collaboration. Accumulated investment patterns determine the availability of a skilled workforce, appropriate infrastructure and potential entrepreneurs with relevant experience. Firms and industries may grow in particular places because this is where suitable labour, institutions and other factors of production happen to be concentrated, or where major customers or parent companies were once located. London has a dominant position in the creative industries, partly because of long-established key anchors of demand such as the BBC. Regional cities in the UK suffer from the long-standing loss of corporate headquarters and high-level R&D functions to the South East.

The general point is that urban and regional development need to be understood as historical, path-dependent processes in which new industries are laid down on and shaped by inherited conditions (MASSEY, 1984; KRUGMAN, 1996; MARTIN and SUNLEY, 1996). Mechanisms of cumulative causation may reinforce existing industrial centres, unless diseconomies emerge, key markets stagnate and the growth process moves into reverse, leaving a legacy of out-dated infrastructure and institutions that may be difficult to turn around. BAILEY and FRENCH (2004) show that history and basic factors of production such as labour and infrastructure are much more important than localized networks in explaining the performance of financial services in most of Britain's cities. Only in the City of London do firms seem to attach much value to shared intelligence and informational networks (BUCK et al., 2002).

The theories of local networks also risk overstating the degree of vertical disintegration that has occurred within industry and portraying it as a one-way process. Mergers, acquisitions and other forms of consolidation of ownership and control have become increasingly important in many branches of the economy, often in response to intensified competition and the rising costs of technological innovation. The most visible signs are the creation of powerful TNCs; 65 000 of them have around 850 000 foreign affiliates, which employ 54 million people and account for one-tenth of the world's Gross Domestic Product and one-third of exports (UNCTAD, 2002). They benefit from substantial *internal* economies of scale, scope and complexity to fund the development of new products and processes, build strong brands and sell them into global markets. The networks that promote knowledge sharing and innovation are likely to be much stronger between different geographical sites *within* TNCs than between smaller firms within particular localities (AMIN and THRIFT, 2002). Collaboration for small firms is usually voluntary and they often have serious reservations about sharing information with potential competitors who may obtain their intellectual property, gain valuable information about their customers or poach their best staff (TUROK, 2003). The most dynamic firms within local 'clusters' may also accept acquisition by TNCs at a certain stage of growth in order to improve access to external capital, managerial skills, technologies and

distribution channels. This weakens local linkages, but strengthens the firms' competitiveness.

It is also important not to assume that vertical disintegration leads to re-agglomeration, or that consolidation means dispersal. The idea that smaller, specialized and flexible firms are more dependent on external economies, knowledge spillovers and face-to-face relationships with other firms and institutions is plausible. However, it may overstate the importance of spatial proximity and 'closure' of the economic system, especially in the context of rising mobility, falling transport costs and developments in information and communication technology (ICT). It may also neglect a wide range of crucial external ties that firms have or need to develop with customers, suppliers and technical collaborators elsewhere in the country and indeed abroad if they are to be successful, as research by SIMMIE et al. (2002) on innovative firms has shown. In addition, the consolidation of firms into larger corporations may have various geographical consequences. It may lead to dispersal of different functions according to their specific locational requirements (e.g. headquarters, R&D or routine services), or to the concentration of activities in one place to integrate separate operations and remove duplication, as BAILEY and FRENCH (2004) show in relation to banks and call centres. It should also be borne in mind that changes in corporate ownership per se may have no significant spatial implications.

The main point is that city-regions need to be understood as part of wider economic systems, networks and resource flows, rather than as self-contained units. This means that the strength of external business connections and the efficiency of external communications and transport links are important, as well as national and international policies and the changing structure of external markets. In addition, city-regions appear to obtain a competitive advantage from the size and diversity of concentrated economic activity, which improves access to markets, suppliers, collaborators and a large labour pool. Localized business networks may be most important for certain kinds of innovative and emerging functions. These advantages cannot be taken for granted since cities – especially older ones – also tend to have higher costs, more congestion and inferior access to the motorway network compared with surrounding areas and some smaller towns. Consequently, an efficient transport system and an effective supply of development land and property are important to avoid cities being disadvantaged.[8]

Acknowledgements – The study on which the present paper is based was part of the Central Scotland Integrative Case Study under the ESRC Cities Programme (Award Number L130251040) with additional support from Scottish Enterprise and the Scottish Executive. Thanks are due to Nick Bailey, Ian Gordon, Alan Harding and John Parr for comments on an earlier version of the manuscript.

NOTES

1. In a report for the UK Government, PORTER and KETELS (2003) argue that this has been the predominant approach over the last two decades and that the UK now needs a new approach focused on improving innovation and skills.

2. Other governments recognize the value of manufacturing because of its interdependence with product innovation and technological development, as well as its disproportionate contribution to the balance of trade and its importance in maintaining a diversified economy. Moreover, service industries are not necessarily immune from relocation overseas, as recent experience with functions such as call centres and data processing has shown.

3. Elsewhere in Europe, there remains a stronger commitment to established regional policies, using instruments such as infrastructure, financial assistance and R&D spending to prioritize development in lagging regions. UK spending on regional grants is less than one-quarter of the European Union average (WREN, 2003).

4. The UK Government recently criticized European Union regional policy for its centralized controls and inflexibility (H. M. TREASURY, 2003a).

5. The calculation might be much simpler in the case of formal competitions for special public resources or to host one-off events, since the organizational bidding costs may be marginal and the direct rewards much more substantial.

6. In recognition of this, the UK Government recently proposed a scheme to reward local authorities for encouraging business in their area by allowing them to retain some of the revenues that arise from growing the business tax base. It is currently consulting on the scale of the incentive to offer and how to ensure that the distributional impact is fair (H. M. TREASURY, 2003b).

7. For a contrary interpretation of Silicon Valley's success, emphasizing federal defence contracts, large corporations and external ties, see GRAY *et al.* (1998) and MARKUSEN (1999).

8. Interestingly, physical infrastructure emerges from the most recent Global Competitiveness Report as the UK's most important economic weakness in relation to other advanced economies, reflecting the low rate of public investment over the last two decades (PORTER and KETELS, 2003).

REFERENCES

AMIN A. (Ed.) (1994) *Post-Fordism: A Reader.* Blackwell, Oxford.

AMIN A. (2002) Ethnicity and the multi-cultural city: living with diversity, *Environment and Planning A* **34**, 959–980.

AMIN A. and THRIFT N. (2002) *Cities: Reimagining the Urban.* Polity, Cambridge.

ANYADIKE-DANES M., FOTHERGILL S., GLYN A., SMITH J. G., KITSON M., MARTIN R., ROWTHORN R., TUROK I., TYLER P. and WEBSTER D. (2001) *Labour's New Regional Policy: An Assessment.* Regional Studies Association, Seaford.

BAILEY N., DOCHERTY I. and TUROK I. (2002) Dimensions of city competitiveness: Edinburgh and Glasgow in a UK context, in BEGG I. (Ed.) *Urban Competitiveness: Policies for Dynamic Cities*, pp. 135–159. Policy Press, Bristol.

BAILEY N. and FRENCH S. (2004) Cities and financial services, in BUCK N., GORDON I., HARDING A. and TUROK I. (Eds) *Changing Cities.* Palgrave, London (forthcoming).

BAILEY N., TUROK I. and DOCHERTY N. (1999) *Edinburgh and Glasgow: Contrasts in Competitiveness and Cohesion.* University of Glasgow, Glasgow.

BASSETT K., GRIFFITHS R. and SMITH I. (2002) Cultural industries, cultural clusters and the city: the example of natural history film-making in Bristol, *Geoforum* **33**, 165–177.

BEATH J. (2002) UK industrial policy: old tunes on new instruments?, *Oxford Review of Economic Policy* **18**, 221–239.

BEGG I., MOORE B. and ALTUNBAS Y. (2002) Long-run trends in the competitiveness of British cities, in BEGG I. (Ed.) *Urban Competitiveness*, pp. 101–133. Policy Press, Bristol.

BREHENY M. (1999) *The People: Where Will They Work?* Town and Country Planning Association, London.

BUCK N., GORDON I., HALL P., HARLOE M. and KLEINMANN M. (2002) *Working Capital: Life and Labour in Contemporary London.* Routledge, London.

BUCK N., GORDON I., HARDING A. and TUROK I. (Eds) (2004) *Changing Cities.* Palgrave, London (forthcoming).

CARLIN W., HASKEL J. and SEABRIGHT P. (2001) Understanding the essential fact about capitalism, *National Institute Economic Review* **175**, 67–84.

CASTELLS M. (1996) *The Rise of the Network Society.* Blackwell, Oxford.

CHESHIRE P. (1999) Cities in competition: articulating the gains from integration, *Urban Studies* **36**, 843–864.

CHESHIRE P. and GORDON I. (1996) Territorial competition and the predictability of collective (in)action, *International Journal of Urban and Regional Research* **20**, 383–399.

CHESHIRE P. and GORDON I. (1998) Territorial competition: some lessons for policy, *Annals of Regional Science* **32**, 321–346.

COE N. and TOWNSEND A. (1998) Debunking the myth of localised agglomerations, *Transactions of the Institute of British Geographers* **23**, 385–404.

COOKE P. and MORGAN K. (1998) *The Associational Economy: Firms, Regions and Innovation.* Oxford University Press, Oxford.

CRAFTS N. (1996) Post-neoclassical endogenous growth theory: what are its policy implications?, *Oxford Review of Economic Policy* **12**, 30–47.

DEPARTMENT OF ENVIRONMENT, TRANSPORT AND THE REGIONS (2000) *Our Towns and Cities: The Future.* DETR, London.

DEPARTMENT OF TRADE AND INDUSTRY (1998) *Our Competitive Future: Building the Knowledge-Driven Economy.* DTI, London.

DEPARTMENT OF TRADE AND INDUSTRY (2001) *Opportunity for all in a World of Change: White Paper on Enterprise, Skills and Innovation*. HMSO, London.

FLORIDA R. (2002) *The Rise of the Creative Class*. Viking, London.

GORDON I. and MCCANN P. (2000) Industrial clusters: complexes, agglomeration and/or social networks?, *Urban Studies* **37**, 513–532.

GRAY M., GOLOB E., MARKUSEN A. and PARK S. (1998) New industrial cities? The four faces of Silicon Valley, *Review of Radical Political Economy* **30**, 1–28.

HALL P. (1998) *Cities in Civilisation: Culture, Technology and Urban Order*. Weidenfeld & Nicholson, London.

HALL S. and JACQUES M. (Eds) (1989) *New Times: The Changing Face of Politics in the 1990s*. Lawrence & Wishart, London.

HILL E. W. and NOWAK J. (2002) Policies to uncover the competitive advantages of America's distressed cities, in BEGG I. (Ed.) *Urban Competitiveness*, pp. 257–282. Policy Press, Bristol.

H. M. GOVERNMENT (1994) *Competitiveness: Helping Business to Win*. HMSO, London.

H. M. GOVERNMENT (1995) *Competitiveness: Forging Ahead*. HMSO, London.

H. M. TREASURY (2001) *Productivity in the UK: 3 – The Regional Dimension*. H. M. Treasury, London.

H. M. TREASURY (2003a) *A Modern Regional Policy for the UK*. H. M. Treasury, London.

H. M. TREASURY (2003b) *Productivity in the UK: 4 – The Local Dimension*. H. M. Treasury, London.

HOUSE OF COMMONS (2003) *Reducing Regional Disparities in Prosperity, ODPM: Housing, Planning, Local Government and the Regions Committee, Ninth Report of Session 2002–03*. HC 492. House of Commons, London.

JACOBS J. (1969) *The Economy of Cities*. Penguin, Harmondsworth.

JACOBS J. (1984) *Cities and the Wealth of Nations*. Random House, New York.

KEARNS A. and TUROK I. (2000) Power, responsibility and governance in Britain's new urban policy, *Journal of Urban Affairs* **22**, 175–191.

KITSON M. and MICHIE J. (2000) *The Political Economy of Competitiveness*. Routledge, London.

KRUGMAN P. (1996) *Pop Internationalism*. MIT Press, Cambridge, MA.

KRUGMAN P. (1998) What's new about the new economic geography?, *Oxford Review of Economic Policy* **14**, 7–17.

LANDRY C. (2000) *The Creative City*. Earthscan, London.

LEADBEATER C. and OAKLEY K. (1999) *The Independents: Britain's New Cultural Entrepreneurs*. Demos, London.

LOGAN J. and MOLOTCH H. (1987) *Urban Fortunes: The Political Economy of Place*. University of California Press, Berkeley.

MACLENNAN D. (2000) *Changing Places, Engaging People*. York Publ. Services, York.

MARKUSEN A. (1999) Fuzzy concepts, scanty evidence, policy distance, *Regional Studies* **33**, 869–884.

MARSHALL A. (1920) *Principles of Economics*, 8th Edn. Macmillan, London.

MARTIN R. and SUNLEY P. (1996) Paul Krugman's geographical economics and its implications for regional development theory: a critical assessment, *Economic Geography* **72**, 259–292.

MARTIN R. and SUNLEY P. (1998) Slow convergence? The new endogenous growth theory and regional development, *Economic Geography* **74**, 201–227.

MASSEY D. (1984) *Spatial Divisions of Labour: Social Structures and the Geography of Production*. Macmillan, London.

MASSEY D., ALLEN J. and PILE S. (Eds) (1999) *City Worlds*. Routledge, London.

MOSS KANTER R. (1995) *World Class: Thriving Locally in the Global Economy*. Simon & Schuster, New York.

OATLEY N. (Ed.) (1998) *Cities, Economic Competition and Urban Policy*. Paul Chapman, London.

OFFICE OF THE DEPUTY PRIME MINISTER (2003) *Second Report from the Working Group of Government Departments, the Core Cities and the Regional Development Agencies*, ODPM, London.

ORGANIZATION FOR ECONOMIC CO-OPERATION AND DEVELOPMENT (2001) *Devolution and Globalisation: Implications for Local Decision-Makers*. OECD, Paris.

PARKINSON M., HUTCHINS M., SIMMIE J., CLARK G. and VERDONK H. (2003) *Competitive European Cities: Where Do the Core Cities Stand?* Report to the Core Cities Working Group. John Moores University, Liverpool.

PARR J. B. (2002) Missing elements in the analysis of agglomeration economies, *International Regional Science Review* **25**, 151–168.

PIORE M. and SABEL C. (1984) *The Second Industrial Divide*. Basic, New York.

PORTER M. (1990) *The Competitive Advantage of Nations*. Free Press, New York.

PORTER M. (1998) Clusters and the new economics of competitiveness, *Harvard Business Review* **December**, 77–90.

PORTER M. (2001) Regions and the new economics of competition, in SCOTT A. J. (Ed.) *Global City Regions: Trends, Theory, Policy*, pp. 139–157. Oxford University Press, Oxford.

PORTER M. and KETELS C. (2003) *UK Competitiveness: Moving to the Next Stage*. Economics Paper 3. Department of Trade and Industry, London.

SASSEN S. (1994) *Cities in a World Economy*. Pine Forge, London.

SAXENIAN A. (1994) *Regional Advantage*. Harvard University Press, Cambridge, MA.

SCOTT A. J. (1988) *New Industrial Spaces: Flexible Production Organisation and Regional Development in North America and Western Europe*. Pion, London.

SCOTT A. J. (Ed.) (2001) *Global City Regions: Trends, Theory, Policy*. Oxford University Press, Oxford.

SCOTT A. J. (2002) Competitive dynamics of Southern California's clothing industry, *Urban Studies* **39**, 1287–1306.

SHAW M., DORLING D., GORDON D. and SMITH G. D. (1999) *The Widening Gap: Health Inequalities and Policy in Britain*. Policy, Bristol.

SIMMIE J., SENNETT J., WOOD P. and HART D. (2002) Innovation in Europe: a tale of networks, knowledge and trade in five cities, *Regional Studies* **36**, 47–64.

STONE C. (2001) The Atlanta experience re-examined, *International Journal of Urban and Regional Research* **25**, 20–34.

STORPER M. (1995) The resurgence of regional economies, ten years later, *European Urban and Regional Studies* **2**, 191–221.

STORPER M. (1997) *The Regional World: Territorial Development in a Global Economy* Guildford, New York.

TUROK I. (2003) Cities, clusters and creative industries: the case of film and television in Scotland, *European Planning Studies* **11**, 549–565.

TUROK I. and BAILEY N. (2004a) The theory of polycentric urban regions and its application to Central Scotland, *European Planning Studies* **12**, 371–389.

TUROK I. and BAILEY N. (2004b) Twin track cities: competitiveness and cohesion in Glasgow and Edinburgh, *Progress in Planning* **63**, 135–204.

TUROK I. and EDGE N. (1999) *The Jobs Gap in Britain's Cities: Employment Loss and Labour Market Consequences.* Policy, Bristol.

TUROK I. and HOPKINS N. (1998) Competition and area selection in Scotland's new urban policy, *Urban Studies* **35**, 2021–2061.

UNITED NATIONS COMMISSION ON TRADE AND DEVELOPMENT (UNCTAD) (2002) *World Investment Report.* United Nations, Geneva.

WEBSTER D. (2000) Scottish social inclusion policy: a critical assessment, *Scottish Affairs* **30**, 30–50.

WIN P. (1995) The location of firms: an analysis of choice processes, in CHESHIRE P. and GORDON I. (Eds) *Territorial Competition in an Integrating Europe*, pp. 244–266. Avebury, Aldershot.

WREN C. (2003) UK regional policy: does it measure up? Mimeo. Department of Economics, University of Newcastle upon Tyne.

Globalization and Competitive Strategy in Europe's Vulnerable Regions: Firm, Industry and Country Effects in Labour-intensive Industries

GORDON L. CLARK★, THEO PALASKAS†, PAUL TRACEY‡ and MARIA TSAMPRA†

★School of Geography & the Environment and Said Business School, University of Oxford, Mansfield Road, Oxford OX1 3TB, UK. Email: gordon.clark@geog.ox.ac.uk

†Department of Economics & Regional Development, Panteion University of Athens, 136 Syngrou Avenue, GR-17671 Athens, Greece. Emails: thpal@panteion.gr, mtsam@geo.aegean.gr

‡Judge Institute of Management, University of Cambridge, Trumpington Street, Cambridge CB2 1AG, UK. Email: p.tracey@jims.cam.ac.uk

(Received November 2003: in revised form May 2004)

CLARK G. L., PALASKAS T., TRACEY P. and TSAMPRA M. (2004) Globalization and competitive strategy in Europe's vulnerable regions: firm, industry and country effects in labour-intensive industries, Regional Studies 38, 1077–1092. European integration has prompted great interest in the adjustment capacities of small and medium enterprises in regions characterized by high levels of unemployment and lower-than-average incomes. At issue, in these circumstances, is the extent to which economic competitiveness can be enhanced by technological change and the resources of European and national governments. Relying upon the results of a detailed survey of small- and medium-sized firm competitive strategies in selected vulnerable regions across Europe, the paper focuses upon firm adjustment strategies in four labour-intensive industries vulnerable to international competition. It draws together the results of these surveys providing econometric and statistical analyses that demonstrate the commonalities and differences apparent in small- and medium-sized firms' responses to changing market competition. Significant insights were gleaned from the pooling of these data. It is shown that there are statistically significant firm, country and industry effects in competitive strategies. Unlike many other related studies, the derived results are quite consistent across Europe. Furthermore, statistically significant relationships are established between changes in market sales, local employment and the adoption of process-specific technologies. The findings provide robust conclusions about the significance of country and industry determinants of European small and medium enterprises' competitive strategies in relation to the expanding European and global economy. In sum, the paper raises doubts about the value of regional development strategies that rely exclusively upon clusters and geographical embeddedness in the face of globalization.

Competitive strategy   Firm   Industry   Country effects

CLARK G. L., PALASKAS T., TRACEY P. et TSAMPRA M. (2004) La mondialisation et la stratégie compétitive dans les régions défavorisées d'Europe: les retombées sur l'entreprise, l'industrie et le pays des industries à forte main-d'oeuvre, Regional Studies 38, 1077–1092. L'intégration européenne a suscité un intérêt important à la capacité d'ajustement des petites et moyennes entreprises dans les régions qui se caractérisent par des niveaux de chômage élevés et par des niveaux de revenu qui sont inférieurs à la moyenne. Dans de telles circonstances, la question qui se pose est la suivante. Jusqu'à quel point peut-on améliorer la compétitivité économique au moyen de l'évolution technologique et à l'aide des ressources dont disposent l'administration européenne et nationale? Puisant dans les résultats provenant d'une enquête détaillée de la stratégie compétitive des PME situées dans certaines régions défavorisées à travers l'Europe, l'article porte sur les stratégies d'ajustement dans quatre industries à forte main-d'oeuvre qui sont exposées à la compétition internationale. A partir des résultats de ces enquêtes, on fournit des analyses économétriques et statistiques, qui démontrent les similarités et les différences qui proviennent des réponses des petites et moyennes entreprises à l'évolution du marché. La mise en commun de ces données a facilité l'obtention d'importants aperçus. On montre que les stratégies compétitives ont des retombées statistiquement importantes sur l'entreprise, le pays et l'industrie. A la différence d'autres études liées, les résultats se sont avérés relativement homogènes à travers l'Europe. D'autres rapports statistiquement plus importants ont été établis entre la variation des ventes, l'emploi local et l'adoption des technologies spécifiques aux procédés. Ces résultats fournissent de solides conclusions quant à l'importance des déterminants nationaux et industriels des stratégies compétitives des petites et moyennes entreprises européennes par rapport au développement des économies européenne et mondiale. En somme, on doute de la valeur des politiques d'aménagement du territoire qui dépendent exclusivement des regroupements et de l'ancrage géographique face à la mondialisation.

Stratégie compétitive   Entreprise   Industrie   Effets nationaux

CLARK G. L., PALASKAS T., TRACEY P. und TSAMPRA M. (2004) Globalisierung und Wettbewerbsstrategie in wirtschaftlich wehrlosen Regionen Europas: Firmen-, Industrie- und Ländereffekte in arbeitsintensiven Industrien, *Regional Studies* 38, 1077–1092. Die europäische Integration hat grosses Interesse an den Anpassungsfähigkeiten kleiner und mittelgroßer Unternehmen (small and medium enterprises – SMSs) in Regionen geweckt, die durch hohe Erwerbslosigkeit und unterdurchschnittlich niedrige Einkommen gekennzeichnet sind. Unter diesen Umständen erhebt sich die Frage, in welchem Ausmaß die wirtschaftliche Konkurrenzfähigkeit durch technologischen Wandel und die Mittel der europäischen und einzelner Länderregierungen aufgebessert werden kann. Unter Verlaß auf die Ergebnisse einer ins Einzelne gehenden Untersuchung von Wettbewerbsstrategien kleiner und mittelgrosser Unternehmen in ausgewählten, wirtschaftlich schwachen Regionen in ganz Europa konzentrieren die Autoren sich auf Anpassungsstrategien von Firmen in vier arbeitsintensiven Industrien, die als wehrlos gegenüber der internationalen Konkurrenz angesehen werden. Die Autoren betrachten die Ergebnisse dieser Untersuchungen im Zusammenhang, wobei ökonomische und statistische Analysen Gemeinsamkeiten und Unterschiede aufzeigen, die in Antworten kleiner und mittlerer Firmen auf die sich wandelnde Marktkonkurrenz erscheinen. Die Kombination dieser Daten gewährt wesentliche Einsichten. Es wird aufgezeigt, daß es statistisch signifikante Firmen-, Länder- und Industrieeffekte in Wettbewerbsstrategien gibt. Im Unterschied zu vielen anderen, verwandten Untersuchungen stimmten die gewonnenen Ergebnisse in ganz Europa überein. Darüberhinaus wurden statistisch signifikante Beziehungen zwischen Veränderungen bei Marktsabsatz, Erwerbstätigkeit am Orte und der Einführung verfahrensspezifischer Techniken festgestellt. Diese Befunde vermitteln überzeugende Schlüsse auf die Bedeutung der Länder– und Industriedeterminanten der Wettbewerbsstrategien der europäischen kleinen und mittelgrossen Unternehmen im Verhältnis zu der sich ausweitenden europäischen und globalen Wirtschaft. Zusammenfassend werden Zweifel am Werte der regionalen Entwicklungsstrategien laut, die sich angesichts der Globalisierung ausschließlich auf Cluster und geographisches Eingebettetsein verlassen.

Wettbewerbsstrategie   Firmen   Industrie- und Ländereffekte

CLARK G. L., PALASKAS T., TRACEY P. y TSAMPRA M. (2004) Globalización y estrategia competitiva en las regiones europeas más vulnerables: efectos empresariales, industriales y del país en la industrias de mano de obra intensiva, *Regional Studies* 38, 1077–1092. La integración europea ha despertado un gran interés en las capacidades de ajuste de las pequeñas y medianas empresas en regiones caracterizadas por altos niveles de desempleo e ingresos que están por debajo de la media europea. En tales circunstancias, una de las cuestiones es el grado hasta el cual se puede mejorar la competitividad económica por medio del cambio tecnológico y de los recursos de los gobiernos tanto europeos como nacionales. Contando con los resultados obtenidos de una encuesta detallada de las estrategias competitivas de las PIMEs en una serie de regiones vulnerables seleccionadas a través de Europa, nos centramos en las estragias de ajuste de las empresas en tres tipos de industrias de mano de obra intensiva vulnerables a la competición internacional. Reunimos los resultados de estas escuestas y ofrecemos análisis econométricos y estadísticos que demuestran las similitudes y diferencias que son aparentes en las respuestas de las pequeñas y medianas empresas con respecto a la cambiante competencia de mercado. Un número de percepciones nuevas se ha derivado de estos datos. Mostramos que existen efectos empresariales, industriales y del país significativos en las estrategias competitivas. A diferencia de muchos otros estudios similares, los resultados obtenidos eran bastante consistentes a través de Europa. Además, se establecieron otras relaciones estadísticas significativas entre los cambios en las ventas al mercado, el empleo local y la adopción de tecnologías específicas de proceso. Estos resultados ofrecen conclusiones robustas en lo que respecta a la significancia de los determinantes industriales y del país de las estrategias competitivas de las PIMEs europeas en relación a la economía global y europea en expansión. En resumen, planteamos una serie de dudas acerca del valor de las estrategias de desarrollo regional que dependen exclusivamente de clusters y de una incrustación geográfica ante la globalización.

Estrategia competitiva   Empressa   Efectos industriales y del país

JEL classifications: L10, O33, R11

INTRODUCTION

As the process of market integration reaches into the most remote corners of the European Union (EU) and beyond, it is increasingly apparent that long-term structural imbalances may be exacerbated by EU expansion and global competition (HUDSON, 2002). Not withstanding case studies of the successful 'exemplary regions' of the Third Italy and Baden-Wurttenburg, Germany, many of Europe's non-metropolitan regions are dominated by labour-intensive industries and high levels of unemployment beset by competition from within and without an enlarged Europe. In many cases, these firms are small family or community-based organizations with low levels of capitalization

and employment. Global competition has placed a premium on the adjustment potential of small- and medium-sized enterprises (SMEs) in these 'vulnerable regions', suggesting a rather bleak map of future European regional growth. Even so, those firms and their regions that can enhance labour productivity through the adoption of technology, innovation and product development may be the winners in global markets, just as those firms not so adept may simply contribute further to existing poor rates of local employment creation and out-migration (MARTIN, 2001).

The present paper looks closely at the adjustment capacity of these types of firms concentrating on SMEs in four labour-intensive industries located in vulnerable regions of Europe. Using EU Objectives 1 and 2[1] status designations, a set of similarly placed regions was identified for five countries including Greece, Italy, Ireland, Spain and the UK (GUERRIERI and IAMMARINO, 2002). As for the industries, these included apparel (18), leather and footwear products (19), electrical and electronic assembly (30–32), and automotive components (34). Based on the results of a large multi-country study of the competitive strategies of SMEs in such settings, a series of important policy-related questions was evaluated. For instance, holding the type of region constant, can consistent patterns of strategic adjustment be identified across countries and within or between industries? Most importantly, the data set allows us to test whether the adoption of labour productivity enhancing technology by SMEs facing heightened market competition has changed the demand for labour in the home region of the firm, and whether government policies have affected the adjustment potentials of such firms.[2]

At the outset, it should be recognized that this paper is less an exercise in the construction of theory and more a systematic analysis of a unique data set for policy-related purposes. Based upon a common questionnaire and survey methodology, a data set on SME competitive strategy has been created covering a range of topics including market conditions, employment, technology and investment. The data set is quite extensive, being designed to aid comparative statistical analysis. The construction of the data set is discussed below and in Appendix 1. At this point, it should be recognized that robust relationships between changing market conditions, the adoption of technology and employment were derived from the present analysis. Furthermore, and unlike many related studies, consistent results were established distinguishing between industry and country effects in driving firm competitive strategy across countries within industries (cf. HAWAWINI *et al.*, 2000). Even so, it was found that there remain significant firm-specific factors that drive labour productivity.[3]

The paper is organized as follows. First, it makes commonplace but necessary observations about the nature of EU regional economic structure. Here, contrasts are drawn between European and North American patterns and expectations. This is followed with the brief specification of a neo-Keynesian 'model' of the firm and its relationship to global commodity and local labour markets. The data set and empirical strategy are then described in detail before subsequent sections discuss the results and the implications of the econometric tests.

SMALL- AND MEDIUM-SIZED ENTERPRISES AND ECONOMIC PERFORMANCE

The paper begins by assuming that SME performance is very sensitive to market revenue and hence their market share. This is an immediate implication of recent theoretical work by GREENWALD and STIGLITZ (1995) and matches the present authors' intuitive understanding of the predicament faced by many of Europe's smallest firms. It could be also suggested that SMEs are more or less 'competitive' if they expand or maintain their sales in existing markets. Of course, there are more extensive definitions of competitiveness that would take into account firm's strategic goals in adding new markets and/or expanding the range of products produced so that their share of market demand may increase over time. By beginning with the firm, its market revenue and market share, it was also assumed that competitiveness is a characteristic of firms and the resources – including geography and history – at their disposal, and is the result of strategic choices made by their owners and managers.[4] It is not the wish of the authors to exaggerate or idealize the scope of firm-based strategic decision-making. If markets are highly competitive, firms' strategic options may be very limited; strategic choice and decision-making in this context may be simply an issue of internal flexibility and adjustment capacity in accordance with market signals (CLARK, 1994).

By focusing upon the firm and its strategic choices, the authors do not mean to ignore the context in which such issues are considered and resolved (CLARK and TRACEY, 2004). In point of fact, as many others would argue, the time and place of strategic decision-making may have significant implications for those options considered as relevant, those ignored and those ultimately taken. But as is known, whatever the local factors involved in decision-making, market scope and prospects have broadened enormously over the past 25 years working up the spatial scale from local to regional and national, and now to Europe and the world beyond. Indeed, just as 'local' firms have had opportunities to expand into markets that have taken them away from their local communities, so too have other firms located in faraway jurisdictions come to the commodity and consumer markets of the developed and developing worlds. Markets are increasingly open to rival producers whatever their location of production (CLARK *et al.*, 2000).

There remain, however, considerable tensions between where firms produce and the ultimate destination of their products. If, at some point in time in the past, the geographical scale of production matched the geographical scale of final markets, it could be argued that there was a symbiotic geographical relationship between the organization of the production process and the configuration of final consumer markets. The literature on regional economic growth assumes that this was once the case and goes on to show that the increasing spatial disjunction between the site of production and the geographical scope of markets has increased the premium placed upon the strategic capacity of those firms that have a distinctive and committed place of origin. While much of the literature focuses upon the mobility of capital in relation to the configuration of final demand, in Europe at least, one should be less sanguine about the prospects of firms relocating in relation to the imperatives of market competition given that in many industries SMEs are the dominant unit of production. In many cases, factor mobility is a less important option compared with designing and implementing changes to the organization of production and the technology of production itself (RICCI, 1999).

It must be recognized, however, that conventional models of regional economic growth begin with rather different assumptions. Being dominated by Anglo-American theoretical presumptions and a distinctive heritage of empirical research, much of the literature assumes high levels of factor mobility and ultimately spatial and economic convergence in measures of employment and welfare (BARRO and SALA-I-MARTIN, 1995). By implication, assumed are national markets and relatively low transaction costs both with respect to the distance to market and to the flow of commodities between firms within related chains of transactions that produce the products brought to market. Obviously, the exemplar case is the US economy. Just as obviously, those that advocate a single integrated European market have in mind an institutional configuration that would at least mimic the US case particularly in terms of enhancing the efficient allocation of capital if not labour between the regions of Europe (KRUEGER, 2000). If European firms are currently 'embedded' in their localities, in the end European integration may transform geographical constraints into extensive geographical and industrial opportunities (cf. ROTEMBERG and SALONER, 2000, who use non-negligible transport costs to help sustain, in theory, a differentiated economic landscape).

These theoretical and empirical expectations have been challenged in recent years by the new economic geography allied with KRUGMAN (1991), but shared with many economic geographers whatever their disciplinary heritage. If increasing returns to scale as opposed to constant returns to scale are introduced, then it is possible that individual firms may wish to concentrate their productive capacity while developing local networks of intensive linkages that in effect share between firms the benefits of increasing returns to scale. If it is assumed that 'learning by doing' characterizes many firms' experience in exploiting their inherited configuration of production, there may be considerable benefits in sticking with past investments while adopting new forms of technology that reinforce their knowledge base. Finally, if knowledge spills over between firms within an industry–region by virtue of the movement of labour between related firms, a firm's labour productivity may develop in accordance with its co-location with other firms. This is a theoretical rationale for linking the competitiveness of firms with

the attributes of industry–regions (COOKE and MORGAN, 1997).[5]

At the limit, firms' competitiveness may be thought dependent upon their location in region- and industry-specific regimes of accumulation. And it is possible that firms' competitive strategies are both enabled and limited by their region–industry setting. However, it should be observed that there are at least two countervailing forces that may undercut long-term region–industry-specific regimes of accumulation. As markets for products have extended beyond communities, regions and even nations, the attributes of products must be seen as increasingly exogenous to region–industry regimes of accumulation. Commodity markets may effectively discount the value of region–industries by homogenizing products, and perhaps even the means by which they are produced. A region–industry complex may control the definition of product quality as it may control the definition of product characteristics. In that case, it may dominate an industry. However, as the geographical scope of commodity markets broadens, there are increasingly more rival region–industry complexes that challenge this kind of hegemony. In any event, it is apparent that, within an industry, product characteristics and the means and methods of producing those products diffuse between jurisdictions over the long term (BREZIS et al., 1993).

With respect to firms' competitiveness, one should expect to find a variety of interaction effects including interaction between firms and regions, firms and industries, and even firms and country settings. These effects are the focus of the present country-specific case studies (CLARK et al., 2002). One should also expect to find distinctive scale effects: as the geographical scope of markets for labour-intensive industries has shifted from region to nation to Europe and the world, the industry affiliation of a firm as opposed to its country and region of origin could now be the dominant and driving force behind strategic choices with respect to competitive advantage. This is the topic of this paper.

MODEL OF THE FIRM (THEORETICAL EXPECTATIONS)

To sustain the present empirical analysis, one should establish an appropriate theoretical reference point. One way to do so would be to invoke a theory of the firm and economy based on real prices and perfect competition. As indicated above, however, there are many reasons to suppose that European product markets, capital markets and labour markets are subject to significant 'imperfections'. A more appropriate theoretical reference point with which to inform empirical analysis of current circumstances would be the literature grouped under the heading of the 'new Keynesian economics' (MANKIW and ROMER, 1991). Therein, due recognition is made of the structural imperfections of markets and institutions that sustain price rigidity, the immobility of capital and labour, and the incremental costs of adjustment. Whether 'perfect markets' are the most appropriate reference point for long-term welfare analysis in the European context is, of course, the subject of considerable intellectual and political debate.

Since much of the paper is devoted to the results of empirical analysis, it does not intend to derive a formal model of the firm based on first principles. However, it is the authors' wish to record their initial expectations about the most important variables, the expected relationships between those variables, and whether they should expect positive or negative signs on the estimated parameters. Also informing the authors' expectations is the work of GREENWALD and STIGLITZ (1995) and HART (1982), as well as the more recent work of DAVIS and WEINSTEIN (1999) on the disputed significance of economic geography for Europe and Organization for Economic Co-operation and Development countries. While there are some significant differences between these writers, especially as regards the status and importance of market efficiency, it is shown empirically that there remain important country and industry effects that dominate the adjustment capacity of European SMEs.[6] The paper will first consider the competitive domain of its firms.

The unit of analysis is SMEs. While the definition of SMEs is a topic of considerable academic research, it is apparent from the present data that many are very small (with less than ten employees). Given their significance as employers for many European countries (especially Greece, Italy and Spain), the competitive strategies of these types of firms have enormous implications for the long-term growth potential of Europe as a whole. In the present study, of course, these firms operate in labour-intensive industries subject to European and global competition. As such, these firms are assumed to adjust to market signals such as the industry price of a commodity and the volume or quantity demanded of such a product demanded by consumers (whether other businesses or final consumers). For these firms, market prices and the quantities demanded may be quite volatile and subject to considerable uncertainty from year to year. Entry into domestic and European industry markets by 'external' producers (notably from South Asia and the Far East) is assumed to be an ever-present threat and reality. In this respect, while market competition may not be 'perfect', it is amongst firms and potential rivals of which none can effectively 'manage' prices and quantities.

On the input side of the equation, the SMEs in this study are assumed to face short-term fixed prices for labour and most inputs to the production process. If market demand rises over time with either constant or increasing real prices, then it could be argued that the inherited configuration of production is probably irrelevant to firms' competitive strategies. The issue

here is the extent to which the principals of firms wish to take advantage of market demand by increasing the volume of output. But this depends upon what assumption is made about the objective function of such firms. Do they maximize sales, profits or some other related measured variable that represents their utility? Or do they seek to protect the flow of income over time and the cash-out value of the firm (wealth) in conditions of market uncertainty? To discriminate between these rival behavioural propositions would require fine-tuned experimental psychology, which is not the topic of the present study. At this juncture, it is sufficient to note that it is assumed that firms seek to maximize sales to achieve their other objectives, namely improved operational efficiency and profit (BAUMOL, 1959). By sales maximization, the present paper does not mean the number of physical units sold, but rather the total revenue achieved by the firm through transactions with customers. As a management objective, sales are more observable and, on one level, easier to manipulate than profits (AMIHUD and KAMIN, 1979; VICKERS, 1985). As Baumol notes, the result is that sales and market share become crucial reference points for firms' strategic decision-making. This is consistent with the position, outlined above, that the performance of SMEs is closely related to their market revenue.

Whereas the 'new economic geography' invokes scale economies as an incentive rewarding the growth of a firm and related networks of local firms, there are reasonable doubts about the existence of increasing returns to scale amongst SMEs. Following BLANCHARD and KIYOTAKI (1987), a more plausible assumption would be to assume constant elasticity of substitution where output is a linear function of inputs of labour and capital (the embedded capital stock and technology of production). By this logic, increasing demand is met in the first instance by increasing output through a fixed combination of labour and capital. Similarly, any decrease in demand (declining sales) is matched by a proportionate decrease in the use of the given inputs to production. In many circumstances, the embedded capital stock (and related technology of production) is rudimentary at best. Declining demand is met, in these circumstances, by decreased hours of labour and decreasing use of capital. Herein, it is assumed that quantity adjustments (rather than price adjustments) dominate SMEs' responses to changing demand.

The present paper is also concerned with the issue of technological adjustment – going beyond immediate capacity adjustment to changing market demand, to longer-term responses that may include changing the inherited configuration of production. The following assumptions are made. First, the adoption of new technology is a function of investment, which is itself a function of the capacity of firms to finance that investment. Given that SMEs are almost always under-capitalized, subsidized sources of finance may be thought an important enabling condition for invest-ment. Second, it is also assumed that the choice of technology is determined by both the expected demand for products differentiated by quality and price, and the rule that firms maximize total revenues and minimize costs. In the end, the choice of technology is one determinant of labour productivity (there being other, perhaps more important, determinants of labour productivity including the implementation and organ-ization of that technology in real production processes; GERTLER, 2001). Third, it is assumed that the adoption of technology has significant implications for the com-position and volume of labour used in the production process. Again, it is assumed that quantity adjustment dominates price adjustment in this case (the embodied skills of labour).

As the nature of the embedded capital and technol-ogy of production changes, one might expect to see firms consider the advantages and disadvantages of increasing output in relation to expected demand. In effect, the issue here is one of firm size and commit-ment to growth. These are not issues of great signifi-cance for this paper. But one would suggest that growth in firm size is not necessarily desired by the owners of SMEs if they are owner–managers and entrepreneurs. In this respect, there may be a significant difference between the value of cash flow (and all that entails for building a firm) and profit (and all that entails for personal and family wealth as reflected in property and consumption). In this respect, the adoption of technology may be as much a defensive competitive strategy designed to protect market share and retain expected profits as it is an expansionary competitive strategy designed to capture market share and thereby enable growth in employment and income. In other words, all things being equal, the adoption of technol-ogy could be associated with increasing or decreasing sales.

DATA AND EMPIRICAL METHODOLOGY

As noted above, this paper relies upon a unique data set developed in collaboration with partners across the EU. The data set was produced through the design and execution of a survey of SMEs in four labour-intensive industries located in vulnerable regions of Europe. Using common questions, a well-defined survey methodology and an agreed coding system, the data set allows for the pooling of data by question across industries and regions. The results of econometric and statistical tests reported below rely upon this pooled data set recognizing that country-specific case studies take advantage of the insights generated by the survey not easily captured in a strictly quantitative approach to the topic. Here, the paper focuses upon quantitative

insights and the arguments generated by the pooled data set are augmented, in conclusion, with relevant insights from the case studies.

Given the significance of understanding competitive strategy across the EU in labour-intensive industries and vulnerable regions, the paper sets out to collect data that was robust enough for comparative econo-metric and statistical analysis. Here, the authors' wish is to summarize the steps taken in this process so as to indicate both the strengths and weaknesses of the derived data (see also Appendix 1).

The first step involved defining 'vulnerable' regions beginning with three criteria: Objective 1 status, a non-metropolitan location (being outside of large centres of urban economic development), and with labour-intensive firms and industries. In the Italian case, the authors' colleagues developed a statistical method for the classification of regions using a wide range of indicators of economic well-being including income and employment opportunities (GUERRIERI and IAMMARINO, 2002). At this point in the procedure, it was ensured that the identification of regions contained enough commonality across countries to make for meaningful comparison and pooling of data. For the precise definition of the regions by country, see the present authors' report on this phase of the project (CLARK et al., 2002).

The second step involved establishing trends of employment, unemployment and incomes by industry and region, paying particular attention to the numbers and sizes of firms in the identified four labour-intensive industries. Those industries, as noted above, included footwear and leather products, apparel, electrical and electronic equipment, and automobile component parts. An assessment was made at this point about the competitive place of these industries in Europe and in the global economy. These industries are significant employers across Europe, and are especially sensitive to market competition accompanying global economic integration.[7]

The third step was to design an appropriate question-naire, linking the firm and its ownership structure to a set of crucial issues having to do with competitive strategy, market conditions, employment, investment and technological change, and government policy. The initial questionnaire was designed to be a scaled attitu-dinal survey instrument built upon overlapping ques-tions allowing for cross-tabular representation of the results. It was based, in part, upon a similar type of survey of Asian SMEs reported by CLARK and KIM (1995). Having developed the questionnaire, it was then tested in a number of countries and the relevant regions. It was found to be too long, too complicated and too demanding in terms of the distinctions of judgement asked of the respondents. The questionnaire was then redesigned so as to identify actions taken as opposed to attitudes while deleting extraneous ques-tions (see Appendix 1).[8]

The fourth step was to implement the questionnaire in each country, region and industry over 6 months (during the first half of 2001). Note that respondents were asked to consider their competitive strategies, market conditions and responses over the past 3–5 years. In many cases, the surveys were executed through on-site interviews with the most relevant firm representative (in many cases being the principal and managing director of the firm). In almost all cases, at least 20 completed responses were produced for each region–industry, being in combination a data set of over 331 completed and consistent questionnaire responses covering more than 25 specific questions regarding European SME industry competitive strategy in the global economy.[9]

The fifth step was to analyse the coded responses. The data set was compiled, cleaned of missing data and ambiguities in response, and then set in a database consistent with facilitating comparative econometric and statistical analysis. In the main, it was found that there were surprising commonalities amongst SMEs in each industry across regions and countries of the EU. At the same time, note that exceptions had to be made to the general rules driving the design and collection of the data. For example, in the UK, the region reference had to be shifted from an Objective 1 to an Objective 2 status region because in the former (Liverpool and surrounding areas), there were simply insufficient firms of an appropriate size in the relevant industries to survey. Similarly, in Ireland, for different reasons in one particular industry there were also insufficient firms to survey. While in Spain, adjustment had to be made between the industries in terms of the proportional share of the industry interviews.

Having developed the database, having ensured its integrity, and having assessed its compatibility within and between regions, within and between industries, and across Europe, the next step was to undertake an analysis of the relationships between competitive strategy, employment, investment and technological change. These tests are reported below.

ECONOMETRIC AND STATISTICAL RESULTS

The results of the various econometric and statistical analyses performed using the entire database of 331 completed survey questionnaires are reported. The results are dependent, of course, upon the integrity of the survey instrument and the collection of the data in each country and the related regions. Where possible, it was ensured that the data-collection process used common protocols and procedures (as described in the Appendix). Given the sparseness of data in some individual country/industry sets (e.g. leather products in Ireland and Italy), care must be taken in assessing the significance of the results.

Analysis of the whole model

To begin, the complete model linking firm decision-making with variables such as changes in sales and employment, as well as the relationships between sales, investment and technological change is analysed. These relationships are clearly highly aggregated, being brought together across the total data set. Even so, knowledge of the robustness of these expected relationships is important in coming to grips with the significance of the subsequent observations. At this point, of most concern were the statistical significance, parameter estimates and overall goodness of fit of the expected relationships. To summarize, the model estimated was as follows:

$$SAL_{fs} = a_{11} + a_{12}\hat{INV}_{fs} + a_{13}XLRM_{fs} + a_{14}XEUM_{fs} + u_{11} \tag{1}$$

$$INV_{fs} = a_{21} + a_{22}\hat{SAL}_{fs} + a_{23}EUPNT_{fs} + a_{24}EUPRT_{fs} + a_{25}LOQP_{fs} + u_{21} \tag{2}$$

$$TECH_{fs} = a_{31} + a_{32}\hat{INV}_{fs} + a_{33}CACF_{fs} + u_{31} \tag{3}$$

$$EMPL_{fs} = a_{41} + a_{42}\hat{SAL}_{fs} + a_{43}L\hat{BSK}_{fs} + a_{44}TE\hat{CH}_{fs} + u_{41} \tag{4}$$

$$LBSK_{fs} = a_{51} + a_{52}E\hat{MPL}_{fs} + a_{53}ATPR_{fs} + a_{54}TE\hat{CH}_{fs} + u_{51} \tag{5}$$

where SAL is sales and $\hat{SAL}$ is identified by exogenous elements, INV is investment and $\hat{INV}$ is identified by exogenous elements, XLRM is exports to local/regional markets, XEUM is exports to EU markets, EUPNT is EU programmes for new technologies, EUPRT is EU programmes for retraining, LOQP is a lack of qualified personnel, TECH is adopted technologies and $TE\hat{CH}$ is identified by exogenous elements, CACF is cost/access to finance (factors inhibiting the adoption of technologies), EMPL is employment and $E\hat{MPL}$ is identified by exogenous elements, LBSK is the need for adequately skilled employees and $L\hat{BSK}$ is identified by exogenous elements, ATPT is the adopted production process technologies, and where f is the interviewed firm in sector s.[10]

In most cross-section econometric models, the most common estimation approach has been the specification of single-equation models to identify and estimate the impact of predetermined variables on endogenous elements. However, the economic relationships of the present model (involving SAL, INV, TECH, EMPL and LBSKL) are interrelated because they are needed for determining the value of the endogenous variables included in the model. Therefore, the present model is a system of simultaneous equations since the adoption of the single-equation method of estimation would lead to biased estimators. This arises because the reduced form of the present specified model shows explicitly that the endogenous variables SAL, INV, TECH, EMPL and LBSK are jointly dependent upon the predetermined variables XLRM,

Table 1. Summary of results for the estimated relationships regarding firm-specific adjustment (sales, investment, technological change, employment and labour force composition) using the total database (331 complete sets of observations)

Dependent variable	Explanatory variables					$F_{statistic}$	Degrees of freedom	$\hat{R}^2$
SAL	Constant	IN̂V	XLRM	XEUM				
	2.338 (12.372)	0.148 (2.590)	0.122 (2.104)	0.137 (2.354)		5.633	292	0.234
INV		SÂL	EUPNT	EUPRT	LOQP			
	2.052 (7.179)	0.155 (2.748)	0.135 (2.274)	0.110 (1.862)	−0.185 (3.279)	7.847	291	0.312
TECH		IN̂V	CACF					
	2.635 (12.542)	0.146 (2.414)	−0.138 (2.215)			4.794	250	0.192
EMPL		SÂL	LB̂SK					
	2.326 (9.368)	0.157 (2.860)	0.203 (3.702)			9.761	318	0.240
LBSK		EMP̂L	ATPR					
	2.595 (12.153)	0.175 (2.903)	0.393 (2.579)			8.953	318	0.294

Notes: *t*-statistics are in parentheses below the estimated values of the parameters.
For an explanation of variables, see the text.

XEUM, EUPNT, EUPRT, LOQP, CACF and ATPR, and the disturbance terms u_{11}, u_{21}, u_{31}, u_{41} and u_{51} of the system. The model was estimated using the two-stage least-squares method (perhaps the best-known single-equation method that can be used; cf. HART-MANN and MASTEN, 2000). The estimates are, in general, given as non-linear functions of the reduced form estimates and inherit all their asymptotic properties. The results are shown in Table 1.

With respect to these results, four observations can be made. First, the signs of the estimated parameters linking, for example, sales, employment and labour composition were as expected (in a neo-Keynesian sense). This is an important finding since it helps one appreciate the significance of commonalities amongst the data and the logic by which the analysis was approached. Second, it is clear that both local and European markets are important driving forces behind firms' changing competitiveness: the European market 'effect' is more important than the local market 'effect'. Market integration and industry competition are a significant issue behind European SME competitive strategy. Third, with respect to the adoption of process technologies designed to enhance SME competitiveness, Table 1 demonstrates the expected relationship between technology and investment (positive) and a most important relationship between technology adoption and the cost of finance (negative), as well as the (positive) relationship between investment and EU programmes designed to enhance access to new technologies and labour skills. Finally, as expected, there is a strong (positive) relationship between technological change and the skill composition of employed labour. While the coefficients of determination are modest, these tests of significance are robust.

The authors were, of course, concerned to test for 'problems' or significant discontinuities in the data, particularly given the apparent differences between the country studies. Two different tests of the coherence of the database were conducted. In the first instance, tests were undertaken on the stability of the estimated parameters from the econometric model. For methodological completeness, the geometric properties, i.e. the mean and variance of the variables used in the econometric estimations and analysis, are presented in Table 2. The variance shows the distribution of the responses around the mean and indicates whether the responses are normally distributed. The mean is calculated for two types of variables. The first type (Table 2a) includes variables derived from responses on the scale 1–5, where 1 = decreased greatly and 5 = increased greatly. The second type are dichotomous variables (Table 2b) with 1 = Yes and 0 = No. Note that variable TECH does not appear among the explanatory variables of the estimated equations (4) and (5) of Table 2; it was

Table 2. Summary of the means and variances of the variables used in the econometric model (as estimated using the entire RASTEI countries and industries database)

Variable	Mean	Variance
2a. Variables where the responses were on the scale 1–5 (where 1 = decreased greatly, 2 = decreased, 3 = remained the same, 4 = increased and 5 = increased greatly)		
SAL	3.11	1.69
INV	2.67	3.32
EMPL	3.38	1.38
TECH	2.76	3.04
LBSK	3.31	1.64
2b. Variables where the responses were 1 = yes and 0 = no		
XLRM	0.59	0.24
XLEU	0.63	0.23
EUPNT	0.17	0.14
EUPRT	0.13	0.12
LOQP	0.32	0.22
CACF	0.46	0.25
ATPR	0.32	0.22

Note: For an explanation of variables, see the text.

omitted because of collinearity with SAL in equation (4) and with ATPR in equation (5).

It was also sought to test whether the exclusion of a country would significantly change the derived econometric and results of the analysis of variance (ANOVA). Using Spain as a test case, the analyses were run with and without this country's survey data. While there were minor differences in the estimated parameter values, there were no instances of changed statistical significance, nor were there any instances of changed signs on the estimated parameters. Further more, with respect to the ANOVA analyses reported below, the exclusion of the Spanish data would not have altered the statistical results significantly. As a result, the authors are confident that the statistical results are robust.

Analysis of variance (ANOVA)

The aim of the ANOVA was to examine whether or not the adjustment capacity of the examined firms – specifically investment in technology and its consequences for competitiveness and employment – differed statistically significantly across the industries and countries in question. The s variance was considered to be the industry/sector, and f was considered to be the interviewed firm located in region r of country h. It was assumed that r was identical with h (although this is not strictly true for Greece).[11] The s variance is described by WA for wearing apparel (18), LP for leather products and footwear (19), EL for electronics (30–32) and TE for transport equipment manufacturing (34). The h variance is described by GR for Greece, EN for England, IT for Italy, SP for Spain and IR for Ireland.

More specifically, given the research objectives, the statistical analysis examines whether and to what extent: (1) the behaviour of the f firms across the h=GR, EN, IT, SP and IR countries differed statistically (H_0 hypothesis: do not differ), independently of the s=WA, LP, EL and TE industries. The s is the basis here for the classification of the f into h subsamples; and (2) the behaviour of the f firms across the s=WA, LP, EL and TE industries differed statistically (H_0 hypothesis: they do not differ), independently of the r=1, 2, 3, ... vulnerable regions, and the h=GR, EN, IT, SP and IR countries. The h is the basis here for the classification of the f into s subsamples. ANOVA is equivalent to the estimation of the $F^\star$ distribution with $v_1=m-1$ and $v_2=N-m$ degrees of freedom given by:

$$F^\star = \frac{\left[\sum_{j=1}^{m} n_j(\bar{Y}_j - \bar{Y})^2\right]\bigg/(m-1)}{\left[\sum_{j=1}^{m}\sum_{i=1}^{nj}(Y_{ji} - \bar{Y}_j)^2\right]\bigg/(N-m)} \qquad (6)$$

where n_i is the size of the jth sample, $N = \Sigma_{j=1}^{m} n_i$ is the size of the 'pooled' (enlarged) sample and m is the number of samples.

The H_0 hypothesis holds at a 95% level of significance as long as the estimated $F^\star$ statistic is smaller than the theoretical specific level of significance given by the degrees of freedom. If the variables s and h that are the basis for the classification of the f's into h and s subsamples, respectively, are important causes of variation in f's behaviour, performance, etc., then the differences among the means of the subsamples will be large: this will be shown by a large dispersion of the means of the subsamples $Y_{f\,s}$ around a common mean $\bar{Y}$, that is by a large variance of the distribution. On the contrary, if h or s is not an important source of variation of the s and h subsamples, respectively, then the differences among the means of the subsamples will be small.

The ANOVA results are summarized in Table 3. The F-statistic and the level of significance for accepting the null hypothesis (H_0) are presented with respect to (i) the mean of the 17 variables across four sectors within the same country do not differ statistically (Table 3, a); and (ii) the mean of the variables across five countries within the same sector do not differ statistically (Table 3, b). More detailed statistical results are available from the authors.[12]

First, the variation in source of employees (variable 1) of the firms is examined for the industries and countries in question. Any identified differences would suggest diversity in the role of firms within the local/regional labour markets. Hypothesis (ii) is examined across the five countries in question, and the test results support the proposition that firms in the sample sectors across the different countries use similar sources of employees, with the exception of leather and footwear products. When hypothesis (i) is examined, the results indicate that the sources of employees across industries do not differ for any of the countries.

The competitive strategy of firms was examined based on change in sales (variable 13) and response to change in sales (variable 3). In other words, whether increases or decreases in sales over the last 3 years are associated with the firm's response by changing production capacity, expanding into new markets, developing products, outsourcing, forming partnerships and acquisitions. Hypothesis (i) is tested first, and the results strongly support the proposition that the change in sales of firms in England, Italy and Ireland over the last 3 years was similar across industries, but different in Greece and Spain. The most important response of firms to the change of sales across the examined industries was similar in Greece, Italy and England, but differed in Spain and Ireland. In other words, the competitive response of firms to changing sales is, in general terms, both country and industry determined.

Tests for hypothesis (ii) suggest that firms in three of the four industries had significantly different sales patterns across the examined countries. In other words,

Regional Competitiveness

Table 3. F-*statistic results of analysis of variance*

Question/variable	3a. F-statistic results testing H_0: (i) Mean of the variables across four sectors within the same country do not differ statistically					3b. F-statistic results testing H_0: (ii) Mean of the variables across five countries within the same sector do not differ statistically			
	Greece	England	Italy	Spain	Ireland	Wearing apparel	Leather and footwear	Electrical and electronic assembly	Automotive components
1. Source of employees	1.887	0.243	0.882	0.823	0.631	0.592	2.453★	0.881	0.107
2. Sales	0.572	5.750★★	1.275	1.061	1.634	5.941★★	1.797	0.881	0.107
3. Response to change in sales	1.452	0.668	1.404	2.758★	2.515★	2.850★★	1.022	0.765	1.555
4. Investment strategies	4.803★★	0.472	0.476	3.287★★	0.957	9.375★★	0.418	1.380	2.085
5. Investment sources	1.101	2.004	1.264	3.462★★	3.741★	2.672★★	4.330★★	2.432★	2.341★
6. Effect on labour	0.248	0.478	0.765	5.369★★	0.312	2.430★	1.153	0.280	3.053★★
7. Desired results of investment	1.316	1.874	1.977	0.420	1.019	2.568★★	1.226	2.873★★	1.330
8. Technologies adopted	2.959★★	2.080	2.791★	2.839★★	0.531	3.359★★	4.567★★	1.373	1.503
9. Sources of technological knowledge	0.448	8.835★★	0.710	0.249	—	2.570★★	0.986	2.266	0.691
10. Ways upgrading skills	0.530	3.460★★	0.567	0.848	0.542	1.973	0.398	1.286	2.507★
11. Development programs	0.935	8.002★★	0.254	1.594	0.240	1.466	0.065	1.511	2.967★★
12. Factors inhibiting technology adoption	2.207	1.830	0.484	0.640	0.746	0.823	0.857	0.172	1.131
13. Δ Sales	2.644★	1.766	0.183	2.728★	0.624	13.735★★	1.207	8.909★★	11.286★★
14. Δ Demand for skilled labour	7.809★★	2.849★★	2.229	6.720★★	0.434	25.627★★	1.208	28.908★★	9.472★★
15. Δ Total employment	5.740★★	2.608★	0.515	4.650★★	1.685	7.713★★	1.988	3.208★★	1.738
16. Δ Per unit labour costs	0.938	2.285	0.691	2.548★	1.916	9.198★★	0.595	0.618	2.279★
17. Δ Total labour costs	0.326	3.285★★	1.145	3.769★	1.356	0.476	1.481	1.891	2.929★★

Notes: Δ = Change in.

Levels of significance: ★★99%, ★95%; otherwise not significantly different from zero (level of significance).

the economic performance of firms appears strongly dependent upon the country from which they operate. The exception is the leather products industry, which appears to be independent from the business environment of each country in terms of sales. With respect to the most important response of firms to changes in sales, in three of four industries, similarity is sustained across countries. However, in the wearing apparel industry, the response of firms to changing sales differs among countries; in other words, the country context appears to be more influential for firms in this industry than for those in the other industries considered.

Next, the analysis focuses on the investment strategies (variable 4) of the firms, and more specifically on their most important investments either in new plants and equipment or in innovation and product development. The investment priorities of the firms are examined along with variable 5, their investment sources (internal, provided by banks, government or EU subsidy) and variable 6, their effects on labour (either displacement or change in demand for skilled/unskilled and part/full-time labour). Moreover, the desired results of investment (variable 7) are taken into account (increased productivity, increased market share, increased profit or increased technological sophistication).

The results for hypothesis (i) show that in three of five countries, the most important investment strategies adopted by the firms do not differ significantly across the examined industries. However, in Greece and Spain, investment decisions differ among the industries. In three of five countries, investment sources appear similar across industries. However, in Spain and Ireland, sources of investment seem to differ among industries. In four countries, the investment impact on the variable effect on labour has a similar pattern across industries. The exception is Spain, where investment implications on labour differ across industries. The most desired investment results do not differ across industries, in all countries.

Tests for hypothesis (ii) suggest that investment strategies are similar in three of four industries across countries, the exception being wearing apparel, where investment choices depend upon the business context; in other words, the place that regional agglomerations hold in the international network of this industry determines their investment strategies. The hypothesis that investment sources are similar in the examined industries across countries is very weak. Investment implications on variable 6, effect on labour, are similar in the leather product and electronic assembly industries across countries, but in the automotive components and wearing apparel industries there are differences between the various contexts. Finally, the results of the most desired investment outcome are mixed: similarity is found for the leather products and transport equipment manufacturing industries across countries, while differentiation is depicted for the wearing apparel and electronics industries among countries.

Having analysed the competitive and investment strategies of firms, the paper attempts to associate the results with the technologies adopted (variable 8) in specific firms. In other words, the analysis examines the most important technologies adopted by the firms in the last 3 years (in product development, inventory control, marketing and communication), and the most important sources of technological knowledge (variable 9) (internal personnel, suppliers and customers, institutional organizations). The test of hypothesis (i) suggests similarity across industries in the most important technologies adopted by firms in Ireland and England, but differences in Greece, Italy and Spain. The sources of technological knowledge are similar in three countries across industries (Greece, Italy, Spain), but in England differentiation is depicted among industries (no data are available for Ireland for this variable).

Tests for hypothesis (ii) suggest that in wearing apparel and leather products, the investment in technology differs across countries. In other words, it depends upon the business context. In the electronics and automotive components industries, investment in technology is less context determined and rather industry focused. With the exception of the wearing apparel industry, the sources of technological knowledge are similar in all industries, independently of the country context.

Next, the paper examines the impact of strategies adopted by firms (response to change in sales, investment, technology adoption) on labour, and more specifically upon: change in demand for skilled labour (variable 14), change in total employment (variable 15), change in per unit labour costs (variable 16) and change in total labour costs (variable 17). Provided that firms apply similar technology strategies (independently of industry and country), the effects of these strategies on labour are interesting. Starting with hypothesis (i), the results suggest that in three of five countries – Greece, England and Spain – the need for adequately skilled employees over the past 3 years differs significantly across industries. The pattern of total employment differs across industries in Greece, Spain and England. The labour cost per unit over the last 3 years evolves along a similar pattern across industries in four countries, the exception being Spain. Finally, total labour costs over the past 3 years differ at the 99% level of significance across industries for England and at the 95% level of significance for Spain, but are similar Greece, Italy and Ireland.

Tests for hypothesis (ii) indicate that the impact on the demand for skilled labour is significantly different across countries in the examined industries – with the exception of leather products. The pattern of change in total employment is similar across countries in leather products and automotive components, but differs for wearing apparel and electronic assembly. With regard to change in per unit labour cost, in wearing apparel and automotive components the pattern differs among countries, but is similar for leather products and electronic assembly. Change in total labour cost is similar across different countries and contexts in all industries apart from automotive components.

The final issue concerns policy implications. Here the paper examined variable ways of upgrading skills (in-firm training or institutionally provided), variable development programmes (loan and credit facilities, tax credits and labour-cost subsidies, or R&D and training grants) and variable factors inhibiting technology adoption (uncertain benefits, cost/access to finance, lack of information, size of market, lack of skilled labour, the desire for a manageable firm size). The results for hypothesis (i) suggest that, in general, the impact of the policy and institutional context on SMEs in the examined countries is similar across industries, with the exception of England, where the ways that firms upgrade skills and use development programmes differ among industries.

The results for hypothesis (ii) indicate that policy measures and institutions affect firms similarly across all countries in the examined industries. The exception is the automotive components industry, where the most important development programmes used by firms in the past 3 years are different.

Summary of the ANOVA results

In an attempt to systemize the results of the statistical analysis of the research data, according to the research hypotheses, the following are concluded:

- Firm economic performance is country defined.
- Investment strategies are defined by the role/place of country-based networks in a world of integrated networks of production.
- Technology adoption and the sources of technological knowledge are country defined; but in less traditional firms, they are industry led.
- Change in a firm's total labour costs is industry determined.
- Total employment of the firm is industry determined.
- Demand for skilled labour is both country defined and industry led.
- Investment impact on firms' workforces is both country and industry led.
- Policy and institutional impacts are country defined and industry determined.
- Competitive strategy is neither country defined nor industry determined; firm-specific factors dominate.
- Labour cost per unit change is neither country defined nor industry determined; firm-specific factors dominate.

CONCLUSIONS

For many years, the economic map of Europe has been characterized by regions of long-term unemployment and concentrated centres of economic growth and employment. A vast array of regional development policies has been used to ameliorate persistent high levels of unemployment, from state aid to a systematic concern with the competitiveness of firms and regions. As European and global integration gathers pace, the economic performance of 'vulnerable' regions and industries in the EU has become more important than before. Many communities and the whole EU have a large stake in the adjustment potential of firms to the swirling winds of market competition. Furthermore, in those non-metropolitan regions dominated by labour-intensive industries, the competitiveness of local SMEs in the global economy has enormous implications for the long-term growth trajectories of those regions.

Competitiveness is commonly thought synonymous with clusters of innovation. Whether associated with the work of PORTER (1990) or the more subtle approaches championed by FELDMAN (2000) and STORPER (2000), amongst others, competitiveness is believed to be a process of enhanced labour productivity through endogenous technological change organized via local networks of information and exchange. While sympathetic to that approach, the present paper has also focused upon the adjustment strategies of SMEs to changes in market demand. The goal was to establish the principal causal factors behind firm-based competitive strategy while making an explicit connection between the local employment consequences of technology-related adjustment strategies. This approach is consistent with a long tradition in economics and in geography, linking the prospects of regions to the adjustment potential of local firms in the face of market competition regionally, nationally and internationally.

By convention, studies of market-related adjustment potential distinguish between the size of the firm, the nature of firm ownership, regional identity, industry identity and even country identity. For instance, it is often contended that a small firm within a distinctive industry and regional milieu has a quite different adjustment capacity to similarly sized firms in different industry and regional settings. Similarly, larger firms are presumed to have a rather different adjustment potential than smaller firms even within the same industry and regional setting. By this logic, 'identity' may be both the objective of analysis and in various ways a means of explaining observed variation in adjustment potential. The present study has attempted to hold constant the size of the firm, the nature of the region and industry affiliation. It has been found, however, that there are significant variations in firms' responses to global competition that can be attributed to the country and the industry of origin.

Remarkably, the paper derived robust econometric relationships of the expected sign between employment and output, between output and investment, between investment and technological change, and between technological change and employment composition. These econometric results across the entire data set are encouraging given the fact that much of the related literature cannot establish such systematic effects (HAWAWINI *et al.*, 2000). The results are not surprising if one takes as a reference point economic theory and certain conventions regarding the nature and structure of firm decision-making in the context of global market competition. But the results are surprising at another level: given the logistics involved in sustaining a comprehensive and coherent fieldwork-based study across five countries, the strength of the derived relationships indicates just how important market competition has become for labour-intensive industries in the context of European and global economic integration.

Having established a robust econometric framework, the paper looked more closely at the significance or otherwise of industry and country effects across a range of issues including competitive strategy and employment composition. Here, a mix of effects and implications were found. For instance, industry effects seem to drive changes in firms' labour costs, whereas investment strategies and the adoption of production technology appear driven by the country setting of the firm. At the same time, there are a number of issues that appear driven by a mixture of country and industry location. For example, the impact of investment on a firm's composition of labour is driven by both factors just as the demand for skilled labour is driven by industry and country effects. These are important results, bearing upon the efficacy of country- and industry-specific occupational and training systems. Even so, whatever the significance of these macro-factors, there remain vital firm and region-specific factors that appear to drive competitive strategy and labour productivity (as might be expected; witness the reports of country-based colleagues given in CLARK *et al.*, 2002, and the arguments of GERTLER, 2001, STORPER and SALAIS, 1997, and others).

Based upon a common questionnaire and survey methodology, well-defined questions focused on the actions taken over the past 3–5 years were used to determine what drives SME decision-making. The survey instrument has been described above and in Appendix 1. What is notable about the survey instrument is that 'vulnerable' regions from very different national circumstances were included – from the Celtic Tiger (Ireland) to Greece. A most important finding from the econometric results was that government policy can make a positive difference to SME market adjustment potential. The derived relationships were empirically robust and indicate that, as might be theoretically expect, SMEs rarely have the internal resources necessary to go it alone in European and global markets. This does not mean, of course, that government policy is a sufficient ingredient in determining 'successful' adjustment potential. But it does indicate that government policy has played an active and positive role in enhancing that capacity (cf. HARTMANN and MASTEN, 2000).

The results of the present study have significant implications for conceptualizing SME performance by region and industry across Europe, as well as implications for the role and status of government policy designed to enhance European and global competitiveness. Just as importantly, the results have implications for the long-term development of vulnerable regions in terms of the demand for labour (quality and quantity). There was a significant relationship between the adoption of new technology and changes in the skills mix of employed labour within local SMEs. That relationship may vary by industry, and there is no doubt that the adoption of new technology may have distinctive 'local' effects not captured by the econometric analysis (as suggested by GERTLER, 2001). Nevertheless, it is apparent that new production technologies increase the complement of skills required and decrease the per unit produced volume of labour. In this respect, as small firms in labour-intensive industries rise to the challenge posed by European and global competition, their role in regions characterized by high rates of unemployment and low relative income will further decline.

There is one further important implication: globalization and market competition create winners and losers. If the present econometric results hold for other labour-intensive industries across Europe, there may be more commonalities amongst 'losers' than might have been imagined based on domestic EU politics. As whole industries respond to global competition, the country–regional concentration of the negative effects of SME competitiveness may reinforce a political-cum-regional sense that integration itself is the driving force behind changing lifetime employment and income opportunities. The authors do not mean to suggest that European and global integration can in any sense be 'stopped' or held in abeyance for a generation. In fact, as other Central and Eastern European countries join the EU and as their labour-intensive industries become exposed to the forces of market competition, it might be imagined that this type of study will be more important than before.

Acknowledgements – The paper was made possible through a European Union FP5 research grant (RASTEI HPSE-1999-00035) and the continuing interest of the authors' European Union project managers Marshall Hsia and Nikolaos Kastrinos. The authors recognize the commitment of their colleagues from Ireland/France (Mary O'Sullivan and Manuela Giangrande), Italy (Paolo Guerrieri and Simona Iammarino), Spain (Pere Escorsa) and the UK (Helen Lawton Smith) to the project including their survey work and comments on a previous draft (at the Barcelona coordination meeting). Their work and that of their research teams made the paper possible. In addition, the authors acknowledge the research assistance on the development and analysis of the data set, including that of Jane Battersby and D. Boutzona. Finally, they thank the referees for comments and assistance.

APPENDIX 1: SURVEY INSTRUMENT

The structure of the questionnaire included the following dimensions specific to the project. In the first instance, the size of the firm (SME), its location (by vulnerable region) and its industry (labour intensive) were aspects of the survey held constant by virtue of the authors' prior agreement about the significance of those issues. The questionnaire began having identified the firm, its location and industry and had eight separate sections as summarized below:

1. Background: the questionnaire began with the responsibility of the respondent, as well as the size of the firm as indicated by sales and the number of employees. The opportunity was taken to ask questions concerning the gender make up of the firm's employees, the split between full- and part-time employment, and the geographical origin of employees.

2. Ownership: the questionnaire sought information about the formal ownership structure of the SME, recognizing that these types of organizations vary in form and in practice between jurisdictions and in relation to related firms. In theory and in practice, the authors began with the assumption that the nature of ownership and management matters a great deal in investment decision-making.

3. Supply and distribution links: it is widely recognized that SMEs are more often than not component parts of extended supply and distribution networks. The questionnaire sought to elicit information about the geographical and functional origin and destination of inputs to production and outputs of production.

4. Competitive strategies: recognizing the rapidly changing competitive circumstances of European industries, their regions and firms, questions were asked so as to understand better the pattern of total sales over the past 3 years as well as the nature of SME response to changes in total sales.

5. Investment strategies: information about investment strategies was needed on the nature of investment, the sources of funds used to finance investment, the effect of investment on employment and the desired results of investment for the firm.

6. Technology adoption: having established the competitive circumstances of the firm, as well as the investment strategies of SMEs, the next section linked explicitly to the adoption of technology (broadly defined). Much is made of technology in the economic development and regional development literature, while at the same time, there is a tendency to exaggerate the nature and sophistication of technology for SMEs. The questionnaire made allowance for the simplest types of technology, including communication technologies.

7. Labour and technological change: the effect of technological change on employment was explicitly

tackled. The goal was to elicit information on the demand for labour in terms of the quantity of labour, skill and productivity.

8. Policy and policy institutions: the connection was made between decisions taken and identified in previous sections and the relevance and usefulness of existing regional, national and EU policy instruments.

Reproduced below is the final version of a question asked about the origin of firm employees. As initially framed, respondents ranked options using a 5 (most important) to 1 (least important) and 9 (irrelevant) code. The revised question asked respondents about the likely actions they may have taken, while nevertheless asking for a judgement about the most significant source of firm's employees:

---

8. Which of the following sources of employees
does the firm use?   Yes   No
    (a) family members
    (b) local community
    (c) people from outside the region
    (d) joint venture partner
    (e) parent firm

9. Of the options selected (YES) for question 8, which is the most important?

NOTES

1. Objective 1 regions are EU regions with a Gross Domestic Product per head less than 75% of the Community average. More than two-thirds of the monies allocated by the EU to regional development is invested in Objective 1 regions. Objective 2 regions are EU regions with a Gross Domestic Product per head close to the Community average and which are experiencing 'structural difficulties', often the decline of industrial activity, leading to higher than average levels of unemployment (for a more detailed description of the EU regional policy context, see http://www.europa.eu.int/comm/regional_policy).

2. In sum, about 25 sets of questions and answers per respondent, about 20 respondents per industry and country. After ensuring the integrity of the derived data, the pooled database is comprised of 331 completed files with the balance of observations drawn from Greece, Ireland and the UK. The completed data files from Italy and Spain are significantly smaller in number (see below).

3. HAWAWINI *et al.* (2000) observed that many studies of firms' profitability find that firm-specific effects far outweigh industry effects. They looked closely at a large US data set covering about 1000 firms from three-digit SIC industries over nearly 20 years. By identifying key firms within these industry groups, they distinguished the effects of firm and industry effects with and without these firms. On balance, having excluded these types of firms from their sample, they identified a significant industry effect. The present paper does not make any such adjustments but finds, nevertheless, significant

country and industry effects behind firm-competitive strategies.

4. Competitiveness is a controversial issue in the social sciences. In part, this is because the very idea of competitiveness contradicts the tenets of neoclassical economics: 'in a world inhabited by "representative firms" operating under perfect information and with no scale effects ... the term competitiveness is meaningless' (REINART, 1995, pp. 26–27). While KRUGMAN (1993) believes that the term should be expunged from social science, PORTER (1990) claims that competitiveness can be thought as a proxy for labour productivity. In this regard, competitiveness is considered here to be about the capacity of firms, industries, regions and countries (being sites of production) to make profits in markets subject to international competition. Competitiveness is an important characteristic of places and industries in the global economy, a conceptual tool whereby one may understand the generation of uneven patterns of wealth and living standards across regions and nations.

5. There is an enormous literature devoted to region-specific case studies and the lessons to be drawn therein (STORPER and SALAIS, 1997). It is also an epistemological issue, being the basis of arguments in favour of capitalist diversity (CROUCH and STREECK, 1997; CROUCH *et al.*, 2001).

6. In their Introduction, MANKIW and ROMER (1991) emphasize research that helps explain how the existence of 'small' imperfections may accumulate into systemic barriers of price flexibility. The European context does not need such subtle theories and inferences; see the compelling arguments made by BLANCHARD and SUMMERS (1987) and KRUEGER (2000) regarding the institutional logic of European labour and product markets.

7. There are, of course, considerable practical issues involved in using common industry classifications across the EU. Most obviously, there may be significant differences within industries between countries and regions due to differences in the precise composition of each 'industry'. Clearly, leather and footwear products vary between Italy and Spain, for example. Even so, for all the apparent significance of such composition effects, their practical importance must be assessed against the derived results and the compromises one must make in any comparative study (on the inevitable qualifications that attach to industry studies, see HAWAWINI *et al.* 2000).

8. The design of the questionnaire was based on the following four principles of comparative studies and related fieldwork: *simplicity*, allowing for variations between jurisdictions and industries in terms of the assumed knowledge of the respondents; *standardization*, ensuring that the questionnaire was relevant to the firms, industries and regions of Europe while recognizing that its implementation in different settings is likely to bring forth complications that arise from different customs and traditions; *coherence*, beginning with the opening questions through to the final questions and adding important pieces of information in a sequence of questions that in combination contribute to the realisation of the project; and *parsimony*, being concerned to keep to a minimum the number of questions asked, not only to ensure that the questionnaires could be implemented

according to the available time for each respondent, but also according to the logic of the project.

9. Note that focus is on those firms that survived over the past 5 years. Missing, of course, are those firms that 'died' before implementation of the present study.

10. The variables SAL, EMPL, TECH and LBSK were scaled using a common structure of 1–5, where 1 is decreased greatly and 5 is increased greatly. The other variables were dichotomous variables set as $0 = NO$ and $1 = YES$ (for more details, see the Appendix).

11. The present paper uses country rather than regional affiliation as a means of distinguishing the relative effects of industry and geography on firm competitive strategy.

It is possible, of course, that the 'country effect' is a proxy for the region effect or even a firm-specific effect. Given the aggregation of the data and the nature of the econometric procedures, it is not possible to make a more sensitive analysis of these issues. Those are left for the case studies reported by CLARK *et al.* (2002).

12. The present paper, however, excludes from its analysis the results for firm ownership and the nature and extent of supply and distribution networks. Neither is directly relevant to the task, although they may contain certain useful insights. Discussion of these and other related issues are left for another time (CLARK *et al.* 2004).

REFERENCES

AMIHUD Y. and KAMIN J. (1979) Revenue and profit maximization: differences in behavior by the type of control and by market power, *Southern Economic Journal* **45**, 838–846.

BARRO R. and SALA-I-MARTIN X. (1995) *Economic Growth*. McGraw-Hill, New York.

BAUMOL W. J. (1959) *Business Behavior, Value and Growth*. Macmillan, New York.

BLANCHARD O. J. and SUMMERS L. H. (1987) Hysteresis in unemployment, *European Economic Review* **31**, 288–295.

BLANCHARD O. J. and KIYOTAKI N. (1987) Monopolistic competition and the effects of aggregate demand, *American Economic Review* **77**, 647–666.

BREZIS E. S., KRUGMAN P. and TSIDDON D. (1993) Leap-frogging in international competition: a theory of cycles in national technological leadership, *American Economic Review* **83**, 1211–1219.

CLARK G. L. (1994) Strategy and structure: the domain of competition and the characteristics of sunk costs, *Environment and Planning A*, **26**, 9–32.

CLARK G. L. and KIM W. B. (Eds) (1995) *Asian NIEs in the Global Economy*. Johns Hopkins University Press, Baltimore.

CLARK G. L. and TRACEY P. (2004) *Global Competitiveness and Innovation*. Palgrave Macmillan, Basingstoke.

CLARK G. L., FELDMAN M. and GERTLER M. S. (2000) Economic geography: transition and growth, in CLARK G. L., FELDMAN M. and GERTLER M. S. (Eds) *The Oxford Handbook of Economic Geography*, pp. 3–17. Oxford University Press, Oxford.

CLARK G. L., PALASKAS T., TRACEY P. and TSAMPRA M. (2004) Market revenue and the scope and scale of SME networks in Europe's vulnerable regions, *Environment and Planning A* **36**, 1305–1326.

CLARK G. L., TRACEY P. and LAWTON SMITH H. (2002) *RASTEI: Report to the European Union*. School of Geography and the Environment, University of Oxford, Oxford.

COOKE P. and MORGAN K. (1997) *The Associational Economy*. Oxford University Press, Oxford.

CROUCH C., LE GALES P., TRIGILIA C. and VOELZKOW H. (Eds) (2001) *Local Production Systems: Rise or Demise?* Oxford University Press, Oxford.

CROUCH C. and STREECK W. (Eds) (1997) *Political Economy of Modern Capitalism: Mapping Convergence and Diversity*. Sage, London.

DAVIS D. R. and WEINSTEIN D. E. (1999) Economic geography and regional production structure: an empirical investigation, *European Economic Review* **43**, 379–407.

FELDMAN M. (2000) Location and innovation: the new economic geography of innovation, spill-overs, and agglomeration, in CLARK G. L., FELDMAN M. and GERTLER M. S. (Eds) *The Oxford Handbook of Economic Geography*, pp. 373–394. Oxford University Press, Oxford.

GERTLER M. S. (2001) Best practice? Geography, learning and the institutional limits to strong convergence, *Journal of Economic Geography* **1**, 5–26.

GREENWALD B. and STIGLITZ J. (1995) Labour-market adjustment and the persistence of unemployment, *American Economic Review* **85**, 219–225.

GUERRIERI P. and IAMMARINO S. (2002) Vulnerability and regions in the European Union: an exercise on the Italian Mezzogiorno. Working Paper 02-17. School of Geography and the Environment, University of Oxford, Oxford.

HART O. (1982) A model of imperfect competition with Keynesian features, *Quarterly Journal of Economics* **97**, 109–138.

HARTMANN G. B. and MASTEN J. (2000) Profiles of state technology transfer and its impact on small manufacturers, *Journal of Technology Transfer* **25**, 83–88.

HAWAWINI G., SUBRAMANIAN V. and VERDIN P. (2000) Is profitability driven by industry- or firm-specific factors? A new look at the evidence. Working Paper 2000/80/FIN. INSEAD, Fontainbleau.

HUDSON R. (2002) Changing industrial production systems and regional development in the new Europe, *Transactions, Institute of British Geographers*, n.s., **27**, 262–281.

KRUEGER A. (2000) From Bismarck to main street: the march to European Union and the labour compact. Working Paper 7456. National Bureau of Economic Research, Cambridge, MA.

KRUGMAN P. (1991) *Geography and Trade*. MIT Press, Cambridge, MA.

KRUGMAN P. (1993) What do undergraduates need to know about trade?, *American Economic Review* **83**, 23–26.

MANKIW N. G. and ROMER D. (Eds) (1991) *New Keynesian Economics*. MIT Press, Cambridge, MA.

MARTIN R. (2001) EMU versus the regions? Regional convergence and divergence in Euroland, *Journal of Economic Geography* **1**, 51–80.

PORTER M. (1990) *The Competitive Advantages of Nations*. Macmillan, London.

REINART E. S. (1995) Competitiveness and its predecessors – a 500-year cross national perspective, *Structural Change and Economic Dynamics* **6**, 23–42.

RICCI L. A. (1999) Economic geography and comparative advantage: agglomeration versus specialization, *European Economic Review* **43**, 357–377.

ROTEMBERG J. J. and SALONER G. (2000) Competition and human capital accumulation: a theory of interregional specialization and trade, *Regional Science and Urban Economics* **30**, 373–404.

STORPER M. (2000) Globalization, localization, and trade, in CLARK G. L., FELDMAN M. and GERTLER M. S. (Eds) *The Oxford Handbook of Economic Geography*, pp. 146–167. Oxford University Press, Oxford.

STORPER M. and SALAIS R. (1997) *Worlds of Production*. Harvard University Press, Cambridge, MA.

VICKERS J. (1985) Deregulation and the theory of the firm, *Economic Journal* **95 (Suppl.)**, 138–147.

Jockeying for Position: What It Means and Why It Matters to Regional Development Policy When Places Compete

EDWARD J. MALECKI

Center for Urban and Regional Analysis and Department of Geography, Ohio State University, 154 North Oval Hall, Columbus, OH 43210-1361, USA. Email: malecki.4@osu.edu

(Received March 2003: in revised form July 2004)

MALECKI E. J. (2004) Jockeying for position: what it means and why it matters to regional development policy when places compete, *Regional Studies* **38**, 1093–1112. The realization that places compete for investment has expanded in recent years to encompass competition among places for the attention of migrants, tourists and media glow as well as investment. The most competitive places have been multidimensional in their attractions and have made the transition to the knowledge-based economy. The latest priority is being placed on attracting mobile workers and mobile investment. Creative workers are the core of the knowledge economy and of its geographies such as 'intelligent places' and 'learning regions'. Knowledge metrics, innovation indices and report cards are increasingly common, each seemingly developed to sort the list of places in a different order. Lists or league tables of 'the best places' for business, to live, retire and visit are key features of economies and societies whose factors of success are highly mobile. Competition in a geographical context and entrepreneurial responses are unlikely to go away, reinforced by an industry comprised of consultancies, the trade press, formal education and other means of learning. Consequently, policy-makers need to grasp the nature of place competition and the critical roles of knowledge and of networks in the strategies of the most competitive places. The standard of competition is complex, comprising innovation indices and cooperation within the network of world cities.

Competition   Regional development   Policy   Knowledge   World cities

MALECKI E. J. (2004) Lutter pour la première place: l'importance de la concurrence interville pour la politique d'aménagement du territoire, *Regional Studies* **38**, 1093–1112. Dans les années récentes, se rendre compte que les villes se font concurrence pour l'investissement s'est élargi pour englober la concurrence interville qui cherche à séduire les migrants, les touristes et les médias ainsi que l'investissement. L'attrait des villes les plus compétitives a été multidimensionnel, et elles se sont transformées en économies basées sur la connaissance. La dernière priorité c'est attirer les travailleurs mobiles ainsi que l'investissement mobile. Les travailleurs créatifs sont au coeur d'une économie basée sur la connaissance et de ses localisations, telles les 'villes intelligentes' et les 'régions d'apprentissage'. Il semble que la mesure de la connaissance, les indices de l'innovation, et les tableaux de bord sont employés de plus en plus afin de classer les villes. Un classement des 'meilleures villes' pour le commerce, la retraite, le tourisme constitue une caractéristique clé des économies et des sociétés dont les facteurs moteurs sont très mobiles. Il est peu probable que la concurrence sur le plan géographique et la réponse de la part des entrepreneurs s'atténuent, ce qui est renforcé par une industrie comportant des cabinets, une presse spécialisée, l'éducation et d'autres moyens d'apprendre. Par la suite, les décideurs devraient saisir la notion de concurrence interville et les rôles décisifs que jouent la connaissance et les réseaux dans les stratégies des villes les plus compétitives. Le niveau de la concurrence est complexe, comportant des indices de l'innovation et de la coopération au sein du réseau des grandes villes de taille mondiale.

Concurrence   Aménagement du territoire   Politique   Connaissance   Grandes villes de taille mondiale

MALECKI E. J. (2004) Bemühungen, sich gut zu plazieren: was es bedeutet, und warum es für die regionale Entwicklungspolitik wichtig ist, wenn Orte miteinander konkurrieren, *Regional Studies* **38**, 1093–1112. Die Erkenntnis, daß Orte um Investierungen kämpfen, hat sich in den letzten Jahren dahingehend ausgeweitet, daß der Wettbewerb unter Ortschaften sich nicht nur auf Investierungen, sondern auch auf die Aufmerksamkeit von Zuwanderern, Touristen und das Rampenlicht der Medien richtet. Die konkurrenzfähigsten Orte sind diejenigen, welche vielfältige Attraktionen anbieten und den Übergang zu einer auf Fachkenntnissen aufbauenden Wirtschaft geschafft haben. Der letzte Schrei in Vorrangstellung ist die Fähigkeit wanderungsfreudige Arbeitskräfte und freies Kapital anzuziehen. Schöpferische Arbeitskräfte bilden den Kern der auf Kenntnissen beruhenden Wirtschaft und ihrer geographischen Bezeichnungen wie 'Intelligenzorte' und 'dazulernende Regionen'. Immer häufiger stößt man auf Messungen des Standes der Fachkenntnisse, Innovationsindexe und Berichterstattungen, die alle anscheinend zum Zweck der Neueinordnung der Ortschaften in Ranglisten geschaffen werden. Listen oder Ligatabellen 'der besten Standorte' für Geschäfte, Wohnort, Ruhestand und Ausflüge sind Hauptmerkmale der Wirtschaften und Gesellschaften, deren zu Erfolg führende Faktoren sich durch hohe Beweglichkeit auszeichnen. Wettbewerb in einem geographischen Zusammenhang und Unternehmerreaktionen werden wahrscheinlich nicht aufhören, sondern eher bestärkt durch eine Industrie, die sich aus Beratern, der Handelspresse, formaler Schulbildung and anderen Lernmöglichkeiten zusammensetzt. Enwicklungspolitiker müssen infolgedessen die Natur der Standortkonkurrenz sowie die kritischen Rollen von Fachkenntnissen und Netzwerken bei den Strategien der konkurrenzfähigsten Orte verstehen. Der Wettbewerbsstandard ist komplex, und umfaßt Innovationsindexe und Zusammenarbeit im Netzwerk der Weltstädte.

Wettbewerb   Regionale Entwicklung   Bestrebungen   Fachkenntnisse   Weltstädte

Malecki E. J. (2004) Maniobrando para conseguir una posición: qué significa y por qué es importante para las políticas de desarrollo regional que los lugares compitan, *Regional Studies* **38**, 1093–1112. La realización de que los lugares compiten por inversión ha aumentado en los últimos años para abarcar la competición entre lugares para atraer la atención de emigrantes, turistas, y periodistas así como para atraer inversiones. Los lugares más competitivos han sido multidimensionales en sus atracciones, y han hecho la transición hacia una economía basada en el conocimiento. La prioridad más reciente se ha dirigido hacia la atracción de trabajadores e inversiones de carácter móvil. Los trabajadores creativos forman el corazón de la economía del conocimiento y de sus geografías como por ejemplo lo son los 'lugares inteligentes' y 'las regiones que aprenden'. Las métricas de conocimiento, los índices de innovación tarjetas de reporte son cada vez màs comunes, cada uno de ellos desarrollados de forma similar para clasificar la lista de lugares siguiendo un órden diferente. Las listas o las tablas de ligas de los 'mejores lugares' para los negocios, para vivir, retirarse y para visitar son rasgos clave de las economías y de las sociedades cuyos factores de éxito son altamente móviles. La competición en un contexto geográfico y las actividades emprendedoras que se producen como respuesta es probable que no desaparezcan, reforzadas por una industria que comprende asesorías, prensa especializada, educación formal y otras formas de aprendizaje. Consecuentemente, los diseñadores de políticas necesitan comprender la naturaleza de la competición entre los lugares y los roles críticos del conocimiento y de las redes (networks) en las estrategias de los lugares más competitivos. El estándar de la competición es un asunto complejo, el cual comprende índices de innovación y co-operación dentro de la red (network) de las ciudades globales.

Competición   Desarrollo económico   Política   Conocimiento   Ciudades globales

JEL classifications: O38, R00, R10, R59

INTRODUCTION

Since the mid-1970s, a higher degree of competition among countries has been evident. Shifting fortunes and the rise of Japan prompted widespread reappraisal of relative national ability, particularly in high-technology industries (Gilpin, 1975; US Department of Commerce, 1983), including a series of over 30 sector-specific studies by the International Trade Administration, US Department of Commerce.[1] Since 1990, the perception is widespread that Europe, Japan (and other Asian countries such as China) and the USA are competing in the global marketplace (De Woot, 1990; Hart, 1992; Jacquemin and Pench, 1997; Office of Technology Assessment, 1991; Stopford and Strange, 1991).

Krugman (1994/96, p. 34) suggests that despite the common use of the term 'competitiveness', 'countries do not compete with each other the way corporations do'. He interprets competition and competitiveness through the lens of an international trade expert, and describes many instances of the misuse of competitiveness as 'careless arithmetic'. For Krugman, the principal reason countries do not compete with each other is that they cannot go out of business.

Camagni (2002b), in a recent critique of Krugman's views in the context of regions, makes two important conclusions. First, regions unlike nations more or less *can* go out of business, becoming so depleted by outmigration that they are at a long-run

competitive disadvantage. Regions and localities do compete for investment, as the chosen location of workers and as the destination of tourists – all of which will be made (either completely or partially) in some places and not in others. Lever and Turok (1999, p. 792) declare that 'cities and other places compete with one another. This takes many different forms – some direct head-to-head competition for particular projects or events; others more indirect, subtle and incremental in nature'. Second, the basis for competitiveness at the regional scale is one of *absolute*, rather than comparative, advantage. Trade theory, on which Krugman's argument relies, based on concepts such as natural resource endowments and relative availability of labour and capital, cannot address adequately 'increasing returns linked to cumulative development processes and the agglomeration of activities' and

> the specific advantages strategically *created* by the single firms, territorial synergies and cooperation capability *enhanced* by an imaginative and proactive public administration, externalities *provided* by local and national governments and the specificities historically built by a territorial culture.
>
> (Camagni, 2002b, p. 2405, original emphases)

Camagni also focuses instead on *non-price competitiveness* and draws on the work of Cooke and Morgan (1998) and of Porter (1990, 2001) to explain the absolute advantages of human capital and infrastructure, which can be measured to some extent, and intangible advantages such as social and relational capital, cooperation, collective learning and untraded interdependencies, which almost certainly cannot be measured. For comparisons among nations, cost and price competitiveness have become less important, increasingly replaced by technological competitiveness and the ability to compete on delivery (indicated by transport equipment and infrastructure) (FAGERBERG, 1988).

Competition among places involves more than marketing or attempting to sell them. It involves the enhancement or improvement in the attributes that make it possible to attract and keep investment and migrants – that is, to become 'sticky places' (MARKUSEN, 1996). In addition, competition raises the level of information – and the factual basis that underlies that information. That is, competition includes marketing but also it connotes more than advertising, which can be based on highly selective if not misleading information.

The following sections lay out some of benefits and problems of competition among places.[2] The next section examines briefly competition among nations, as embodied in annual competitiveness rankings. The paper then turns to competition among subnational territories and cities, contrasting imitative 'low-road' policies with 'high-road', knowledge-based policies. The final sections turn to an assessment of the disadvantages and benefits of competition among places. The disadvantages of competition mainly concern the perils that low-road strategies build so that no strengths can prevail over the long term, which presents particular difficulties for regions trying to catch up in the context of territorial competition based on knowledge. There are many benefits of scanning (i.e. looking over the environment systematically for new knowledge), which aids in learning and absorbing knowledge to be put to use as conditions change (HOWELLS, 2002; JOHANNESSON *et al.*, 1997).

COMPETITIVENESS AND COMPETITION AT THE INTERNATIONAL SCALE

Whether or not nations can or do compete, their competitiveness can be measured. International comparisons have become commonplace, and indeed two competing groups provide annual rankings of national economies based on measures of competitiveness. The first, the WORLD ECONOMIC FORUM's (WEF, 2003) Global Competitiveness Programme, since 1979 has published annual competitiveness reports covering the major economies of the world, now 80 countries. The WEF hypes its *Global Competitiveness Report (GCR)* (CORNELIUS and SCHWAB, 2003) as 'the most authoritative and comprehensive assessment of the comparative strengths and weaknesses of national economies around the world' (WEF, 2003, p. 1). Specific dimensions of competitiveness are also the

focus of separate reports, such as *The Global Information Technology Report 2002–2003* (DUTTA *et al.*, 2003), a new series that began in 2002, and *Environmental Performance Measurement: The Global Report 2001–2002* (ESTY and CORNELIUS, 2002), a (so far) one-off report that focuses on measuring national environmental sustainability and national environmental performance.[3]

All of the WEF reports now centre on country rankings or 'league tables' on two dimensions of competitiveness: growth competitiveness, or prospects for the next 5–8 years, and microeconomic competitiveness, which refers to a country's effective use of its current stock of resources, based on the four elements of PORTER's (1990) 'diamond' framework. Growth competitiveness includes three component indices: technology, public institutions and macroeconomic environment, and the indices themselves have sub-indices. For example, technology itself is comprised of sub-indices on innovation, information and communication technology (ICT) and technology transfer, and the public institutions index consists of sub-indices for contracts and law and for corruption.

Perhaps appropriately for the concept of competitiveness, the WEF has a competitor in the production of annual competitiveness rankings. Since 1989, the International Institute for Management Development has produced a direct competitor to the GCR, the *World Competitiveness Yearbook (WCY)*. Both annual reports include both 'hard data' and data from surveys of executives. Without the series of offspring that now revolve around the GCR, and including fewer countries (50), the WCY analyses a larger number (314) of different criteria, grouped into four 'competitiveness factors': economic performance, government efficiency, business efficiency and infrastructure (INTERNATIONAL INSTITUTE FOR MANAGEMENT DEVELOPMENT, 2002). The 2003 edition for the first time includes regional economies – Bavaria (Germany), California (USA), Catalonia (Spain), Ile-de-France (France), Lombardy (Italy), Maharashtra (India), Rhone-Alps (France), Scotland (UK), and Zhejiang (China) – separately from their national economies.

There might well be advantage in having competition among competitiveness rankings, since they provide distinct information (ROESSNER *et al.*, 2002; YGLESIAS, 2003). Both the GCR and the WCY have added items related to technology and infrastructure in recent years. Analyses of the high-technology competitiveness of countries suggest that inputs and outputs can be tracked over the long term, with predictive power (PORTER *et al.*, 2001; ROESSNER *et al.*, 1996). There remains a bias toward rich countries seen in the neoliberal policy prescriptions implicit in them (LALL, 2001).

Although a country's overall ranking reflects a combination of factors or variables combined in some manner, their combination is not the same as *systemic competitiveness* (BRADFORD, 1994; MEYER-STAMER, 1997). This concept suggests that sustained industrial competitiveness rests not only on firms' capabilities (the micro-level) and a stable economic framework (the macro-level), but also on a tissue of supporting, sector-specific and specialized institutions and targeted policies (the meso-level), and on governance structures that facilitate problem-solving between state and societal actors (the meta-level). Clearly, this bears strong resemblance to the concept of systems of innovations (or innovation systems), on which much has been written, particularly at the national scale (EDQUIST, 1997; LUNDVALL, 1992; NELSON, 1993). Some aspects of institutions are found in both the *GCR* and the *WCY*, but the nested (micro, macro, meso, meta) levels of the systemic competitiveness approach envisions institutions as more than merely variables in a large empirical analysis.

REGIONAL COMPETITION: THE LOW ROAD

The distinctiveness of regional economies has been evident at least since the publication of PORTER (1990) and NAM *et al.* (1990), reinforced by OHMAE (1995) and SCOTT (1998). The *WCY* is the first of the global rankings to examine several regional economies, despite the presence among the *GCR* team of Porter, who has recognized regional clusters as the heart of national competitiveness since 1990. The European Commission also assessed regional competitiveness at the same time, identifying several factors as most important to regional economies: proximity to markets, the communication system, financial institutions and product life-cycle stage (NAM *et al.*, 1990). This list goes a step beyond traditional, cost-based factors that lead to low-road, race-to-the-bottom, policies.

Perhaps the height of interregional competition of the low-road variety took place in the 1970s in the USA, when 'the second war between the states' was announced by BUSINESS WEEK (1976) magazine. This label, repeated throughout the 1980s (RYANS and SHANKLIN, 1986), was reinforced by acrimonious competition among states to attain high rankings on the annual *General Manufacturing Business Climates* rankings of the 50 US states by the accounting firm Alexander Grant (subsequently renamed *General Manufacturing Climates* and the *Grant Thornton Manufacturing Climates Study*). These annual rankings served to define what was meant by a good business climate during the 1980s. Just as business climate was interpreted in various ways, labour 'skill' took on meanings beyond technical qualifications. Skill 'more often means the behavioural characteristics of labour: 'qualities as "good company employees," in terms of attendance, flexibility, responsibility, discipline, identification with the company and, crucially, work rate and quality' (MORGAN and SAYER, 1985, p. 390). These behavioural traits or 'soft skills'

are subtle qualities that frequently outweigh the conventional, measurable 'hard' skills (MOSS and TILLY, 1996).

Competition on the basis of low wages, docile labour and low taxes, which perpetuate an inability to upgrade to an economic base of higher skill and higher wages, had been common in the US South since the 1930s (COBB, 1993). The Grant Thornton business climate's focus on variables related to costs and taxes brought a devastating critique by the CORPORATION FOR ENTERPRISE DEVELOPMENT (CfED, 1986). The CfED's *The Development Report Card for the States* (1987) proposed an alternative set of guidelines for state economic development: performance, business vitality and development capacity as the organizational framework for 71 measures of each state economy (Table 1) (CfED, 2003a, b). The Grant Thornton studies ended in 1993; the annual *Development Report Cards* continue.

Competition among regions of the low-road variety, unfortunately, has not yet died out, especially among regions desperate to land scarce mobile investment such as auto assembly plants. Subsidies of all kinds are tossed out to attract these facilities, mediated by site location consultants who assess the 'business climate' and 'labour climate' of communities to justify providing incentives. Not only smokestacks, but also corporate headquarters are sought in this way, recently including US$61 million to Boeing by the city of Chicago, Illinois, to choose the city as its new headquarters location (KHAN, 2002).

If territories compete for a relatively small number of large investment projects, THOMAS (2003) demonstrates they are in a Prisoners' Dilemma game: there is no incentive for them to cooperate or not to continue to compete by offering subsidies and other incentives to investors. The problem is lessened, Thomas suggests, in areas where a strong central government, or supranational government such as the European Union, can control and restrain such competition. The degree of such control may well be an illusion reinforced by distance. DICKEN (1990, p. 181) concluded that:

> there is no clear and systematic UK policy towards inward investment. Investment promotion is carried on by what can reasonably be called a 'confusion' of different agencies and institutions, a hierarchy of various levels between which there are substantial tensions and within which there is intense competition. ... The territorial development agencies of Scotland, Wales, and Northern Ireland, with their stronger identity, institutions and interests, are able to compete strongly for investment in part on the strength of their research and analytical skills.

'Smokestack chasing' was thought to have died out, replaced by third- and fourth-wave 'entrepreneurial' policies in cities and regions (CLARKE and GAILE, 1998; EISINGER, 1988; FOSLER, 1988; HAIDER, 1986; ISSERMAN, 1994; LEICHT and JENKINS, 1994; SCHMANDT and WILSON, 1990). Supply-side policies

Table 1. *Measures used in the* Development Report Card for the States, *2002*

Indicators	Performance: how well is the state's economy providing opportunities for employment, income and an improving quality of life?	Business vitality: how dynamic are the state's large and small businesses?	Development capacity: what is the state's capacity for future development?
Sub-indicators	Employment: measuring the extent to which the economy is providing work for those who seek it: long-term employment growth, short-term employment growth, unemployment rate, mass layoffs	Competitiveness of existing businesses: measuring the strength of a state's traded sector and whether businesses are being sustained: traded sector strength, change in traded sector strength, business closings, competitiveness index, manufacturing capital investment	Human resources: identifying the education and skill levels of the workforce: basic educational skills, proficiency – reading, basic educational skills proficiency – mathematics, average teacher salary, K-12 education expenditures, high-school graduation, high-school attainment, college attainment
	Earnings and job quality: measuring how well people are compensated for the work they do: average annual pay, average annual pay growth, employer health coverage, working poor, involuntary part-time employment	Structural diversity: determining if the economic base of the state is sufficiently varied so the state can grow even if the market for products produced by any industry changes: sectoral diversity, dynamic diversity	Financial resources: focusing on the availability and use of capital to meet the full range of business needs: income from dividends, interest and rent, venture capital investments, Small Business Investment Companies (SBIC) Program financing, loans to small businesses
	Equity: identifying the extent to which the opportunity to attain a high standard of living is widely shared: poverty rate, income distribution, income distribution change, rural/urban disparity	Entrepreneurial energy: evaluating the extent to which new firms are generated and whether they are contributing to employment growth: new companies, change in new companies, new business job growth, technology jobs, initial public offerings	Infrastructure resources: measuring the conditions of a state's physical infrastructure: highway deficiency, bridge deficiency, urban mass transit, sewage treatment needs, digital infrastructure
	Quality of life: examining the non-material aspects of a high standard of living, such as social conditions and civic capacities to determine: net migration, infant mortality, uninsured low-income children, teen pregnancy, heart disease, homeownership rate, charitable giving, voting rate, crime rate		Amenity resources and natural capital: assessing quality of life and the sustainability of natural resources: energy costs, urban housing costs, health professional shortage areas, conversion of cropland to other uses, air quality
	Resource efficiency: identifying the intensity of finite natural resource use to evaluate sustainability: per capita energy consumption, renewable energy, toxic release inventory, vehicle miles travelled, recycling rate, greenhouse gas emissions		Innovation assets: measuring technical knowledge and technological resources: PhD scientists and engineers, science and engineering graduate students, households with computers, university research and development, federal research and development, private research and development, SBIR grants, royalties and licenses, patents issued, university spin-outs

Source: CORPORATION FOR ENTERPRISE DEVELOPMENT (2003b).

to attract businesses were supplemented by demand-side policies aimed at the retention of existing businesses and, to a lesser degree, by policies to support the creation of new firms and the expansion of existing businesses (EISINGER, 1988; FOSLER, 1988). However, it is clear that low-road competition still exists (LEVINE, 1995; LOVERIDGE, 1996; RAINES, 2000). Impact studies project unrealistic impacts to justify larger bundles of 'incentives' (CONNAUGHTON and MADSEN, 2001), firms overstate their future employment to receive incentives (GABE and KRAYBILL, 2001) and land-use planning is tailored to the needs of investors (TEWDWR-JONES and PHELPS, 2000).

Local economic development practitioners continue to focus on traditional location factors such as land,

labour, capital, infrastructure and location. Only after those are softer intangible factors considered: institutional capacity, business culture, community identity and image, and quality of life. Knowledge and technology lie in between, but behind traditional factors. WONG (1998) interprets this as suggestive of a lingering supply-side orientation.

Competitiveness and interlocal competition: marketing and glurbanization

At the urban scale, territorial competition combines the concerns of property-oriented growth machines with those of newer city marketers who manipulate images and repackage the 'place product' (CHESHIRE and GORDON, 1996). Particularly striking are the similarities in the images projected by cities as they compete for business investment, shoppers, tourists and new residents (HOLCOMB, 1994). Indeed, consultants and 'how to' texts effectively ensure that this will be the case (e.g. KOTLER *et al.*, 1993). Places not only can be sold, but also the 'place product' can be branded, launched and repositioned for the appropriate demographic segments (ASHWORTH and GOODALL, 1990; HEATH and WALL, 1992; KOTLER *et al.*, 1993). In the context of tourism, for example, the built infrastructure consists of facilities that 'are similar from city to city' because they are aimed at the same market segments: meetings and conventions, sports, entertainment, and shopping. 'Few cities can forgo competition in each of these sectors' (JUDD, 2003b, p. 14).

HARVEY's (1989, p. 12) review of urban entrepreneurialism identified characteristics that remain largely intact:

> Many of the innovations and investments designed to make particular cities more attractive as cultural and consumer centers have quickly been imitated elsewhere, thus rendering any competitive advantage within a system of cities ephemeral. ... Local coalitions have no option, given the coercive laws of competition, except to keep ahead of the game thus engendering leap-frogging innovations in life styles, cultural forms, products and service mixes, even institutional and political forms if they are to survive.

Even as they advise localities on how to compete, KOTLER *et al.* (1993, p. 15) acknowledge that 'the escalating competition ... for business attraction has the marks of a zero-sum game or worse, a negative-sum game, in that even the winner ultimately becomes the loser'. SWYNGEDOUW (1992, p. 58) observes that 'frenzied' and 'unbridled' competition results in over accumulation and the threat of devaluation. Worse perhaps is the fact that the economics of urban redevelopment projects are so flawed that cities 'face the possibility of being caught in a vicious cycle of having to provide larger subsidies to finance projects that deliver even fewer public benefits' (LEITNER and GARNER, 1993, p. 72). So why do places compete if the benefits are so few and uncertain? In short, because 'all places are in trouble, but some are in more trouble than others' (KOTLER *et al.*, 1993, p. 3; SHORT and KIM, 1998). Moreover, because interurban competition never relents, regeneration must be repeated, because 'all places are in trouble now, or will be in the near future' (KOTLER *et al.*, 1993, p. 346).

Despite similar motivations from place to place, local conditions vary sufficiently (varying degrees of 'trouble', perhaps) that, despite apparent similarities, there is no convergence on a single urban/regional policy in the USA and the UK, even if each can be characterized as a form of competitive regionalism (JONAS and WARD, 2002). Regulatory and institutional structures are 'built within the locality' (SWYNGEDOUW, 1992, p. 57). JESSOP and SUM (2000, p. 2295) call the local tailoring of policies *glurbanization*, the urban counterpart to glocalization. These are 'entrepreneurial strategies that are concerned to secure the most advantageous insertion of a given city into the changing interscalar division of labour in the world economy'.

But is it entrepreneurial?

The shift during the 1980s from managerialism to entrepreneurialism, focusing 'on investment and economic development with the speculative construction of place rather than amelioration of conditions within a particular territory ... is entrepreneurial precisely because it is speculative' (HARVEY, 1989, pp. 7–8). Rather than being merely reactive, cities compete for production of goods and services, for consumption (including tourism and retirement, arts and festivals), for command and control functions, and for redistribution of surpluses through central governments. Because so many places are chasing the same goal, 'serial reproduction of similar forms of urban redevelopment' is inevitable (HARVEY, 1989, p. 10). LOVERING (1995) insists, however, that the urban 'package' is commodification rather than entrepreneurial activity; entrepreneurship implies that a product is something new or innovative. Indeed, HARVEY (1989, p. 11) acknowledges that 'the search to procure investment capital confines innovation to a very narrow path'.

The speculative or entrepreneurial qualities of urban investments derive from the inability to predict exactly which package will succeed in luring mobile production, financial and consumption flows into a particular space (HARVEY, 1989, p. 11). The inability to predict outcomes has led JESSOP and SUM (2000, p. 2290) to suggest five possible types of innovative urban forms and functions:

- Introduction of new types of urban place or space for producing, servicing, working, consuming, living, etc. (e.g. technopoles, intelligent cities, cross-border cities, multicultural cities).
- New methods of space or place production to create location-specific advantages for producing goods/ services.
- Opening new markets, including modifying the spatial division of consumption through enhancing the quality of life for residents, commuters or visitors (e.g. culture, entertainment, spectacles, new cityscapes, gay quarters, gentrification).
- Finding new sources of supply to enhance competitive advantages, such as new sources of immigration, new sources of funding from the central state, attracting inward investment or reskilling the workforce.
- Refiguring or redefining the urban hierarchy and/or altering the place of a given city within it, such as

world or global city position, regional gateways, hubs, cross-border regions and 'virtual regions'.

The elites in entrepreneurial cities, particularly bankers, newspaper publishers and other location-bound businesses, remain in control of the images of their cities (HALL and HUBBARD, 1996; LOVERING, 1995; RACO, 1998). The local dependence of firms can lead to the formation of local business coalitions to promote local economic development. These local business coalitions appeal to the local population and its local consumption/status needs, e.g. orchestras, professional theatre companies, major sports franchises, shopping malls and bricked streets (COX and MAIR, 1988, p. 320).

Media attention

Competition among cities for the attention of investors, tourists and new residents also requires attention to media images and rankings. Annual 'Best cities for business' rankings of *Fortune* magazine have been joined by the *Forbes–Milken Institute Best Places Ranking Index* (MILKEN INSTITUTE, 2002). Other publications, such as ENTREPRENEUR (2002) and INC. (2000), whose readership is comprised of entrepreneurs, produce lists of the *Best Cities to Start and Grow a Company in Now.* Even *AméricaEconomía* has begun an annual ranking of cities in Latin America, in which Miami ranks far out in front of São Paulo, Brazil, the second-ranked city (ABARCA, 2002).

While not a completely new phenomenon, place-marketing has taken on a larger importance as media outlets proliferate. Places see a need to advertise their attractions to target markets, such as visitors, residents and workers, business and industry, and export markets. For each of these, a marketing programme can include creation of a positive image, developing attractions, and improving local infrastructure and quality of life (GOLD and WARD, 1994; KOTLER *et al.*, 1993; RYANS and SHANKLIN, 1986). Maintaining – or creating – a positive image is perhaps most important to the largest, or global, cities, including London, New York and Tokyo. In recent bidding for the 2012 Olympic Games, both London and New York are in the running primarily to stay in the media eye in a positive light. In general, the cities that compete the most are those that are most competitive (SHOVAL, 2002).

McCANN (2004) emphasizes the relationships between media discourse and urban politics in his analysis of *Money* magazine's 'best places to live' in the USA. There are such lists, compiled annually by various publications and organizations, frequently with the objective of selling new publications. McCann shows that these rankings are a genuine focus of local policy-makers and business leaders, wherein the objective to improve a city's ranking becomes a centrepiece of local growth strategy and its discourse.

The discourse of interurban competition, crystallized in the popular media's images and rankings, sustains and encourages ideological conformity about what it takes to 'win' in this competition. Established strategies – redevelopment of central cities, convention centres, sports facilities, and shopping and restaurant districts – are being supplemented by concern for the 'people climate' (amenities and culture), rather than only the business climate of a place (FLORIDA, 2002). The centrality of quality of life to attract and keep mobile professionals – some of whom might start new firms – broadens the scope of 'best places for business' to include amenities and other 'quality of life' considerations. This is the latest in a wave of entrepreneurial strategies to address competition in a geographical context. Such responses are unlikely to go away, reinforced as they are by an industry comprised of consultancies, trade press, formal education and other means of learning (PAINTER, 1998).

Tourism and regional competition

Amenities also figure prominently in efforts to attract tourists. Indeed, the same amenities – a cultural 'scene' incorporating architecture, art and history, and diverse restaurants and shops – are among the local attributes seen as desirable for both local residents and visitors. Tourism is an ill-defined sector that has risen in importance as both business tourism and leisure tourism have expanded greatly, sparking policies and building 'urban entertainment amenities' explicitly to attract visitors (EISINGER, 2000). The 'infrastructure of play' includes renovated waterfronts, shopping areas, and entertainment and cultural districts that demand local investment (JUDD, 2003a). Business tourism, which encompasses conferences, conventions, and sector-specific exhibitions and fairs, also demands local investment and marketing (BRADLEY *et al.*, 2002; CUADRADO-ROURA and RUBALCABA-BERMEJO, 1998; LAW, 2002).

Tremendous competition also has emerged for 'hallmark events', such as blockbuster touring art exhibitions and periodic sporting events such as the Olympic Games and the Football (soccer) World Cup (LAW, 2002; SHOVAL, 2002). Such hallmark events can take place in only one location and only every 2 or 4 years, so they are a classic scarce resource for which cities (and their regions and countries) compete with one another. More frequent, perhaps annual sports championships may induce competition among a small band of cities in a single country, such as the Super Bowl of American football and the Final Four college basketball tournament in the USA. More prominent are attempts to land the Olympics as a high-profile hallmark event. Such efforts, even if not successful, direct media attention toward new symbols – of the 'cultural capital' in a post-modern city (Sydney, Australia) (WAITT, 1999), or of new image for a city and its nation-state (Cape Town, South Africa) (HILLER, 2000).

More generally, sports tourism and mega events and hallmark events are part of a constant competition between cities and regions attempting to draw in mobile capital (JONES, 2001). Big entertainment projects, whether sports or eating, drinking and shopping, generally place the concerns of visitors to cities above those of the those who reside in the city (EISINGER, 2000).

European cities have not blindly followed the US model, particularly with regard to tourism, for several reasons. European cities are structurally unique, and the accumulation of cultural capital such as distinctive architecture is itself a tourist attraction. Moreover, European urban cores retain a mix of functions, including residential, which means that large sports and convention facilities (typical in downtown areas of US cities) are not feasible (VAN DEN BERG et al., 2003). Nonetheless, PERRY (2003, p. 21) insists that 'privatizing discourses' are 'being carried on in every city in the world in one way or another'. The 'essential equipment' of a 'first-class' tourist city includes a sports stadium or arena, a convention centre and major convention hotels, all paid for by the citizens of the city (PERRY, 2003, pp. 35–36). Some of this is the discourse of entrepreneurialism, which may have relatively little connection with who will benefit and who will not from popular policies (EISINGER, 2000).

While the bundle of attractions and the involvement of public financial support remains largely as HARVEY (1989) described it, a glimmer of local uniqueness has entered. Local culture and history are incorporated into restaurant and entertainment district redevelopment, if only to implant some authenticity (FLORIDA, 2002; JUDD et al., 2003).

KNOWLEDGE POLICIES: COMPETITION ON THE HIGH ROAD

It is more difficult for cities and regions to aim for the 'high road' rather than the 'low road' in development. The nuances operating in regional and local systems of innovation are scarcely the traditional factors of production in economics. Even agglomeration, a seemingly simple concept, has proven very difficult to untangle in its various guises (GORDON and McCANN, 2000).

Urban and regional competitiveness is inherently multidimensional, including both traditional factors of production, infrastructure and location, as well as economic structure and more 'ethereal' factors, such as quality of life and environmental urban amenities. Competitiveness also reflects effective governance, urban strategy, public–private cooperation, and institutional flexibility (KRESL, 1995; DEAS and GIORDANO, 2001). Least likely to be understood and reflected

in local strategies are high-road policies to promote entrepreneurship and technology-based economic development. Three sets of prominent examples have attracted international attention. First, the success of industrial districts in Italy and Denmark – 'competitively advantaged regions', as COOKE (1996a, p. 162) calls them – demonstrate that a high-road strategy to regional development is possible (ASHEIM, 1996; COOKE, 1995). There are few such regions where learning, associational behaviour and working clusters operate. Silicon Valley, California, is on the list, as is Baden-Württemberg, Germany (a 'model region'), Emilia-Romagna, Italy, and the UK's Motor Sport Valley (COOKE and MORGAN, 1998; COOKE, 2002a). Second, a few 'new economy' clusters have emerged, including the Telecom Corridor in Richardson, Texas, biotechnology in Cambridge, Massachusetts, and biotech and ICT clusters in Cambridge, UK. Third, newly created, policy-led clusters with promising beginnings have emerged in Oulu, Finland, and winners of a German BioRegio competition centred in Cologne, Heidelberg, Munich, and Jena. The German competition among regional innovation systems is a rare case of a competition among regions initiated, encouraged and carried out by a national ministry, the German Ministry of Education, Science, Research and Technology (BMBF), and focused on the ability of regions to meet objectives to commercialize biotechnology (COOKE, 2002a; DOHSE, 2000).

The economic base of cities is increasingly producer services, which respond not simply to access to markets, inputs or a fixed supply of labour, but to up-to-the-minute information, specialized services and a quality life that facilitates recruitment of skilled and highly mobile professionals. FLORIDA (2002) and NEVAREZ (2003) suggest that elite labour sustains the new industrial space, with quality of life as a locational asset. In this context, urban and regional competitiveness aimed at becoming learning regions, working clusters and knowledge economies with functioning regional or local innovation systems, may be the preferred goal (COOKE, 2002a). These objectives are less sporadic or ephemeral than permanent, incremental and focused on long-term development – development *of* regions rather than *in* regions (LOVERING, 2001). Such an objective combines structural change, such as incorporation of the information economy (DRENNAN, 2002), and the imperatives of lifestyle and amenities to attract the creative workforce of the new economy (FLORIDA, 2002). It has been clear for some time that urban amenities – more than climate – attract tourists as well as mobile professional workers (FLORIDA, 2002; MALECKI and BRADBURY, 1992). People with higher knowledge and skill, whether labelled as 'symbolic analysts' (REICH, 1991) or 'the creative class' (FLORIDA, 2002), also are more capable of entrepreneurship, a key part of the process of continual regional rejuvenation.

FLORIDA's (2002, pp. 223–234) description of quality of place resonates with the soft, intangible qualities used to describe knowledge economies and innovative milieus: an interrelated set of experiences: what is there, who is there, what is going on. Quality of place does not occur automatically; it is an ongoing dynamic process that thrives on authenticity, diversity and interaction. Entrepreneurial cities seem unable to create the 'buzz' found in centres of cultural creativity (STORPER and VENABLES, 2002). There are several reasons: the factors are too soft; the needs of each industry are different; each industry agglomerates in a different district or 'quarter' of the urban area; and each creative person and firm uses the locality in different ways (DRAKE, 2003; SCOTT, 2000).

Despite attempts by cities to be creative (FLORIDA, 2002), innovative (BEGG, 2002; Simmie, 2001) and intelligent (KOMNINOS, 2002), innovative regions are not found everywhere. Large cities in Europe's core region (however defined; NIJKAMP, 1993) have much – but not all – of Europe's innovative activity (MATTHIESSEN and SCHWARZ, 1999; PACI and USAI, 2000; RODRÍGUEZ-POSE, 1999). Europe's regions have originated in different ways: via top-down regionalization (as in France) or bottom-up regionalism (as in Belgium and in Spain). The top-down creations are less able to muster the assemblage of features common to 'accomplished regional economies': agglomeration economies, institutional learning, associative governance, proximity capital and interactive innovation (COOKE *et al.*, 2000; COOKE, 2002a).

COOKE (2002b) argues the case for regional innovation systems using agglomeration economies, institutional learning, associative governance, proximity capital and interactive innovation. Criteria for innovation at the regional level include *infrastructural* (finance, hard infrastructures such as telecom and transport, and soft knowledge infrastructures) and *superstructural* (institutions and organizational aspects of both firms and policy). If regional systems of innovation are a standard to be attained, it is perhaps in the soft superstructural dimensions where regions vary most (COOKE *et al.*, 1998, 2000). The organizational elements that involve firms are perhaps the softest of all. Here, COOKE *et al.* (1998) list trustful (rather than antagonistic) labour relations, workplace cooperation, worker-welfare orientation, mentoring (versus 'sink or swim'), externalization and innovation (in contrast to adaptation) as characteristics of strong potential for regional systems of innovation. These characteristics are similar to those diffused among the suppliers of a firm that chose 'soft' transfer or 'competitiveness transfer' of technology, one which recognizes the human relations requirements of new technology (ETTLINGER and PATTON, 1996). In innovative milieus, equally soft and invisible dynamics are at work: learning and interaction, both of which are difficult to measure and therefore difficult for policy to create, maintain or

change (MAILLAT, 1995). Particularly difficult to influence are the cognitive aspects of a regional system, which strongly affect the ability to adapt to new conditions (GRABHER, 1993; MAILLAT, 1996). Thus, strategies should be aimed at the intensification of the productive capacities of the cities and regions in which they are based through the construction of 'territorially rooted immobile assets' (BRENNER, 1998, pp. 15–16).

It is easier, however, to create science parks and technopoles as symbols of local innovativeness than it is to create communication and technology transfer (KOMNINOS, 2002). It seems to be as difficult, if not impossible, for regional leaders truly to 'get it' with regard to innovation as it is for them to understand the appeal of diversity (FLORIDA, 2002). LEITNER and SHEPPARD (1998) fear that places that cannot attain high-road competitiveness automatically and instinctively tend to shift to low-road, low-wage strategies.

In small communities, which often cannot afford the costly, highly visible projects of large cities, 'soft' cultural and social variables matter most for regional development: institutions, leadership, culture, community (McDOWELL, 1995). In all places, the popular cluster concept has been widely misapplied as merely the collection of sectors that have traded interaction, indicated by input–output linkages. Not measured in input–output matrices are the links between firms and organizations and institutions (AUSTRIAN, 2000, PORTER, 1998a, b). These links and other intangible, untraded interdependencies among firms are often more important than input–output relations (CHESNAIS, 1986; PENEDER, 2001; STORPER, 1997).

Innovation indices

Silicon Valley arguably stands as the leader in the global race; attempts to replicate its success stretch back decades (MICKLETHWAIT, 1997; MICKLETHWAIT and WOOLDRIDGE, 2000; MILLER and COTÉ, 1987; ROGERS and LARSEN, 1984; ROSENBERG, 2002). Although each region has its own set of strengths, including localized tacit knowledge, that cannot be replicated elsewhere, successful regions such as Silicon Valley do not stand still. In general, the superior organizing capacity of strong regions enables them to initiate new efforts as well as to maintain older successful policies (CHESHIRE and GORDON, 1996; VAN DEN BERG and BRAUN, 1999). Since the mid-1990s, i.e. before the recent dot-com meltdown, JOINT VENTURE: SILICON VALLEY NETWORK (2003) has worked to deal with growth, rejuvenation and issues that in Europe would be called cohesion, such as housing affordability, civic involvement, health and quality of life. An annual *Index of Silicon Valley* tracks indicators of the region's economy and quality of life.

Other regions have begun to emulate the practice of annual benchmarking. The Minneapolis–St Paul region, Minnesota, through the Great North Alliance, has recently released its third *Great North Opportunity Forecast* (PETTY, 2002), which expanded its comparison base from seven other urban regions in 2000 to 11 regions in 2001. INNOVATION PHILADELPHIA (2002) has completed an extensive *Innovation and Entrepreneurial Index* that compares Philadelphia with several other places with which the city-region competes, such as Baltimore (Maryland), Boston (Massachusetts), New York (New York), Pittsburgh (Pennsylvania), Raleigh–Durham–Chapel Hill (Research Triangle, North Carolina), San Diego (California) and Washington, DC. The mixed results (Is our glass half empty or half full?) are refreshingly honest. Table 2 compares aspects of Silicon Valley, the Great North and Innovation Philadelphia.

In Canada, Ontario has published an *Ontario Innovation . . . Index* since 2000, including 'benchmarking

Table 2. Categories and measures used by three regional organizations in the USA

Region	Silicon Valley, California, 2010	Great North Alliance, Minneapolis, Minnesota	Innovation Philadelphia, Pennsylvania
Categories and measures	Innovative economy	Performance Prosperity Regional personality Pull Resource flow	Knowledge
	Liveable environment	Innovation capacity Inspiration Invention Entrepreneurial introduction	Capital
	Inclusive society	Development capacity Minds Means Economic momentum	Location
	Regional stewardship		
Total number of indicators	31	58	29
Comparison regions		Chicago, IL Boston, MA Atlanta, GA Dallas, TX Seattle, WA Phoenix, AZ Denver, CO Austin, TX Orange County, CA Salt Lake City, UT Research Triangle, NC	New York, NY Boston, MA Research Triangle, NC San Diego, CA Pittsburgh, PA Baltimore, MD Washington, DC/Northern Virginia

Sources: INNOVATION PHILADELPHIA (2002); JOINT VENTURE: SILICON VALLEY NETWORK (2003); PETTY (2002).

comparisons' with three other Canadian provinces (Alberta, British Columbia, Quebec), four states in the USA (California, Massachusetts, Illinois, Michigan) and one country (Sweden) (ONTARIO SCIENCE AND INNOVATION COUNCIL, 2002). NovaKnowledge has published the *Nova Scotia Knowledge Report Card* since 1998 to define and monitor the progress of Nova Scotia's knowledge economy, mainly in comparison with other Canadian provinces (NOVAKNOWLEDGE, 2002).[4] These are relatively traditional compilations of science and technology indicators. Other regions, especially in the USA, have begun to address more subtle aspects of regional success, such as attracting and keeping young people (FOCUS ST LOUIS, 2002).

Objective comparisons of data for a region and its primary competitors were somewhat rare until recently. The STATE SCIENCE AND TECHNOLOGY INSTITUTE (SSTI, 2002) compiles and critiques the reports available for states and for urban regions, as well as several reports at the national scale in the USA. The SSTI suggests several benefits of innovation indices or report cards. First, an index, particularly in a traditional industrial economy, may help increase the population's recognition of what is necessary to thrive in an economy that is more knowledge based, technologically more sophisticated and globally more competitive. Second, an index can help to identify the areas that warrant the most immediate attention of targeted programmes and policies. Third, an index offers the political opportunity and supporting evidence to engage in longer-term policies and programmes than typically can result when leaders are motivated by short election cycles. Fourth, researchers and policy-makers can assess the direction of a region's or a state's economy if the index includes multi-year data and is done regularly to measure change. Finally, an index may provide data to support 'branding' and other promotional marketing strategies of a region or city.[5]

Currently, seven nation-wide indices in the USA rank states on innovation, technology and knowledge. Perhaps the best known are *The State New Economy Index* (newly updated for 2002 to compare with the original in 1999) and *The Metropolitan New Economy Index* (ATKINSON *et al.*, 1999; ATKINSON and GOTTLIEB, 2001; ATKINSON, 2002). Both indexes use five key economic dimensions of state and/or local: knowledge jobs, globalization, economic dynamism, digital economy and innovation capacity (Table 3).

Such reports are elaborate indeed, with broad frameworks for what constitutes a knowledge base and a range of well-documented data sources. At the same time, LEVER (2002) shows there are no straightforward links between knowledge and innovation at the city scale and economic growth in Europe. FLORIDA (2002) suggests a strong link in the USA, centred around the role of the 'creative class' of mobile professionals who increasingly determine the locations of firms.

Regional (multi-state) organizations also get into

Table 3. Indicators in the New Economy Index

Dimension	Indicator
Knowledge jobs	Information technology jobs (per cent of total jobs)
	Jobs held by managers, professionals and technicians (per cent of total workforce)
	Workforce education level (weighted measure of advanced degrees, bachelor's degrees, associate's degrees and some college coursework)
	Education level of the manufacturing workforce
Globalization	Export focus of manufacturing (per cent of jobs dependent on exports)
	Foreign direct investment (per cent employed by foreign companies)
Economic dynamism	Gazelle jobs (per cent of jobs in fast-growing companies – those with sales revenue that has grown 20% or more for 4 straight years)
	Job churning (business start-ups and failures as a per cent of all firms)
	Initial Public Offerings (their value as a per cent of gross state product)
Transformation to a digital economy	Online population (per cent of adults with Internet access)
	Commercial Internet domains (number per firm)
	Education technology (weighted measure of the per cent of classrooms wired for the Internet, teachers with technology training and schools with more than 50% of teachers with school-based e-mail accounts)
	Digital government (a measure of digital technologies in state governments)
	Online agriculture
	Online manufacturers
	Broadband telecommunication
Technological innovation capacity	Number of high-technology jobs (jobs in electronics, software and computer-related services, and telecommunications as a per cent of total employment)
	Number of scientists and engineers (per cent of workforce)
	Number of patents issued (per '000 workers)
	Industry investment in research and development (per cent of GSP)
	Venture capital (per cent of GSP)

Note: GSP, gross state product.
Source: ATKINSON (2002).

regional assessments. The Southern Growth Policies Board, formed by 13 governors of states in the US South in 1971, has long tracked innovation and technology through its Southern Technology Council. In 2000, the board began to publish an annual *Southern Innovation Index* to promote innovation, entrepreneurship and economic growth in the South. The index identifies 56 benchmarks and compares each state against the US average and against a target figure. Less a regional index than a compilation of those of the various states, it is a typical data-rich report that provides regular comparisons on measures believed to be related to regional development. As an annual index, the *Southern Innovation Index* and other compilations of 'indicators' can provide policy guidance in contrast to 'mere data' (GODIN, 2003).

The creation of indices is not the work of consultants or of local or regional boosters alone. Federal government agencies have weighed in, such as the Technology Administration of the US Department of Commerce, which has prepared a report of *State Science & Technology Indicators* in 2000 and 2001; this report did not appear in 2002 (US DEPARTMENT OF COMMERCE, TECHNOLOGY ADMINISTRATION, 2001). These studies used 37 different metrics that assess research and development (R&D), educational attainment, scientists and engineers, finance, and high-technology industry in each state. For the past decade, the US NATIONAL SCIENCE FOUNDATION (2002) has produced for several years the basic raw material for this and other

studies, the Science and Engineering State Profiles. These are somewhat less comprehensive than the internationally focused *Science Indicators* (since 1987 *Science and Engineering Indicators*) (GODIN, 2003).

One of the more elaborate studies is the *State Science and Technology Index*, commissioned by TechVentures Network, formerly Bay Area Regional Technology Alliance, with support from the California Technology, Trade and Commerce Agency. This study uses 73 components for each of the 50 states, providing a look at each 'ecosystem of economic development and sustainability' (DEVOL, 2002, p. 8). Such an index approaches the goal to embody the degree to which a national or regional 'economy is able to adapt to structural change, or, in the more favourable case, to internally anticipate it' (DUNN, 1994, p. 307).

Rankings and analyses of data at the regional scale in the UK have only recently begun (HUGGINS, 2003). Huggins notes that the most striking feature of the 12-region *UK Index of Regional Competitiveness* is the continuance of a north–south divide in economic fortunes. Indeed, this can be seen as a signal that the *Index* is accurate. The index components that measure knowledge-based business growth exhibit the highest correlation with regional output growth from 1993 to 1999 ($r = 0.62$). It appears, however, that the UK Department of Trade and Industry has decided to combine the *Regional Competitiveness Indicators* with its 'State of the Regions' *Core Indicators* (WHITE *et al.*, 2003). Significantly, regional indicators related to the knowledge economy appear to have been dropped from the new indicator set.

Cooperation, competition and world cities

Because places are not islands, cities and regions and their institutions should have an explicit local 'foreign policy' (CAPPELLIN, 1998). For some cities, to attain the status of a world city is itself an objective. Although world-city status reflects more than simply the concentration of foreign firms or an agglomeration of producer services, these are among the objects of competition, perhaps particularly in Asia (DOUGLASS, 2000; WU, 2000). A city's foreign policy is its various connections with other cities, based on the non-local or extra-local links within spatial innovation systems (OINAS and MALECKI, 2002). Such links are ever more necessary, as 'cities are no longer enclosed within relatively autocentric national economies, but embedded ever more directly within trans-state urban hierarchies and inter-urban networks' (BRENNER, 1998, p. 18). In other words, world cities not only compete with one another, but also they must cooperate and coordinate (BEAVERSTOCK *et al.*, 2002).

Beaverstock *et al.* make the notion of a city's 'foreign policy' more explicit, suggesting that four sets of actors or 'attendants' – firms, sectors, cities, states – work to maintain flows through the network of world cities. Firms operate with the 'communities' of sectors; cities operate within the communities of states (including national and international bodies). World cities comprise a network more than (or as well as) a hierarchy, and the interaction between cities is differentiation rather than zero-sum competition (DOEL and HUBBARD, 2002). Similar thinking is seen in the four roles that CAMAGNI (2001) sees the city as playing: cluster, milieu, interconnection and symbol. While the first two are somewhat inward in orientation, a cluster and/or a milieu as a territorial production system must be outward looking, focused to a large degree on non-local links and knowledge. The latter two roles, as interconnection and as symbol, are more explicitly outward in orientation. Symbols alone are insufficient. 'No amount of local asset manipulation and window-dressing will guarantee world-cityness' (DOEL and HUBBARD, 2002, p. 361).

Seen as a network of places simultaneously competing and cooperating, the world city network is but one example of how networks 'evolve in response to, yet also shape, hierarchies and markets' (LEITNER *et al.*, 2002, p. 288). Viewed as part of a network, the prosperity of a world city is not determined by its 'competitive advantage' over its rivals. World cities work together to maintain flows through the network (BEAVERSTOCK *et al.*, 2002, p. 115). As urban economies become more specialized, they require horizontal links rather than, or in addition to, vertical links with larger cities (CAMAGNI and SALONE, 1993).

Policy-makers and politicians should 'replace their place-based way of thinking with a focus on connectivity, performance and flow', i.e. 'how they can extend city networks through time and space to attain (and perform) world-cityness' (DOEL and HUBBARD, 2002, p. 363). For example, an airport is not enough; also needed are flows of air traffic, meaning airlines and their flights, passengers, and international freight.

Airports are an acknowledged aspect of urban 'foreign policy'. 'For the last forty years, airports have determined the hierarchy of cities, by determining their accessibility from medium and long distances'. Intermediate cities have developed transversal or non-radial international and interregional connections with other intermediate cities. This has enlarged the action area of business and offered better access to distant markets (CAPPELLIN, 1998, p. 75). SMITH and TIMBERLAKE's (2002) analysis suggests that although the air travel network has become more hierarchical, with one pre-eminently dominant city (London), a larger number of cities have become well linked.

Many other networks also operate across national borders, including political, social, cultural, criminal, and flows of money and of immigrants (LEITNER *et al.*, 2002; SASSEN, 2001). JESSOP and SUM (2000) describe the less structured diaspora network, the Hong Kong–Silicon Valley Association, set up to enhance global-local flows of knowledge, expertise and manpower. SAXENIAN and LI (2003) describe similar strong links, including co-investment, between Taiwanese in Silicon Valley and Taiwan.

DRAWBACKS OF COMPETITION

Not all competition is good. The most oft-noted drawback of inter-territorial competition is serial reproduction, the imitation and replication of the same ideas from place to place. Resources (financial and human) are diverted into advertising and marketing rather than into systemic change. The 'civic peacockery' associated with mega-events and monumental spaces may have little lasting value (DOEL and HUBBARD, 2002). The old-style competition, embodied in subsidies, incentives and low-road policies, led to low wages and low taxes as a basis for competition. Consequently, this had the effect of reduced revenue for public services, diminishing quality of life. A priority on competition also reduces the likelihood that places will cooperate toward common goals.

Indeed, even the simplest, and most common, form of competition, promotion and marketing, is fundamentally zero-sum in nature, responding primarily 'to the short-term demands of "global but leaderless" capitalism' (LOVERING, 1995, pp. 122–124). Even if there is widespread benefit from local efforts in territorial competition, many benefits will accrue only to some, such as 'rent earners' and firms entrenched in the local economy, rather than to others (CHESHIRE and GORDON, 1996; COX, 1995; COX and MAIR, 1988).

Research on competitiveness is generally mixed with a concern for cohesion (a term hardly used in the USA) and inequality (e.g. BODDY, 2002; HALL *et al.*, 2001; JACQUEMIN and PENCH, 1997; POTTS, 2002). As but one example, the reconfiguration of Copenhagen, Denmark, as a creative city may well be 'business-as-usual urban redevelopment' (LUND HANSEN *et al.*, 2001). In other words, attracting talent and improving quality of place may be euphemisms for displacement and gentrification (ASHEIM and CLARK, 2001). MOULAERT and SEKIA (2003, p. 295) generalize further: 'There is no reference to improving the non-(market) economic dimensions of the quality of life in local communities or territories'.

While core–periphery contrasts remain within Europe, the core region has expanded to include a larger number of 'islands of innovation' than was the case in earlier configurations (LEVER, 1999). Even in a time of growing innovation and knowledge networks, peripheral locations are likely to become even more peripheral (CAMAGNI, 2002a; POLÈSE *et al.*, 2002). Weak or lagging territories – in terms of competitiveness, internal/external accessibility, quality of human and environmental factors, internal synergy, and learning capability – 'risk exclusion and decline to a larger extent than in the past'. The ingredients needed for development (knowledge, human capital, management and organization, co-operation and networking) 'are rare and not at all ubiquitous' (CAMAGNI, 2002a, p. 88).

Peripheral and smaller cities compete in very different ways from large cities, with a more restricted set of policies and no chance to match national capitals and world cities (LÖFGREN, 2000). The fact that places compete does not mean that they compete equally. Because the playing field is uneven, the dynamics of competition are fraught with negative rather than with positive connotations, particularly for disadvantaged places (LEITNER and SHEPPARD, 1998; SHEPPARD, 2000; LEIBOVITZ, 2003).

BENEFITS OF COMPETITION

In the context of decisions of firms, of mobile skilled workers and of tourists, and given the constraints of a limited investment budget for plants, offices and other facilities, companies and people can choose only a small number of locations, and often only one in the short one. Hence, the benefit to those making location decisions of information found in the *GCR* and the *WCY*, as well as the results of TRANSPARENCY INTERNATIONAL (2003) on corruption.

Competition among places can also lead to strengthened technology, boosting the absorptive capacity of places for new technologies and enabling foresight concerning future technologies. Technology foresight programmes and technology-scanning activities embody an ongoing absorptive capacity of a region (FOSS, 1996; MARTIN and JOHNSTON, 1999; VAN WYK, 1997). COOKE (1996b) identifies Emilia-Romagna as a rare region with capability in foresight.

Beyond media attention and infrastructural improvements that can be touted to the media, part of urban competition is the compilation and distribution of information and data about a place. Internet websites are now the standard mode of such information, typically providing links to complete reports and documents that a decade ago would have been difficult if not impossible to find and distributed in very limited quantities. Even now, such documents rarely find their way onto the shelves of traditional libraries.

The website of a city or region is an important means to form initial impressions – positive or negative – based in part on how informative and easy to navigate the site. Websites are important as a constantly available source of information. They may reduce but not entirely put an end to the disadvantages faced by small or poor regions and the information asymmetries created by smaller staff size and smaller advertising budgets that favour large, rich regions. However, there is little hard evidence on this to date. To compete, all places – large and small – must make the effort to prepare reports and other material to put on their websites; this is a relatively larger burden for small places. Some relation exists between country wealth and the size of city websites among 20 large cities, but there is no clear relation between city size and the structure or content of the website (URBAN, 2002). The website of a city or region is not for outsiders alone, and it communicates to local residents as well as to prospective residents and others, such as researchers. E-governments attempt to provide a '24/7' service, as citizens have come to expect in their role as consumers.

Network-enhancing policies, which incorporate soft as well as hard networks (MALECKI, 2002), can add to the more familiar growth-enhancing policies (Table 4). Territorial competitiveness, if it engages public administrations and local communities in the creation of a

Table 4. Some territorially competitive policies

Zero sum	Growth enhancing	Network enhancing
Pure promotion	Training	Internal networking
Capturing mobile investment	Fostering entrepreneurship	External (non-local) networks
Investment subsidies	Helping new firms	Benchmarking assessments
Subsidized premises	Business advice	Airline and air freight links
	Uncertainty reduction	Scanning globally for new knowledge
	Coordination	
	Infrastructure investment	

Source: Columns 1 and 2 are from CHESHIRE and GORDON (1998, p. 325); column 3 has been added.

widening spectrum of 'preconditions' – from hard to soft, from competitive to cooperative – need not mean a wasteful zero-sum game. Competitiveness reached through territorial quality and public service efficiency brings benefits to all local economic and social activities. Competitiveness attained by creating local synergies among local actors, or integrating external firms in the local relational web, exploits spillovers and increasing returns that are at the very base of economic development, in its positive-sum, 'generative' sense (CAMAGNI, 2002a, p. 89).

Attempts to create positive-sum strategies are now becoming commonplace at both the state and local levels in the USA. The assessments made of science and technology, with benchmarks and honest comparisons with other places, are realistic and produce more candid marketing efforts. Local leaders 'see themselves as others see them' as they search for local attributes to advertise, as they capture their economy's weaknesses as well as its strengths in regularly monitored indicators, and as websites make good as well as bad data far more accessible than in the past.

CONCLUSION

Competition among places has evolved considerably from crass attempts to offer the lowest cost to prospective investors and migrants to, more recently, sophisticated self-assessments that reflect honest analysis and comparison. All places must content with being ranked by external bodies (governmental, media or research organizations). In part because the criteria used in each ranking are different, no place is objectively 'best' or first in each league table. When ranking with annual updates, on the other hand, rankings inevitably show change rather than stability over time.

As research has proliferated on regional and local innovation systems and other territorial innovation models, serial replication of the high road policies that lead to learning regions and knowledge economies is recommended but hardly anticipated (COOKE et al., 2000; COOKE, 2002a). Internal conditions (R&D, strong but flexible institutions, a culture of trust and networking, etc.) and broad capabilities to capture and absorb external knowledge suggest that only a very small number of regions can attain the characteristics needed to be a 21st-century economy. A large number of the necessary ingredients (i.e. in particular, those that are not ubiquitous) cannot simply be imposed from the top down, but grow out of the region or community, and this can take a long time (COOKE and MORGAN, 1998; MASKELL et al., 1998; MOULAERT and SEKIA, 2003).

What does competition mean for policy? Competition has pushed local and regional policy toward the easy solution: homogenization of the 'place product' because the market is the same (globalized) set of investors, tourists, consumers. Entrepreneurship in the

sense that the product is something new or innovative is much more rare and may be shrouded in conflicts between competing discourses. In Hong Kong, for example, a traditional place-based discourse competes against a vision of the city as a networked 'urban economic space that will manage ever-expanding global–regional–local flows of production and exchange' (JESSOP and SUM, 2000, p. 2302). Hong Kong is not alone in attempting to create such a vision, suggesting that serial replication of best practices is not likely to end.

To some degree, learning and external (even global) scanning are what 'intelligent' cities and regions are doing, adding to the list of tasks needed to keep up. Continual monitoring and periodic benchmarking of what 'the competition' is doing are demanded.

The growing divergence between strong and weak territories is largely a divergence in orientation toward innovation-prone and -averse regions (RODRÍGUEZ-POSE, 1999). In innovation-prone regions, infrastructure, innovation support for firms and innovation policy vision are present (COOKE et al., 2000). Lack of innovativeness also is symptomatic of a lack of external orientation – the degree to which firms and public-sector organizations receive, learn, absorb and adapt experience, knowledge and expertise from elsewhere. In short, the challenge from competition is a daunting one, which can provide many opportunities for fruitless packaging and marketing of places as products. Although imitation of high-road development is much more difficult than was imitation of low-road policies, competition provides opportunities for places to learn how they might specialize and form new links with other places – to their mutual benefit.

Acknowledgements – Research was partially supported by a grant from the Mershon Center, The Ohio State University. The paper benefited from the helpful comments of Peter Maskell and of three anonymous referees.

NOTES

1. Although not cited here, the title of each begins with *A Competitive Assessment of the . . . Industry* or *Competitive Assessment of the . . . Industry.*
2. The present paper does not deal with the large literature on competitiveness of firms, whether small or large, except to the degree that they contribute directly to a region's development. Nearly all research on firm competitiveness focuses on the dependence of firms, especially small- and medium-sized firms, on their local and regional environment (CONTI et al., 1995; HITCHENS et al., 1996; MASKELL et al., 1998). National and regional economies are largely the assemblage of the firms that operate within their borders, along with other actors and institutions in the national or regional economic system (COX, 1995; PORTER, 1990).

3. Regional reports also have begun to appear on the Arab world (SCHWAB and CORNELIUS, 2003), on Europe (WARNER, 2002) and on Latin America (VIAL and CORNELIUS, 2002). Reports on Africa and on Asia have not been done recently (see http://www.weforum.org/site/homepublic.nsf/Content/Global + Competitiveness + Programme%5Creports).

4. Some dubious facts emerge from such reports. The 2001 NovaKnowledge report places Nova Scotia's R&D as 'lagging and stuck', the lowest of four categories of 'How are we doing?', whereas a year later, the 2002 report rates R&D as having jumped to 'leading', the highest category. This is a rapid turnaround by any measure.

5. The SSTI (2002, p. 1) suggests there are 'characteristics of good indices' of innovation. According to the SSTI, a good index would contain some, if not all, of the following: (1) public involvement and wide ownership of the selection of the measures included and the weighting, if any, for the indicators; (2) a clear explanation of how factors are measured or calculated and any weighting that may be used; (3) an explanation of the goals of the index and why certain indicators are included (and possibly why others are not); (4) an examination of trends in the measures over time instead of one-time snapshots; (5) a public dissemination of results; (6) specific recommendations for action from the study, including identification of responsible parties; (7) follow-up assessment of improvement (every 2–3 years); and (8) a proper citation of sources.

REFERENCES

ABARCA F. (2002) Un imán llamado: Sao Paulo (Ranking de ciudades 2002). *AméricaEconomía* **16 May**, 20–24 (available at: http://www.americaeconomia.com/FilesMC/CiuSP-02.pdf).

ASHEIM B. and CLARK E. (2001) Creativity and cost in urban and regional development in the 'new' economy, *European Planning Studies* **9**, 805–811.

ASHEIM B. T. (1996) Industrial districts as 'learning regions': a condition for prosperity, *European Planning Studies* **4**, 379–400.

ASHWORTH G. and GOODALL B. (Eds) (1990) *Marketing Tourism Places*. Routledge, London.

ATKINSON R. D. (2002) *The 2002 State New Economy Index: Benchmarking Economic Transformation in the States*. Progressive Policy Institute, Washington, DC (available at: http://www.neweconomyindex.org/states).

ATKINSON R. D., COURT R. H. and WARD J. M. (1999) *The State New Economy Index: Benchmarking Economic Transformation in the States*. Progressive Policy Institute, Washington, DC (available at: http://www.neweconomyindex.org/states/).

ATKINSON R. D. and GOTTLIEB P. D. (2001) *The Metropolitan New Economy Index: Benchmarking Economic Transformation in the Nation's Metropolitan Areas*. Progressive Policy Institute, Washington, DC (available at: http://www.neweconomyindex.org/metro).

AUSTRIAN Z. (2000) Cluster case studies: the marriage of quantitative and qualitative information for action, *Economic Development Quarterly* **14**, 97–110.

BEAVERSTOCK J. V., DOEL M. A., HUBBARD P. J. and TAYLOR P. J. (2002) Attending to the world: competition, cooperation and connectivity in the world city network, *Global Networks* **2**, 111–132.

BEGG I. (Ed.) (2002) *Urban Competitiveness: Policies for Dynamic Cities*. Policy Press, Bristol.

BODDY M. (2002) Linking competitiveness and cohesion, in BEGG I. (Ed.) *Urban Competitiveness: Policies for Dynamic Cities*, pp. 33–53. Policy, Bristol.

BRADFORD C. I. (1994) The new paradigm of systemic competitiveness: why it matters, what it means and implications for policy, in BRADFORD C. I. (Ed.) *The New Paradigm of Systemic Competitiveness: Toward More Integrated Policies in Latin America*, pp. 41–65. Organisation for Economic Co-operation and Development, Paris.

BRADLEY A., HALL T. and HARRISON M. (2002) Selling cities: promoting new images for meetings tourism, *Cities* **19**, 61–70.

BRENNER N. (1998) Global cities, global states: global city formation and state territorial restructuring in contemporary Europe, *Review of International Political Economy* **5**, 1–37.

BUSINESS WEEK (1976) The second war between the states, *Business Week* **17 May**, 92–114.

CAMAGNI R. (2001) The economic role and spatial contradictions of global city-regions: the functional, cognitive, and evolutionary context, in SCOTT A. J. (Ed.) *Global City-regions: Trends, Theory, Policy*, pp. 96–118. Oxford University Press, Oxford.

CAMAGNI R. (2002a) Territorial competitiveness, globalisation and local milieux, *European Spatial Research and Policy* **9**, 63–90.

CAMAGNI R. (2002b) On the concept of territorial competitiveness: sound or misleading?, *Urban Studies* **39**, 2395–2411.

CAMAGNI R. P. and SALONE C. (1993) Network urban structures in Northern Italy – elements for a theoretical framework, *Urban Studies* **30**, 1053–1064.

CAPPELLIN R. (1998) The transformation of local production systems: international networking and territorial competitiveness, in STEINER M. (Ed.) *Clusters and Regional Specialisation: On Geography, Technology and Networks*, pp. 57–80. Pion, London.

CHESHIRE P. C. and GORDON I. R. (1996) Territorial competition and the predictability of collective (in)action, *International Journal of Urban and Regional Research* **20**, 383–399.

CHESHIRE P. C. and GORDON I. R. (1998) Territorial competition: some lessons for policy, *Annals of Regional Science* **32**, 321–346.

CHESNAIS F. (1986) Science, technology and competitiveness, *Science Technology Industry Review* **1**, 85–129.

CLARKE S. E. and GAILE G. L. (1998) *The Work of Cities*. University of Minnesota Press, Minneapolis.

CLINTON J., DORON S., JAMES K. and WARREN J. (2002) *Invented Here: The 2002 Southern Innovation Index*. Southern Growth Policies Board, Research Triangle Park, NC (available at: http://www.southern.org/pubs/ih2002/invented%20here%202002.pdf).

COBB J. C. (1993) *The Selling of the South: The Southern Crusade for Industrial Development, 1936–1990*, 2nd Edn. University of Illinois Press, Urbana.

CONNAUGHTON J. E. and MADSEN R. A. (2001) Assessment of economic impact studies: the cases of BMW and Mercedes-Benz, *Review of Regional Studies* 31, 293–303.

CONTI S., MALECKI E. J. and OINAS P. (Eds) (1995) *The Industrial Enterprise and its Environment: Spatial Perspectives*. Avebury, Aldershot.

COOKE P. (1995) Keeping to the high road: learning, reflexivity and associative governance in regional economic development, in COOKE P. (Ed.) *The Rise of the Rustbelt*, pp. 231–245. UCL Press, London.

COOKE P. (1996a) The new wave of regional innovation networks: analysis, characteristics and strategy, *Small Business Economics* 8, 159–171.

COOKE P. (1996b) Building a twenty-first century regional economy in Emilia-Romagna, *European Planning Studies* 4, 53–62.

COOKE P. (2002a) *Knowledge Economies: Clusters, Learning and Cooperative Advantage*. Routledge, London.

COOKE P. (2002b) Biotechnology clusters as regional, sectoral innovation systems, *International Regional Science Review* 25, 8–37.

COOKE P., BOEKHOLT P. and TÖDTLING F. (2000) *The Governance of Innovation in Europe: Regional Perspectives on Global Competitiveness*. Pinter, London.

COOKE P. and MORGAN K. (1998) *The Associational Economy*. Oxford University Press, Oxford.

COOKE P., URANGA M. G. and ETXEBARRIA G. (1998) Regional systems of innovation: an evolutionary perspective, *Environment and Planning A* 30, 1563–1584.

CORNELIUS P. K. and SCHWAB C. (2003) *The Global Competitiveness Report 2002–2003*. Oxford University Press, Oxford.

CORPORATION FOR ENTERPRISE DEVELOPMENT (1986) *Taken for Granted: How Grant Thornton's Business Climate Index Leads States Astray*. Corporation for Enterprise Development, Washington, DC.

CORPORATION FOR ENTERPRISE DEVELOPMENT (1987) *Making the Grade: The Development Report Card for the States*. Corporation for Enterprise Development, Washington, DC.

CORPORATION FOR ENTERPRISE DEVELOPMENT (2003a) *Development Report Card for the States*. Corporation for Enterprise Development, Washington, DC (available at: http://drc.cfed.org/ and http://www.cfed.org).

CORPORATION FOR ENTERPRISE DEVELOPMENT (2003b) *Development Report Card for the States: Measures*. Corporation for Enterprise Development, Washington, DC (available at: http://drc.cfed.org/measures/).

COX K. R. (1995) Globalisation, competition and the politics of local economic development, *Urban Studies* 32, 213–224.

COX K. R. and MAIR A. (1988) Locality and community in the politics of local economic development, *Annals of the Association of American Geographers* 78, 307–325.

CUADRADO-ROURA J. R. and RUBALCABA-BERMEJO L. (1998) Specialization and competition amongst European cities: a new approach through fair and exhibition activities, *Regional Studies* 32, 133–147.

DEAS I. and GIORDANO B. (2001) Conceptualising and measuring urban competitiveness in major English cities: an exploratory approach, *Environment and Planning A* 33, 1411–1429.

DE WOOT P. (1990) *High Technology Europe: Strategic Issues for Global Competitiveness*. Basil Blackwell, Oxford.

DEVOL R. (2002) *State Science and Technology Index: Comparing and Contrasting California*. Milken Institute, Santa Monica (available at: http://www.milken-inst.org/nst/nst.pdf).

DICKEN P. (1990) Seducing foreign investors – the competitive bidding strategies of local and regional agencies in the United Kingdom, in HEBBERT M. and HANSEN J. C. (Eds) *Unfamiliar Territory: The Reshaping of European Geography*, pp. 162–186. Avebury, Aldershot.

DOEL M. and HUBBARD P. (2002) Taking world cities literally: marketing the city in a global space of flows, *City* 6, 351–368.

DOHSE D. (2000) Technology policy and the regions – the case of the BioRegio contest, *Research Policy* 29, 1111–1133.

DOUGLASS M. (2000) Mega-urban regions and world city formation: globalisation, the economic crisis and urban policy issues in Pacific Asia, *Urban Studies* 37, 2315–2335.

DRAKE G. (2003) 'This place gives me space': place and creativity in the creative industries, *Geoforum* 34, 511–524.

DRENNAN M. P. (2002) *The Information Economy and American Cities*. Johns Hopkins University Press, Baltimore.

DUNN M. H. (1994) Do nations compete economically? A critical comment on Prof. Krugman's essay 'Competitiveness: a dangerous obsession', *Intereconomics* 29, 303–308.

DUTTA S., LANVIN B. and PAUA F. (2003) *The Global Information Technology Report 2002–2003*. Oxford University Press, Oxford.

EDQUIST C. (Ed.) (1997) *Systems of Innovation*. Pinter, London.

EISINGER P. (2000) The politics of bread and circuses: building the city for the visitor class, *Urban Affairs Review* 35, 316–333.

EISINGER P. K. (1988) *The Rise of the Entrepreneurial State: State and Local Economic Development Policy in the United States*. University of Wisconsin Press, Madison.

ENTREPRENEUR (2002) *Entrepreneur and Dun & Bradstreet's 9th Annual Best Cities for Entrepreneurs*. October (available at: http://www.entrepreneur.com/bestcities/1,5271,00.html).

ESTY D. and CORNELIUS P. K. (2002) *Environmental Performance Measurement: The Global Report 2001–2002*. Oxford University Press, Oxford.

ETTLINGER N. and PATTON W. (1996) Shared performance: the proactive diffusion of competitiveness and industrial and local development, *Annals of the Association of American Geographers* 86, 286–305.

FAGERBERG J. (1988) International competitiveness, *Economic Journal* 98, 355–374.

FLORIDA R. (2002) *The Rise of the Creative Class, and How It's Transforming Work, Leisure, Community and Everyday Life*. Basic Books, New York.

Focus St Louis (2002) *Preparing St. Louis for Leadership in the 21st Century.* Focus St Louis, St Louis (available at: http://www.focus-stl.org/prio/pdf/econreport2002.pdf).

Fosler R. S. (Ed.) (1988) *The New Economic Role of American States.* Oxford University Press, New York.

Foss N. J. (1996) Higher-order industrial capabilities and competitive advantage, *Journal of Industry Studies* 3, 1–20.

Gabe T. M. and Kraybill D. S. (2001) The effect of state economic development incentives on employment growth of establishments, *Journal of Regional Science* 42, 703–730.

Gilpin R. (1975) *Technology, Economic Growth, and International Competitiveness.* US Government Printing Office, Washington, DC.

Godin B. (2003) The emergence of S&T indicators: why did governments supplement statistics with indicators?, *Research Policy* 32, 679–691.

Gold J. R. and Ward S. V. (Eds) (1994) *Place Promotion: The Use of Publicity and Marketing to Sell Towns and Regions.* Wiley, Chichester.

Gordon I. R. and McCann P. (2000) Industrial clusters: complexes, agglomeration and/or social networks?, *Urban Studies* 37, 513–532.

Grabher G. (1993) The weakness of strong ties: the lock-in of regional development in the Ruhr area, in Grabher G. (Ed.) *The Embedded Firm: On the Socioeconomics of Industrial Networks*, pp. 213–241. Routledge, London.

Haider D. (1986) Economic development: changing practices in a changing US economy, *Environment and Planning C: Government and Policy* 4, 451–469.

Hall R., Smith A. and Tsoulakis L. (2001) *Competitiveness and Cohesion in EU Policies.* Oxford University Press, Oxford.

Hall T. and Hubbard P. (1996) The entrepreneurial city: new urban politics, new urban geographies?, *Progress in Human Geography* 20, 153–174.

Hart J. A. (1992) *Rival Capitalists: International Competitiveness in the United States, Japan, and Western Europe.* Cornell University Press, Ithaca.

Harvey D. (1989) From managerialism to entrepreneurialism: the transformation of urban governance in late capitalism, *Geografiska Annaler* 71B, 3–17.

Heath E. and Wall G. (1992) *Marketing Tourism Destinations: A Strategic Planning Approach.* Wiley, New York.

Hiller H. H. (2000) Mega-events, urban boosterism and growth strategies: an analysis of the objectives and legitimations of the Cape Town 2004 Olympic bid, *International Journal of Urban and Regional Research* 24, 439–458.

Hitchens D. M. W. N., O'Farrell P. N. and Conway C. D. (1996) The competitiveness of business services in the Republic of Ireland, Northern Ireland, Wales, and the South East of England, *Environment and Planning A* 28, 1299–1313.

Holcomb B. (1994) City make-overs: marketing the post-industrial city, in Gold J. R. and Ward S. V. (Eds) *Place Promotion: The Use of Publicity and Marketing to Sell Towns and Regions*, pp. 115–131. Wiley, Chichester.

Howells J. (2002) Tacit knowledge, innovation and economic geography, *Urban Studies* 39, 871–884.

Huggins R. (2003) Creating a UK competitiveness index: regional and local benchmarking, *Regional Studies* 37, 89–96.

Inc. (2000) Best cities to start and grow a company in now. *Inc. Magazine* **1 December** (available at: http://www.inc.com/magazine/20001201/21110.html).

Innovation Philadelphia (2002) *Innovation and Entrepreneurial Index 2002: Is Our Glass Half Empty or Half Full?* Innovation Philadelphia, Philadelphia (available at: http://www.ipphila.com/index.cfm/fuseaction/document.download/documentID/9/doc/Innovation%20%26%20Entrepreneurial%20Index.pdf).

International Institute for Management Development (2002) *World Competitiveness Yearbook 2002.* IMD, Lausanne (available at: http://www02.imd.ch/wcy/).

Isserman A. M. (1994) State economic development policy and practice in the United States: a survey article, *International Regional Science Review* 16, 49–100.

Jacquemin A. and Pench L. R. (1997) *Europe Competing in the Global Economy.* Edward Elgar, Cheltenham.

Jessop B. and Sum N.-L. (2000) An entrepreneurial city in action: Hong Kong's emerging strategies in and for (inter)urban competition, *Urban Studies* 37, 2287–2313.

Johannesson J.-A., Dolva J. O. and Olsen B. (1997) Organizing innovation: integrating knowledge systems, *European Planning Studies* 5, 331–349.

Joint Venture: Silicon Valley Network (2003) *Joint Venture's 2003 Index of Silicon Valley: Measuring Progress Toward the Goals of Silicon Valley 2010.* Joint Venture: Silicon Valley Network, San Jose (available at: http://www.jointventure.org/2003index/2003index.pdf).

Jonas A. E. G. and Ward K. (2002) A world of regionalisms? Towards a US–UK urban and regional policy framework comparison, *Journal of Urban Affairs* 24, 377–401.

Jones C. (2001) A level playing field? Sports stadium infrastructure and urban development in the United Kingdom, *Environment and Planning A* 33, 845–861.

Judd D. R. (2003b) Building the tourist city: editor's introduction, in Judd D. R. (Ed.) *The Infrastructure of Play: Building the Tourist City*, pp. 3–16. M. E. Sharpe, Armonk, NY.

Judd D. R. (Ed.) (2003a) *The Infrastructure of Play: Building the Tourist City.* M. E. Sharpe, Armonk, NY.

Judd D. R., Winter W., Barnes W. R. and Stern E. (2003) Tourism and entertainment as local economic development: a national survey, in Judd D. R. (Ed.) *The Infrastructure of Play: Building the Tourist City*, pp. 50–74. M. E. Sharpe, Armonk, NY.

Khan M. (2002) Bidding for economic development: the role of site location consultants, *Corporate Research E-Letter* **no. 22** (available at: http://www.goodjobsfirst.org/crp/mar02.htm).

Komninos P. (2002) *Intelligent Cities: Innovation, Knowledge Systems and Digital Spaces.* E & FN Spon, London.

KOTLER P., HAIDER D. H. and REIN I. (1993) *Marketing Places: Attracting Investment, Industry, and Tourism to Cities, States, and Nations.* Free Press, New York.

KRESL P. K. (1995) The determinants of urban competitiveness: a survey, in GAPPERT G. and KRESL P. K. (Eds) *North American Cities and the Global Economy*, pp. 45–68. Sage, Thousand Oaks.

KRUGMAN P. (1994) Competitiveness: a dangerous obsession, *Foreign Affairs* **73**, 28–44; repr. KRUGMAN P. (1996) *Pop Internationalism*, pp. 3–24. MIT Press, Cambridge, MA.

LALL S. (2001) Competitiveness indices and developing countries: an economic evaluation of the Global Competitiveness Report, *World Development* **29**, 1501–1525.

LAW C. (2002) *Urban Tourism: The Visitor Economy and the Growth of Large Cities*, 2nd Edn. Continuum, London.

LEIBOVITZ J. (2003) Interrogating 'Enterprise Europe': issues of coordination, governance and spatial development in the European Union's emerging enterprise policy, *International Journal of Urban and Regional Research* **27**, 713–722.

LEICHT K. T. and JENKINS J. C. (1994) Three strategies of state economic development: entrepreneurial, industrial recruitment, and deregulation policies in the American states, *Economic Development Quarterly* **8**, 256–269.

LEITNER H. and GARNER M. (1993) The limits of local initiatives: a reassessment of urban entrepreneurialism for urban development, *Urban Geography* **14**, 57–77.

LEITNER H. and SHEPPARD E. (1998) Economic uncertainty, inter-urban competition and the efficacy of entrepreneurialism, in HALL T. and HUBBARD P. (Eds) *The Entrepreneurial City: Geographies of Politics, Regime and Representation*, pp. 285–307. Wiley, Chichester.

LEITNER H., PAVLIK C. and SHEPPARD E. (2002) Networks, governance, and the politics of scale: inter-urban networks and the European Union, in HEROD A. and WRIGHT M. W. (Eds) *Geographies of Power*, pp. 274–303. Blackwell, Oxford.

LEVER W. F. (1999) Competitive cities in Europe, *Urban Studies* **36**, 1029–1044.

LEVER W. F. (2002) Correlating the knowledge-base of cities with economic growth, *Urban Studies* **39**, 859–870.

LEVER W. F. and TUROK I. (1999) Competitive cities: introduction to the review, *Urban Studies* **36**, 791–793.

LEVINE M. V. (1995) Globalization and wage polarization in U. S. and Canadian cities: does public policy make a difference?, in GAPPERT G. and KRESL P. K. (Eds) *North American Cities and the Global Economy*, pp. 89–111. Sage, Thousand Oaks.

LÖFGREN A. (2000) A thousand years of loneliness? Globalization from the perspective of a city in a European periphery, *Geoforum* **31**, 501–511.

LOVERIDGE S. (1996) On the continuing popularity of industrial recruitment, *Economic Development Quarterly* **10**, 151–158.

LOVERING J. (1995) Creating discourses rather than jobs: the crisis in the cities and the transition fantasies of intellectuals and policy makers, in HEALEY, P., CAMERON, S., DAVOUDI, S., GRAHAM, S. and MADANI-POUR A. (Eds) *Managing Cities: The New Urban Context*, pp. 109–126. Wiley, Chichester.

LOVERING J. (2001) The coming regional crisis (and how to avoid it), *Regional Studies* **35**, 349–354.

LUND HANSEN A., ANDERSEN H. T. and CLARK E. (2001) Creative Copenhagen: globalization, urban governance and social change, *European Planning Studies* **9**, 851–869.

LUNDVALL B.-Å. (Ed.) (1992) *National Systems of Innovation.* Pinter, London.

MAILLAT D. (1995) Territorial dynamic, innovative milieus and regional development, *Entrepreneurship and Regional Development* **7**, 157–165.

MAILLAT D. (1996) Regional productive systems and innovative milieux, in *Networks of Enterprises and Local Development: Competing and Co-operating in Local Productive Systems*, pp. 67–80. Organization for Economic Co-operation and Development, Paris.

MALECKI E. J. (2002) Hard and soft networks for urban competitiveness, *Urban Studies* **39**, 929–945.

MALECKI E. J. and BRADBURY S. L. (1992) R&D facilities and professional labour: labour force dynamics in high technology, *Regional Studies* **26**, 123–136.

MARKUSEN A. (1996) Sticky places in slippery space: a typology of industrial districts, *Economic Geography* **72**, 293–313.

MARTIN B. R. and JOHNSTON R. (1999) Technology foresight for wiring up the national innovation system: experiences in Britain, Australia, and New Zealand, *Technological Forecasting and Social Change* **60**, 37–54.

MASKELL P., ESKELINEN H., HANNIBALSSON I., MALMBERG A. and VATNE E. (1998) *Competitiveness, Localised Learning and Regional Development: Specialisation and Prosperity in Small Open Economies.* Routledge, London.

MATTHIESSEN C. W. and SCHWARZ A. W. (1999) Scientific centres in Europe: an analysis of research strength and patterns of specialisation based on bibliometric indicators, *Urban Studies* **36**, 453–477.

MCCANN E. J. (2004) 'Best places': inter-urban competition, quality of life, and popular media discourse, *Urban Studies* **41**, 1909–1929.

MCDOWELL G. R. (1995) Some communities are successful, others are not: toward an institutional framework for understanding the reasons why, in SEARS D. W. and REID J. N. (Eds) *Rural Development Strategies*, pp. 269–281. Nelson-Hall, Chicago.

MEYER-STAMER J. (1997) New patterns of governance for industrial change: perspectives for Brazil, *Journal of Development Studies* **33**, 364–391.

MICKLETHWAIT J. (1997) Future perfect? A survey of Silicon Valley, *Economist* **29 March**.

MICKLETHWAIT J. and WOOLDRIDGE A. (2000) *A Future Perfect: The Challenge and Hidden Promise of Globalization.* Crown Business, New York.

MILKEN INSTITUTE (2002) *Forbes–Milken Institute Best Places Ranking* (available at: http://www.milkeninstitute.org/research/research.taf?cat=indexes&function=detail&ID=16&type=FMI).

MILLER R. and COTÉ M. (1987) *Growing the Next Silicon Valley.* Lexington Books, Lexington, MA.

MORGAN K. and SAYER A. (1985) A 'modern' industry in a 'mature' region: the remaking of management–labour relations, *International Journal of Urban and Regional Research* **9**, 383–404.

MOSS P. and TILLY C. (1996) 'Soft' skills and race: an investigation of black men's employment problems, *Work and Occupations* **23**, 252–276.

MOULAERT F. and SEKIA F. (2003) Territorial innovation models: a critical survey, *Regional Studies* **37**, 289–302.

NAM C. W., NERB G. and RUSS H. (1990) *An Empirical Assessment of Factors Shaping Regional Competitiveness in Problem Regions*. Main Report. Commission of the European Communities, Luxembourg.

NATIONAL SCIENCE FOUNDATION (2002) *Science and Engineering State Profiles: 1999–2000*. NSF, Arlington (available at: http://www.nsf.gov/sbe/srs/nsf02318/htmstart.htm).

NELSON R. R. (Ed.) (1993) *National Innovation Systems*. Oxford University Press, Oxford.

NEVAREZ L. (2003) *New Money, Nice Town: How Capital Works in the New Urban Economy*. Routledge, London.

NIJKAMP P. (1993) Towards a network of regions: the united states of Europe, *European Planning Studies* **1**, 149–168.

NOVAKNOWLEDGE (2002) *Nova Scotia Knowledge Report Card 2002*. NovaKnowledge, Halifax (available at: http://www.novaknowledge.ns.ca/media/documents/reportcard_2002.pdf).

OFFICE OF TECHNOLOGY ASSESSMENT (1991) *Competing Economies: America, Europe, and the Pacific Rim*. US Congress, OTA, Washington, DC.

OHMAE K. (1995) *The End of the Nation State: The Rise of Regional Economies*. Free Press, New York.

OINAS P. and MALECKI E. J. (2002) The evolution of technologies in time and space: from national and regional to spatial innovation systems, *International Regional Science Review* **25**, 102–131.

ONTARIO SCIENCE AND INNOVATION COUNCIL (2002) *Ontario Innovation 2002 Index*. Ministry of Enterprise, Opportunity and Innovation, Toronto (available at: http://www.ontariocanada.com/ontcan/en/downloads/reports/report_dec_2002_innovation_index.pdf).

PACI R. and USAI S. (2000) Technological enclaves and industrial districts: an analysis of the regional distribution of innovative activity in Europe, *Regional Studies* **34**, 97–114.

PAINTER J. (1998) Entrepreneurs are made, not born: learning and urban regimes in the production of entrepreneurial cities, in HALL T. and HUBBARD P. (Eds) *The Entrepreneurial City: Geographies of Politics, Regime and Representation*, pp. 259–273. Wiley, Chichester.

PENEDER M. (2001) *Entrepreneurial Competition and Industrial Location: Investigating the Structural Patterns and Intangible Sources of Competitive Advantage*. Edward Elgar, Cheltenham.

PERRY D. C. (2003) Urban tourism and the privatizing discourses of public infrastructure, in JUDD D. R. (Ed.) *The Infrastructure of Play: Building the Tourist City*, pp. 19–49. M. E. Sharpe, Armonk, NY.

PETTY D. (2002) *Great North Opportunity Forecast 2002–2003*. Great North Alliance, Minneapolis (available at: http://www.thegreatnorth.com/reports/2002_2003_Opportunity_Forecast_Appendix.pdf).

POLÈSE M., SHEARMUR R., DESJARDINS P.-M. and JOHNSON M. L. (2002) *The Periphery in the Knowledge Economy: The Spatial Dynamics of the Canadian Economy and the Future of Non-Metropolitan Regions in Quebec and the Atlantic Provinces*. Institut National de la Recherche Scientifique – Urbanisation, Culture et Société and Canadian Institute for Research on Regional Development, Montreal.

PORTER A. L., ROESSNER J. D., JIN X.-Y. and NEWMAN N. C. (2001) Changes in national technological competitiveness: 1990, 1993, 1996 and 1999, *Technology Analysis and Strategic Management* **13**, 477–496.

PORTER M. E. (1990) *The Competitive Advantage of Nations*. Free Press, New York.

PORTER M. E. (1998a) Clusters and competition: new agendas for companies, governments, and institutions, in PORTER M. E. *On Competition*, pp. 197–287. Harvard Business School Press, Boston.

PORTER M. E. (1998b) Clusters and the new economics of competition, *Harvard Business Review* **76**, 77–90.

PORTER M. E. (2001) Regions and the new economics of competition, in SCOTT A. J. (Ed.) *Global City-regions*, pp. 139–157. Oxford University Press, Oxford.

POTTS G. (2002) Competitiveness and the social fabric: links and tensions in cities, in BEGG I. (Ed.) (2002) *Urban Competitiveness: Policies for Dynamic Cities*, pp. 55–80. Policy, Bristol.

RACO M. (1998) Assessing 'institutional thickness' in the local context: a comparison of Cardiff and Sheffield, *Environment and Planning A* **30**, 975–996.

RAINES P. (2000) Regions in competition: inward investment and regional variation in the use of incentives, *Regional Studies* **34**, 291–296.

REICH R. B. (1991) *The Work of Nations*. Alfred A. Knopf, New York.

RODRÍGUEZ-POSE A. (1999) Innovation prone and innovation averse societies: economic performance in Europe, *Growth and Change* **30**, 75–105.

ROESSNER D., PORTER A. L., NEWMAN N. and JIN X.-Y. (2002) A comparison of recent assessments of the high-tech competitiveness of nations, *International Journal of Technology Management* **23**, 536–557.

ROESSNER J. D., PORTER A. L., NEWMAN N. and CAUFFIEL D. (1996) Anticipating the future high-tech competitiveness of nations: indicators for twenty-eight countries, *Technological Forecasting and Social Change* **51**, 133–149.

ROGERS E. M. and LARSEN J. (1984) *Silicon Valley Fever*. Basic Books, New York.

ROSENBERG D. (2002) *Cloning Silicon Valley*. Reuters, London.

RYANS J. K. and SHANKLIN W. L. (1986) *Guide to Marketing for Economic Development: Competing in America's Second Civil War*. Publishing Horizons, Columbus, OH.

SASSEN S. (2001) Global cities and global city-regions: a comparison, in SCOTT A. J. (Ed.) *Global City-regions: Trends, Theory, Policy*, pp. 78–95. Oxford University Press, Oxford.

SAXENIAN A. and LI C.-Y. (2003) Bay-to-bay strategic alliances: the network linkages between Taiwan and the US venture capital industries, *International Journal of Technology Management* **25**, 136–150.

SCHMANDT J. and WILSON R. W. (Eds) (1990) *Growth Policy in the Age of High Technology: The Role of Regions and States.* Unwin Hyman, Boston.

SCHWAB C. and CORNELIUS P. K. (2003) *The Arab World Competitiveness Report 2002–2003.* Oxford University Press, Oxford.

SCOTT A. J. (1998) *Regions and the World Economy.* Oxford University Press, Oxford.

SCOTT A. J. (2000) *The Cultural Economy of Cities: Essays On the Geography of Image-Producing Industries.* Sage, Thousand Oaks.

SHEPPARD E. (2000) Competition in space and between places, in SHEPPARD E. and BARNES T. J. (Eds) *A Companion to Economic Geography*, pp. 169–186. Blackwell, Oxford.

SHORT J. R. and KIM Y.-H. (1998) Urban crises/urban representations: selling the city in difficult times, in HALL T. and HUBBARD P. (Eds) *The Entrepreneurial City: Geographies of Politics, Regime and Representation*, pp. 55–75. Wiley, Chichester.

SHOVAL N. (2002) A new phase in the competition for the Olympic gold: the London and New York bids for the 2012 games, *Journal of Urban Affairs* **24**, 583–599.

SIMMIE J. (Ed.) (2001) *Innovative Cities.* E & FN Spon, London.

SMITH D. and TIMBERLAKE M. (2002) Hierarchies of dominance among world cities: a network approach, in SASSEN S. (Ed.) *Global Networks, Linked Cities*, pp. 117–141. Routledge, London.

STATE SCIENCE AND TECHNOLOGY INSTITUTE (2002) Special Issue: A look at innovation indices & report cards. *SSTI Weekly Digest* **1 November** (available at: http://www.ssti.org/Digest/2002/110102.htm).

STOPFORD J. and STRANGE S. (1991) *Rival States, Rival Firms.* Cambridge University Press, Cambridge.

STORPER M. (1997) *The Regional World.* Guilford Press, New York.

STORPER M. and VENABLES A. J. (2002) Buzz: the economic force of the city. Paper presented at the DRUID Summer Conference, 'Industrial Dynamics of the New and Old Economy – Who is Embracing Whom?', Copenhagen/Elsinore, Denmark, 6–8 June 2002 (available at: http://www.druid.dk/conferences/summer2002/Papers/STORPER.pdf).

SWYNGEDOUW E. A. (1992) The mammon quest. 'Glocalisation', interspatial competition and the new monetary order: the construction of new scales, in DUNFORD M. and KAFLAKAS G. (Eds) *Cities and Regions in the New Europe*, pp. 39–67. Belhaven, London.

TEWDWR-JONES M. and PHELPS N. A. (2000) Levelling the uneven playing field: inward investment, interregional rivalry and the planning system, *Regional Studies* **34**, 429–440.

THOMAS K. (2003) Geographic scales and the competition for economic growth, *American Behavioral Scientist* **46**, 987–1001.

TRANSPARENCY INTERNATIONAL (2003) *Global Corruption Report 2003.* TI, Berlin (available at: http://www.globalcorruptionreport.org/index.shtml).

URBAN F. (2002) Small town, big website? Cities and their representation on the Internet, *Cities* **19**, 49–59.

US DEPARTMENT OF COMMERCE (1983) *An Assessment of U. S. Competitiveness in High Technology Industries.* US Department of Commerce, International Trade Administration, Washington, DC.

US DEPARTMENT OF COMMERCE, TECHNOLOGY ADMINISTRATION (2001) *State Science & Technology Indicators* (available at: http://www.ta.doc.gov/reports/TechPolicy/StatesIndicators2.pdf).

VAN DEN BERG L. and BRAUN E. (1999) Urban competitiveness, marketing and the need for organizing capacity, *Urban Studies* **36**, 987–999.

VAN DEN BERG L., VAN DEN BORG J. and RUSSO A. P. (2003) The infrastructure of urban tourism: a European model? A comparative analysis of mega-projects in four Eurocities, in JUDD D. R. (Ed.) *The Infrastructure of Play: Building the Tourist City*, pp. 296–319. M. E. Sharpe, Armonk, NY.

VAN WYK R. J. (1997) Strategic technology scanning, *Technological Forecasting and Social Change* **55**, 21–38.

VIAL J. and CORNELIUS P. K. (2002) *The Latin American Competitiveness Report 2001–2002.* Oxford University Press, Oxford.

WAITT G. (1999) Playing games with Sydney: marketing Sydney for the 2000 Olympics, *Urban Studies* **36**, 1055–1077.

WARNER A. M. (2002) *The European Competitiveness and Transition Report 2001–2002: Ratings of Accession Progress, Competitiveness, and Economic Restructuring of European and Transition Economies.* Oxford University Press, Oxford.

WHITE P., DOUGLAS A. and STILLWELL D. (2003) *Regional Competitiveness & State of the Regions.* Department of Trade and Industry, London (available at: http://217.154.27.195/sd/rci/download_document.htm).

WONG C. (1998) Determining factors for local economic development: the perception of practitioners in the North West and Eastern regions of the UK, *Regional Studies* **32**, 707–720.

WORLD ECONOMIC FORUM (2003) *Global Competitiveness Report 2002–2003* (available at: http://www.weforum.org/site/homepublic.nsf/Content/Global+Competitiveness+Programme%5CReports%5CGlobal+Competitiveness+Report+2002–2003).

WU F. (2000) The global and local dimensions of place-making: remaking Shanghai as a world city, *Urban Studies* **37**, 1359–1377.

YGLESIAS E. (2003) Porter vs. Porter: modeling the technological competitiveness of nations, *Scientometrics* **57**, 281–293.

The Economic Performance of Regions

MICHAEL E. PORTER

Institute for Strategy and Competitiveness, Harvard Business School, Soldiers Field Road, Boston, MA 02163, USA.
Email: mporter@hbs.edu

(First received February 2003; in revised form April 2003)

PORTER M. E. (2003) The economic performance of regions, *Reg. Studies* **37**, 549–578. This paper examines the basic facts about the regional economic performance, the composition of regional economies and the role of clusters in the US economy over period of 1990 to 2000. The performance of regional economies varies markedly in terms of wage, wage growth, employment growth and patenting rate. Based on the distribution of economic activity across geography, we classify US industries into traded, local and resource-dependent. Traded industries account for only about one-third of employment but register much higher wages, far higher rates of innovation and influence local wages. We delineate clusters of traded industries using co-location patterns across US regions. The mix of clusters differs markedly across regions. The performance of regional economies is strongly influenced by the strength of local clusters and the vitality and plurality of innovation. Regional wage differences are dominated by the relative performance of the region in the clusters in which it has positions, with the particular mix of clusters secondary. A series of regional policy implications emerge from the findings.

Regional economic performance   Clusters   Competitiveness   Industrial location

PORTER M. E. (2003) La performance économique des regions, *Reg. Studies* **37**, 549–578. Cet article cherche à examiner les principes fondamentaux de la performance économique régionale, de la structure des économies régionales, et du rôle des groupements dans l'économie des Etats-Unis de 1990 à 2000. La performance des économies régionales varie sensiblement du point de vue des salaires, de la croissance des salaires, de la hausse de l'emploi, et du nombre des brevets. A partir de la répartition de l'activité économique géographique, on classe les entreprises industrielles aux Etats-Unis sous les rubriques commerciale, locale, et dépendante des ressources. Les entreprises industrielles à vocation commerciale n'expliquent qu'un tiers de l'emploi mais laissent voir des salaires nettement plus élevés, des taux d'innovation bien plus importants, et influent sur les salaires locaux. Employant des distributions de localisations partagées à travers les Etats-Unis, on délimite des groupements d'entreprises industrielles à vocation commerciale. La structure des groupements varie sensiblement suivant la région. La performance des économies régionales est fortement influencé par la force des groupements locaux et par la vitalité et par la pluralité de l'innovation. Les écarts des salaires réels s'expliquent primordialement par la performance relative de la région quant aux groupements où elle est présente, la structure particulière des groupements n'étant que d'une importance secondaire. Il en résulte toute une série d'implications pour la politique.

Performance économique régionale   Groupements   Compétitivité   Localisation industrielle

PORTER M. E. (2000) Die wirtschaftliche Leistungskraft von Regionen, *Reg. Studies* **37**, 549–578. Dieser Beitrag analysiert Kerndaten regionaler Wirtschaftsräume in den Vereinigten Staaten, insbesondere ihre wirtschaftliche Leistungskraft, ihre Zusammensetzung und die Rolle regionaler Cluster. Die Regionen der Vereinigten Staaten unterschieden sich in den Jahren 1990 bis 2000 deutlich in ihrer wirtschaftlichen Leistungskraft gemessen an Lohnniveau und – wachstum, Beschäftigungsentwicklung, und Patentrate. Basierend auf der geographischen Konzentration öknomischer Aktitivtät klassifizieren wir Industriezweige als überregional ('traded'), lokal oder abhängig von der Präsenz von Naturschätzen. Cluster überregionaler Industrien beschäftigen nur circa ein Drittel äller Erwerbstätigen, verzeichnen aber überdurchschnittliche Löhne und signifikant höhere Innovationsraten als die Gesamtwirtschaft. Die relative Bedeutung einzelner Cluster innerhalb der Gruppe überregionaler Industrien unterscheidet sich deutlich im regionalen Vergleich. Der wirtschaftliche Erfolg einer Region wird stark von der relative Leistungskraft und Innovationsstärke der dort angesiedelten überregionalen Cluster beeinflusst. So hat das relative Lohnniveau in den überregionalen Clustern in einer Region einen dominanten Einfluss auf das regionale Lohnniveau, während die spezifische Identität dieser Cluster nur eine sekundäre Rolle spielt. Der Beitrag entwickelt aus dieser Analyse eine Reihe von Implikationen für die Wirtschaftspolitik.

Regionale Wirtschaftsleistung   Cluster   Wettbewerbsfähigkeit   Industriestandort

Studies of competitiveness and economic development have tended to focus on the nation as the unit of analysis, and on national attributes and policies as the drivers. As regional scientists and economic geographers have long understood, however, there are substantial differences in economic performance across regions in virtually every nation. This suggests that many of the essential determinants of economic performance are to be found at the regional level.

There is a substantial theoretical literature on regional economic development, and numerous case studies have explored the influences on economic development and performance in particular regions. SCOTT, 2000, provides a comprehensive review of the economic geography literature over the past half century. FELDMAN, 2000; GLAESER, 2000; and HANSON, 2000, provide additional literature review. Despite this rich tradition, empirical studies of large samples of regions have been comparatively rare. A recent body of work has examined various hypotheses about regional performance in large samples of cities, most notably the respective influence of economic specialization and diversity.[1] In this paper, we aim to contribute to this empirical literature with a complementary approach. Using a newly assembled dataset covering every metropolitan area, economic area and state in the US, and new statistical methods to derive the composition of regional economies and the boundaries of clusters of linked industries, we seek to explore the basic facts about regional economies in the US. In particular, we explore the overall economic performance of regions, the composition of regional economies, and the role of clusters in composition and performance.

Our primary aim here is not to test a particular theory, but to examine facts and relationships that have been implicit or explicit in many theories.[2] How much do regions vary in wages, employment growth and patenting rates? How important is size or industry specialization in performance? Does the particular composition of industries in a region matter? What are the groups of industries that are linked in geographically concentrated clusters, and how does cluster position and mix relate to a region's performance? Those and many other questions are examined, employing basic statistical tests. In-depth analyses of particular hypotheses are the subject of other papers.[3]

The core dataset is the annual County Business Patterns (CBP) data, covering employment, establishments and wages by county at the four-digit SIC (Standard Industrial Classification) level.[4] The newer NAICS system offers some improvements because it is less aggregated, but the changes affect a modest number of industries. We utilize the SIC system in this analysis because of the availability of a decade of historical data. The CBP data excludes government and military employment but covers the great majority of the private sector, excluding only agricultural workers, railroad workers and household employment.

To the CBP data we matched patent data from the US Patent and Trademark Office and CHI Research, which is allocated to SIC codes using an algorithm developed by Silverman (SILVERMAN, 1999). Patents are the best available measure of innovative activity across all regions, and we explore the patterns of patenting across geography and its relationship with industry location.[5] All our data covers the 1990 to 2000 time period.

The primary geographic unit used in the analysis is the Economic Area (EA) as defined by the Bureau of Economic Analysis. There are 172 EAs covering the entire US, which are generally smaller than states but larger than most metropolitan statistical areas or MSAs (see Appendix A). We utilize EAs, rather than MSAs which have been the focus of much of the statistical literature, because EAs cover the entire US, have stable definitions over time and, most importantly, better reflect true economic boundaries of regions because they capture the actual patterns of market exchange that often cross arbitrary MSA borders. We utilized states (51 including Washington, DC) as the geographic unit for some analyses due to less data suppression. All of the analyses here have been replicated using all three geographic units and, by and large, the results are similar.

The first section of this paper focuses on differences in overall regional economic performance in terms of wages, wage growth, employment growth, and patenting. The next section uses the actual patterns of industry employment across geography to decompose regional economies into traded, local, and resource-dependent industries, and we explore their respective roles in economic performance. We then employ statistical methods to derive clusters of traded industries that co-locate.[6] We explore the attributes, overlap, and distribution of clusters across the US economy and the relationship between the mix of clusters in a region and its performance. A final section provides a summary and conclusions.

DIFFERENCES IN REGIONAL ECONOMIC PERFORMANCE

A region's overall average wage[7] is perhaps the most basic measure of its economic performance and most associated with its standard of living. In 2000, the average wage in US EAs was $27 533. There is a striking variation in average wages among EAs, ranging from $19 228 in North Platte, NE-CO to $52 213 in San Francisco-Oakland-San Jose, CA (see Fig. 1).

The average EA experienced an $8403 wage increase from 1990 to 2000, or about 44% of the 1990 average wage (a compound annual growth rate (CAGR) of 3.7%). However, wage growth also varied markedly across regions, with the CAGR over the 1990 to 2000 period ranging from 7.1% in Austin-

San Marcos, TX to 1.8% in Wheeling, WV-OH (see Fig. 2).

Regional wage inequality increased somewhat over the 1990–2000 period, with the wage GINI coefficient increasing from 0.0774 to 0.0940 over the period. However, wage growth was only weakly related to starting wage level (see Fig. 3). Hence, success or failure in growing wages in not determined by starting level but is affected by other influences that will be explored.

Another way of exploring the change in average regional wages over time is to group the EAs into wage deciles in 1990 and 2000 and examine the mobility between starting and ending decile groups (see Fig. 4).[8] Roughly half of the EAs (43.6%) remained in the same decile, 27.9% rose to a higher decile, and 28.5% fell to a lower decile, with no strong pattern related to starting level. Regions moving up two or more wage deciles included Fort Myers-Cape Coral (FL), Sioux City, Omaha, San Antonio, and Boise City, while regions moving down included Wheeling (WV-OH), Charleston (WV), Johnson City-Kingsport-Bristol (TN-VA), Erie (PA), and Champaign Urbana (IL).

Employment growth, another important attribute of economic performance, also varied markedly across regions, with employment CAGRs over the 1990–2000 period ranging from 6.49% for Austin-San Marcos to −0.08% for Syracuse. Employment growth had only a weak statistical relationship with starting employment size (see Fig. 5). Neither large nor small regions

were more successful overall in growing employment in the 1990s. There was also no discernable relationship between employment growth and starting average wages (Fig. 6). There was a relatively weak but significant positive relationship between wage growth and employment growth (see Fig. 7). It appears that regions that were improving their economic fundamentals benefited both in terms of jobs and wages.

It is a common assertion in economic development circles that large regions that support diverse economies will be advantaged. Average wages do tend to be higher in larger regions measured by employment size, even after excluding the outliers New York and Los Angeles (see Fig. 8). However, the relationship between employment size and wage growth is much weaker (see Fig. 9). Once again, the data reveal that both large and small regions experienced success in growing wages; and both large and small regions experienced problems.

A third, more forward-looking measure of regional performance is patenting. While the patent system does not capture all innovative activity (e.g. in services, software, etc.), patenting is the best available and comparable measure of innovative activity across regions.[9] We mapped patents to regions by assigning each patent to the region in which the inventor resides. In the case of multiple inventors from different regions, patents were assigned fractionally to each region.

Patenting intensity, measured by patents per 100 000

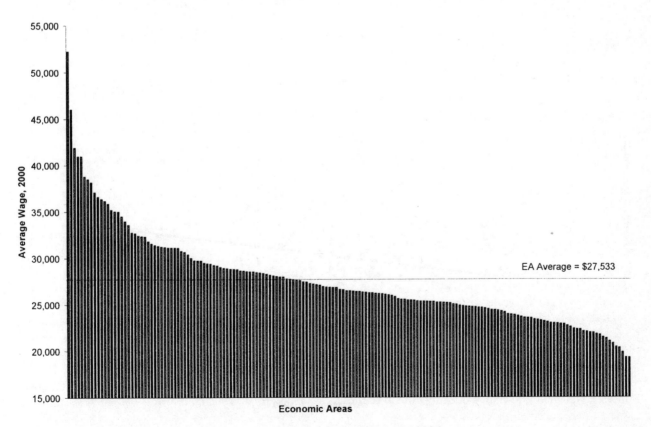

Fig. 1. Average wages by economic area, 2000

Sources: County Business Patterns; Cluster Mapping Project, Harvard Business School.

Regional Competitiveness

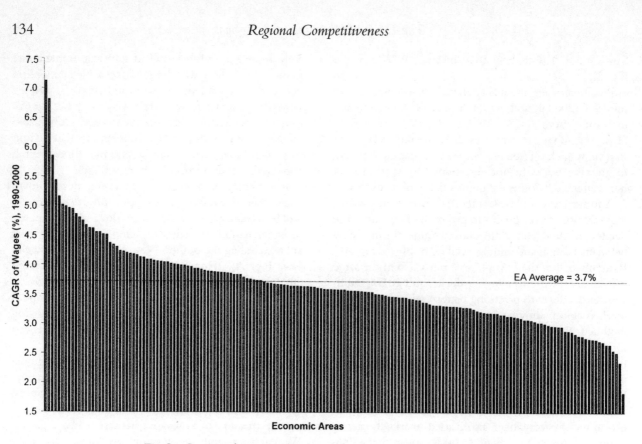

Fig. 2. *Compound average wage growth by economic area, 1990–2000*
Sources: County Business Patterns; Cluster Mapping Project, Harvard Business School.

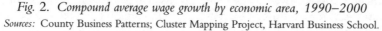
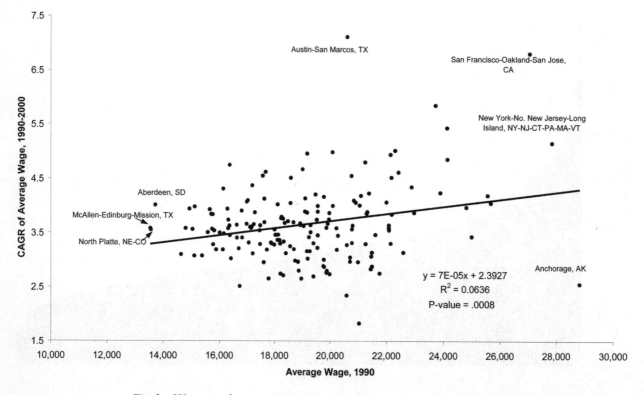

Fig. 3. *Wage growth vs. starting average wage by economic areas, 1990–2000*
Sources: County Business Patterns; Cluster Mapping Project, Harvard Business School.

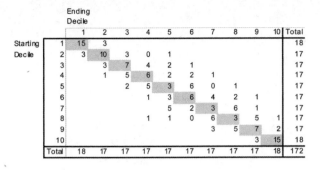

Fig. 4. *Changes in economic area wage deciles, 1990–2000*
Sources: County Business Patterns; Cluster Mapping Project,
Harvard Business School.

inhabitants in 2000, ranges from essentially 0 patents per 100 000 inhabitants in Abilene, TX to over 250 in Boise City (see Fig. 10). The variation in patenting across regions far surpasses the variation of average wages and employment growth. Compound annual growth in patenting per capita from 1990 to 2000 also varied markedly, ranging from 28.2% in Boise City to −4.8% per year in Shreveport-Bossier City, LA–AR (see Fig. 11). There is no relationship between the starting level of patenting and patent growth over the 1990s. A scatter plot of patenting per capita vs. the size of a region is provided in Fig. 12. We utilized negative binomial regression to examine the relationship between patenting per capita and employment size, and find the coefficient of employment size to be statistically significant.

There was no statistical relationship between the rate of employment growth and starting patenting (see Fig. 13). However, a region's patenting intensity is strongly associated with average wages (see Fig. 14), with patenting intensity accounting for almost 30% of the variation across regions in average wage. High patenting signals more advanced products and processes and higher productivity that support a higher wage. Patenting intensity remains highly significant after controlling for regional size.

We would expect that the relationship between patenting and average wages to be affected by whether patenting is widespread or concentrated in a small number of firms or institutions. Patenting distributed among many inventors would yield greater spillovers across innovators and be associated with higher productivity in numerous fields.[10] Using Patent and Trademark Office data on patenting organizations, we computed a Herfindahl-Hirschman Index (HHI) of patentor concentration.[11] Increasing patentor HHI (higher concentration) is negatively related to average wages (see Fig. 15). Note that large regions will tend to have more patentors, tending to reduce patentor HHI. However, the concentration of patentors has a negative and significant relationship with average wages even after controlling for regional size. We explore some of these relationships in more detail in a related paper (see PORTER, 2003).

Given the differing challenges of urban and rural economic development, it is of interest to see how

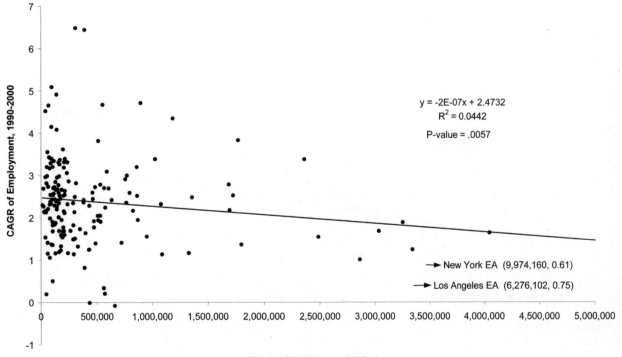

Fig. 5. *Employment growth vs. starting employment by economic area, 1990–2000*
Sources: County Business Patterns; Cluster Mapping Project, Harvard Business School.

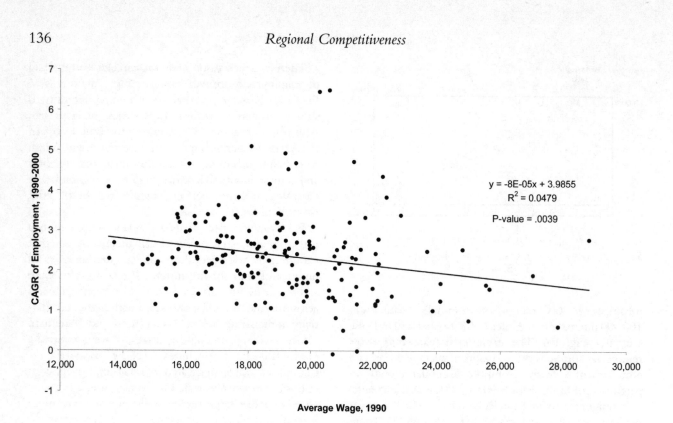

Fig. 6. *Employment growth vs. starting average wage by economic area, 1990–2000*
Sources: County Business Patterns; Cluster Mapping Project, Harvard Business School.

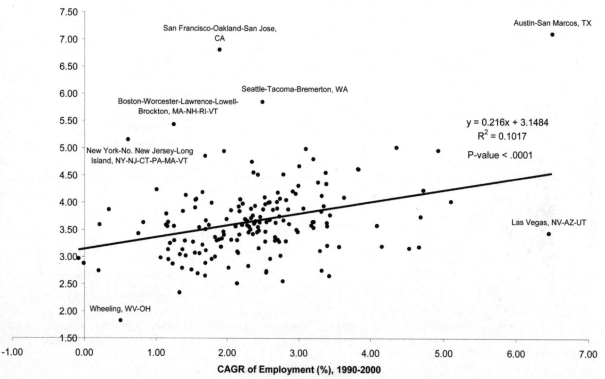

Fig. 7. *Wage growth vs. employment growth by economic area, 1990–2000*
Sources: County Business Patterns; Cluster Mapping Project, Harvard Business School.

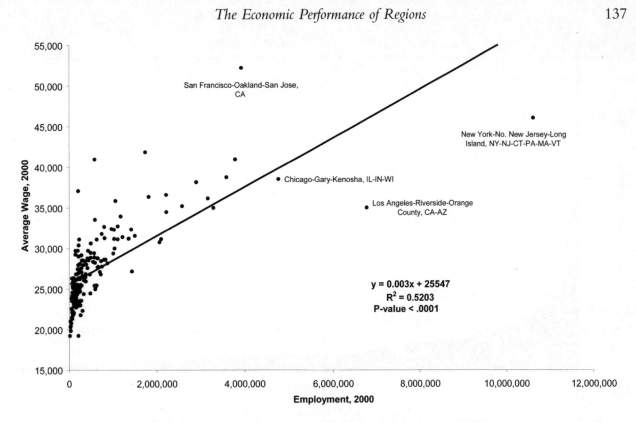

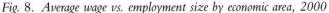

Fig. 8. *Average wage vs. employment size by economic area, 2000*

Note: Since the employment sizes of the Los Angeles and New York EAs are substantially larger than the size of the rest of the regions, we also examined the results after dropping these two observations. R^2 rises to 0.6145 and the coefficient of size remains positive but is somewhat higher.

Sources: County Business Patterns; Cluster Mapping Project, Harvard Business School.

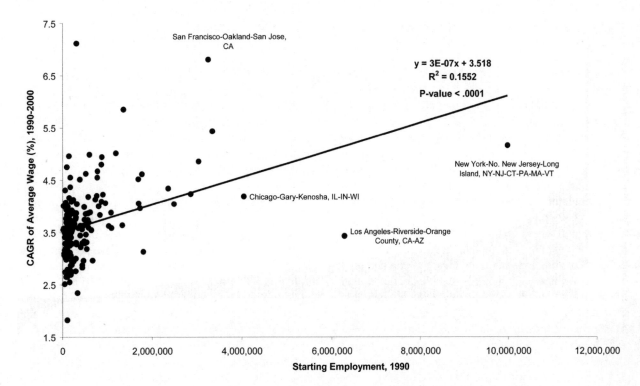

Fig. 9. *Average wage growth vs. starting employment by economic area, 1990–2000*

Note: Since the employment sizes of the Los Angeles and New York EAs are substantially larger than the size of the rest of the regions, we also examined the results after dropping these two observations. R^2 rises to 0.2379 and the coefficient is again moderately higher.

Sources: County Business Patterns; Cluster Mapping Project, Harvard Business School.

Regional Competitiveness

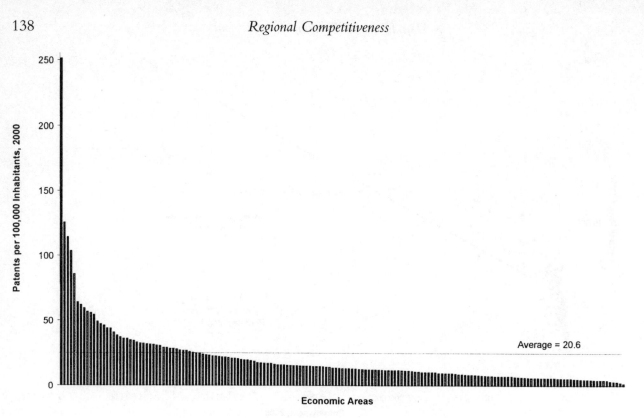

Fig. 10. *Patents per 100,000 inhabitants by economic area, 2000*
Sources: US Patent and Trademark Office; CHI Research; Cluster Mapping Project, Harvard Business School.

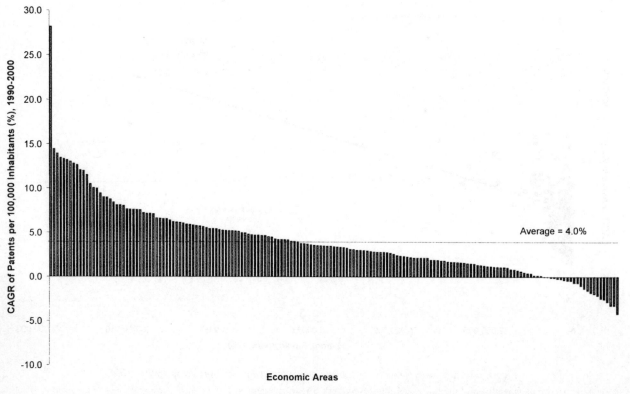

Fig. 11. *Growth in patents per 100,000 inhabitants by economic area, 1990–2000*
Sources: US Patent and Trademark Office; CHI Research; Cluster Mapping Project, Harvard Business School.

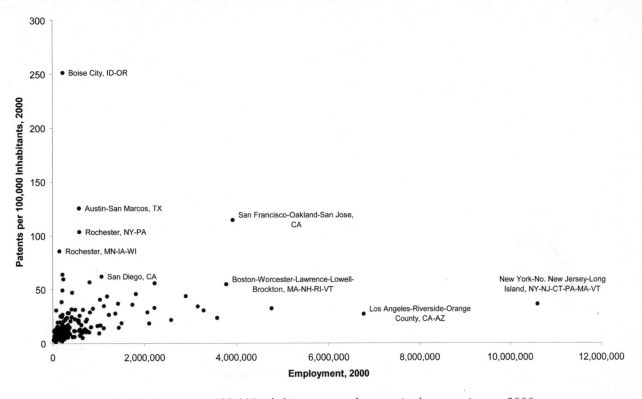

Fig. 12. *Patents per 100,000 inhabitants vs. employment size by economic area, 2000*

Sources: US Patent and Trademark Office; CHI Research; County Business Patterns; Cluster Mapping Project, Harvard Business School.

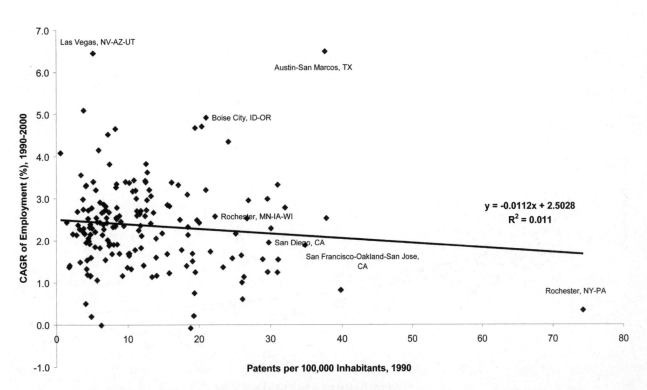

Fig. 13. *Employment growth vs. starting patents per 100,000 inhabitants by economic area, 1990–2000*

Sources: US Patent and Trademark Office; CHI Research; County Business Patterns; Cluster Mapping Project, Harvard Business School.

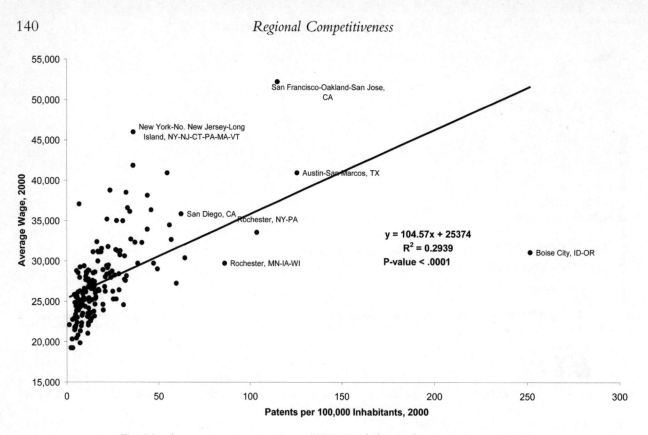

Fig. 14. *Average wage vs. patents per 100,000 inhabitants by economic area, 2000*
Sources: US Patent and Trademark Office; CHI Research; County Business Patterns; Cluster Mapping Project, Harvard Business School.

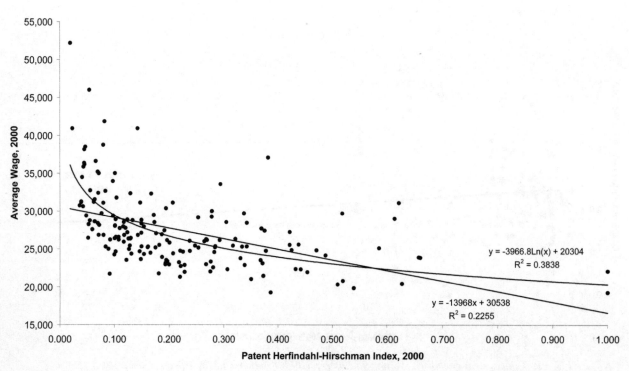

Fig. 15. *Average wage vs. patent HHI by economic area, 2000*
Sources: US Patent and Trademark Office; CHI Research; County Business Patterns; Cluster Mapping Project, Harvard Business School.

various measures of economic performance differ in urban versus rural areas. While a full analysis of this question is beyond the scope of this paper, we divided all US counties into those that are part of a metropolitan area (847) and those that are not (2293). Metropolitan (urban) counties account for 80.4% of US population in 2000 and 85.6% of private employment in 2000. The average metropolitan county wage was $35 716 in 2000, far higher (49%) than the $24 004 average in non-metropolitan counties. The CAGR of wages over the 1990 to 2000 period in metropolitan counties was 4.82% versus 3.81% in non-metropolitan counties. However, the CAGR of employment between 1990 and 2000 in metropolitan counties was 2.19%, less than the 2.34% in non-metropolitan counties.

THE COMPOSITION OF REGIONAL ECONOMIES

To explore these marked differences in regional performance further, we examine the differing types of industries that constitute a regional economy. The distribution of economic activity by industry over geography reveals three different broad types of industries, with very different patterns of spatial competition and different drivers of locational behavior. Distinguishing them is essential in testing hypotheses about regional performance.

The first type of industry in regional economies is *local* industries. In these industries, employment that is evenly distributed across all regions – that is, employment is roughly proportional to regional population. Local industries provide goods and services primarily to the local market, or the region in which the employment is located.[12] Such industries compete in only a limited way with other regions. Most are services including local health services, most utilities, retailing and many types of construction. A few goods producing industries are revealed as local, including bottled and canned soft drinks, newspapers, concrete products and ready-mixed concrete.

A second type of industry is *resource dependent* industries. Employment in these industries is located primarily where the needed natural resources are found, but these industries compete with other domestic and international locations. Examples of such industries include uranium ore, logging, beet sugar, and freight transportation on the Great Lakes.

The third type of industries in regional economies is *traded* industries that are not resource dependent. These industries sell products and services across regions and often to other countries. They locate in a particular region based not on resources but on broader competitive considerations, and employment concentration varies markedly by region. Examples of traded industries include aircraft engines and engine parts, motion picture and videotape production, and automobile assembly.[13]

We utilize the actual distribution of employment by industry to separate industries into these three groups, using data for 1996.[14] The CBP data *understates* the true geographic concentration of traded industries by region because the employment related to the local sales, service, distribution and other support activities of traded industries based elsewhere are counted in the local region in which the employment appears, even though the primary and headquarters activities are based elsewhere. This might be termed the local portion of traded industries. We utilize three measures of the variation of industry employment across geography to separate industries: the share of national employment for all states with LQ $\geqslant 1$; the mean location quotient (LQ) for the top five states ranked by LQ; and the employment GINI coefficient.

After examining the pattern of employment across geography in many industries, cutoffs were established for each variable: employment in states with LQ $\geqslant 1$ of $\geqslant 50\%$ of total employment; mean LQ of the top five states $\geqslant 2$; and employment GINI of 0.3. The vast majority of the 879 industries in the SIC system were clearly traded or local based on all three criteria. For the industries that met two but not all three criteria, we examined the actual distribution of employment as well as the industry definitions. Of those 62 industries, 18 were categorized as traded and the rest as local. We also identified a number of industries that were traded based on all three criteria but were local based on the industry definition (mostly retailers). We classified all of those as local after examining the employment distribution.

This process resulted in 241 local industries out of 879. Of the 638 traded industries, 48 had locational distributions and industry definitions tied heavily to the location of resource endowments. Our designation of resource-dependent industries was conservative, and only industries clearly dominated by resource endowments were included. This left 590 non-resource dependent traded industries. Table 1 gives a further breakdown of these industries categorized into goods and services. While the cutoff points used in developing the classifications were arbitrary, modifying the cutoffs led to only minor changes in the results.

Local industries prove to account for by far the largest share of US private employment, or 67%, which is perhaps surprising in an era where geographic borders are seen as having limited economic significance.[15] Even in a global economy and in a nation (the US) with completely open internal borders, two-thirds of

Table 1. *Mix of goods and services by industry type*

	Traded	Local	Natural endowment dependent
Goods	441	7	37
Services	149	234	11

Table 2. Composition of the US economy by type of industry

	Traded industries	Local industries	Natural endowment dependent industries
Share of employment (%)	31.8	67.4	0.80
Employment growth, 1990–2000 (CAGR) (%)	1.7	2.8	−1.0
Average wage ($)	45 040	27 169	32 129
Relative wage	137.0	82.6	97.7
Wage growth, 1990–2000 (CAGR) (%)	5.0	3.6	1.9
Relative productivity	144.1	79.3	140.1
Patents per 10 000 employees	21.1	1.3	7.0
Number of SIC industries	590	241	48

Notes: 2000 data, except relative productivity which is 1997 data. Relative wage equals the average wage of the class relative to the overall average (average = 100). Relative productivity equals productivity of the class relative to overall average productivity (average = 100).
Source: Cluster Mapping Project, Institute for Strategy and Competitiveness, Harvard Business School.

employment is heavily tied to the local market. The ownership of the parent company in local industries may be based elsewhere, but almost all these jobs are inherently local. It should be noted that while the designation as a local industry always reflects the vast majority of industry employment, there are a relatively few cases where a small segment of a local industry is traded.[16] The disproportionate position of Delaware in commercial banks (SIC 6060), for example, reflects Delaware's role as the state of incorporation for many national companies. Our data do not account for these cases.

Traded industries account for about 32% of employment (see Table 2). Natural endowment dependent industries account for only about 1% of employment. In a highly advanced economy such as the US, industries heavily dependent on natural endowments have declined to a minor part of employment, unlike the case in many developing economies.

While local industries account for the majority of employment, however, traded industries are fundamental to prosperity.[17] The average traded industry wage is $45 040 in 2000 versus $27 169 for local industries. Traded industries also have higher wage growth, much higher productivity and much higher patenting rates (see Table 2).

We calculated average productivity by industry, defined as sales/receipts/shipments per employee, using data from the 1997 Economic Census. While the data is imperfect due to some data suppression and is only available for 1997, traded industries are revealed to have much higher productivity than local industries, consistent with their higher patenting rates and higher wages. Resource dependent industries fall in between.[18]

Traded industries, then, appear to heavily influence the relative prosperity of regions. Competitive success

in traded industries creates demand for local industries serving commercial customers, while the higher wages paid by traded industries heavily influence local household demand.

The ratio of traded employment to total employment varies by EA, ranging from 18% in Sarasota–Bradenton, FL (a region with many retirees) to 47% in Hickory–Morganton, NC–TN in 2000 where the wood furniture cluster is located. A plot of total employment versus percentage of traded employment (Fig. 16) reveals no significant relationship, an interesting finding. Most regions tend to fall within a range of traded to total employment of between 26% and 37%, with smaller regions more likely to fall outside the range. This suggests that the presence of an unusually high or low proportion of traded employment may often be due to the misdefinition of true economic regions. Smaller regions, for example, may obtain local products and services from adjacent regions, reducing local employment share. Alternately, some regions may have large communities of retirees or higher proportions of individuals below working age, which can drive up the share of local employment.

There has been a meaningful shift in the composition of the US economy over the last decade, with the percentage of local employment rising from 64.9% in 1990 to 67.4% in 2000. Upon first reaction, this also appears contradictory to the globalization of competition. The rising proportion of local employment may be the result of several factors, including the higher productivity growth of traded industries and the fact that demand for local services tends to go up with prosperity (the 1990s were especially prosperous). An ageing population may also play a part. Also, the trend to greater outsourcing of services arbitrarily shifts the classification of some employment from manufacturing to services. Since many services are local, this boosts local share. Finally, overly broad industry definition may bury traded services in aggregates involving industries that are predominately local. For example, semiconductor chip design, which is traded and highly concentrated geographically, is part of 'engineering services', much of which is geographically dispersed.

The average level of local wages in a region is strongly associated with the average level of traded wages,[19] as shown in Fig. 17. On average, local wage is 66% of traded wage. Yet, the proportion of traded employment to total employment has a weak relationship with the regional average wage. This suggests that the average wage achieved in a region's traded industries tends to determine the local wage and hence drives the region's overall average wage. Hence the causality appears to go from traded wages to local wages, not vice versa.

In order to more precisely explore the role of a region's mix of traded versus local employment in regional average wage, we calculate a mix and level effect. The mix effect sets the average wage of traded

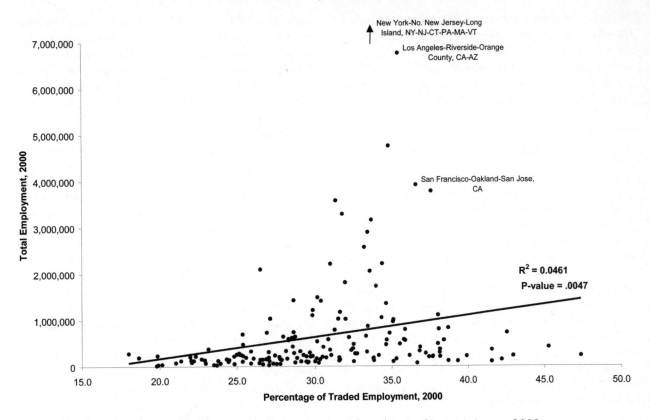

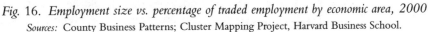

Fig. 16. *Employment size vs. percentage of traded employment by economic area, 2000*
Sources: County Business Patterns; Cluster Mapping Project, Harvard Business School.

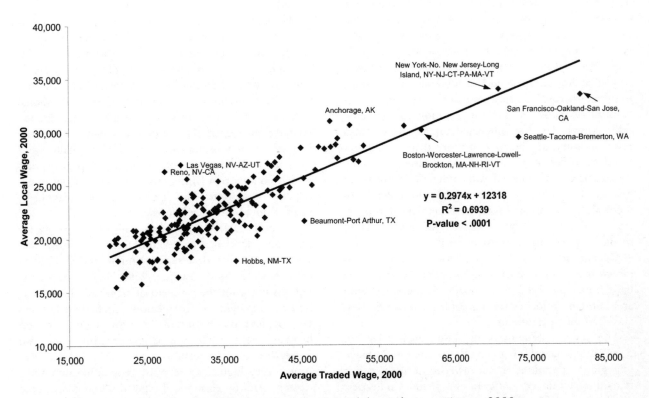

Fig. 17. *Average local wages vs. average traded wage by economic area, 2000*
Sources: County Business Patterns; Cluster Mapping Project, Harvard Business School.

and local industries at the national averages to isolate the effect of a region's traded–local employment mix on its average wage. The level effect measures the contribution to a region's average wage of the differences between its traded wage and local wages and the national averages weighted by the region's actual mix of traded and local employment. The level effect dominates, accounting for 79.4% of the variation in determining average wages across regions, while the mix effect accounts for just 20.6%. The key for a region, then, is to develop the conditions for supporting high wages in its traded industries, rather than attempting to grow the traded share of the economy.

Finally, we explored the differences in the composition of regional economies between urban and rural areas. Metropolitan counties and non-metropolitan counties prove to have similar shares of traded and local employment. Both traded and local wages are much lower in non-metropolitan areas, while the ratio of traded to local wages is moderately higher in metropolitan counties. Interestingly, the average wages for national endowment industries are nearly identical in urban and rural areas. Metropolitan counties account for a much lower proportion of natural endowment industries than non-metropolitan counties.

CLUSTERS OF TRADED INDUSTRIES

One of the most striking features of regional economies is the presence of clusters, or geographic concentrations of linked industries.[20] We define a cluster as a geographically proximate group of interconnected companies, suppliers, service providers and associated institutions in a particular field, linked by externalities of various types. Examples of clusters are financial services in New York (Wall Street), medical devices in Boston, and IT in Austin, Texas and Silicon Valley. Clusters are important because of the externalities that connect the constituent industries, such as common technologies, skills, knowledge and purchased inputs. Note that a given industry can be part of more than one cluster based on different patterns of externalities. Software, for example, is connected with other IT industries in terms of technology and demand, but also linked with medical devices because software is embedded in many types of devices and software development is crucial to medical device product development.

Recent academic and practitioner literature has placed increasing emphasis on industry clustering as a basic feature of regional and national economies, with an important influence on innovation, competitiveness and economic performance.[21]

The concept of clusters also bears on a debate in economic geography between the relative importance of regional specialization and diversity. This debate is framed predominantly in terms of individual industries. As characterized by Glaeser and colleagues (GLAESER *et al.*, 1992), the so-called MAR framework posits that

regional performance will be driven by specialization in a few industries because specialized regions will advance more quickly down the earning curve.[22] Others, notably JACOBS, 1969, argue that regional diversity in a wide array of industries will spark creativity and innovation. We have been associated with MAR. Previous statistical tests, using MSAs as the unit of geography, have mixed results.[23]

The cluster perspective suggests that these hypotheses are too simple, and offers a third hypothesis in between the two extremes. The industry may not be the appropriate unit of analysis because of the externalities across related industries within clusters. The relevant knowledge spillovers that affect innovation and performance should be strongest within cluster and among related industries. Hence, specialization in clusters, not in industries *per se*, should lead to higher performance. Diversity of clusters in a region rather than diversity of industries may also be a more meaningful diversity measure (KETELHÖHN, 2002). A diverse array of overlapping clusters (see below) should be associated with better performance than a diversity of clusters that are unrelated.

A major constraint to the analysis of clusters has been the lack of a systematic approach to defining the industries that should be included in each cluster and the absence of consistent empirical data on cluster composition across a large sample of regional economies. Lack of large sample empirical data is understandable, since knowledge spillovers and other positive externalities are difficult if not impossible to measure directly.

We proceed indirectly, using the locational correlation of employment across traded industries to reveal externalities and define cluster boundaries. For example, if computer hardware employment is nearly always associated geographically with software employment, this provides a strong indication of locational linkages. Such a methodology exploits the unique characteristics of the US economy which is by far the largest economy in the world, in which virtually every industry and cluster in any economy is present, and which consists of a large number of distinct but interdependent regions. This approach is not feasible in most if not all other countries.

We utilized states as the base unit of geography for computing locational correlations for two reasons. First, states involve less data suppression in the CBP data than EAs. Second, starting with larger geographic regions mitigates the problem of artificially high locational employment correlation coefficients when employment in a given traded industry is small or zero in many regions. The use of small regions, then, can cause locational correlation across many industries to appear very high. The relevant geographic unit for a cluster varies by cluster and region. Clusters are often concentrated within a state and, conversely, clusters sometimes cross state lines. However, states are large enough and sufficiently diverse in economic landscape to reveal clusters. After defining clusters using states, we repeated the analysis using EAs. While the correlations were generally higher for EAs, the patterns were nearly identical to clusters defined using states.

Using CBP data for 1996, we identified pairs and then groups of tightly linked industries based on statistically significant locational correlations.[24] Standard clustering algorithms proved inadequate to revealing the multiple patterns of linkages across industries. To build up clusters, then, we proceeded pragmatically, beginning with small groups of obviously related industries and then tracing correlation patterns to others.

The major complexity arises because of spurious correlation, which can occur for several reasons. First, SIC industry definitions tend to be overly broad, hence two industries may be correlated overall though only a small portion of one industry involves the linked products or services. Second, the CBP data do not distinguish between employment in headquarters activities and that employment dispersed to serve local markets. This overstates true traded industry employment in many locations. Third, industries with a major presence in large employment states like California and New York can appear highly correlated with each other even though there is no economic relationship. Fourth, small industries can register small or zero employment in many locations, making them appear correlated. Finally, industries can register high locational correlation if they are part of different clusters that appear in some of the same larger states, either by chance or for historical reasons related to natural resources. The strong position in Michigan of both automotive industries and industries related to office and commercial furniture, for example, creates a statistical correlation between the two groups of industries even though they are located in different parts of the state and have little or no economic relationship with each other.

We employed a sequence of steps to eliminate spurious correlation. First, we used detailed four-digit SIC industry definitions and lists of products included in each industry, together with industry knowledge, to reveal the likely presence of logical externalities. Focused case studies were conducted in unfamiliar industries to better understand the possible externalities present. Second, where there were no apparent externalities, we utilized the National 1992 input–output (I-O) accounts from the Bureau of Economic Analysis to look for meaningful cross-industry flows.[25] Note that input–output links are just one of many forms of externalities or linkages between industries within a cluster, but have the advantage that systematic data is available even though industry definitions in the I-O tables are more aggregated than the four-digit SIC codes we employ. Where there was no logical externality *and* the I-O data revealed no meaningful product flows, a correlation pair was excluded as spurious. Through this sequence of steps, we eliminated those

pairs of correlated industries where there was no apparent basis for linkages.

This process resulted in 41 traded clusters in the US economy, with an average of about 29 industries each.[26] Each cluster has a different geographic pattern of employment. Clusters often contain both manufacturing and service industries as well as industries from various parts of the SIC system. Clusters, then, represent a different way of dividing the economy than is embodied in conventional industrial classification systems that are based primarily on product type and similarities in production.

We expected overlap of industries across clusters, and such overlap was indeed present empirically. Total cluster employment including overlap is 204% of total traded employment in 2000. So that, on average, each industry is part of about two clusters. Fig. 18 provides a schematic representation of those clusters with substantial overlap. Some clusters are linked with several others, such as education and knowledge creation (significant overlap with eight other clusters) and analytic instruments (significant overlap with seven other clusters). Other clusters (e.g. textiles forest products, distribution services) are relatively independent.

The presence of overlapping industries across clusters leads to double counting of employment. In order to eliminate double counting for some analyses, we designated *broad* and *narrow* cluster definitions. Broad cluster definitions include all the industries included in a cluster. Narrow cluster definitions involve assigning each industry to the single cluster with which it has the strongest locational correlation. Here clusters are mutually exclusive.

We also subdivided each cluster into *subclusters*. Subclusters are subgroups of industries *within* the cluster whose locational correlations with each other were higher than with remaining industries. Subclusters are important because they can differ in sophistication, wage and patenting rates. Different regions often have differing concentrations in some subclusters relative to others.

Separate subclusters were defined for the set of industries included in the narrow cluster definition and those in the remaining industries. In most cases, subclusters were quite sharply delineated. In other cases, judgements based on detailed industry definitions were made or subclusters were designated with only one constituent industry. In all, there were 264 subclusters for narrowly defined clusters, or an average of 6.4 subclusters per cluster. There were a total of 550 subclusters for broadly defined clusters, or an average of 13.4 (see Appendix B).

Table 3 lists the 41 clusters together with some key parameters of each cluster using narrow cluster definitions. The clusters vary substantially in employment, average wages, employment growth and wage growth. The largest cluster is business services, which employed 4 667 320 in 2000. The average cluster

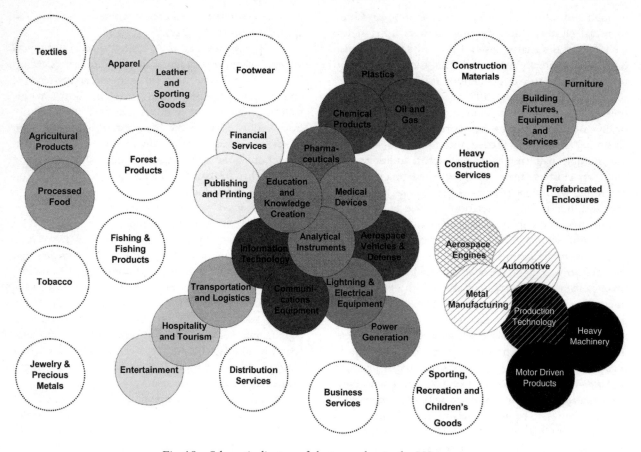

Fig. 18. *Schematic diagram of cluster overlap in the US economy*

Note: Clusters with overlapping borders or identical shading have at least 20% overlap (by number of industries) in both directions.

employed 854 352 workers. The smallest cluster, footwear, employed only 23 962 workers in 2000. Average cluster wages in 2000 ranged from $93 024 in information technology to $21 229 in hospitality and tourism (see Table 3).

Clusters normally designated as 'high-tech' – aerospace engines, aerospace vehicles and defence, analytical instruments, biopharmaceuticals, communication equipment, information technology and medical devices – account for just 8.9% of traded employment and 2.8% of total US private employment. The average high-tech cluster wage is $63 972 versus $43 183 for other clusters. The proportion of high-tech employment has a meaningful impact on a region's average wage, which explains 27.0% of the variation in regional average wages. However, high-tech share explains 12.5% of the variation in the average wage in *non*-high-tech clusters, and 14.4% of the variation of *local* wages. Hence success in high-tech clusters does not just raise wages directly, but signals an ability to compete productively and sustain higher wages elsewhere in the economy.

We found that regional high-tech share had no meaningful relationship with employment growth. Also, regions that are growing their high-tech share do not have higher wage *growth* in the region as a whole,

nor is growth in high-tech share associated with higher wage growth in non-high-tech clusters.

Rather than focusing solely on developing 'high-tech' clusters, then, our data reveal that regions need to upgrade *all* the clusters that are present. This conclusion is verified by a statistical partitioning of the sources of regional wage differences to be discussed below.

A given cluster can register substantially different average wages in different regions, due to differences in its sophistication and productivity, patterns of unionization and cost of living. In the automotive cluster, for example, Michigan's 296 002 workers in 2000 earned an average wage of $58 799 versus $34 655 in California, $32 814 in Tennessee and less than $30 000 in Georgia and Alabama (see Table 4). Regional sophistication is revealed in part by the particular subclusters in which the region is strong.

Patenting rates also vary markedly by cluster (see Fig. 19). Measured by patenting per 10 000 employees, the communications equipment cluster has the highest patenting rate of 205 in 2000; the patenting rate in a number of service clusters is negligible in part due to the fact that patents are not the leading form of intellectual property protection in these clusters. The patenting intensity of a given cluster also varies substantially across regions, as shown for the biopharmaceuticals cluster (see

Table 3. Traded clusters in the US economy: narrow cluster definition

Cluster	Employment, 2000	CAGR of employment, 1990–2000	Job growth rank	Average wage, 2000 ($)	Wage rank	CAGR of average wage, 1990–2000	Wage growth rank
1 Business services	4 667 320	5.6	1	56 699	5	6.0	4
2 Financial services	3 242 151	2.4	12	74 237	2	7.8	2
3 Hospitality and tourism	2 565 077	2.5	10	21 229	41	4.4	11
4 Education and knowledge creation	2 246 974	3.4	4	33 453	29	5.0	8
5 Distribution services	1 962 523	3.3	5	51 110	10	5.4	5
6 Heavy construction services	1 883 271	3.1	7	37 123	21	3.0	36
7 Transportation and logistics	1 644 641	3.1	8	36 642	23	2.3	41
8 Metal manufacturing	1 412 368	0.4	19	38 052	20	3.0	34
9 Processed food	1 388 073	0.2	22	33 646	28	3.0	35
10 Automotive	1 386 153	1.6	15	45 941	15	3.3	29
11 Entertainment	1 057 193	5.1	2	38 668	19	4.2	14
12 Publishing and printing	983 152	−0.1	24	41 369	17	4.2	15
13 Plastics	874 482	1.9	13	34 328	27	3.1	32
14 Information technology	860 230	3.1	6	93 024	1	9.7	1
15 Analytical instruments	744 832	−1.6	35	53 247	9	4.8	9
16 Building fixtures, equipment and services	670 048	1.7	14	30 286	33	3.4	27
17 Production technology	665 382	0.3	20	40 452	18	3.5	25
18 Apparel	559 276	−5.1	39	21 444	40	3.9	17
19 Chemical products	438 967	−1.7	36	48 974	11	3.6	24
20 Communications equipment	425 332	−0.3	26	56 884	4	6.2	3
21 Heavy machinery	411 940	−0.4	30	36 987	22	2.9	37
22 Motor driven products	408 427	−0.4	28	35 601	25	3.1	33
23 Textiles	402 839	−3.3	37	28 962	35	3.7	23
24 Forest products	392 080	−0.4	27	42 222	16	2.7	38
25 Furniture	379 108	0.2	21	24 904	38	3.9	18
26 Medical devices	372 442	2.5	11	47 880	13	5.2	6
27 Oil and gas products and services	370 192	−1.2	33	53 734	7	4.4	12
28 Aerospace vehicles and defence	367 315	−6.3	40	56 118	6	3.8	20
29 Lighting and electrical equipment	329 723	−0.2	25	36 178	24	3.7	22
30 Prefabricated enclosures	317 080	2.6	9	32 206	30	2.6	39
31 Power generation and transmission	290 896	3.6	3	57 272	3	5.0	7
32 Agricultural products	265 260	0.1	23	29 405	34	3.3	30
33 Biopharmaceuticals	264 319	0.8	16	48 452	12	3.4	28
34 Construction materials	199 051	0.6	18	31 120	32	3.4	26
35 Leather products	133 253	−1.6	34	27 789	36	4.2	16
36 Jewellery and precious metals	126 621	−0.4	29	34 393	26	3.9	19
37 Sporting, recreational and children's goods	107 064	0.8	17	31 577	31	4.4	13
38 Aerospace engines	94 360	−4.2	38	53 277	8	3.8	21
39 Fishing and fishing products	51 222	−0.7	31	27 320	37	3.3	31
40 Tobacco	43 843	−1.0	32	47 703	14	2.6	40
41 Footwear	23 962	−9.3	41	22 323	39	4.7	10
Total traded employment	35 028 441						
Average cluster employment	854 352						
Standard deviation of cluster employment	967 019						

Fig. 20). This reflects differences in sophistication and subcluster mix by region. Also, cluster employment in regions without a strong cluster in that field tends to be dominated by the local activity of companies based elsewhere. Such activity, including sales and customer support, often does not involve R&D and innovation. Regions with small absolute employment and LQ ⩽ 0.5 are areas where employment in a cluster is not usually a sign of competitive advantage.

Differences in cluster position across regions

Most states register some employment in many clusters, in part due to the reporting of local employment of companies based elsewhere. In most clusters, there is employment in at least 40 states and 160 (of 172) EAs. Footwear, the least represented cluster, has employment in just 24 states and 86 EAs in 2000.

About 83% of traded employment in the average EA is concentrated in its top 15 clusters in 2000, and 71% is concentrated in the top 10 clusters. This is modestly higher than the concentration of traded

Table 4. Automotive cluster employment and wages in 2000: selected states

State	Average wage, 2000 ($)	Employment, 2000	Share of national cluster employment (%)
Michigan	58 799	296 002	21.4
Ohio	49 160	182 687	13.2
Indiana	47 981	134 534	9.7
Illinois	42 125	57 728	4.2
Wisconsin	39 859	54 307	3.9
Pennsylvania	39 804	36 289	2.6
Minnesota	37 847	19 270	1.4
Kentucky	35 242	56 257	4.1
North Carolina	35 037	43 315	3.1
California	34 655	66 625	4.8
South Carolina	34 243	32 231	2.3
Tennessee	32 814	71 455	5.2
Missouri	30 508	44 601	3.2
Georgia	29 622	31 617	2.3
Alabama	28 935	16 357	1.2
US automotive cluster average	45 941	1 386 153	

employment by the top 10 and 15 clusters for the economy as a whole.

The mix of clusters, however, varies markedly across regions. Of the 41 clusters, 24 are the largest cluster for at least one EA in 2000, and 12 are the largest cluster for at least one state. The average standard deviation of employment rank of a given cluster in a region minus the US rank for that cluster is 7.3 for states and 8.5 for EAs. Business services, the largest cluster, is ranked number one in just 38 of 172 EAs and ranks as low as 19. Other examples are the information technology cluster whose rank ranges from 1 to 40; agricultural products 1 to 37; and plastics 3 to 38.[27]

Variation in regional specialization over time

To explore whether regions are becoming more or less specialized by cluster, we calculated GINI coefficient measuring the inequality of the *employment* distribution among the 41 traded clusters within states and EAs. The majority of states (35) had a positive change in the GINI coefficient over the 1990–2000 period signifying greater specialization, while 16 had a negative change. The corresponding figures for EAs are 72 and 100. State economies are tending to become more specialized by cluster, while EAs, which are smaller, are more mixed.[28]

Fig. 21 plots the change in employment GINI versus wage growth by state for the 1990 to 2000 period. States that are becoming more specialized have higher wage growth, with the proportion of explained variance 25.5% (the results are similar for EAs). This provides provocative though not definitive evidence that specialization of a region in an array of stronger traded clusters boosts regional performance.

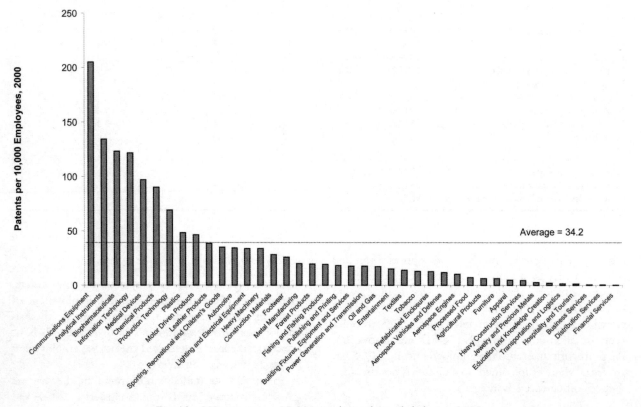

Fig. 19. US patents per 10,000 employees by traded cluster, 2000

Sources: US Patent and Trademark Office; CHI Research; Cluster Mapping Project, Harvard Business School.

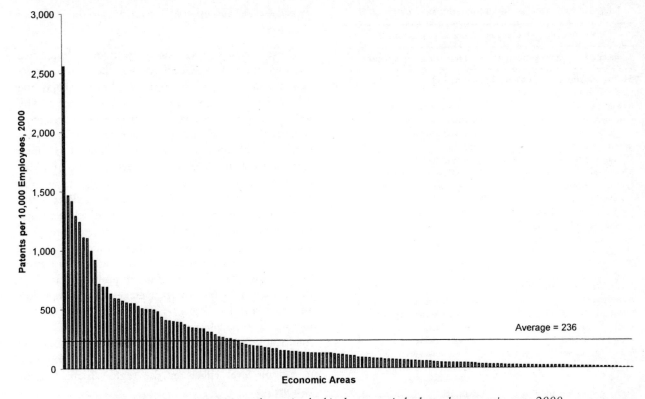

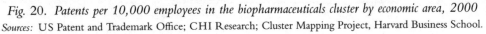

Fig. 20. *Patents per 10,000 employees in the biopharmaceuticals cluster by economic area, 2000*
Sources: US Patent and Trademark Office; CHI Research; Cluster Mapping Project, Harvard Business School.

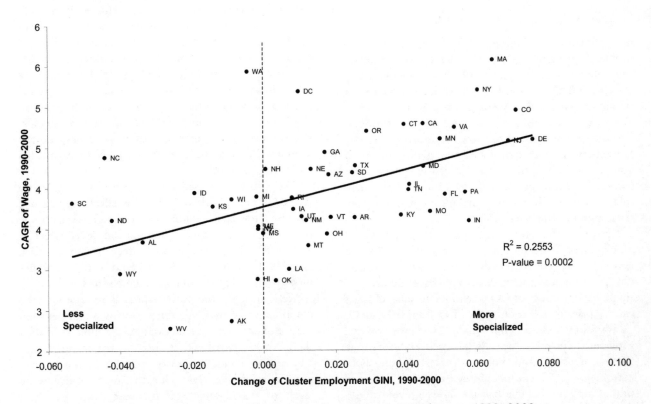

Fig. 21. *Wage growth vs. change of cluster employment GINI by state, 1990–2000*
Sources: County Business Patterns; Cluster Mapping Project, Harvard Business School.

Table 5. Variation in cluster concentration, 1990–2000

Strong cluster employment defined as LQ > = 0.8	
Concentrating in fewer regions	Dispersing across regions

Strong cluster employment defined as LQ > = 1

Concentrating in few regions

Aerospace engines	Aerospace vehicles and defence
Education and knowledge creation	Agricultural products
	Chemical products
Entertainment	Footwear
Fishing and fishing products	Forest products
Metal manufacturing	Hospitality and tourism
Oil and gas products and services	Information technology
	Motor driven products
Production technology	Prefabricated enclosures
Publishing and printing	
Sporting, recreational and children's goods	

Dispersing across regions

Analytical instruments	Apparel
Automotive	Biopharmaceuticals
Financial services	Building fixtures, equipment and services
Heavy construction services	
Haevy machinery	Business services
Jewellery and precious metals	Communications equipment
Leather products	Construction materials
Plastics	Distribution services
Power generation and transmission	Furniture
	Lighting and electrical equipment
Processed food	Medical devices
Transportation and logistics	Textiles
	Tobacco

Variation in cluster concentration over time

To explore whether clusters themselves are becoming more or less concentrated in a few regions over time, we calculate the share of regions with strong employment in the cluster (LQ ⩾ 0.8 or LQ ⩾ 1.0 using narrow cluster definitions) to total US employment in the cluster.[29] We use these cutoffs, lower than in some investigations, because the presence of the downward bias in LQ due to the pervasive presence of local employment of cluster companies with headquarters located elsewhere. This means that most regions will have some employment in almost every cluster even though the region has no meaningful competitive position.

Clusters with a positive change in the proportion of employment in strong clusters from 1990 to 2000 are getting more concentrated. Those with a negative change are getting more dispersed. Since the use of a single cut-off value for LQ is sensitive to small changes on the margin (e.g. a change of LQ from 0.99 to 1.0 can shift strong cluster employment share), we explored a range of cut-off values. As shown in Table 5, nine clusters are becoming more concentrated using both cutoffs, while 12 clusters are getting more dispersed using both cutoffs. The balance show different trends for each cutoff, suggesting a shifting distribution of cluster positions across regions.

Explaining regional wage differences: cluster mix vs. relative wage level

Since the average wage varies by traded cluster, we explored the relative contribution to the regional average traded wage of the mix of clusters versus the relative level of wages achieved for given clusters.[30] The level of wages for a given cluster can also vary across regions due to differences in sophistication, productivity and subcluster structure. The cluster mix effect is the sum of the differences in each cluster's employment share versus the national average times the cluster's national average wage. The level effect is the sum of the difference between the region's cluster wage and the national average cluster wage times the region's employment in the cluster (see Appendix C).

The Las Vegas EA provides a striking demonstration of the two effects. Competing disproportionately in the cluster with the lowest average wage, hospitality and tourism, Las Vegas is ranked 171 out of 172 regions on the cluster mix effect. However, Las Vegas significantly outperforms the national average in hospitality and tourism cluster average wage, contributing to a high level effect for the region (ranked tenth nationally).

On average, the level effect accounts for 75.7% of the variation in average wages across regions, versus 24.3% for the cluster mix effect. The reason is that mix differences do not account for large enough shifts in employment to move a region's average wage relative to the impact of overperformance or underperformance in terms of wages in each cluster. A region's ability to compete in its array of clusters with higher productivity (e.g. better product quality, more advanced service delivery) has the decisive influence on the region's prosperity. This finding carries important implications of economic development. Many regional economic development initiatives focus heavily on shifting the mix to more 'desirable' clusters. An equally if not more important policy focus is to upgrade the productivity of *all* the clusters in which the region has a meaningful position.

The cluster mix and level effects for all EAs are plotted in Fig. 22. Many of the level effects are negative because a few large regions have a higher average wage than the US average – the median level effect is −$13 387. The average mix effect is also negative (−$3622) because large regions tend to have a higher proportion of higher average wage clusters.

We can apply the same approach to examine the components of the large difference in wages between metropolitan and non-metropolitan counties. Traded share of employment is not a major influence. The overwhelming majority (82.3%) of the metro–non-metro differences is due to lower relative wage levels in traded and local industries, not the share of each. Hence, the imperative for non-metropolitan counties is to develop the conditions for supporting

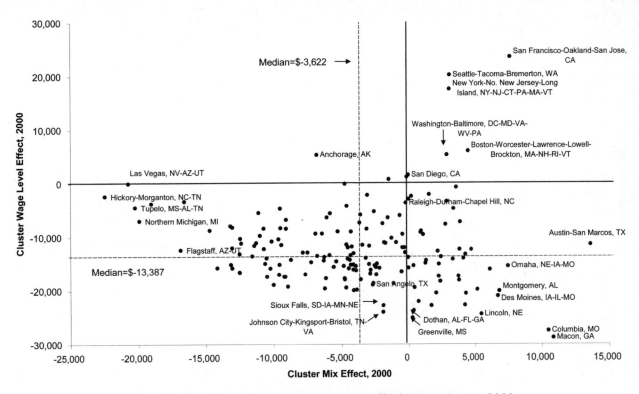

Fig. 22. Cluster wage level effect vs. cluster mix effect by economic area, 2000
Sources: County Business Patterns; Cluster Mapping Project, Harvard Business School.

high wages in their traded industries. Metropolitan and non-metropolitan counties have substantially different traded cluster composition, and skewed toward lower wage clusters. The cluster mix effect accounts for 52.3% of the difference in average traded wages between metropolitan and non-metropolitan counties, while the level effect accounts for 47.7%. For non-metropolitan counties, then, shifting the mix to more 'desirable' clusters is of about equal priority to raising the relative level of the wages of the clusters they have positions in.

The importance of leading clusters and regional performance

It is widely believed by practitioners and some economic development thinkers that reliance on a few clusters is dangerous for regional economic development because it exposes a region to shocks and business cycles. Many regions, then, set a goal of diversifying the clusters present. Fig. 23 reveals that this hypothesis is not borne out by the data, at least in its simplest form. There is no clear relationship between the importance of the leading clusters (measured by the employment of the top three clusters as a percentage of total traded employment), and average wages. The same is true of wage growth, employment growth and patenting. The results are nearly identical using the top five clusters.

Cluster strength and regional wages

We constructed several measures of the strength of a region's array of clusters, measured by the proportion

of traded employment accounted for by strong clusters (LQ ⩾ 0.8 or LQ ⩾ 1.0) using both narrow and broad cluster definitions. The use of broad cluster definitions to measure cluster strength gives weight to the industries that overlap within a region's clusters, and measure crudely the extent of potential cross-cluster spillovers. The proportion of strong clusters in the economy should be positively related to productivity and hence average wages.

All four measures of cluster strength have a positive and mostly statistically significant relationship with average wages as well as other measures of regional performance metrics. Interestingly, cluster strength measured using broad cluster definitions has a stronger and markedly more significant positive relationship with regional wages, shown in Fig. 24.

Regional patenting rates by cluster

Patenting rates should increase with the size and depth of clusters due to more vigorous competition and greater spillovers among firms and institutions in the region.[31] We utilize the proportion of traded employment in strong clusters (LQ ⩾ 0.8) using broad cluster definitions as an overall measure of the strength and depth of clusters since it measures not only strength within each cluster but also the extent of overlap among a region's clusters and hence spillovers among them. Fig. 25 reveals a positive and significant relationship between the patenting rate and the share of traded employment in strong clusters using negative binomial regression.

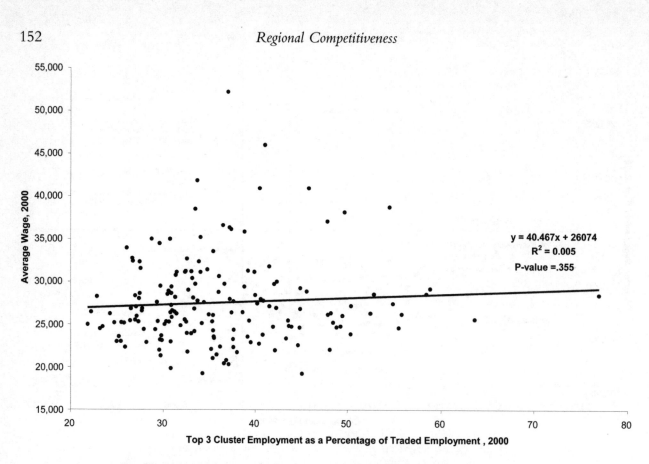

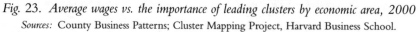

Fig. 23. *Average wages vs. the importance of leading clusters by economic area, 2000*
Sources: County Business Patterns; Cluster Mapping Project, Harvard Business School.

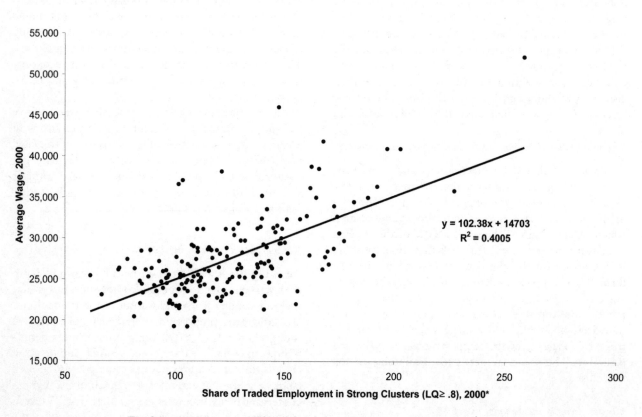

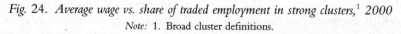

Fig. 24. *Average wage vs. share of traded employment in strong clusters,[1] 2000*
Note: 1. Broad cluster definitions.
Sources: US Patent and Trademark Office; CHI Research; County Business Patterns; Cluster Mapping Project, Harvard Business School.

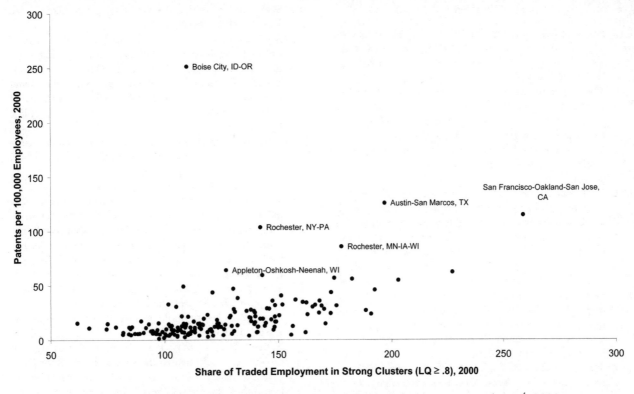

Fig. 25. Patents per 100 000 inhabitants vs. share of traded employment in strong clusters,[1] 2000

Note: 1. Broad cluster definitions.

Sources: US Patent and Trademark Office; CHI Research; County Business Patterns; Cluster Mapping Project, Harvard Business School.

SUMMARY AND CONCLUSIONS

This paper reveals the striking importance of regional economies to the overall performance of nations, using the data from the US economy. The performance of regional economies varies markedly in terms of wages, wage growth, employment growth and patenting. National performance, then, is a composite of very different levels of regional performance. Regional economies differ moderately in their proportion of traded, resource-dependent and local industries, and differ markedly in the mix of clusters present. Regional economic performance is strongly influenced by the traded clusters which appear to shape wages in local industries. Relative wages in traded industries drive regional wage differences, dominating the influence of differences in the proportion of traded employment. Regional economic performance is strongly affected by the strength of clusters and the vitality and plurality of innovation. Regional performance differences are dominated by relative wage levels in the array of clusters that are present in a region, rather than the particular mix of clusters itself.

Our findings suggest that regional analysis must become far more central to research and policy formulation in competitiveness and economic development. Our results reveal the need for much of economic policy to be decentralized to the regional level. Since many of the essential determinants of economic performance appear to reside in regions, national policies will

be necessary but not sufficient. The importance of regions may explain why countries with greater economic decentralization, such as Germany and the US, have been historically successful. It may also explain why countries such as India and China are making notable economic progress in particular states or provinces relative to others.

Our findings highlight the need for regional economic development policies to be particularly attuned to traded clusters, because these not only support higher wages but also appear to drive local employment and especially local wages. Regions should focus on upgrading the productivity of all clusters in which they have a meaningful position, rather than attempting to migrate to more 'desirable' clusters. Also, the importance of building innovative capacity at the regional level is strongly revealed, as is the benefits of diversifying the companies and institutions that generate innovative output.

Acknowledgements – This paper has benefited greatly from sustained research over a multi-year period by Daniel Vasquez, Elisabeth deFontenay, and especially Weifeng Weng in assembling the dataset, statistically deriving the composition of regional economies, defining clusters and performing the numerous analyses contained here. We are grateful to the Harvard Business School and Sloan Foundation for supporting the Cluster Mapping Project from which the paper is drawn, and to the editors and anonymous referees for helpful comments.

NOTES

1. See especially GLAESER *et al.*, 1992; HENDERSON *et al.*, 1995; HARRISON *et al.*, 1996; BAPTISTA *et al.*, 1998; FELDMAN *et al.*, 1999; HENDERSON, 1999; and KETELHÖHN, 2002.

2. There is some empirical literature on regional performance. The work of BORTS and STEIN, 1964, is one of the earliest and best-known efforts to test neoclassical explanations of regional growth disparities.

3. For example, see PORTER, 2003, for further statistical findings on regional differences in wages, wage growth and patenting.

4. CBP data is suppressed if the disclosure would compromise the data for a particular company. CBP data is made available at the county, state and US level. Economic area and metropolitan statistical area data are built up from the county file, which has the most data suppression problems. The state file has fewer suppression problems, mostly at cluster level. The national data is virtually free of suppression. When data is suppressed, a range is reported for the employment data. We utilize the mid-point in the range in our data. For payroll data, no information is provided when data is suppressed. Employment figures are therefore less affected than wage data.

5. The US Patent and Trademark office requires inventors to list their home address. CHI Research assigns patents to counties based on the county in which the inventor's residence is located. We would prefer attributing the patent to the work address, but this information is not available. In practice, the difference due to the use of home versus work addresses is quite small. Using EAs as the unit of analysis largely alleviates the problem since almost all of the commuting is within EAs.

6. Co-location of industries does not guarantee interaction or spillovers, but consistent co-location across many regions creates a strong presumption that such interactions are present.

7. Both full-time and part-time employees are reported in CBP. Since there is no reason to expect major differences in the mix of full-time and part-time workers across regions, there should be little bias introduced in examining the key relationships. However, reported wage differences across clusters may be affected, especially in the hospitality and tourism cluster.

8. For each year, EAs are sorted in descending order by average wage, then grouped into deciles. All decile groups contain 17 EAs, except for the first and last, which contain 18. The decile group with the lowest wages is marked as group 1, and the one with the highest wage is group 10.

9. Discussions of the relative merits of using patents as a proxy for innovative activity can be found in GRILICHES, 1984, 1990; JAFFE, 1986; DOSI *et al.*, 1990; and TRAJTENBERG, 1990. Some have used occupational data to explore patterns on innovation, but such data is only available for regions as a whole and, unlike patents, cannot be assigned to individual industries. Also, output oriented measures of innovation such as patenting offer advantages over input measures.

10. This is an implication of the theory of clusters, which is discussed in PORTER, 1998.

11. Patents filed by individuals unaffiliated with a specific organization are excluded in the patentor analysis.

12. Such industries have been termed residentiary – see VINING, 1946; NORTH, 1955.

13. Such industries have been termed export industries, although the definition of these varies from industries that export internationally to industries that export across regions. We define traded industries statistically using locational patterns. The export-based theory can be dated to INNIS, 1920. See ARMSTRONG and TAYLOR, 1985; LEICHENKO and COULSON, 1999; and LEICHENKO, 2000; for comprehensive reviews. Past studies have examined broadly defined sectors or manufacturing as a whole. Our focus is on the cluster and industry level.

14. The categorization is highly stable from year to year.

15. VINING, 1946, finds that employment in residentiary industries was about 55% of a state's total employment. Our figure is higher, which is consistent with the somewhat faster employment growth in local industries for the decade of the 1990s for possible reasons discussed in the paper.

16. This is a case of overly aggregated industry definitions, which will be discussed further below.

17. There was a debate on the relative importance of export and residentiary industries between North and Tiebout in the 1950s. NORTH, 1955, 1956, states that regional growth 'is closely tied to the success of its exports and may take place either as a result of the improved position of existing exports relative to competing areas or as a result of the development of new exports.... 'Since residentiary industry depends on income within the region, the expansion of such activity must have been induced by the increased income of the region's inhabitants.' On the other hand, TIEBOUT, 1956, argues that there is no reason to assume that exports are the sole or even the most important factor in regional growth, and 'in terms if causation, the nature of the residentiary industries will be a key factor in any possible development'. Our findings support North's view.

18. Data on productivity by industry at the individual region level is significantly affected by data suppression, especially for EAs and MSAs. We did not make use of this data in most of the analysis herein.

19. Data suppression is more common for industry level wage data than for employment data. Also, where wage data is suppressed no information is given, while for counties where employment is suppressed a range of employment is reported. We calculated a likelihood ratio test to explore whether data suppression caused a bias in the relationship between traded and local wages. The test examined whether the coefficients of the relationship between traded and local wages was the same in the sample of half of EAs with less suppression at the industry level versus the entire EA sample. The null hypothesis, i.e. no difference, cannot be rejected – an indication that wage data suppression does not introduce a major bias in the results.

20. It is well known that industries are often geographically concentrated in certain regions. The level of the concentration and the reasons for the persistence of industrial concentration are explored in ENRIGHT, 1990; KRUGMAN, 1991; DUMAIS *et al.*, 1997; ELLISON *et al.*, 1997, KIM, 1998; and ELLISON *et al.*, 1999.

21. There is a growing literature on clusters; see PORTER, 1998, for a brief survey.

22. MARSHALL, 1920; ARROW, 1962; and ROMER, 1986.
23. There is a related hypothesis about the role of competition. MAR sees competition as bad because it reduces the rate of progress down the learning curve. PORTER, 1990, argues that competition is good because it stimulates innovation and dynamism; JACOBS, 1969, is associated with this view although there is no explicit discussion of competition in her book. Previous results, again using industries and MSAs as units of analysis, support the positive role of competition.
24. This analysis was based on 1996, the most recent year then available. Replicating the analysis using more recent years revealed no material differences.
25. Application of the input–output method can be found in TIEBOUT, 1956; MIERNYK, 1965; NEVIN *et al.*, 1966; YAN, 1969; RICHARDSON, 1972; LEWIS and MCNICOLL, 1978; PULLEN and PROOPS, 1983; and others. See ARMSTRONG and TAYLOR, 1985, for the summary on the input–output approach.
26. Amended clusters have been defined using NAICS data which prove to be very similar in composition but include a moderate number of additional industries. We do not utilize NAICS clusters here due to lack of historical data.

27. The standard deviation of relative rank fell modestly between 1990 and 2000.
28. We also calculated the time trend of the employment GINI: $GINI = \alpha + \beta * t$, where t represents the year and ranges from 1990 to 2000. If the time coefficient is positive, this indicates that the state is becoming more specialized and vice versa. The findings were similar to the results for simple changes in GINI. More than half (32) of the states have a positive coefficient, and the rest have a negative coefficient. For EAs, 72 (of 172) have a positive coefficient. Most of the trend coefficients are statistically significant.
29. An LQ cutoff for cluster strength of $\geqslant 1.0$ means that the cluster's employment in the region is equal to or greater than the region's share of total national employment. We also employ a somewhat lower cutoff ($\geqslant 0.8$) to capture clusters with a substantial position in the region that from list – please add may fall just below LQ of 1.
30. The notion of cluster mix vs. relative wage level is similar in concept to shift-share analysis, which was originally proposed by DUNN, 1960, and has many applications in regional studies.
31. See JAFFE *et al.*, 1993.

APPENDIX A: US ECONOMIC AREAS

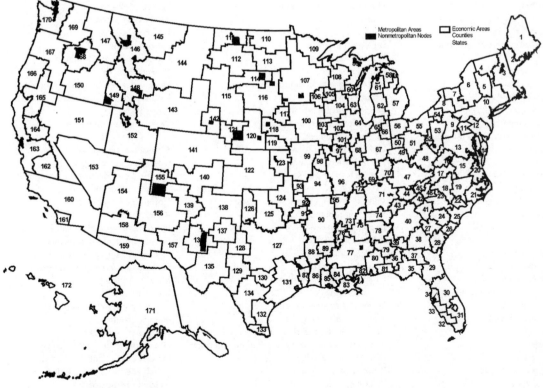

Fig. A1. *US economic areas: BEA economic areas and component economic nodes*[1]

Notes: 1. Established as of February 1995. Metropolitan areas are the MSAs defined by the Office of Management and Budget as of December 1997.

Source: Prepared by Regional Economic Analysis Division, Economics and Statistics Administration, Bureau of Economic Analysis, US Department of Commerce.

APPENDIX B: LIST OF TRADED CLUSTERS AND SUBCLUSTERS

Table B1. List of traded clusters and subclusters

Aerospace engines
Aircraft engines
Precision metal products
Engine and other instruments
Parts and components
Foundries
Parts processing
Nonferrous processing
Machine tools
Aircraft and parts

Aerospace vehicles and defence
Aircraft
Missiles and space vehicles
Defence equipment
Distribution and wholesaling
Metallic parts
Electronic parts
Instruments
Semiconductors and computers
Related equipment
Communications equipment
Software and computer services
Research

Agricultural products
Farm management and related services
Soil preparation services
Irrigation systems
Packaging
Fertilizers
Agricultural products
Wine and brandy
Cigars
Milling and refining
Product distribution and wholesaling
Malt beverages
Related processed foods
Related ingredients
Animal health products
Fish products
Agricultural chemicals
Supplies distribution and wholesaling
Related financial services
Transportation and logistic services
Marine transportation services
Bulk packaging
Packaging and packaging machinery
Related services

Analytical instruments
Laboratory instruments
Optical instruments
Process instruments
Search and navigation equipment
Electronic components
Distribution and wholesaling
Electronic parts
Other parts
Medical equipment
Related process equipment
Related equipment
Computer and software services
Research organizations

Apparel
Men's clothing
Women's and children's clothing
Hosiery and other garments
Accessories
Knitting and finishing mills
Gloves
Hats
Other accessories
Related garments
Outwear

Automotive
Motor vehicles assembly
Automotive parts
Automotive components
Forgings and stampings
Flat glass
Production equipment
Small vehicles and trailers
Marine, tank and stationary engines
Related parts
Motors and generators
Related vehicles
Metal processing
Machine tools
Related process machinery
Industrial trucks and tractors
Die-castings

Biopharmaceuticals
Biopharmaceutical products
Health and beauty products
Containers
Drug and related wholesaling
Biological products
Specialty chemicals
Packaging
Instruments and laboratory apparatus
Diagnostics
Surgical instruments and supplies
Dental instruments and supplies
Medical equipment
Ophthalmic goods
Patent owners and lessors
Research organizations

Building fixtures, equipment and services
Plumbing products
Drapery hardware
Fabricated materials
Heating and lighting
Furniture and fittings
Clay and vitreous products
Floor coverings
Steam and air-conditioning
Stone and tile work
Wood cabinets, fixtures and other products
Concrete, gypsum and other building products
Distribution and wholesaling
Plating and polishing
Lighting products
Ceramic tile
Elevators and moving stairways
Related electrical products
Furnishings
Other vitreous products

Mobile and motor homes
Related parts
Construction materials
Hardware
Millwork
Related fixtures
Steel work

Business services
Management consulting
Online information services
Computer services
Computer programming
Photocopying
Marketing related services
Professional organizations and services
Engineering services
Laundry services
Facilities support services
Freight arrangement
Surveying services
Media related services
Catalog and mail-order
Insurance

Chemical products
Intermediate chemicals and gases
Packaged chemical products
Other processed chemicals
Refractories
Leather tanning and finishing
Ammunition
Special packaging
Treated garments
Hydrocarbons
Petrochemicals
Plastics, resins and products
Pharmaceuticals
Diagnostics and biological products
Related consumer products
Other packaging
Processing instruments

Communications equipment
Communications equipment
Electrical and electronic components
Specialty office machines
Communications services
Related services
Distribution and wholesaling
Wiring, coils and transformers
Semiconductor and optical devices
Software and computer services
Metal processing
Cabinets
Power transmission equipment
Storage batteries
Computer equipment
Household audio and video equipment
Guided missiles and space vehicles
Search and navigation equipment
Related instruments
Research institutions

Construction materials
Tile, brick and glass
Plumbing fixtures
Wood products
Cut and crushed stone
Gum and wood chemicals
Rubber products
Adhesives and sealants
Insulation and roofing
Plastic sheet
Synthetic rubber
Steel pipe and tubes
Flooring and veneer
Sand and gravel
Concrete block and brick
Other wood products

Distribution services
Merchandise wholesaling
Apparel and accessories wholesaling
Catalogue and mail-order
Food products wholesaling
Farm material and supplies wholesaling
Transportation vehicle and equipment distribution
Special warehousing and storage
Jewellery and precious stones wholesaling
Construction machinery wholesaling

Education and knowledge creation
Educational institutions
Research organizations
Educational facilities
Patent owners and lessors
Supplies
Research related instruments
Pharmaceuticals
Publishing
Printing
Communications services
Marketing and information services
Online information services
Computer services
Prepackaged software
Computer and software wholesaling and services
Computer equipment

Entertainment
Video production and distribution
Recorded products
Entertainment equipment
Entertainment related services
Entertainment venues
Distribution and wholesaling
Marketing and promotional service
Related attractions
News syndicates
Audio and video equipment

Financial services
Depository institutions
Securities brokers, dealers and exchanges
Insurance products
Health plans
Risk capital providers
Investment funds
Real estate investment trusts
Passenger car leasing

Information providers
Computer and communication services
Printing services
Patent owners and lessors
Marketing related services
Research organizations

Fishing and fishing products
Fish products
Fishing and hunting
Processed seafoods
Seafood distribution and wholesaling

Footwear
Footwear
Speciality footwear
Footwear parts
Other leather goods
Related materials

Forest products
Paper products
Paper mills
Paper industries machinery
Prefabricated wood buildings
Wood partitions and fixtures
Paperboard and boxes
Process equipment
Hoists and cranes
Paper related machinery and instruments
Stationery products
Brooms and brushes

Furniture
Furniture
Wood materials and products
Furnishings
Tableware and kitchenware
Furniture related parts
Metal household furniture
Office furniture
Mattresses and bedsprings
Related household fixtures
Mobile homes
Other wood products
Power tools
Woodworking machinery
Millwork

Heavy construction services
Final construction
Subcontractors
Primary construction materials
Ceramic tiles
Equipment distribution and wholesaling
Fabricated metal structures and piping
Explosives
Transportation services
Chemical and related products
Glass and clay
Related equipment and components
Elevators and moving stairways
Related services
Tiling and glazing

Heavy machinery
Construction machinery
Farm machinery
Railroad equipment and rental
Mining machinery

Machinery components
Valves and pipe fittings
Hoists and cranes
Forgings, castings and metal parts
Engines
Related parts
Compressors and fans
Tires and inner tubes

Hospitality and tourism
Tourism attractions
Tourism related services
Water passenger transportation
Accommodations and related services
Boat related services
Ground transportation
Other local transportation
Related professional services
Other attractions
Air services
Vehicle distribution and wholesaling
Facilities support services

Information technology
Computers
Electronic components and assemblies
Peripherals
Software
Communications services
Distribution and wholesaling
Other electronic components and parts
Recording media services
Online information services
Computer services
Instruments
Communications equipment
Research organizations

Jewellery and precious metals
Jewellery and precious metal products
Costume jewellery
Cutlery
Collectibles
Distribution and wholesaling
Precious metal related financial services

Leather products
Leather products
Fur goods
Coated fabrics
Related products
Accessories
Women's footwear
Men's clothing
Women's clothing and accessories

Lighting and electrical equipment
Lighting fixtures
Electric lamps
Batteries
Switchgear
Electrical parts
Metal parts
Related electrical equipment
Instruments to measure electricity
Electric services
Glass and ceramics products
Wire
Related electronic parts
Other lighting equipment

Medical devices
Surgical instruments and supplies
Dental instruments and supplies
Ophthalmic goods
Medical equipment
Diagnostic substances
Biological products
Laboratory apparatus
Electronic components
Plastic parts
Metal parts
Software
Online information services
Precision instruments
Computer equipment
Pharmaceutical products
Research organizations

Metal manufacturing
Fabricated metal products
Metal alloys
Primary metal products
Precision metal products
Fasteners
Wire and springs
Metal processing
Iron and steel mills and foundries
Nonferrous mills and foundries
Metal furniture
Environmental controls
Pumps
Saw blades and handsaws
General industrial machinery
Laundry and cleaning equipment
Metal armaments
Measuring and dispensing pumps
Tools, dies and fixtures
Paints and allied products
Lubricating oils and greases
Abrasive products
Metalworking machinery and components
Related metal processing
Industrial furnaces and ovens
Automotive parts and equipment
Hoists and cranes
Related metal products
Motorcycles and bicycles

Motor driven products
Motors and generators
Batteries
Motorized equipment
Refrigeration and heating equipment
Appliances
Specialized pumps
Specialized machinery
Tires and inner tubes
Marine, tank and stationary engines
Motorcycles and bicycles
Metal processing
Related appliances
Hoists and cranes
Printing trades machinery
Elevators and moving stairways
Air and gas compressors
Power transmission, motors and pumps
Control devices

Oil and gas products and services
Oil and gas machinery
Hydrocarbons
Oil and gas exploration and drilling
Oil pipelines
Petroleum processing
Oil and gas trading
Water freight transportation services
Forgings and fittings
Turbines and turbine generators
Lubricating oils
Intermediate chemicals
Plastics and related materials
Barrels and drums
Other transportation services

Plastics
Plastic materials and resins
Plastic products
Paints and allied products
Synthetic rubber
Plastics distribution and wholesaling
Organic chemicals
Alkalies and chlorine
Inorganic chemicals
Related plastic products
Hydrocarbons
Petroleum processing
Surface active agents
Adhesives and sealants
Process equipment

Power generation and transmission
Electric services
Turbines and turbine generators
Transformers
Porcelain, carbon and graphite components
Electronic capacitors
Electrical apparatus and instruments
Motors, generators and electric fans
Switchgear, controls and components

Prefabricated enclosures
Recreational vehicles and parts
Mobile homes
Trucks and trailers
Caskets
Elevators and moving stairways
Office furniture
Household refrigerators and freezers
Aluminum processing
Non-ferrous processing, except aluminum
Aluminum forging and other processing
Steel springs
Railroad equipment
Other furniture and cabinets

Processed food
Milk and frozen desserts
Baked packaged foods
Coffee
Processed dairy and related products
Meat and related products and services
Flour
Specialty foods and ingredients
Milling
Candy and chocolate

Malt beverages
Paper containers and boxes
Metal and glass containers
Food products machinery
Distribution and wholesaling
Packaging materials
Bulk packaging

Production technology
Machine tools and accessories
Process equipment sub-systems and
components
Hoists and cranes
Process machinery
Industrial patterns
Fabricated plate work
Industrial trucks and tractors
Ball and roller bearings
Production machinery and components
Blast furnaces and steel mills
Household appliances
Abrasive products
Metal heat treating
Process equipment
Vehicle and heavy stamping
Construction machinery
Casting, forgings and metal alloys

Publishing and printing
Publishing
News syndicates
Signs and advertising specialties
Photographic services
Photographic equipment and supplies
Radio, TV, publisher representatives
Printing services
Printing inputs
Paper products
Speciality paper products
Inked paper and ribbons
Office equipment and supplies
Marketing related services
Printing-related machinery
Online information services
Computer services
Research organizations
Research facilities

Sporting, recreational and children's goods
Sporting and athletic goods
Games, toys, and children's vehicles
Motorcycles and bicycles
Dolls and stuffed toys
Fabricated metal products
Toys and hobby goods wholesaling
Metal processing

Textiles
Fabric mills
Speciality fabric mills
Speciality fabric processing
Textile machinery
Yarn and thread mills
Carpets and rugs
Wool mills
Fibres
Finishing plants

Speciality apparel components	Tobacco processing	Airports
Women's and children's underwear	Specialty packaging	Bus terminals
Tyre cord and fabrics		Passenger transportation
Process chemicals	*Transportation and logistics*	Communication equipment and services
Coated fabrics	Air transportation	Rental of railroad cars
Home furnishings	Bus transportation	Computer services and equipment
	Marine transportation	
Tobacco	Ship building	
Cigarettes	Transportation arrangement and warehousing	
Other tobacco products	Trucking terminal	

APPENDIX C: MIX AND LEVEL EFFECT ON REGIONAL AVERAGE TRADED WAGE

Variable definitions

$RITA$ = regional employment in cluster i

$RITA_i^{Pr}$ = predicted employment in cluster i (see below)

$TRITA$ = total regional traded employment

$RITD_i$ = regional wage of cluster i

$NITD_i$ = national wage of cluster i

$TNITD$ = national traded wage

The predicted employment in cluster i is defined as:

$$RITA_i^{Pr} = NITA_i * \left(\frac{TRITA}{TNITA} \right)$$

with the term in parentheses being the region's share of traded employment.

National-level variables are aggregated from the regional CBP files, not taken from the US CBP file, in order to ensure that the wage and level effects add up to the actual difference between the region's average wage and the overall average wage. For the same reason, the employment variables contain only non-flagged employment

Cluster mix effect

$$\frac{\sum_{i=1}^{41} [(RITA_i - RITA_i^{Pr}) * (NITD_i - TNITD)]}{TRITA}$$

Level effect

$$\frac{\sum_{i=1}^{41} [(RITA_i * (RITD_i - NITD_i)]}{TRITA}$$

Discussion

The cluster mix and level effects add up to the actual difference between a region's average wage and the national average wage. The cluster mix component represents the portion of this wage difference that can be explained by the region's particular employment distribution across clusters. For instance, a region with above average employment in a nationally high-wage cluster will raise its average wage.

The level effect measures the portion of the wage difference that can be attributed to the region's having higher or lower wages for particular clusters than the national average for those clusters.

REFERENCES

ARMSTRONG H. and TAYLOR J. (1985) *Regional Economics and Policy.* Philip Allan, Oxford.

ARROW K. J. (1962) The economic implications of learning by doing, *Rev. Econ. Studies* **29** (June), 155–73.

BAPTISTA R. and SWANN P. (1998) Do firms in clusters innovate more?, *Research Policy* **27**, 525–40.

BORTS G. H. and STEIN J. L. (1964) *Economic Growth in a Free Market.* Columbia University Press, New York.

DOSI G., PAVITT K. and SOETE L. (1990) *The Economics of Technical Change and International Trade.* New York University Press (distributed by Columbia University Press, New York).

DUMAIS G., ELLISON G. and GLAESER E. L. (1997) Geographic concentration as a dynamic process, NBER Working Paper 6270, pp. 1–47, National Bureau of Economic Research, Cambridge, MA.

DUNN E. S. (1960) A statistical and analytical technique for regional analysis, *Pap. Proc. Reg. Sci. Ass.* **6**, 97–112.

ELLISON G. and GLAESER E. L. (1997) Geographical concentration in US manufacturing industries, *J. Pol. Econ.* **105** (October), 889–927.

ELLISON G. and GLAESER E. L. (1999) The geographic concentration of industry: does natural advantage explain agglomeration?, *AEA Pap. & Proc.* **89** (May), 311–16.

ENRIGHT M. J. (1990) Geographic concentration and industrial organization, Ph.D. dissertation, Harvard University.

FELDMAN M. P. (2000) Location and innovation: the new economic geography of innovation, spillovers and agglomeration, in CLARK G., FELDMAN M. and GERTLER M. (Eds) *The Oxford Handbook of Economic Geography*, pp. 373–94. Oxford University Press, Oxford.

FELDMAN M. P. and AUDRETSCH D. B. (1999) Innovation in cities: science-based diversity, specialization and localized competition, *Europ. Econ. Rev.* **43**(2), 409–29.

GLAESER E. L. (2000) The new economics of urban and regional growth, in CLARK G., FELDMAN M. and GERTLER M. (Eds) *The Oxford Handbook of Economic Geography*, pp. 83–98. Oxford University Press, Oxford.

GLAESER E. L., KALLAL H. D., SCHEINKMAN J. A. and SHLEIFER A. (1992) Growth in cities, *J. Pol. Econ.* **100** (December), 1126–52.

GRILICHES Z. (1984) *R&D, Patents, and Productivity.* University of Chicago Press, Chicago, IL.

GRILICHES Z. (1990) Patent statistics as economic indicators: a survey, *J. Econ. Lit.* **92**, 630–53.

HANSON G. H. (2000) Scale economies and the geographic concentration of industry, NBER Working Paper 8013, National Bureau of Economic Research, Cambridge, MA.

HARRISON B., KELLEY M. and GANT J. (1996) Specialization versus diversity in local economies: the implications for innovative private-sector behavior, *Cityscape: A Journal of Policy Development and Research* **2** (May), 61–93.

HENDERSON V. (1999) Marshall's scale economies, NBER Working Paper 7358, National Bureau of Economic Research, Cambridge (MA).

HENDERSON V., KUNCORO A. and TURNER M. (1995) Industrial development in cities, *J. Pol. Econ.* **103**(5), 1067–87.

INNIS H. (1920) *The Fur Trade in Canada.* Yale University Press, New Haven, CT.

JACOBS J. (1969) *The Economy of Cities.* Random House, New York.

JAFFE A. B. (1986) Technological opportunity and spillovers of R&D: evidence from firms' patents, profits, and market value, *Am. Econ. Rev.* **76**(5), 984–1001.

JAFFE A. B., TRAJTENBERG M. and HENDERSON R. (1993) Geographic localization of knowledge spillovers as evidenced by patent citations, *Quart. J. Econ.* **108**, 577–98.

KETELHOHN N. W. (2002) *The Role of Clusters as Sources of Dynamic Externalities.* DBA dissertation, Harvard University.

KIM S. (1998) Economic integration and convergence: US regions, 1840–1987, *J. Econ. Hist.* **58** (September), 659–83.

KRUGMAN P. (1991) *Geography and Trade.* MIT Press, Cambridge, MA.

LEICHENKO R. (2000) Exports, employment and production: a causal assessment of US states and regions, *Econ. Geogr.* **76**, 303–25.

LEICHENKO R. and COULSON E. (1999) Foreign industrial exports and state manufacturing performance, *Growth & Change* **30**, 479–506.

LEWIS T. M. and MCNICOLL I. H. (1978) *North Sea Oil and Scotland's Economic Prospects.* Croom Helm, London.

MARSHALL A. (1920) *Principles of Economics*, 8th edition. Macmillan, London.

MIERNYK W. H. (1965) *The Elements of Input–Output Economics.* Random House, New York.

NEVIN E., ROE A. and ROUND J. I. (1966) *The Structure of the Welsh Economy.* University of Wales Press.

NORTH D. C. (1955) Location theory and regional economic growth, *J. Pol. Econ.* **63**(3), 243–58

NORTH D. C. (1956) Exports and regional economic growth: a reply, *J. Pol. Econ.* **64**(2), 165–68.

PORTER M. E. (1990) *The Competitive Advantage of Nations.* The Free Press, New York.

PORTER M. E. (1998) Clusters and competition: new agendas for companies, governments, and institutions, in PORTER M. E. *On Competition*, pp. 197–287. Harvard Business School Press, Boston, MA.

PORTER M. E. (2003) Determinants of regional economic performance, Harvard Business School, Harvard University (mimeo).

PULLEN M. J. and PROOPS J. L. R. (1983) The North Staffordshire regional economy: an input–output assessment, *Reg. Studies* **17**(3), 191–200.

RICHARDSON H. W. (1972) *Input–Output and Regional Economics.* Weidenfeld & Nicolson, London.

ROMER P. M. (1986) Increasing returns and long-run growth, *J. Pol. Econ.* **94**, 1002–37.

SCOTT A. J. (2000) Economic geography: the great half-century, in CLARK G., FELDMAN M. and GERTLER M. (Eds) *The Oxford Handbook of Economic Geography*, pp. 18–44. Oxford University Press, Oxford.

SILVERMAN B. S. (1999) Technological resources and the direction of corporate diversification: toward an integration of the resource-based view and transaction cost economics, *Mgt. Sci.* **45**(8), 1109–24.

TIEBOUT C. M. (1956) Exports and regional economic growth, *J. Pol. Econ.* **64**(2), 160–64.

TRAJTENBERG M. (1990) *Patents as Indicators of Innovation, Economic Analysis of Product Innovation.* Harvard University Press, Cambridge, MA.

VINING R. (1946) Location of industry and regional patterns of business-cycle behavior, *Econometrica* **14**(1), 37–68.

YAN C. (1969) *Introduction to Input–Output Economics.* Holt, Rinehart & Winston, New York.

INDEX

168   *Index*

  performance 144
  positioning 114, 116, 118
  strategy 102, 104–5
small and medium-sized enterprises (SMEs) 46–50,
    88, 90, 96–98, 100, 105–7
Smith, Adam 29
smokestack chasing 114
Soci, A. 3, 57
social capital 18–19, 89
social cohesion 1, 7, 56, 58, 71, 119, 123
social networks 4–5, 12, 16, 44
soft factors 20
Soskice, D. 17
South Africa 118
South Asia 99
Southern Growth Policies Board 121
Southern Innovation Index 121
Southern Technology Council 121
Spain 47, 60, 68, 97, 99, 101, 103–5, 113, 119
spatial structure 6, 36
special interests 83
specialization 15–18, 20–21
  cities 82, 85–86, 88–90
  concepts 29, 31, 34
  networks 45–47
  performance 132, 144, 148
  positioning 114, 118
  productivity 60, 62, 66, 70
spillovers 27, 30, 32, 34–35
  cities 82, 86, 89–90
  performance 135, 144, 151
  positioning 124
  productivity 60, 68
spin-offs 19–20, 22
sports 117–18
stability 18–20
stagnation 83, 86, 90
Standard Industrial Classification (SIC) 132, 145
The State New Economy Index 120
'State of the Regions' Core Indicators 121
State Science & Technology Indicators 121
State Science and Technology Index 121
State Science and Technology Institute (SSTI) 120
statistical analysis 100–105
sticky places 113
Stiglitz, J. 97, 99
Storper, Michael 2, 4, 88, 106
stress 87
Structural Fund 70, 75
subclusters 145, 147, 150
subcontracting 48
subsidies 20, 81, 84, 100, 104–5, 114, 116, 122
Sum, N.-L. 116, 122
Sunley, P. 4
Super Bowl 117
superstructure 119
suppliers 27, 40, 44–45, 48–50, 86, 107

supply-side policies 6, 30, 114–15
survey instrument 107–8
sustainability 85, 113, 121
Sveikauskas, L. A. 60
Sweden 65, 68, 120
Swyngedouw, E. A. 116
Syracuse 133
systemic competitiveness 113–14

Taiwan 122
taxation 20, 81, 83, 105, 114
teamwork 41
technology 4, 7, 13, 18–21
  cities 81–82, 84, 86–90
  concepts 27, 29–31, 34
  networks 41–48, 50
  performance 144, 146
  positioning 112–13, 115, 118–21, 123–24
  productivity 57, 59–60, 64, 66, 68, 71, 74–75
  strategy 96–107
Technology Administration 121
technopoles 116, 119
TechVentures Network 121
Telecom Corridor 118
Tennessee 146
territorial competition 27–31, 56, 115, 123
theoretical expectations 98–100
Third Italy 19, 47, 50, 96
Thomas, K. 114
Tokyo 117
top-down policies 82, 119, 124
total factor productivity (TFP) 3, 34–35, 59
total quality management 35
tourism 82, 85, 112, 116–18, 123, 146
Tracey, Paul 95–110
tradables 57, 66
trade 2, 4, 26–30, 32–35, 66–68
  associations 41, 44, 47, 89
  cities 80, 86, 89
  positioning 112, 117
traded industries 141–42, 144–53
training 43–44, 47, 82, 86, 105–6
Transactions Cost Economics 27
transactions costs 34, 36, 41–43, 47–48, 98
transnational corporations (TNCs) 80, 84, 89–90
transnational firms 48–50
Transparency International 123
transport 32, 34, 42, 68
  cities 80–83, 85–87, 90
  positioning 113, 119
  strategy 98, 103
Treasury 1, 3, 5–6, 84
trust 43–44
Tsampra, Maria 95–110
turnaround 27, 30
Turok, Ivan 79–93, 112
Tyler, Peter 1–9, 31–32, 55–77
Tyson, L. 57